The Army of the Republic

*The Place of the Military in the
Political Evolution of France, 1871-1914*

The Army of the Republic

The Place of the Military in the
Political Evolution of France, 1871–1914

David B. Ralston

The M.I.T. Press

Massachusetts Institute of Technology
Cambridge, Massachusetts, and London, England

To my wife and to my parents

Preface

The present work is a somewhat shortened and revised version of my doctoral dissertation, defended in February 1964 at Columbia University. It has its origins in a tutorial paper that I wrote in the spring of 1955, while studying at the University of Grenoble under the auspices of the Korean G. I. Bill. At that time and since then, I have been aided in many ways by many people, and I am beholden to them all. MM. Ambroise Jobert of the University of Grenoble, Henry Contamine of the University of Rennes, and Raoul Girardet of the Institut des Sciences Politiques, Paris, have probably forgotten the casual conversations they had with me on various matters pertaining to the French army under the Third Republic. Nevertheless, they helped me to understand certain questions which would otherwise have remained obscure. General Joseph Revol, historian of the French army, was kind enough not only to allow me to examine his unpublished memoirs but also to discuss at some length the whole subject of this study.

In France, most of my research in printed sources was done at the library of the Ministry of War. Mlle. Madeleine Lenoir, Director of the library, kindly granted me the full use of their fine collection. Assistance of a special nature was rendered by the staff of the library, in particular Mme. Berger and MM. Besson and Fournier. Because of their good-humored willingness to put up with my many importunities, great and small, my periods of research at the Ministry of War were much facilitated. The Service historique de l'Armée gave me permission to examine the minutes of the Conseil supérieur de la Guerre for the years 1871–1914, and also the memoirs of General Millet, which are now on microfilm in the Archives of the Ministry of War at Vincennes.

An undertaking such as the present study can seldom be completed without financial assistance from some outside source. I am pleased to record my gratitude to the Samuel S. Fels Fund for the generous fellowship awarded to me for the academic year 1959–1960, during which I was able to do full-time research in France. The Department of Humanities at M.I.T. gave me two summer grants, one for further research in France in 1965 and the other in 1966 for the final preparation of this work for publication. From the same source, I also received considerable financial assistance to help defray the cost of typing both the dissertation and the final manuscript for publication. Mrs. Martha Robinson typed the dissertation, not only displaying her usual technical proficiency, but also providing welcome assistance to me in the form of suggestions and criticisms as to style, grammar, and spelling. Miss Ofelia Ruiz did a fine job of retyping my revised manuscript on very short notice.

Professors Emmet Larkin of the University of Chicago and Lynwood Bryant and Bruce Mazlish of M.I.T. read the manuscript either in whole or in part and contributed both encouragement and a number of valuable suggestions. Above and beyond my thanks to Professor Shapard B. Clough for sponsoring my dissertation, I owe him a special debt of gratitude. Like so many other candidates for the Ph.D. in European history at Columbia, I have found him to be not only a fine and knowing teacher but, what is perhaps more vital for a graduate student, a wise councilor and a friend. Without his continual encouragement, his occasional prodding, and his unfailing acts of kindness to me over the past ten years, this work would have taken much longer to complete, while my career in my chosen profession could not have been launched with so few discouraging setbacks.

If all of the afore-mentioned persons had a part in making this book a better one, none of them, of course, is to be blamed for its shortcomings, its omissions, or its errors in fact and interpretation. They are my responsibility.

Through the various stages of my career as a graduate student and in my first years as a teacher, my wife has been constant in her sympathy and her patience. She made the creation of this book a pleasanter experience than it would have otherwise have been, and I am deeply grateful.

DAVID B. RALSTON

Boston, Massachusetts
September 1966

Contents

xi

PART IV

THE ENTENTE RESTORED

Introduction

With the emergence of the Third Republic in the 1870's, France found herself confronted by a novel and unprecedented political problem: the coexistence of a republican regime, increasingly democratic in form and spirit, and a large standing army, led by a caste of professional officers. The great historian Leopold von Ranke noted at the time that it would be a curious experiment to follow.[1] Ranke was not alone in doubting that a parliamentary republic, by definition a weak form of government, would be able to exercise effective control over a large standing army, of necessity organized on authoritarian, hierarchical lines and officered by men who tended to be antidemocratic in outlook. A number of elements made the problem particularly acute in the case of France.

The supposedly inherent weaknesses of any democratic parliamentary regime were for the Third Republic accentuated by the circumstances of its birth. The Republic was based not on any great groundswell of enthusiasm within the nation but rather on the inability of the conservative, predominantly monarchist deputies to the National Assembly of 1871 to agree on who should be king. If a majority of Frenchmen soon came to favor a republican form of government, it was simply because they recognized the truth of the ironic remark of Adolphe Thiers: "The Republic divides us least."

The historical precedents for the success of France's third experiment in republican government were not reassuring.

[1] H. Contamine, *La Revanche* (Paris: Berger-Levrault, 1957), p. 20.

The Republic of 1792, having momentarily profited by a surge of revolutionary enthusiasm to expel the invader from French soil, quickly degenerated into the corruption of the Directory. Bonaparte cut short its existence in 1799. The Republic of 1848 began as the slightly ludicrous by-product of a street riot. When Louis Napoleon, the President of the Republic, staged the *coup d'état* that overthrew it in December 1851, few regretted its passing. In the plots leading to the downfall of both of these regimes, elements of the army played a vital role. That the army might again be made the instrument of a *coup d'état* or that it might become the focus of sentiment for the strong antirepublican forces within the country was a very real fear for the leaders of the new regime during the first uncertain decades of its existence.

Because of their memories of 18 Brumaire and December 2 and their consequent distrust of the army, the republican chiefs could well have believed it elementary prudence to reduce the army's strength, or at least to make it more democratic in spirit. They did neither, for the possibility that a large standing army might endanger the new political institutions of France was offset by the necessities of national defense. The defeat of France in 1870 and the appearance on the European scene of a united Germany gave a new importance to the army. French military policy in the halcyon days before 1870 had been based on the assumption that France as the strongest state in Europe was safe from aggression. The primary function of the army was not so much to defend the national soil but rather to assert the country's interests in various foreign expeditions. Now, however, the safety of the state was seen to depend on its efficiency.

Instead of reducing its strength, republicans had no choice but constantly to reinforce the army. They dared not change its form, for no one before the turn of the century would argue that a "democratic" army was a more effective instrument of national defense than one constituted according to traditional principles. A profound and far-reaching program of military reform was among the earliest preoccupations of the newly founded regime. The three decades after the defeat of 1870 were to witness a thorough reorganization of French military institutions. If this was, above all, the result of the efforts of the soldiers, it was at every step encouraged by the civilian leaders of France, who appropriated the huge sums of money that were necessary and who enacted such laws as were required.

Yet the problem posed for the new regime by the existence of the army was more acute in appearance than in fact. For all the structural and spiritual incompatibility between the Republic and the army, they managed to live together over the years between 1871 and 1914 and to evolve a satisfactory, but thoroughly pragmatic, relationship. There were a number of factors that facilitated such an understanding. The first generation of republican politicians recognized the tenuousness of their position only too well to want to create additional trouble by needlessly threatening the army, especially since their own well-being ultimately depended on its ability to carry out its mission of defending the country. There was, it is true, always a vague sense of fear and distrust underlying the attitude of the republican government toward the army. The politicians tended to think of the military as forming something of an alien body within the state, a group living according to a particular code and devoted to an ideal that was fundamentally antithetical to that cherished by the Republic; but so long as they felt no overt danger from the army, they were willing to leave it alone.

The army, for its part, would show itself to be the docile, obedient servant of the Republic. It was, above all, a passive instrument of state policy. To the degree that the military had a will of their own with regard to the regime, their primary desire was for independence within their own special sphere. This did not necessarily preclude governmental intervention in, or surveillance over, military affairs. The soldiers never thought to question the prerogatives of the state in such matters as conscription, budgetary appropriations, or the over-all organization of the army. All such matters had political ramifications. On the other hand, there was a vast terrain where the military believed that, in the interest of the nation and of the army, the civilian government should intrude as little as possible. With regard to these more purely military matters, involving both the long-term institutional interests of the army and its ability to discharge its technical mission, the soldiers wanted to maintain a high degree of autonomy.

The distinction between questions that were primarily military and those having political implications was not always easy to make, but over a period of a quarter century at least, following the defeat of 1870, the army and the state managed on most occasions to reach some accommodation as to what was expedient and proper. This entente was based less on mutual sympathy and comprehension than on a common devotion to the same patriotic vision. Whatever differences there might be between the democratic and the authoritarian ideal, particularly with regard to internal affairs, the politician and the soldier were agreed on what should be the primary goals in foreign policy: the reestablishment of the place of France in Europe, the ending of her diplomatic isolation, and ultimately the revision of the Treaty of Frankfurt, *la Revanche*.

The military tended to regard the advent of the Republic as but the latest of the periodic changes in regime that seemed to be the outstanding characteristic of French political life in the nineteenth century. The attitude of the soldier toward the state in the nineteenth century was determined less by the shape and spirit of the regime of the moment than by the fact that it was probably ephemeral. The military had learned to take an attitude of disciplined detachment toward political matters and had come to see the danger of committing themselves too wholeheartedly to any particular regime. For the soldier, the essence of his duty lay not so much in giving the government his active support as in obeying whatever orders he received from it.

The present work seeks to examine, and possibly to explain, how the French army and the Third Republic managed to reach an effective and workable understanding. Without this entente, the defense of the national soil could not have been assured. This will not be a study of the French army as a social institution. As far as the author knows, such a work is lacking for the period in question, although the relevant chapters of Raoul Girardet's splendid essay *La société militaire dans la France contemporaine, 1815-1939* are very suggestive. Nor does the author pretend to give a full account of the military developments of the era, in particular the series of technical reforms that during the decades after 1870 constituted a veritable renaissance within the army. Such purely technical questions will be treated only insofar as they bear on the problem of the place of the army within the state.

Much has been written on the defects and the shortcomings of the Third Republic. It may be that students have not paid enough attention to the areas where it worked, and often very well indeed. Though there were numerous political, social, and economic problems that the republican system of parliamentary government ignored, or could not solve, there were numerous others that were dealt with as a matter of course. For the first four decades of its existence, one such problem was that of national defense, and to consider it the touchstone of effective government is to exaggerate only slightly. The Republic managed to assure the military security of France and also to resolve whatever political problems were thereby created down until 1914. This is certainly one measure of its efficacy as a system of government, and perhaps even of its peculiar glory.

PART I

THE PRECEDENTS

CHAPTER ONE

The Army and the State: 1815-1870

The military force of the Third Republic was a "national" army consisting chiefly of conscripts called to the colors for a comparatively short period of time. The army of the constitutional monarchies and the Second Empire had been a corps of long-term professionals. Yet, even with this significant change in the shape of French military institutions, there was an underlying continuity between the old and the new. Having inherited the defeated and battered army of Napoleon III, the Third Republic altered the method of recruitment for the men in the ranks and by stages introduced a system of universal conscription. The new regime could not so easily replace the personnel or transform the spirit of the professionals who constituted the real nucleus of the army. Because the officer corps had survived the Franco-Prussian War more or less intact, the army of the Third Republic was from the beginning commanded by men molded in outlook and attitude by the old army. They gave a decisive imprint to the army of the Republic.

In the years from 1815 to 1870, the French army as a whole led an existence completely apart from the rest of the nation. In contrast to the exhilarating years of the Revolutionary and Napoleonic wars, with their unceasing saga of military glory, and in contrast to the period after 1870, when the French people "cherished their army with a love that was slightly child-

9

ish . . . ,"[1] during the middle years of the nineteenth century the army was something unknown, something outside the main currents of national life. The great majority of the French people, possibly worn-out by the martial clamor of the Napoleonic era, simply seemed to have no interest in military affairs. The middle classes grew accustomed "like the Chinese . . . to look on soldiering as the lowest of human occupations."[2] The pay of an officer was low, life in a series of dreary garrison towns was monotonous, and, in time of peace, promotion for all but the very gifted or the very lucky was slow. It was difficult for an officer to marry or to establish any kind of reasonable home when each regiment changed garrison on the average of every twelve or eighteen months.[3] Under these circumstances, a military career was not a very attractive one.

The men in the ranks were recruited from those too poor to buy their way out. The annual contingent of conscripts generally numbered about 30,000 out of the 300,000 who each year became eligible for military service.[4] Conscription was regulated by drawing lots. Men who drew "good" numbers were exempt from all but the most nominal and unlikely reserve obligation, but the ones with "bad" numbers were liable for induction. Even so, the possessor of a "bad" number was not automatically obliged to serve, for if he could find a substitute and pay him an adequate premium, he could still escape the army. Companies were set up to ensure people against drawing a "bad" number and to procure substitutes for those who did.[5] Naturally enough, the sons of even the moderately well-to-do never experienced military life as conscripts. For those

[1] H. Contamine, *La Revanche* (Paris: Berger-Levrault, 1957), p. 20.

[2] A. Kovacs, "French Military Legislation in the Third Republic," *Military Affairs,* January 1949, p. 1.

[3] Ch. de Gaulle, *France and Her Army,* F. L. Dash, trans. (London: Hutchinson, 1945), p. 61.

[4] J. Monteilhet, *Les institutions militaires de la France* (Paris: Alcan, 1932), p. 23.

[5] Col. J. Revol, *Histoire de l'armée française* (Paris: Larousse, 1929), p. 187.

who were inducted, the term of service was at first eight and later seven years. So long a period of time was usually sufficient to break a young man of all binding attachments to civilian life. In seven years a recruit could develop a taste for military life, could grow to think of himself as having no other home than the army. He could also expect to be made a noncommissioned officer, a further inducement for him to remain in uniform.

There was a remarkable homogeneity in the army of the constitutional monarchies and of the Second Empire. Between the officers and the troops, there was much less class distinction than was to be found in either the Prussian or the British armies of the time. More than half the officer corps was recruited from the men in the ranks, for there were never enough young men from the educated classes, who entered the army via the great military schools, Saint-Cyr and Polytechnique, to fill the available billets.

If the majority of the French people systematically scorned or ignored the army, the military in turn were glad to segregate themselves from what they considered to be the corrupt and enervating influences of civilian life. The conditions of a soldier's existence—the distinctive uniform, the low scale of pay, the constant changes of garrison, the special code of justice and discipline—all conspired to keep him on the margin of French society in the nineteenth century. The great stirrings in French intellectual and scientific life passed him by, as did also the political developments of the era. The latter is particularly significant because in the period just ended the army had come to be an accepted path to political preferment, the outstanding example here being Napoleon Bonaparte. Despite the actions of a few ambitious officers in the *coup d'état* of December 2, 1851, the army was behind none of the changes of regime in the nineteenth century.[6] To the degree that the soldiers found themselves involved in the political turmoil, it was

[6] R. Girardet, *La société militaire dans la France contemporaine, 1815–1939* (Paris: Plon, 1953), p. 144.

as involuntary participants, drawn in against their better judgment.

Prior to 1870 every soldier was bound by his oath of fidelity to the sovereign. This oath was a remnant of the old personal feudal contract between lord and vassal, and for most officers and enlisted men it committed their honor, in itself an effective brake on any seditious sentiments that one might harbor toward the powers that be. But a problem arose for a soldier as to how far he was bound by his oath when his sovereign was deposed and replaced by another. This had taken place with great frequency during the years of revolution, from 1789 to 1814, and was to continue to do so down until 1870. Under the circumstances, where the nation periodically repudiated the sovereign whom the soldiers had sworn to uphold, a new concept of military honor had to come into existence. The revolution of July 1830 supplied a particular impetus to this evolution.

Under the restored Bourbons, the officer corps had consisted of an uneasy amalgam of Napoleonic veterans and members of the old privileged classes, many of them *émigrés*. Never absolutely certain of the sentiments of the men from the *Grande Armée,* and with some justification, considering their behavior during the One Hundred Days, the government had systematically sought to assure the devotion of the army to the regime by reserving the more important posts for former *émigrés,* although many were lacking in military experience. Though the oath of fidelity was sufficient to prevent any overt reaction to this policy so long as the regime lasted, its collapse in July 1830 appeared to release the pent-up discontent of many soldiers. As a result the morale of the officer corps was profoundly shaken. In certain garrisons the soldiers spontaneously destroyed the white flags and other insignia of the Bourbons and refused to obey orders emanating from men too closely involved in the fallen regime. On the other hand, some officers adhering to traditional values interpreted their oath of loyalty to the legitimate sovereign in the most literal fashion and resigned their commissions. In all, about two thousand officers quit the army in the wake of the Revolution of 1830.[7]

Those officers who remained in the army might well ask themselves how their oath of personal fealty to Charles X could be reconciled with the fact that there was now a new king on the throne, placed there by a band of revolutionaries. In due course, the military were obliged to swear allegiance to Louis Philippe, and this could be taken as superseding any former oath. Still a malaise persisted among the officers. An individual oath of personal fidelity to the sovereign could not alone provide adequate assurance for the solidity or the moral cohesiveness of the officer corps. Though it did guarantee to the government that in normal times its orders would be obeyed throughout the military hierarchy, it did not guarantee to the soldiers themselves that the necessary bonds of mutual trust and camaraderie would not again be subjected to a terrible strain.

To meet this problem, there evolved the ideal of passive obedience to orders from above. Military honor was to be based not merely on the concept of personal fealty to the sovereign but also on the principle of absolute obedience pure and simple to whomever should be in a position of supreme power. If it is a truism that no army can function effectively or even exist without discipline, it is a necessary corollary that discipline is seriously endangered when political events force the soldier periodically to question the legitimacy of the ultimate authority in the state and therefore the validity of the orders that he is told to obey. The instinctive need of the soldier to have a clearer and more binding concept of obedience was enshrined in military regulations three years after the advent of the July Monarchy. Colonel Pierre Chalmin in his remarkable study *L'officier français de 1815 à 1870* pinpoints this change in the principle of obedience as having been effectuated through a minor revision in the general military regulations covering discipline.

[7] *Ibid.,* p. 129.

Before the Revolution of 1830, the principle of subordination had been defined as follows: "Discipline being the principal basis of military strength . . . the right of protest is permitted to the one who has obeyed." Apparently the military authorities sensed some degree of ambiguity here, for by the ordinance of November 2, 1833, the regulations were amended to read: "The right to protest is permitted to a subordinate only after he has obeyed." [8] Henceforth a soldier was allowed no doubts concerning orders no matter how legitimate or well-founded these doubts might be. We may surmise that the military were happy to have their initiative so circumscribed. The situation of the officer vis-à-vis the state was further defined by a number of measures enacted at a relatively early date in the July Monarchy. The chief sin of the Bourbon dynasty as far as the army was concerned had been its unjust and heavy-handed efforts to put in place a military personnel specifically devoted to its cause. To protect soldiers against the arbitrary, politically motivated policies of any future government and also against their own inclination to profit by such policies, Marshal Soult, one of the abler lieutenants of Napoleon and twice Minister of War under Louis Philippe, sponsored two laws, one stating the conditions under which an officer was to be promoted and another defining and giving legal protection to his professional status.

By the promotion law of April 14, 1832, the government sought to reconcile the larger needs of the army with the vital interests of each individual officer. Every officer was guaranteed his rights to promotion by strict seniority up to the rank of *commandant* or major, but the law also enabled a fixed percentage of evidently gifted men to be advanced more rapidly, after having served a specified minimum of time in each rank. This last provision was meant to permit the men capable of commanding a division or an army to reach the higher ranks at a reasonably young age, while they still had their mental and physical vigor, rather than spending their best years vege-

[8] Col. P. Chalmin, *L'officier français de 1815 à 1870* (Paris: Rivière, 1957), pp. 251–252.

tating as captains or majors.[9] The 1832 law was to remain in effect until World War I.

Even more significant in terms of the place of the army within the French state was the law of May 19, 1834, on the status of the officer. By this law, a fundamental distinction was made between the rank of an officer and his assignment or post. Rank, since it was conferred on an officer by governmental decree, became his property, something of which he could be deprived only under exceptional circumstances and in accordance with legal forms. His military assignment, on the other hand, depended on the needs of the moment as understood by the government. Such legal protection against the vagaries of politics gave the officer unusual security and even moral independence, compared to the other servants of the French state, and he was to be much envied by the other functionaries.[10] All of the afore-mentioned measures and the point of view they reflected within the army meant that the abstract concept of the state was replacing the more specific, personal idea of the sovereign as the focus of military loyalties and as the guarantor of a soldier's honor. The obligations of an officer toward a particular regime could last only as long as the regime did, but his obligations with regard to the state, and his rights as a servant of the state, endured as long as he was an officer. The consequences of such an attitude were to be seen as early as the Revolution of February 1848.

The military were distressed by the fall of the Orléans dynasty, and they regarded the advent of the Republic of 1848 with real distaste. The troops of the Paris garrison did their best to uphold the regime against the mob in the streets, but once the abdication of Louis Philippe had made the situation hopeless, no one in the army thought to raise a hand on his behalf.[11] More striking yet was the reaction of the Duc d'Aumale, younger son of Louis Philippe, and Governor Gen-

---

[9] Revol, op. cit., p. 176.

[10] L. Thile, Pouvoir civil et pouvoir militaire (Paris: Rousseau, 1914), p. 222.

[11] Chalmin, op. cit., p. 258.

eral of Algeria. When he received word in Algiers of the
events of February 1848, he did nothing, though he might
have exploited the tremendous prestige he enjoyed within the
Army of Africa in the interests of his dynasty. "Irreproachable
soldier and functionary according to the strict definition given
by the era to these terms, he withdrew, thus setting the example of submission and obedience to the new legal power." [12]

The new regime lasted less than four years, its existence cut
short by the brilliantly planned *coup d'état* of the President of
the Republic, Louis Napoleon Bonaparte. With this act of violence, carried out by the troops of the Paris garrison, he broke
a three-year-long constitutional deadlock between the legislative and the executive branches. Although the coup of December 2, 1851, most certainly represented an incursion by the military into the political life of the country, one would err in seeing it as an example of a classic *pronunciamiento* on the Spanish model. As Chalmin points out, the word is not a French
one, nor is there any equivalent to it in the French language.[13]
Rather than seeking to impose their own solution in the conflict between the Prince-President and the conservative Assembly, the soldiers were drawn into the conflict in spite of themselves. "Solicited by both parties, the army, in the very name of
the obedience it owed the constituted authorities, could not refuse to take sides." [14]

In his contest with the Assembly, Louis Napoleon possessed
one important trump: by the terms of the Constitution he was
the Commander in Chief of the armed forces. Even so, the
majority of the more eminent generals owed their careers to
the House of Orléans and were thus in some degree opposed
to the ambitions of the present Bonapartist pretender. Knowing that he had little support within the highest ranks, Louis
Napoleon had to replace the overscrupulous commanders of

[12] Girardet, *op. cit.,* p. 132.

[13] Chalmin, *op. cit.,* pp. 360–361.

[14] Girardet, *op. cit.,* p. 138.

the Paris garrison with younger, more ambitious officers, recruited mainly in Algeria. For all the careful sounding of opinions carried out by Major Fleury, aide-de-camp to the Prince-President, only one man could be found to assume responsibility for the military end of the *coup d'état,* Saint-Arnaud. At the time an obscure brigadier general, he was hardly typical in spirit or outlook of the French officer of the period. Other generals, such as Castellane, Magnan, Vaillant, Regnault Saint-Jean d'Angély, and Baraguey d'Hilliers,[15] obviously favored the enterprise and declared themselves willing to carry out orders, but no one except Saint-Arnaud would take the necessary initiative. Even after he was placed in command of one of the divisions of the Paris garrison, Saint-Arnaud in a moment of faintheartedness wanted to back out of the undertaking. It was only when his meteoric rise was climaxed by his nomination as Minister of War, that is, as chief of the French army, that he was able to overcome his scruples, thus permitting the operation to be launched.[16]

Once the *coup d'état* was successful, the army rallied to Louis Napoleon with enthusiasm and obvious joy. A new Bonapartist regime implied governmental attention to the needs and desires of the army, as well as particular favors to those who had early given witness to their belief in Louis Napoleon's "star." The new Emperor went to great lengths to show that even if he lacked the military genius of his uncle, he was nevertheless a Bonaparte with a profound affection for the army and a great concern for its well-being. He raised the pay of the soldiers and increased their pensions; he created the Military Medal for the men in the ranks; he reinstituted the Imperial Guard. Napoleon III wore a uniform and staged frequent reviews and parades, all meant to restore to the army its splendor and its éclat and to give a military aura to the re-

[15] B. D. Gooch, *The New Bonapartist Generals in the Crimean War* (The Hague: M. Nijhoff, 1959), pp. 13–17.

[16] Girardet, *op. cit.,* p. 140.

fine physique, good health, and an impeccable appearance, these were sufficient, with some luck and a little backing, for a man to make a career." [22]

During the first half of the nineteenth century, France was at war far more often than any other European power. The French soldiers were thus afforded abundant occasions to display their warlike qualities, particularly during the conquest and pacification of Algeria. The best of them won rapid promotion, with the result that the army of Napoleon III was led by a group of dashing and courageous soldiers. Their laurels had been won at the head of small units in pell-mell encounters with the Arabs, and they had an ill-disguised contempt for any graduate of the Staff School who really thought that there might be another dimension to warfare. Nothing in the Crimean or Italian wars disturbed their confidence that they knew more about the realities of war than any other soldiers in the world. Of the three armies involved in the Crimea, the French turned out to be considerably less incompetent and poorly organized than either the British or the Russians.[23] In 1859, the indolence of the Austrians prevented them from taking advantage of the blunders of the French high command prior to Magenta and Solferino. French soldiers, and not the French generals, won the two bloody victories of 1859.

The rapid Prussian victory in the 1866 war against Austria revealed to the more prescient of the French officers that there might be more to warfare than the "Africans" cared to admit. A few tentative steps were taken to remedy the obvious insufficiency in advanced military planning. In 1867, at the initiative of the Emperor, the most eminent officers of the army were called together at the Châlons encampment to undertake a *Kriegspiel* on the Prussian model. No one there was capable of evolving a general theme for the exercise. No one

[22] Gen. Weygand, *Histoire de l'armée française* (Paris: Flammarion, 1953), p. 284.
[23] M. Howard, *The Franco-Prussian War* (New York: Macmillan, 1961), p. 17.

knew how to analyze a military situation or how to give the necessary orders. In the presence of so complete an inability on the part of his generals, "the Emperor adopted the course of asking General Trochu to read aloud from the work of Thiers on *The History of the Consulate and the Empire.*" [24]

A far more significant response to the rising Prussian menace than this belated attempt to teach his generals about warfare on a grand scale was the plan of reform sponsored by Napoleon III which called for a general broadening of military service. The project involved an increase in the size of the active army and the effective organization of the reserves much in the manner of the Prussians. The Emperor found no real support for his ideas either within the army or in the country at large. The soldiers were frankly doubtful that short-term conscripts, such as those in the Prussian army, were of any real military value at all. A conscript began to be worth something only after he had served a few years and regimental life had broken him of all civilian ways. Marshal Randon declared: "These proposals will give us only recruits. It is soldiers we need." [25] The bourgeois did not want their sons wasting their time in the army, while the peasants still preferred to take their chances on drawing a "good" rather than a "bad" number. In the end, Marshal Niel, the Minister of War and the author of the law, was able to do no more than have the term of service reduced to five years, thereby giving military training to a slightly larger percentage of the population than formerly. Elaborate provisions were also made for the organization of the reserves, but these were still a dead letter in 1870 when war broke out. The Niel law of 1868 was a pale reflection of what Napoleon III and his more farsighted advisers demanded. It did little to improve the state of the army on the eve of the Franco-Prussian War.

A simple narrative account of the French performance in the War of 1870 makes it difficult to believe that France had

[24] De Gaulle, *op. cit.,* p. 64.
[25] *Ibid.,* p. 66.

been the preeminent military power on the European conti-
nent for the past fifty years. The confusion of mobilization
was probably no worse than it had been in 1859, as described
by General Trochu in his work *L'armée française en 1867*, or
at the time of the Crimean War. The enemy, however, was of
a caliber different from the Russians or the Austrians. The
causes of the French defeat in 1870 are numerous. In numbers
of men mobilized, the French with 250,000 soldiers could not
match the 400,000 in the army of Prussia and her allies, not to
mention the 100,000-man reserve and a large force of militia.
The French artillery was inferior in quantity to that of the
Prussians and shorter in range. The French army had no plan
of campaign, other than to rush the troops headlong to the
frontier, in the vague hope of invading South Germany. The
Prussian war plan was carefully worked out in advance, with
due allowances made for unforeseen contingencies. Since no
unit in the French army larger than a regiment had an organized peacetime existence, brigades, divisions, army corps, and
armies had to be created at the time of mobilization, their
components drawn from the farthest parts of France and their
command structures improvised in haste.[26] In the Prussian
army all such things had been carefully worked out in advance and tested in numerous *Kriegspielen.*

Despite all its organizational and material deficiencies, the
French army might yet have made a respectable showing in
the war but for one irremediable defect. The army had no
leadership. There was no general in unquestioned command
of the armies in the field who was able to impose his will on
his higher-ranking subordinates or on the government, as
Pélissier had done in the Crimea. The command of the main
French field army changed hands three times in the course of
six weeks. None of the subordinate commanders displayed any
initiative, possibly because absolute obedience had become so
ingrained in their mentality that very few of them dared to
make a move without first receiving a specific order. The

[26] Howard, *op. cit.*, pp. 63–71.

French generals were profoundly ignorant of war on a grand scale; thus the years of careful peacetime planning necessary to mobilize an army and to launch a campaign were completely lacking as was also the training required to manage the movements of an army in the field. The confusion caused by the intellectual deficiencies of the generals in command was heightened by the personal enmity many of them felt toward each other.

The French chiefs were all mutually jealous and ready to abandon one another at the moment of danger. A sovereign, sick and lacking in prestige, could not through fear suppress their rivalries. Opposed to them were to be seen the chiefs of the German army, possessing not only the most brilliant qualities, but also a perfect sense of solidarity, which led them to rush to the help of each other and to move spontaneously, without orders, toward the sound of cannon fire in order to render mutual support. . . .[27]

Bravery was not lacking in the French army, either among the generals or the men in the ranks. Badly provisioned through the incompetence of the military commissariat, suffering terrible losses in battle, and then subjected to the crushing fatigue of marches and countermarches as the generals tried to evolve or improvise a plan of campaign, the soldiers fought with traditional verve and courage. On occasion, by their fierceness and their tenacity, they would win a temporary local advantage, only to have their generals throw it away. In the recent past, the French soldier had been able to win his own battles while his chiefs did little more than stand aside observing the slaughter, but it was to no avail against the superior numbers and the methodical maneuvers of the Prussian armies.

To climax the list of mistakes committed by the French in the war, Napoleon III insisted on accompanying the armies, although he was in such pain that he often seemed hardly

[27] Gen. du Barail, *Mes souvenirs* (3 vols.; Paris: Plon, 1894–1896), Vol. III, p. 239.

aware of what was taking place around him. He could do little to impose any order on the quarreling generals, while the Regency Council under the incompetent direction of the Empress tried to run the war from Paris. Napoleon III was not a soldier as his uncle had been. The sight of the slaughter at Solferino and Magenta had sickened him.[28] His presence with the armies added nothing, while his absence from Paris was a disaster. After the opening defeats the only salvation for the French army lay in a retreat to Paris. Here it could dig in and regroup its forces, but for political reasons the Empress vetoed even the return of Napoleon III to Paris, let alone the army.[29] The hastily formed Army of Châlons, accompanied by the Emperor, thus wandered into the encirclement of Sedan. Had Napoleon III remained in Paris, he would perhaps have taken the political risk of withdrawing his army back on the capital.

Napoleon III had come to power because he had known how to exploit the ambitions and the sentimental Bonapartism of certain officers to his own political advantage. Once the Empire was reestablished, he showered favors on the military in an effort to keep any current antipathetic to himself from gaining strength. In the matter of choosing the men to lead the armies, much depended on how well the general in question stood with the imperial couple. "Gallantry in the field and an agreeable personality were the passports to court favour and court favour was the passport to high command." [30] Public opinion also had to be heeded in the choice of generals, as was the case with Bazaine. His reputation may have been tarnished by certain of his actions during the Mexican campaign, but as a promoted ranker, he was a favorite of the more advanced opposition.[31] After the fact, few would deny that the Emperor's constant interference in the affairs of the army, be it for personal reasons or motives of state policy, had contributed greatly to the disasters of 1870.

[28] Guérard, *op. cit.,* p. 172.
[29] Howard, *op. cit.,* pp. 133–134.
[30] *Ibid.,* p. 65.
[31] Guérard, *op. cit.,* p. 174.

The more prescient soldiers asked of the emerging Republic that they be given the greatest possible latitude in the management of their own affairs. In making such a request, they were not acting out of any desire to resist the general policies of the government, or because of their supposedly innate antirepublicanism. Rather their experiences under the Second Empire had indicated that too much politically motivated interference was incompatible with the primary function of an army in time of peace: preparing for war. Republican politicians could never overcome completely their distrust of the army, but most of them over the years came to see the soundness of the military argument and to allow the soldiers to make the institutional arrangements necessary to profit by the increased autonomy of the army within the state. This was to be one of the constant themes in the evolution of the relationship between the Third Republic and the French army.

PART II

THE PERIOD OF PEACEFUL ACCOMMODATION

CHAPTER TWO

The Army and the Founding of the Republic: 1871-1879

The National Assembly and the Rebuilding of the Army

Following the elections to the National Assembly in February 1871 and the organization of a provisional republic, the political institutions of France hung in abeyance for five years. Unable to agree on the constitution of a monarchical regime and unwilling to found a republican one, the predominantly conservative deputies to the National Assembly postponed considering the problem for as long as possible. Only when it was apparent that the Republic represented the solution most acceptable to all factions within the country, did they vote the constitutional laws confirming its existence. This slowness on the part of the National Assembly in reaching a political solution is in notable contrast to the dispatch with which it reestablished the army. The three fundamental laws governing its existence under the Third Republic had been voted by 1875, before discussion of the Constitution even began. At a moment when the shape of the new regime could be only dimly perceived, the military institutions of the Third Republic were in existence and beginning to function. The immediate reason for their speedy reconstitution was the Paris Commune of 1871.

With the regular army in captivity and the levies of the Government of National Defense led by Léon Gambetta in the process of dissolution, the newly organized provisional Republic, under the presidency of Adolphe Thiers, had no military forces at all. In order to deal with the insurrection in Paris, which apparently portended the disintegration of the political and social fabric of the nation, Thiers skillfully negotiated the release of the French troops imprisoned in Germany. To have requested that the German troops in occupation around Paris crush the rebellion would have seriously compromised his political situation, while the remnants of the armies of Gambetta appeared hardly reliable. As had often happened throughout the nineteenth century, the regular army was called upon to repress internal disorder and to avert the danger of social revolution. Organized as the Army of Versailles, under the command of Marshal MacMahon, the freshly liberated regulars stormed the city and in a week of bitter fighting subdued the Communards. The Army of Versailles lost about a thousand men killed. At least 20,000 of the insurgents died in the fighting or before a firing squad.

By the exemplary brutality with which it suppressed the Commune, the army established firmly the authority of the provisional government. On June 29, 1871, at Longchamps, the 120,000 troops of the Army of Versailles passed in review before Thiers, to be greeted by the tumultuous cheers of the assembled crowd. The French army had been reborn. As the *Moniteur de l'armée* declared: "Today we show to Europe an army of 100,000 men, full of courage, and admirably led, which has just saved civilization." [1]

The Paris Commune as the climactic event of the *année terrible* had a profound effect on the conservative National Assembly, to whom chance had given the mission of reorganizing the country. One may justifiably wonder which of the two great catastrophes of the year just past had shocked them more, the defeat of France at the hands of the upstart Prussians or the civil war fought out under the sardonic gaze of the occupying enemy. Considering themselves to be the

[1] *Moniteur de l'armée,* July 1, 1871.

spokesmen of an older and better France, the deputies to the National Assembly held definite views as to the needs of the country. A majority of them had been *émigrés* from public life since 1830 or 1848 and were thus untainted by the corruption supposedly rampant under the Second Empire. It would be their mission not only to reform the political institutions of France but also to reestablish the bases of a healthy society. Their political and social program can best be summed up in the title taken for itself by the Broglie ministry of 1873, the "Government of Moral Order." In the conservative vision of a society founded on the precepts of moral order, the army as an institution devoted to the complementary ideals of obedience and authority was bound to figure prominently. Its reorganization was therefore an issue of great immediate importance.

Even before seriously broaching the question of military reform, the National Assembly moved to reestablish some kind of hierarchical order within the newly constituted army and, in effect, to reapply the laws that traditionally governed its existence. In their efforts to raise and to organize new armies to fight the Prussians, the delegation of the Government of National Defense at Tours had had to go to extreme lengths to find the officers necessary to command these units. Thus, by the decree of October 13, 1870, the measures concerning promotion then in force were suspended for the duration of hostilities.[2] Numerous persons were commissioned outright, while many officers were jumped several ranks to fill the need. Then came the return from captivity of the officers of the regular army, who felt that their vital interests had been endangered by the wholesale promotions of the Government of National Defense. As a result, there was an excess of some 50 per cent in the officer ranks.[3] A commission was therefore set up by the National Assembly to examine each case individually

---

[2] *Journal Officiel de la République française* (hereafter referred to as *J.O.*), (1871), p. 2385.

[3] "De la situation actuelle des officiers de l'armée française," *Correspondant*, August 10, 1871, pp. 554–555.

on its merits and to decide whether the promotion given had been deserved or not. It was also to pass on the retention in the army of those men who, having received temporary commissions, wished to remain as officers. The decisions of the Commission were to be final and without appeal.

Under the chairmanship of General Changarnier, a noted royalist and one of the leading lights of the old army, the Commission claimed to be guided in its decisions by the "rule of equity and good faith" and the "old and healthy traditions of the French army." If the Commission could not act in accordance with the strict letter of the 1832 law, "which had no provision for the annihilation of entire armies, it always took into consideration the spirit of our military regulations." [4] Particularly blameworthy were those who, having pledged their word to their captors not to attempt to escape, had not been placed under guard and who had thereupon fled back to France to rejoin the fight. In so doing, these officers, in the estimation of the Commission, forgot what they owed to themselves and to the good name of their corps and their country. Neither the violations of international law attributed to the Prussians nor the call of patriotism was "a sufficient excuse for the violation of one's word of honor." [5]

The Commission, by basing its estimation of where the duty of an officer lay on canons of military honor rather than of patriotism, would seem to have been setting up the needs and standards of a mere corporate body against those of the nation as a whole. One may also see the blame attached to those men who evaded captivity to join the Government of National Defense as another blow aimed at Gambetta. His assumption of the role of radical dictator after Sedan had frightened many conservatives. Even the conservative, Catholic review *Correspondant,* in noting the attitude of those officers who for reasons of military honor had stood aside as the Government of National Defense went down under the blows of the enemy,

---

[4] *J.O.* (1872), p. 2736.
[5] *Ibid.,* p. 2737.

wondered if "duties towards the Prussians were the only ones that a French soldier had to fulfill!"[6]

Assuming the conservative nature of the Commission, and indeed of the National Assembly itself, along with its avowed intention of restoring the authority of the 1832 law, one should not be surprised that the men of the regular army were favored over those who had served under Gambetta. Where General du Barail, despite his irritation at the pretensions of a civilian commission to meddle in a strictly military matter, found its decisions to be essentially sound,[7] another officer, the staunch republican General Iung, found them to be "bizarre."[8] Many officers who had fought for the Government of National Defense or who had republican sentiments felt that the Commission had injured their vital interests, and there were many letters to *République française,* Gambetta's paper, from these men.[9] That the avowed intention of the Commission to maintain the rules of equity and good faith were perhaps realized after all may be gathered from the fact that its accomplishments were also denounced by at least one fiercely anti-republican officer.[10]

Whatever the rights or wrongs done to republican and anti-republican officers, the chief result of the labors of the Commission was the restoration, virtually intact, of the officer corps of the Second Empire. The men in command of the French army over the next two or three decades would all have begun their careers under Napoleon III or even before. In themselves, they perpetuated during the first decades of the Third Republic the military traditions of the pre-1870 era, despite all the re-

---

[6] *Correspondant,* August 10, 1871, p. 559.

[7] Gen. du Barail, *Mes souvenirs* (Paris: Plon, 1894–1896), Vol. III, pp. 303–304.

[8] Gen. Iung, *La République et l'armée* (Paris: Charpentier, 1892), p. 140.

[9] E. Katzenbach, "Charles Louis de Saulces de Freycinet and the Army of Metropolitan France" (unpublished Ph.D. dissertation, Princeton University, 1953), p. 207.

[10] Gen. Castex, *Ce que j'ai vu* (Paris: Capiomont, 1898), p. 159.

forms undertaken by the National Assembly and succeeding legislatures.

That the National Assembly had an imperative mandate to undertake a program of military reform was admitted by all, including the many officers who were deputies. No one could deny that the French army had been shown to be inferior to the Prussian army and that efforts had to be made to improve it. The real question before the National Assembly and before the country was one of degree. Had French military institutions shown themselves to be so defective that nothing less than a complete renovation was necessary, or was the defeat caused by the malfunctioning of certain parts of what was generally a healthy organism? The deputies to the National Assembly tended to lean toward the second view. Whatever the failings of the regular army in the recent war, it had vigorously and successfully defended the established order against the forces of social chaos represented in the Paris Commune. Wisdom dictated that the legislators not tinker too radically with an institution of such proved ability. Then, too, the experts in military matters in the National Assembly were, naturally enough, the generals who had been elected as deputies. They were reluctant to admit that there was anything basically wrong with the institution that had nurtured them. Everyone, however, admitted one defect: the numerical insufficiency of the French in the recent war. Thus, the enactment of a new conscription law to increase the size of the army was the first major item in the program of military reform of the Assembly.

A conscription law, since it decrees what part of the civil population of a country is to undergo military service and under what conditions, is a piece of social as well as military legislation. It can profoundly affect the lives of a large portion of the people in a nation by removing its young men at an especially impressionable age from their traditional routines of family and livelihood and by subjecting them for an extended period of time to a totally new way of life. This particular aspect of the conscription law was of especial interest to those deputies who were concerned with the moral reform of French society and who saw in the army a possible means to this end.

The system of recruitment considered to be best suited to the needs of the country was universal conscription. As one of the fundamental military institutions of Prussia, it had proved its efficacy in the three wars of national unity. It was also hoped that to subject every young man in the country to the rigors of military service "would be a moral antidote for the anarchy of the times." [11] The reporter for the law, the Marquis de Chasseloup-Laubat, stressed the double aim of the men who had drawn it up. "The law is not only in our opinion a military law, it is also a social institution, upon which will be based, let us hope, important reforms in our morals, our customs, and our laws." [12] Universal military service was a necessary complement to the growing democratic spirit of the era. The more the institutions of a nation were based on democratic principles, the more the nation needed that "obedience to one's superior which is military discipline, and that submission to the law which is civil discipline. . . . Order and liberty are to be had only at that price." [13]

In their emphasis on the need for social regeneration, the deputies appeared to be blind to the actual causes of the defeat of 1870. The fact that the evils besetting the country stemmed primarily from the inability of the high command of the army to understand the realities of modern warfare did not occur to them. Instead, they considered the army to be "beyond all praise . . . ," [14] the one national institution untarnished by the events of the *année terrible*. Then, too, it was easier to blame the departed politicians of the Empire, or even the French people as a whole, for the misfortunes that had befallen the country, rather than to risk wounding the feelings

[11] R. D. Challener, *The French Theory of the Nation in Arms* (New York: Columbia University Press, 1955), p. 35.

[12] *J.O.* (1872), p. 2396.

[13] *Ibid.*, p. 2383.

[14] *Ibid.*, p. 3637.

of the nineteen generals sitting in the Assembly. At all times, the army was mentioned only in terms of the greatest respect. The semiofficial *Moniteur de l'armée* noted with satisfaction "the well-merited praises" bestowed upon the army during the parliamentary discussions of the conscription law. "These panegyrics were vigorously applauded by the National Assembly, which thus vindicated the army for the unjust denigration of which it has been the victim. . . ." [15]

The republican minority in the National Assembly also advocated universal conscription, but for different reasons. Whereas the conservatives saw it as a means to further their cherished principles of hierarchical social organization, the republicans saw it as a natural concomitant to the regime they hoped to found. Thus, universal conscription was admitted by practically everyone in the National Assembly as a fundamental principle in the military reorganization of France. But as Jules Simon, Minister of Education in the Thiers cabinet, pointed out: "The difficulty did not lie in establishing the principle of universal military service, but in organizing it; and that difficulty was considerable." [16] Here factors that were primarily military applied, although the problem had social overtones as well. All members of a conscript class could serve an equal length of time, which would necessarily be short, or the class could be divided into two contingents, one serving for a longer period of time than the other. In deciding which of these two alternative methods to enact into law, the deputies were influenced chiefly by the opinions and the parliamentary tactics of Adolphe Thiers.

Thiers was, without a doubt, the dominant figure in the National Assembly. The events of 1870 had only proved how prescient he was in his trenchant criticisms of the foreign policy of Napoleon III. He had not actively participated in the Government of National Defense and had thus not been implicated in its failure to salvage anything tangible after Sedan.

---

[15] *Moniteur de l'armée*, June 4, 1872.

[16] J. Simon, *Le gouvernement de M. Thiers* (Paris: Calmann-Lévy, 1878), p. 59.

In February 1871, Thiers was elected Chief of the Executive Power, to which title was added that of President of the Republic later in the same year. As "the most heeded orator, the most popular personage, the elect of two million voters, and supremely the indispensable man . . . , he spoke whenever he wanted, and by threatening to resign, he generally got whatever he asked for." [17] His indispensability was accentuated by the fact that he was one of the few contemporaries that Bismarck would recognize as a statesman. As long as France remained a conquered land, with the indemnity to be paid and German troops in occupation of her soil, no faction in the National Assembly was strong enough or had the courage to try to unseat him.

In addition to his political and administrative talents, Thiers considered himself an expert in military affairs. He took them "as seriously as any graduate of Saint-Cyr." [18] In the midst of all his other labors, Thiers busied himself with military matters in order to become better acquainted with the actual condition of the army. He put himself in touch with high-ranking officers in every branch, receiving frequent reports from them and thus gaining a detailed knowledge of all aspects of the military situation.[19] General Trochu, who was to be his most determined opponent in the coming debate over conscription, believed that Thiers had so immersed himself in his studies of the Revolutionary and Napoleonic wars that he had almost come to think that he himself was maneuvering the armies from "the most glorious period in French military history . . . and that to be a general was his true vocation." [20]

Recent events had not demonstrated to Thiers that universal

[17] C. Seignobos, *Le déclin de l'Empire et l'établissement de la IIIe République*, Vol. VII of *Histoire de France contemporaine*, E. Lavisse, ed. (10 vols.; Paris: Hachette, 1920–1922), p. 324.

[18] Challener, *op. cit.*, p. 39.

[19] A. Thiers, *Memoirs, 1870–1873*, F. M. Atkinson, trans. (London: Allen & Unwin, 1915), p. 231.

[20] Gen. L. Trochu, *Oeuvres posthumes* (Tours: Alfred Maine, 1896), Vol. I, p. 609.

conscription and mass armies were necessarily the answer to France's military problem. Charles de Freycinet, the lieutenant of Gambetta in the Delegation at Tours, quotes Thiers as having declared to him: "Your numbers are nothing; if the armies had been well led and constituted, as they should have been, we would have beaten the Prussians." [21] The French defeat in 1870 was thus caused not by her numerical inferiority to the Germans but rather by her unpreparedness, her strategic blunders, and the incredible frivolity of the government in thinking that the army could be mobilized in six days. "It is not the Prussian system which vanquished the French system; it is the Prussian government which defeated the French government." [22] French military institutions, founded on the conscription law of 1832, were basically sound; the fault lay with Napoleon III.

Thiers saw the problem as a choice between quality and quantity. The French army, made up of long-term professionals, emphasized quality, while the Prussians, with their masses of conscripts and reserves, had only quantity. One could not make a real soldier in three years. It was only after years of training and rigid discipline had broken a man of all civilian habits and attitudes that he could be trusted on a field of battle. This was "military education," the instilling of "military spirit," as opposed to mere "training." For many senior officers, it was an article of faith. Thiers passionately believed that to sacrifice quality for quantity, the seasoned veteran for the raw conscript, would be folly. The army of the July Monarchy was still his ideal. According to one historian: "By 1872, certain generals were less attached than this civilian to the old professional army." [23]

The conscription bill was drawn up by a special commission, consisting of forty-five deputies, including nine generals, four admirals, and four colonels. Instituted in May 1871, the

[21] C. de Freycinet, *Souvenirs* (Paris: Delagrave, 1912), Vol. I, p. 292.

[22] *J.O.* (1872), pp. 3862–3863.

[23] R. Dreyfus, *La République de M. Thiers* (Paris: Gallimard, 1936), p. 195.

Commission of Forty-Five spent over a year in writing the bill. At the start, the majority of the Commission were in favor of adopting the Prussian system "in all its details, without omitting anything." [24] Generals Billot, Chanzy, Martin de Pallières, and Ducrot all began by advocating a much shortened term of service on the Prussian model, with a consequent increase in the number of trained men in the country. Possibly the fact that several of them had led armies under the Government of National Defense had something to do with their belief. Thiers worked ceaselessly to convince the Commission of the soundness of his ideas. He spoke before it several times and buttonholed individual members on every possible occasion in an effort to win them over to his view. [25] As Thiers claims to have foreseen, wiser ideas began to find support within the Commission. Two of its most influential members, Generals Chanzy and Ducrot, after being strongly opposed to the ideas of Thiers, came to see that two or three years were not enough time adequately to train a soldier. They rallied to a longer period of service. [26] Their conversion was of some significance, for both men enjoyed great prestige and influence within the army and the National Assembly.

Thiers would have preferred eight, or at least seven, years as the term of service, but such was out of the question. In the end, the Commission settled on five years, the same as had been set by the Niel law of 1868. For financial reasons alone, it was impossible to induct a whole conscript class for five years, but universal compulsory service was still advocated by everyone, "except," as Thiers claimed, "some very few men of unusual good sense." [27] So "to win the reality of things, we had to sacrifice words." [28] The principle of compulsory service would be set on the frontispiece, but it would receive no more

[24] Thiers, *op. cit.,* p. 232.
[25] Simon, *op. cit.,* p. 64.
[26] Thiers, *op. cit.,* pp. 232–233.
[27] *Ibid.,* pp. 198–199.
[28] *Ibid.,* p. 233.

than lip service in the actual provisions of the law. Every young man in a conscript class not qualifying for an exemption was to be elegible for military service and to be a member of the active army for five years. At the end of the first year, however, in accordance with the needs of the army as decided by the Minister of War, only a portion of the class would remain under the colors. The rest, although still legally members of the active army, would return home. They were to be considered as being at the disposition of the Minister of War and therefore liable for reviews and military exercises. Whether a man would remain in the army one or five years would be determined by a drawing of lots at the start of his service.[29]

The Commission of Forty-Five displayed its concern for the social and educational needs of the state, as well as for the demands of equity and justice, in permitting a number of exemptions. A particular point, however, was made of the fact that these exemptions were not to be had for a price.[30] Students at certain specified professional schools, if they contracted to spend ten years in a career in the service of the state or if they were training to be teachers and priests, were either exempted from all military service except in time of war or were obliged to spend only one year in the army. Young men who were the sole support of a widow or who were indispensable to the operation of a family business or farm were also exempted.[31] Education received a further boon with the provisions made for one-year volunteers, a concept introduced from the Prussian army. A young man who had passed his baccalaureate and who was enrolled in the university would be permitted to volunteer for one year of service in the active army on condition that he pay for his uniforms and his maintenance. He would be expected to pass a special examination

[29] *J.O.* (1872), pp. 2397–2398.
[30] *Ibid.*, p. 2385.
[31] *Ibid.*, p. 2397.

at the end of a year to show that he had acquired sufficient military training.[32] The reporter for the law went to particular pains to stress that this was not simply a disguised form of the supposedly discredited systems of substitution or exoneration. Rather, it would be a "potent stimulant to serious study," protecting those careers considered to be "in the interests of society" and, within the army itself, provoking "an ardent desire for self-instruction" on the part of the other soldiers and N.C.O.'s.[33]

The debate in the National Assembly over the conscription law was remarkable for the unanimity of patriotic sentiment which seemed to motivate the deputies. The reconstruction of the army was looked upon as a noble mission, and political considerations were not allowed to intrude, or at least not explicitly. The religious and educational exemptions ran counter to the principle of universal military service, and this fact might have provided the grounds for a highly partisan debate if the deputies had not really been intent on the great work of restoring the military strength of France as rapidly as possible. The articles concerning the future priests and schoolteachers were voted without any serious objections being raised after only a minimum of discussion.[34]

The question of the one-year volunteers did cause a certain amount of debate, although only a few orators attacked it as a measure favoring the rich to the detriment of the poor.[35] To meet such objections, the Commission inserted an amendment permitting the Minister of War to waive payment of expenses in the case of a volunteer who fulfilled all the intellectual and educational conditions but whose family was poor.[36] Rather than being bothered by the antiegalitarian aspects of the pro-

[32] *Ibid.*, p. 2394.
[33] *Ibid.*, p. 2388.
[34] *Ibid.*, pp. 3958–3968.
[35] *Ibid.*, p. 4113.
[36] *Ibid.*, p. 4174.

gram, the deputies seemed to be more concerned with widening its scope, to include a greater number of categories of schools. In particular, it was felt that students in the agricultural schools should benefit.[37] It would appear that the majority of the deputies actually believed that the program of one-year volunteers, if applied with the strictness envisioned by the Commission, would be beneficial not only to the treasury but also to society and to the army.

The core of the conscription law and the question that elicited the most debate concerned the length of service. Where the exemptions were motivated by social considerations, the length of service was primarily a military matter with only incidental social implications. Many deputies, soldiers included, were not willing to accept on faith the bill as written by the Commission. They still believed that a shorter term of service would result in a stronger army, and they sought to amend the bill from the floor. Their most eloquent spokesman was General Trochu. Disputing the contention that without a solid nucleus of long-term conscripts the army would have no inner cohesion, Trochu declared that units consisting of men serving for five years alongside those who were in for only six months or one year would be sadly lacking in a spirit of camaraderie. The military spirit that people hoped to see inculcated by five years of service would be ruined.[38] Trochu maintained that for a conscript, the optimum period of service was three years. It was just long enough for him to acquire and to retain his military "form." After that, a conscript would begin to be bored by routine and to lose his suppleness and his vigor.[39]

The solidity and cohesiveness that the proponents of the five years' service felt could come only with men living and working together over a long period of time Trochu found in the Prussian army, where men were recruited locally rather than nationally. Conscripts from the same region served in the

[37] *Ibid.,* pp. 4139–4141.
[38] *Ibid.,* p. 3811.
[39] *Ibid.,* p. 3812.

same units. Local patriotism complemented the solidarity and the *esprit de corps* imposed by military discipline. Regional recruitment was also a potent factor in the speed and effectiveness of the mobilization of the Prussian army.[40] Thiers recognized the incontestable advantages that the Prussians derived from regional recruitment, but he felt that it could not be introduced in France. To have regiments made up of men solely from Brittany, Provence, Burgundy, or Picardy would be to risk destroying the unity of the nation, the greatest achievement of the French Revolution.[41] With the Commune and its various manifestations in the provinces still a very recent memory, such an argument had undoubted force.

Thiers stated his case before the National Assembly in a long, brilliant speech. He lauded the Commission for having done its best to make "universal service . . . as harmless as possible." [42] He then went on to scorn the concept of the nation in arms, which, as a matter of fact, no one in the National Assembly explicitly advocated, as being worthy only of a barbarian tribe. The true principle of military organization, Thiers stated, for the modern Prussians as for the ancient Romans, was to maintain permanently under arms "a part of the nation, carefully chosen, thoroughly trained, hardened to danger by constant observation of the great spectacle of war. . . ." [43] Even if one were to call on the whole nation to defend the soil of France, one still would need a solid backbone or cadre of trained men, and this cadre could not be formed without a long term of service. The secret of the military success of Napoleon, in the estimate of the historian of the wars of the Consulate and the Empire, was to combine his hardened veterans with raw recruits in the proportion of two to one. That was the army of Austerlitz.[44] As another deputy

[40] *Ibid.,* pp. 3870–3871.
[41] *Ibid.,* p. 3865.
[42] *Ibid.,* p. 3861.
[43] *Ibid.,* p. 3864.
[44] *Ibid.,* pp. 3867–3868.

pointed out, the legend of the volunteers of 1793, which was supposed to be historical proof of the efficacy of a mass army inspired by pure patriotism, should be discounted. It was not until 1794, when Carnot had integrated the volunteers with experienced troops of the line, soldiers from the royal army, that the legendary armies of the Revolution took shape.[45] Thiers was not impressed by mere numbers, and he speculated that if Napoleon had invaded Russia with 250,000 men, instead of 642,000, his campaign might have been a success.[46] Thiers would appear to have convinced the National Assembly, for the moment at least, of the soundness of his views. Trochu and three other deputies each introduced an amendment reducing the term of service to three years. The four amendments were rejected in a block by a vote of 455 to 227.[47]

The crucial point in the debate over the length of service came with the amendment introduced by General Chareton, a member of the Commission. He proposed a reduction in the service to an indefinite term of not more than four years and not less than one.[48] In the opinion of Jules Simon, this was the only amendment that had any chance of success, and for a time it seemed as if the National Assembly might seriously consider adopting it.[49] At this juncture Thiers did not fail. After reiterating his belief in the absolute necessity of at least a five-year term of service, Thiers climaxed his speech by announcing that he would not accept the responsibility for enforcing a law in which he did not believe. If the National Assembly did not vote the five years' service, he would be forced to resign, "deeply wounded."[50]

By threatening to resign, Thiers changed what had been a technical military problem into a political question. The re-

---

[45] *Ibid.,* p. 3808.
[46] *Ibid.,* p. 3912.
[47] *Ibid.,* p. 3871.
[48] *Ibid.,* p. 3900.
[49] Simon, *op. cit.,* p. 65.
[50] *J.O.* (1872), p. 3913.

publican minority in the National Assembly could not in good conscience vote for so obvious a perversion of egalitarian principles as would result from the application of the five years' service. Yet they could not reject what was in 1872 still their greatest single political asset, Thiers in the presidency. The noted publicist Joseph Reinach feels that at this crucial moment many conservative deputies who actually favored a long term of service would have voted with the republicans for the Chareton amendment just to get rid of Thiers. In order to block such an eventuality Gambetta announced that the only patriotic course for the republicans was to abstain.[51] Faced by the ultimatum from Thiers, Chareton withdrew his amendment, but it was immediately reintroduced by another general, Martin de Pallières, who claimed that all the generals on the Commission of Forty-Five were in favor of it.[52] When put to a vote, it was rejected 455 to 56, with 196 abstentions.[53] Among the fifty-six who voted for the amendment were three generals, most notably Chanzy, while five generals abstained.[54]

The conscription law of 1872 was a conservative measure. The Marquis de Chasseloup-Laubat, the reporter for the law, had said that the Commission of Forty-Five hoped to write a law of transition, one that would "carefully preserve as much as is possible of existing legislation, insofar as it does not interfere with our stated aims . . . the defense and order of the country."[55] He could be well satisfied with the results. As was noted in *Moniteur de l'armée,* with regard to the composition of the army, the new law would not noticeably change "the results heretofore obtained by the laws of 1832 and 1868."[56] Because of the overwhelmingly conservative sentiments of the National Assembly and the generally accepted conservative

[51] J. Reinach, *La vie politique de Léon Gambetta* (Paris: Alcan, 1918), pp. 281–282.

[52] *J.O.* (1872), p. 3913.

[53] *Ibid.,* p. 3916.

[54] Dreyfus, *op. cit.,* p. 196.

[55] *J.O.* (1872), pp. 3916–3917.

[56] *Moniteur de l'armée,* June 25, 1872.

view about the necessity of the army as a defense against social revolution and as an instrument of moral order, it was to be expected that the deputies would retain as much as possible from the old army. What is striking about the enactment of the 1872 law is the docile way in which the republicans accepted the resurrection of the old army and the obvious inequalities of the five years' service. If a republican military program existed in 1872, it was not readily discernible in the debates over the law.[57] Gambetta may have denounced the law in his paper *République française* on the day that it was finally voted, and he may have proclaimed in his political speeches that the Republic would "eventually establish a military system in which neither wealth nor privilege would have special benefits." [58] He was curiously silent, however, on these matters in the debates themselves. Gambetta did raise an objection to certain contemplated exemptions for members of religious teaching orders, and he spoke at some length on the subject of deferments for the less fortunate groups in society, but he never made any audible objections to the essential point of the law, the five years' service and the inequality that it caused. The best defense of what one might have expected to be the republican view on conscription was made by a soldier, General Trochu, on purely military grounds.

There are several possible explanations for the quiescence of Gambetta in the 1872 debates and for the docility of the republicans in general. The military realities that Gambetta was obliged to face as the dictator of Tours when he had tried to combat the Prussian war machine with raw levies must have given him second thoughts about the suppression of standing armies, "the cause of ruin in our finances . . . the source of hatred between peoples . . ." that he had advocated in the Belleville Program of 1869.[59] Against the Prussian army, revolutionary *élan* and patriotic enthusiasm had shown themselves

[57] Katzenbach, *op. cit.,* p. 181.
[58] Challener, *op. cit.,* pp. 44–45.
[59] Seignobos, *op. cit.,* Vol. VII, p. 75.

to be inadequate substitutes for military discipline and training. Reinach also believes that Thiers had convinced Gambetta of the necessity of the longer term of service. According to his account, Thiers was so adamant on the subject of the five years' service because he feared that a sudden attack by Germany was possible in the near future. To meet such an attack, he wanted to be able to throw into battle immediately two or three trained classes, which would only be possible at that time if the five years of the 1868 law were retained. Reinach is sure that Thiers, having informed Gambetta of his fears, obtained his assent to their retention, at least temporarily, "in order to have without delay an army ready for all eventualities." [60]

Even if the republican deputies represented the left wing of the National Assembly, they were not a very radical group in their social ideas. Arguments that stressed the army as the defender of the existing social order appealed to these spokesmen of the French middle classes. Over the next three decades, there was to be a constant demand from the French people for reducing and equalizing the burden of conscription, and the republicans would heed the political imperatives of this demand. In 1872, however, they had no real reason to object to the long term of service and the exemptions and the inequalities that it necessitated. The specter of a really radical reform of the army was not even raised. No one advocated the resurrection of the nation in arms or the abolition of the standing army as certain republicans had before 1870.

Through the conscription law and the efforts of the Commission for the Revision of Officers' Ranks, the National Assembly gave to the army a physiognomy that was not essentially different from what it had been under the Second Empire. The personnel of the officer corps was practically the same, and the term of service had not been reduced. The only significant reform was the abolition of substitution. The sons of the well-to-do were no longer able to buy their way out of

[60] Reinach, *Gambetta,* pp. 279–281.

all military service, but the exemptions that there were and the program of one-year volunteers were still postulated primarily on education, and in nineteenth-century France education was very much the privilege of the wealthier classes. As a result, a disproportionately large share of the military burden continued to rest on the shoulders of those who had grown well accustomed to support it: the peasants and the healthier members of the urban working classes.

The importance of the conscription law of 1872 as a military reform lay as much in the spirit in which it was debated as in any profound effect its individual provisions had on French military institutions. Thus the fact that universal military service was accepted in principle turned out to be more significant in the long run than the efforts made by Thiers and others to pervert that principle in operation. Thiers intended to retain as much as possible of the old professional army, and in this he was highly successful; but eventually the force of public opinion as represented in parliament, along with the younger, more progressive elements in the army itself, worked to negate his accomplishment. The avowed aim of the conservatives in the National Assembly, that the army be an instrument of moral reform and social uplift, was also thwarted. The era of moral order, whose salutary ideals and splendid hopes universal military service was meant to further, ended in 1877 or 1878. Universal military service was to have a profound effect on French society, perhaps even a moral one, taking the peasant from his field, often permanently, and throwing men from various social classes and groups together for better or for worse; but as an instrument of moral betterment and for the inculcation of hierarchical social ideals, it was to fail.

Although the conscription law was a conservative measure in its immediate effects, the other two great military laws enacted by the National Assembly were not. The fundamental military institutions of France having been stabilized, people could set about making the necessary reform in them.

With the law of July 24, 1873, on the organization of the army, the National Assembly made two innovations. By the law, the army in time of peace was provided with an organization and a structure of command that, for all but the largest units, corresponded with its wartime needs. Whereas prior to 1870 no unit larger than a regiment had had a distinct corporate existence in time of peace, now there were to be brigades, divisions, and army corps, all organized and all furnished with the appropriate command structures and auxiliary services. All that remained to be constituted at the outbreak of war were the armies and groups of armies. The French army was thus organized in such a manner as to be able "to go into the field in the shortest possible time, by passing from its peacetime to its wartime footing through a simple increase in the number of troops." [61] For the army, this represented a considerable advance.

The second innovation lay in the fact that by enacting a law on the organization of the army, the National Assembly assumed a competence and a responsibility that were new for a French legislative body. While conscription, as a question having important social and political ramifications in addition to its military significance, had always been regulated by law, all matters touching military organization had heretofore been looked upon as being purely technical, and hence beyond the competence of a legislative assembly. Under the constitutional monarchies and the Second Empire, they were therefore governed by executive decree. The justification advanced for this innovation was that the National Assembly was the sovereign power in France and that the executive power of the state was separate from it. The organization of the armed forces, being defined as one of the attributes of the sovereign power, could not be regulated by executive decrees or ordonnances, as was done in a monarchy where the executive and sovereign powers were in the same hands. In a state where the two powers were

[61] *J.O.* (1873), p. 4551.

them in number and organization?" [69] That is to say, when in doubt as to some military question, it was best to follow the German example. The French army, then, would consist of eighteen army corps.

Neither the government nor the Commission believed that any unit larger than an army corps should be organized in time of peace. The grouping of army corps into armies was believed to depend on too many contingent factors that would remain unknown until the outbreak of war, in particular, the size, nature, and organization of the enemy forces. Beyond that, to organize five or six armies on a permanent peacetime basis, creating a few supremely important positions in the hierarchy, "would have as a consequence the subalternization of the army corps commands and thus the erection of an obstacle to the development of individual initiative in those officers who might some day be called upon to exercise supreme command." [70] Without doubt, this argument had great validity, but it should also be noted that in the German army at that time there was no larger peacetime unit than the army corps. This was in itself an adequate reason for the French to adopt a similar plan.

Having provided for the organization of eighteen army corps, the authors of the bill were rather ambiguous in their attitude toward the men who in the future would command them. A general commanding an army corps would occupy, after the Minister of War, the most eminent position in the army. Yet the law made the command of an army corps an essentially temporary job, one entailing no increase in rank. A man with the rank of general of a division was to command an army corps for a term of four years, at the end of which he would revert back to the command of a division. An army corps was to be, rather than the highest position of command responsibility, the training ground for those who in time of war would lead the armies and groups of armies.

[69] *J.O.* (1873), p. 4752.
[70] *Ibid.*, p. 4553.

The idea that a general at the head of an army corps was not really exercising a command but instead serving a glorified apprenticeship did not appeal to the more eminent of the military. To limit arbitrarily and automatically the tenure of a general commanding an army corps was, in the estimation of the Duc d'Aumale, "an encroachment on the rights of the executive . . ." in that the Minister of War, as the responsible chief of the army, would not be able to act as he thought best with regard to the most important positions of command.[71] The interests of the army and of the country would be better served if the government and the Minister of War could choose the best men and keep them in place as long as they were competent. As one general put it, a limited command would never be well exercised.[72] The argument of the Commission, in wanting to insert this provision in the law, was that the government needed an additional legal weapon against aging corps commanders whose proprietary pretensions to their posts would be of a tenacity that was "irresistible."[73]

The military chose to see in this provision limiting the tenure of an army corps commander a thinly disguised fear that some generals might try to play a political role once they were firmly ensconced in their posts and certain of their ascendancy over their troops. Such implicit fears were regarded as insulting to the army. As du Barail put it, the nation should have faith in the army and "give it the full confidence it merits. If a few chiefs might plan to play a political role and to transform their troops into a Praetorian Guard, the four-year limit imposed on their term of command is more than sufficient."[74] Both Generals de Chabaud Latour and Chareton, members of the parliamentary Commission for the law, declared before the Conseil supérieur de la Guerre that politi-

[71] C.S.G., "Reg. dél.," No. 2 (1873–1874), p. 65.

[72] *Ibid.*, p. 67.

[73] *J.O.* (1873), p. 4812.

[74] C.S.G., "Reg dél," No. 2 (1873–1874), p. 66.

cal fears had contributed to the provision limiting the term of command even if they were not the decisive factor. A majority in the Commission, according to Chabaud Latour, had argued that in order to prevent a corps commander from becoming a "political personage," it was best if he did not continue indefinitely in a position where he would exercise such vast powers.[75] These fears, however, were not to be reflected in the report on the law.[76]

In the project as originally presented to the National Assembly by the Commission, the term of a general commanding an army corps was set at four years. There was no provision made for extending it.[77] Faced with strong objections from the military and the government, the Commission agreed to compromise, accepting an amendment by General Billot. Henceforth, the term of command would be three years, unless the general in question was maintained in his post by a special decree handed down by the Council of Ministers.[78] It was expected that such prolongations would be exceptional, and if they became too frequent, parliament could always interpellate the Minister of War on the subject.[79]

In fact, the exception became the rule. Over the next four decades, any general not yet of retirement age who had completed his three years as commander of an army corps was almost invariably kept in his post by the government, even if a certain amount of sophistry was sometimes necessary to maintain the letter of the law. Thus in 1882 a number of generals, upon reaching the end of their term of command, were placed in *disponibilité* for a period of twenty-four hours and then renamed to the posts they had just vacated. In that way none of them would be exercising the same command for more

[75] *Ibid.*, p. 65.
[76] *Ibid.*, p. 78.
[77] *J.O.* (1873), p. 4589.
[78] *Ibid.*, p. 4839.
[79] *Ibid.*, p. 4840.

than three years.[80] In 1884, General Chagrin de Saint-Hilaire, having been at the head of the Sixteenth Army Corps at Montpellier, stepped down and accepted the command of a division. His spirit of military devotion and his courage in voluntarily accepting what seemed to be a demotion attracted much favorable attention, although, as an anonymous article in *Spectateur militaire* pointed out, he was doing no more than his duty according to law.[81] Du Barail considered that many of the younger military members of the National Assembly, unlike the more senior officers, actually favored setting a term to the command of an army corps, and he saw this as evidence of their ambition to reach the summit of the military hierarchy as quickly as possible and of their unwillingness to have the way blocked. Once these younger officers arrived at the top, he noted ironically, they were quite willing that the government ignore this particular provision of the law.[82]

Though the authors of the law did have certain officially unstated motives for limiting the term of command of an army corps, their main objective was still what they said it was, namely to give as many as possible of the divisionary generals a chance to develop and to demonstrate their capabilities in the command of a large unit. Only in this way could the government be sure who was best suited to lead the armies and groups of armies in time of war. Undeniably, it showed an ignorance of elementary psychology for anyone to believe that a general would voluntarily step down to a subordinate position after he had devoted thirty-five or forty years to trying to reach the top. Nevertheless, the fact that the report specifically stated the need for the largest number of generals possible to develop "individual initiative" and the "habit of

[80] *Spectateur militaire* (hereafter referred to as *S.M.*), February 1882, p. 438.

[81] L.S., "Le commandement des corps d'armée," *S.M.*, May 15, 1884, p. 264.

[82] Du Barail, *op. cit.*, Vol. III, pp. 499–500.

responsibility" [83] indicated that it was the memory of the summer of 1870, when an inert and incompetent high command had failed completely, that was paramount in the thinking of the Commission and not fears of another December 2 or 18 Brumaire.

The law of July 24, 1873, on the organization of the army was primarily a military reform, and, as such, it represented a vast improvement in the efficiency of the French army. Even so, it still contained evidences of the social and political preoccupations that had loomed so large in the deliberations of the National Assembly on the subject of conscription. Once again the National Assembly rejected the Prussian scheme of regional recruitment. Conscripts were still to be inducted on a national basis, as the bugbear of civil war was once more raised, always a possibility "in a country which is as divided, as prone to factionalism as ours." [84] This rather lame political rationale was reinforced with an equally lame argument of a sociomilitary nature. Given the diverse temperaments of the natives of the various provinces and their innately different military abilities, one would run the risk of having whole divisions or army corps of inferior soldiers if regional recruitment was instituted in France. It was therefore better to mix them up, to let the solidity and tenacity of the Breton find its natural complement in the *élan* and mercurial qualities of the Provençal.[85] As for the reserves, in interests of military efficiency, they were to be inducted at the moment of mobilization into the unit stationed nearest their place of domicile.[86] Separatist tendencies in the reserves were evidently not considered to be dangerous.

Although the National Assembly considered the regulation of the over-all organization of the nation's armed forces an attribute of its sovereign power, this did not mean that

[83] *J.O.* (1873), p. 4553.
[84] *Ibid.*, pp. 1916–1917.
[85] *Ibid.*, pp. 4751–4752.
[86] *Ibid.*

civilians were now presuming to dictate to the soldiers concerning technical military matters. In fact, the military members of the Assembly dominated the debate. Monteilhet deprecates the manner in which the National Assembly, "after having rendered a platonic homage to parliamentary supremacy, resigned in favor of the military." [87]

The third and last of the important military reforms undertaken by the National Assembly before its dissolution was the law of March 13, 1875, on the cadres and effectives. Whereas the 1873 law had set up the general principles and broad outlines of the peacetime organization of the army, the law on the cadres filled in the details and went so far as to stipulate the number, size, and composition of the companies in the different branches of the army.[88] That the internal constitution of every unit in the army should be governed by statute was justified on primarily pragmatic grounds. In the past, the effectiveness of the units themselves and the welfare of the officers, men, and even the treasury had all suffered from the unstable system of executive decrees.[89] In the estimation of General Billot, the organization of the permanent cadres of the army would benefit greatly from the stability that could only be assured through a law. A law on the subject would also hinder future governments from making the composition and size of the permanent units of the army secondary to the demands of the budget.[90]

The more traditionally minded of the generals and their civilian advocates in the National Assembly did not approve of parliament assuming responsibility for the technical details of the organization of the army. General Changarnier looked upon it as but another step in "a dangerous slope which leads to a confusion of powers. . . . Soon you will be asked to

---

[87] Monteilhet, *op. cit.,* p. 180.
[88] *J.O.* (1875), pp. 220 ff., 243 ff., 270 ff.
[89] *J.O.* (1874), p. 7515.
[90] *J.O.* (1875), p. 266.

decide upon the number of rural constables in each of the 35,000 communes in France." [91] A civilian deputy, the noted royalist Émile Keller, echoed this view when he presented a motion that would remove the decision as to the number of companies in an infantry battalion from the province of parliament and would leave to the executive "the necessary liberty to direct, as in every other country, the details of army life." [92] Both men were displaying a perfectly legitimate lack of confidence in the ability of a parliamentary body to weigh the technical aspects of the problem. Answering them, Gambetta declared that such a line of argument would lead to nothing less than the suppression of the legislative authority of the Assembly. The great matters that as a whole "constitute the social economy of an entire people . . ." were made up of details and were thus "technical questions which must be decided by law." [93] That many in the National Assembly shared the doubts of Keller about their own competence was demonstrated by the narrow margin by which the motion was rejected, 327 to 325.[94]

There was possibly implicit in the reservations of a Changarnier or a Keller the fear that the deputies might not recognize or be sympathetic with the vital personal and professional interests of the officer corps.

In Germany, Austria-Hungary, Russia, and England, the officers were to a far larger extent than in France mandatories of ruling classes. . . . The French army was far more distinctly professional and therefore the interests of the officers were more immediately effective in army organization and doctrine.[95]

The most vivid example of the vested interest of the officer corps in a specific kind of organization could be seen in the debate over the number of companies that there should be in

[91] *Ibid.*, p. 260.

[92] *Ibid.*, p. 299.

[93] *Ibid.*, p. 302.

[94] *Ibid.*, p. 336.

[95] A. Vagts, *Militarism: A History* (New York: Norton, 1937), pp. 239–240.

an infantry battalion. Prior to 1870, the French infantry regiment had consisted of four battalions, each with six companies. The Commission now proposed a regiment of three battalions of four companies, which would make the wartime strength of each company 250 men. The old companies had contained between 150 and 160 men.[96]

There were valid military arguments for either the large or the small company. The Commission felt that a large company would be a more effective tactical unit in battle. Against a German company of 250 men, the 150-man French companies would be inferior in firepower. On the other hand, the battalion made up of six smaller companies lent itself to a greater variety of tactical combinations. One member of the Conseil supérieur de la Guerre questioned the ability of a captain to control 240 or 250 men in battle, while Marchal Canrobert feared that these companies would be too large to be a "family."[97] The Commission sharply rebutted all those who worried about the inability of a French captain to lead 250 men by declaring that it was up to him to develop the necessary skills.[98] The newspaper *Avenir militaire,* which claimed, as its title suggests, to speak for the more progressive elements in the army, expressed some annoyance at the idea that a French captain could not effectively command so large a company when his counterpart in Germany, Russia, and Italy was considered capable of it.[99] General du Barail, at the moment Minister of War, claimed that, of the thirteen army corps commanders whom he consulted on the matter, seven wanted to retain the six-company battalion, while five, including Ducrot and Chanzy, were in favor of four companies, and one of them had no opinion on the subject.[100]

Since the arguments of a purely military nature on both

[96] J. G. Carnes, "The French Army Officers and the Establishment of the Republic, 1876–1889" (unpublished Ph.D. dissertation, Cornell University, 1949), p. 90.

[97] C.S.G., "Reg. dél.," No. 2 (1873–1874), pp. 185–186.

[98] J.O. (1874), pp. 7520–7521.

[99] *Avenir militaire,* November 26, 1874.

[100] C.S.G., "Reg. dél.," No. 2 (1873–1874), p. 186.

sides were inconclusive, the Commission looked to see what
the Germans did and thus adopted the four-company battalion. The government, hearkening to the anxiety of many
subaltern officers, at the last moment hastily produced a
counterproposal featuring the battalion of six companies.[101]
The government plan did not include specific articles covering
the internal organization of the battalion, since it was stated
that such details should be governed by executive decree.
Nevertheless, the government did declare itself in favor of the
smaller companies for reasons of tactical efficiency and control
in battle.[102] Although the Minister of War placed himself on
strictly military grounds in advocating the smaller companies,
the underlying motive for the project lay in the particular interests of the captains and the lieutenants which might be
interpreted as constituting a "general interest."[103] Fewer
companies would mean fewer billets for the captains and
forced retirement for some of them, while the lieutenants
would face much slower promotion to that rank. *Moniteur de
l'armée* lauded the Minister for being "more practical than the
Commission" and, in a matter that could not be decided with
"mathematical rigor," for looking to the "legitimate interests"
of the officer corps and to its "glorious traditions, sanctioned
by long experience."[104]

In an effort to resolve this conflict between the vested interests of the officer corps and the demands of military progress,
the Commission insisted that there would be no need for any
captain to retire prematurely and that there would be billets
for all. When these assurances still did not calm the fears of
the officers, General Chareton, reporter for the law, produced a
new article providing that each battalion would have four
companies and each company two captains, one as commanding officer and one as *capitain à second* to oversee the ever-

[101] *Avenir militaire*, December 1, 1874.
[102] *J.O.* (1874), pp. 7951–7952.
[103] *Moniteur de l'armée*, November 21, 1874.
[104] *Ibid.*

increasing administrative chores that would naturally result from the larger companies. Chareton argued that this arrangement would actually result in an economy, since the battalion would now have sixteen rather than eighteen officers, two second lieutenants having been eliminated.[105] The lieutenants, who had been anxious over the suppression of two captaincies per battalion, could now contemplate with pleasure the creation of two new ones.

In the last reading of the law, the *capitain à second* was suppressed. The featherbedding inherent in such a concept was too blatant, while the problem of what the second captain would actually do in a company could not be satisfactorily answered. An amendment was then proposed, calling for a battalion of four companies with one captain and three lieutenants, but it was rejected by the National Assembly.[106] The article in question was returned to the Commission, and a few days later it reappeared in yet another guise. Chareton now quite frankly stated that the four-company battalion would mean the suppression of 1,200 captains' billets. The government and the Commission, not wishing to harm any vested interests or to "introduce a damaging perturbation into the constitution of the infantry," sought a way to retain the potentially unemployed captains, and they found it through the introduction of the special organization of the Algerian regiments into France. Each Algerian regiment consisted of four battalions (as opposed to the three battalions in a metropolitan regiment); so too would the French regiments. The National Assembly adopted the article without delay.[107] Not only would there now be billets for every captain, but new ones would be created for the majors, which naturally enough increased the chances of promotion for the captains. According to *Avenir militaire,* this solution to a nagging problem came from a suggestion by General Billot to his colleagues in

---

[105] *Avenir militaire,* January 21, 1875.
[106] *J.O.* (1875), pp. 1810, 1815.
[107] *J.O.* (1875), p. 1900.

the Commission. Billot argued that while the present regimental structure was adequate to supply the cadres for the peacetime contingents, it would not be sufficient for the 800,000 men who would march at the moment of mobilization.[108] In considering the matter from that point of view, the Commission was still able to reconcile the particular interests of the captains with its avowed intention of enacting a military reform.

The creation of the fourth battalion was used by Bismarck as an excuse for the "war in sight" incident of 1875. There was another inconvenience of a more prosaic kind that was eventually to lead to their suppression some twenty years later. The permanent cadre of the army was now too big for the number of conscripts that it had to incorporate and train. As was predicted by *Avenir militaire,* the companies and platoons became so undermanned that effective and realistic training was all but impossible.[109] This problem was to be present for the next forty years and was inherent in the peculiar institutional requirements of the French army. There always had to be enough officers on hand, even in time of peace, to meet the greatly expanded need of war. As General du Barail declared: in time of war, "there are never too many officers." [110] At the same time, the ratio between officers and conscripts had to be such that training would be realistic and that there would be something for all the officers to do. The one possibly effective solution, the development of an adequate program of well-trained reserve officers, never had much appeal for the French military.

The laws of 1872, 1873, and 1875 provided the essential framework within which French military institutions were to function and to evolve for the next forty years. The conscription law would be changed three times, while the laws on the organization of the army and on the cadres would be frequently modified and even disregarded, but the general shape

[108] *Avenir militaire,* March 16, 1875.
[109] *Ibid.,* March 21, 1875.
[110] Du Barail, *op. cit.,* Vol. III, p. 489.

of the army would remain the same until 1914. The next order of parliamentary business following the enactment of the law on the cadres and effectives was the discussion of the first of the three laws that together made up the Constitution of 1875. It would seem almost as if the conservatives in the National Assembly had waited until the foundations of the army were firmly laid before acquiescing in the inevitable creation of a republican regime.

The Army and the New Regime

The Third Republic was born of the constitutional travail of a parliamentary body, two thirds of whose members favored restoration of the monarchy. As paradoxical as this phenomenon may have seemed, it did correspond to a growing current of republicanism throughout the country. Still, that sentiment was not so profound nor were republican politicians so securely in control of the levers of power within the state that they could dismiss the possibility of some kind of coup against the Constitution by the conservatives. From the beginning of the 1875 regime the republicans had a majority in the Chamber, but their adversaries held the Senate by a slim margin, while MacMahon, a firm believer in monarchy, was President of the Republic. Then, too, the leading posts in the public administration and in the judiciary were held by men of conservative or Bonapartist views who owed their careers to Napoleon III. Whatever the elections may have indicated about the attitude of the country at large, the antirepublican forces controlled a number of strategic positions should they contemplate an attempt to "guide" political developments along more congenial lines.

In particular, republican anxieties were directed toward the army. Memories of the *coup d'état* of December 2 were still too fresh, and the attachment of many high-ranking officers to the Bonapartist dynasty was too well known, for the republicans in these early years to be able to dismiss the possibility that certain of the military might make common cause with the other conservative forces in the state. Under the circumstances, it is not surprising that the republicans went to considerable lengths to be precisely informed about the political opinions of the officer corps. Not only in the voluminous police files of the period but also in a number of unofficial dossiers and registers, apparently compiled from private resources, there are numerous detailed reports on the political attitudes and the behavior of individual officers, all indicative of the importance the republicans attached to the matter.[111]

Because of the temper of the army and its tradition of political neutrality, republican fears were for the most part groundless. A few members of the officer corps may have looked with equanimity, or even approval, on the prospect of the army participating in some kind of conservative coup, but the vast majority were appalled at the idea. They were thus extremely anxious to avoid the slightest cause for suspicion about their loyalty to the regime and to have it clearly understood that *pronunciamientos* in the Spanish style were emphatically not part of the French military tradition. If most of the politicians hoped that, in the interests of orderly and stable government, the military would not enter the political arena, the soldiers in their turn believed that to introduce into the army the factional quarrels wracking the nation would destroy its cohesion and consequently its effectiveness.

In an effort to reinforce the political neutrality of the military there was included in the conscription law of 1872 a pro-

---

[111] See P. B. Gheusi, *La vie et la mort singulière de Gambetta* (Paris: Albin Michel, 1932), pp. 120 ff. Gheusi quotes at length from a dossier supposedly dating from 1876, in which the views of the leading men of the army are reported at length and in precise detail. Also, F. Bédarida, "L'armée et la République: Les opinions politiques des officers français en 1876–1878," *Revue historique,* Vol. 232 (July–September 1964), pp. 119 ff. Bédarida analyzes at length two manuscript volumes uncovered by him at the Quai d'Orsay. In these volumes, there are regiment-by-regiment reports covering much of the army and providing specific information on individual officers. He is of the opinion that one of them served as the basis for the document referred to by Gheusi. They were apparently compiled for the use of Gambetta.

vision disenfranchising all men on active service. For the conscript this meant merely the deprivation of his political rights during his term of service, but the officers and the permanent cadre of N.C.O.'s were barred from the polls until they retired. The authors of the law believed that discipline would suffer if, by the act of voting, the troops could on a particular day attain equality with their superiors, and perhaps even think of themselves as political adversaries, "without, however, ceasing to be under their orders." [112] Speaking for the army, General de Cissey, Minister of War at the moment, declared that a soldier under arms was to be considered as the embodiment of force in the service of the law. It was imperative therefore that "he remain a stranger to all factions and to all political struggles." [113] Among others, Gambetta concurred in this view, that for a soldier to exercise his civic rights as a French citizen interfered with the proper discharge of his military duty.[114]

In addition to being disenfranchised, the military were progressively barred from serving in parliament. The electoral law of November 30, 1875, denied them the right to sit in the Chamber of Deputies although they could still be elected to the Senate. Then, by the law of December 9, 1884, all but a few of the highest-ranking and most-distinguished officers were excluded from election to the second chamber as well.[115] As one author notes, the soldiers were far more in favor of these restrictions on their political eligibility than were the politicians, who considered that the potential harmful effects on discipline that might possibly be caused by soldier deputies and soldier senators were far outweighed by the benefits to be derived from having them on hand for military questions.[116]

---

[112] Quoted in L. Thile, *Pouvoir civil et pouvoir militaire* (Paris: Rousseau, 1914), p. 194.

[113] *Ibid.*, p. 195.

[114] *Ibid.*, p. 198.

[115] R. d'Ornano, *Gouvernement et haut commandement sous régime parlementaire français* (Aix-en-Provence: Pensée universitaire, 1958), p. 121.

[116] *Ibid.*, pp. 119–120.

With this almost superstitious distrust of "politics" on the part of the military and their ardent desire to keep political questions out of the army, their sensitivity to even the most insignificant incidents becomes understandable. When, in 1872, certain officers in garrison at Grenoble were confined to quarters and then transferred as a consequence of having taken part in a political demonstration, *Moniteur de l'armée* approved completely. Noting that the comrades of these officers concurred as to the justice of the sanctions taken against them, the paper went on: "The role of the army within the state consists in defending the law and maintaining order, which excludes any political preoccupations; it is necessary that all those who have the honor to wear a uniform never forget this." [117]

In 1874 Admiral la Roncière Le Noury, a commander of the French Mediterranean squadron and a Bonapartist deputy to the National Assembly, wrote a rather inflammatory letter to be read at a Bonapartist banquet at Evreux. In it, he condemned the weakness of the present political organization of France and further declared that he would serve the Mac-Mahon government only so long as it followed a conservative policy. MacMahon sacked him without further ado. Writing for the fortnightly chronicle in the *Revue des deux mondes,* the conservative Charles de Mazade lauded MacMahon for his prompt action. In his estimation, the moral of the incident was that there was "a real incompatibility between the political functions of a deputy and the military functions of a man on active duty." [118]

Despite the assertions by the military of their disinterest in political matters, the republicans could never quite overcome their suspicions in this regard. That they might be justified was indicated by the crisis that opened on May 16, 1877, and that lasted for the rest of the year. The *Seize-mai,* as it came to

[117] *Moniteur de l'armée,* October 6, 1872.

[118] *La Revue des deux mondes* (hereafter referred to as *R.D.M.*), September 15, 1874, pp. 455–460.

be called, was the most dramatic confrontation of the decade between the emerging republican regime and the conservative forces within the state. Essentially, it was a conflict between the President of the Republic and the Chamber of Deputies over their respective attributes, with the Senate more or less reluctantly siding with the President. The whole affair revolved around the ambiguities and lacunae in the constitutional laws of 1875 concerning the powers of the different branches of the state and the relationship between them. What made the affair dangerous in republican eyes was the possibility that Mac-Mahon would choose to disregard the verdict of universal suffrage in deciding the color and policy of the government. The Constitution was silent on how such a deadlock was to be resolved, and it could well be that the President might try to break it with military force. According to Article 3 of the constitutional law of February 25, 1875, the President of the Republic had at his disposal the armed forces of the state, the implication being that he commanded them if he so wished.[119] Certainly MacMahon, as President of the Republic, considered the army to be his particular preserve and brooked no interference from the deputies or senators, while the fact that he was a Marshal of France made him more than just a symbolic head of the army in the estimation of the military.

MacMahon had accepted the presidency in 1873 out of a sense of military duty at the behest of the conservative majority in the National Assembly. They had hoped that the underlying conservative forces in the nation would coalesce around him and thus stop the steady drift toward revolutionary republicanism. After the Republic had come into existence despite their efforts, MacMahon felt duty bound to remain at the helm and to use the considerable powers given him by the Constitution to keep France from falling into the hands of the Radicals. In the spring of 1877 he could not find a ministry that would defend the true conservative interests of the country as he understood them and that could command a

[119] D'Ornano, *op. cit.*, pp. 100–101.

majority in the Chamber of Deputies. Acting in accordance with the Constitution, he called upon the Senate to decree the dissolution of the lower house. The Senate acceded to his request by a vote of 149 to 130, with 12 abstentions.

In the election campaign that followed the dissolution of the Chamber, the government went to great lengths, sponsoring official candidates and using its extensive powers of coercion and repression, to return a Chamber favorable to the Marshal.[120] Both the civil administration and the judiciary were used in thoroughly partisan fashion. When, despite all these efforts, the elections of October 1877 resulted in a majority hostile to the conservatives, the victorious republicans understandably enough feared that a government which had thus far shown few scruples about constitutional niceties would not hesitate to use armed force to annul the recorded will of the people. Should MacMahon choose to do so, he was in an excellent situation to attempt a *coup de force* relying on the army. Louis Napoleon in 1851 had had carefully to place men favorable to himself in the crucial commands. Marshal MacMahon would have to make no such prior arrangements, for the majority of the generals commanding the army corps were already devoted to him.

Contemporary observers tended to agree that MacMahon himself would not of his own accord move against the Constitution. The danger lay in his conservative advisers, including some of his military cronies,[121] who might yet convince him that it was his duty to disregard the elections of October 1877 and either to declare a state of siege and rule by military force or to call for a second dissolution. In the case of the second alternative, there might be outbreaks of violence inspired by the Radicals, necessitating the use of the army to maintain order. No matter how they analyzed the situation, the republicans felt that they had reason to fear the army.

[120] See the report of Brisson on the elections of October 1877, *J.O.* (1879), pp. 2558 ff.

[121] J. Silvestre de Sacy, *Le maréchal de MacMahon* (Paris: Internationales, 1960), p. 348.

The most outspoken of the antirepublican generals was Ducrot. Possessing a brilliant military reputation by virtue of his conduct prior to Sedan and during the siege of Paris,[122] he was also one of the acknowledged chiefs of the Legitimist faction in the National Assembly and so fervent in his Catholicism that he began the 1876 maneuvers of his army corps with a great open-air Mass, attended by all the troops under his command.[123] Ducrot was constant in the advice that he offered to MacMahon, namely to follow a firm and vigorous conservative line of conduct with regard to all political questions and to rely on the army if necessary to carry it out.[124] He thus saw no real difficulties for the government at the time of the *Seize-mai* crisis. It had only to act decisively, jailing the leading figures of the Left for having committed an insurrectional act in objecting to the dissolution of the Chamber and thereby obtaining the desired results from the electorate through a kind of "surprise attack." In his estimation, "the voters generally admire and instinctively follow a government which in a straightforward fashion shows them the way and resolutely leads them toward it." [125] MacMahon was somewhat disconcerted by such clarion calls to vigorous action. At one point during the crisis, when someone suggested Ducrot for the post of Minister of War, he reacted violently, declaring that this would mean "the restoration of the monarchy within four weeks." [126]

Following the defeat of the conservatives in the elections of October and November 1877, it did seem for a moment as if MacMahon were about to take the advice of such men as Ducrot. Having requested that the very moderate Dufaure form a ministry and having found his terms unacceptable, MacMahon attempted to govern through an extraparliamen-

[122] Trochu, *op. cit.*, Vol. I, pp. 250–252.

[123] Vicomte de Chalvet-Nastrac, *Les projects de restauration monarchique et le général Ducrot, d'après ses mémoires et sa correspondance* (Paris: Alphonse Picard, 1909), pp. 253 ff.

[124] *Ibid.*, pp. 246–247.

[125] *Ibid.*, pp. 268–269.

[126] *Ibid.*, pp. 277–278.

tary combination. On November 24 he called upon his old friend and comrade in arms, General de Rochebouet, who commanded the Eighteenth Army Corps at Bordeaux, to accept the portfolios of Minister of War and President of the Council of Ministers.

It is difficult to know what MacMahon had in mind in constituting the Rochebouet cabinet. If, as has been claimed, he had already decided to give in to the verdict of universal suffrage,[127] the nomination of an essentially nonparliamentary ministry only alarmed and confused the republicans needlessly. If, on the other hand, MacMahon was contemplating a second dissolution, he would understandably want a government on which he could count to act vigorously and decisively in case of an outbreak of violence. It is possible that, faced with the agitated and divided counsel of the conservatives, MacMahon turned to a man he could understand and trust, a soldier, to run things until the situation settled down, until the conservatives were able to patch together some kind of majority in the Chamber. At the end of three weeks, during which the Chamber withheld its support from the Rochebouet ministry, MacMahon capitulated and accepted Dufaure on his own terms.

Throughout the crisis of *Seize-mai,* the republicans watched the army with some anxiety. The antirepublican sentiments of many of its chiefs, including MacMahon, were well known. Still, the republicans could take some comfort from the fact that of all the great branches of the state, the army alone was not involved in the electoral pressure "in which all the others have been employed by the same people whose duty it was to protect them."[128] The commentator in *Revue politique et littéraire* praised the manner in which the army had been defended by its chief, General Berthaut, Minister of War. He would not permit it to be drawn into politics, and he would not consent that it be "anything other than the army of the

[127] Silvestre de Sacy, *op. cit.,* p. 352.
[128] *Revue politique et littéraire,* November 17, 1877, p. 477.

law." [129] The rigidly nonpartisan attitude of Berthaut angered many conservatives who preferred to see at the head of the army a "man of action." [130] The replacement of Berthaut by Rochebouet doubtless reminded many of the arrival of Saint-Arnaud at the Ministry of War a quarter century before.

Despite the antirepublican sentiments of so many of the leading generals, Gambetta, at least, professed not to be alarmed at the possibility of a *coup de force* by the army. He felt that the men in command were very much divided over the matter and that it would be inconceivable for them "to risk such an adventure without the certitude of being obeyed by absolutely everyone." [131] Indeed, Gambetta may even have believed that if a coup of some kind was attempted, the army would side with the Chamber in its struggle against the President, although his grounds for so thinking are not quite clear.[132] It is nevertheless certain that Gambetta enjoyed immense prestige within the army. According to the unpublished journal of the future Dreyfusard, Senator Scheurer Kestner, the Duc d'Aumale had journeyed incognito on May 18 to Paris from Besançon, where he commanded the Seventh Army Corps,[133] to discuss with Gambetta the dangers of a *coup d'état,* while Generals Clinchant, Campenon, Farre, Lecointe, and Galliffet had all placed themselves at the disposal of the leader of the republicans, in case the government should attempt anything illegal.[134]

Following the capitulation of MacMahon and the triumph of the republicans, an inquiry concerning the elections of October 1877 was ordered by the Chamber. The reporter for the

[129] *Ibid.*

[130] *Avenir militaire,* October 26, 1877.

[131] Letter of August 20, 1877. Quoted in Bédarida, *op. cit.,* p. 139.

[132] E. de Marcère, *Le seize-mai et la fin du septennat* (Paris: Plon, 1900), p. 211.

[133] Following his return from exile in 1871, the Duc d'Aumale had presided with great dignity at the trial of Bazaine and had then been assigned the command of the important Seventh Army Corps.

[134] Silvestre de Sacy, *op. cit.,* p. 350.

inquiry, Henri Brisson, concluded that Rochebouet, actively seconded by General Ducrot in particular, was laying the plans for a military coup against the Constitution and even that the "orders to set it in motion were given." [135] The material gathered by the Commission of Inquiry and incorporated into the report of Brisson could indeed be interpreted as evidence of a governmental plot against the "national will." Certainly the obvious satisfaction of Ducrot on hearing that MacMahon had failed to set up a constitutional government under Dufaure may be taken as corroborating this interpretation.[136] On the other hand, all the material presented regarding the military measures ordered by the government is perfectly consonant with the thesis that MacMahon was still contemplating a second dissolution, or even that he did not know what course to follow, and that as a soldier he was simply taking all the necessary preliminary steps for the maintenance of order. The more intelligent soldiers were certainly not sanguine about the chances for a *coup d'état*. Their attitude was well summed up by the possibly apocryphal words of General de Cissey: "I admit that it might be successful— and afterwards? . . ." [137] The *coups d'état* of the year VIII and of 1851 would not have succeeded if the active participation of a number of soldiers had not received the tacit consent of the great majority of Frenchmen. In 1877 the latter element was lacking.

Despite all the very real anxiety felt by the republicans, the regime was in no danger during the crisis of *Seize-mai*. Its surest defense was probably to be found in the legal narrow-mindedness of MacMahon. He was, in the words of one observer, "obsessed by his concern for legality." [138] The more

---

[135] *J.O.* (1879), p. 2560.

[136] *Ibid.*

[137] Marcère, *op. cit.,* p. 212.

[138] E. Daudet, *Souvenirs de la présidence du Maréchal de MacMahon* (Paris: Dentu, 1880), p. 171.

hotheaded conservatives, who advocated resistance no matter
what the cost, were to find the Marshal's precise sense of the
duties and prerogatives of his office as frustrating as had the
Count of Chambord in 1873. Once MacMahon was convinced
that constitutional "regulations" did not permit him to disregard the stated will of the French people as expressed in the
elections of October 1877, he gave in and accepted Dufaure as
President of the Council of Ministers.

Whatever the inclinations of certain of its chiefs, the army
took no active part in the evolution of the crisis. The most
fervent wish of the great majority of the soldiers was to be
kept out of the affair. The author of the monthly chronicle in
the respected review *Spectateur militaire* expressed the hope
that should the government feel obliged by circumstances to
substitute its own policy for the normal functioning of the
Constitution, the army would not be used to engineer any
such solution. "The army belongs to the country, not to a specific faction, no matter how respectable that faction claims to
be and no matter how mistaken it considers the majority of
Frenchmen." [139] Had the President heeded his conservative
advisers and decided to use force against the Chamber of
Deputies and against the will of the nation, the army would
certainly have done his bidding, for he was its commander by
the constitutional laws of 1875. Any order of this nature given
by MacMahon would have been obeyed, probably even by republican officers, who preferred this course of action to setting
themselves up as "interpretors of legality." [140] Nevertheless,
there is evidence that many officers were profoundly shocked
at even the idea of such an act.[141] Many in the army had a
deep distaste for the regime of frock-coated provincial lawyers
and journalists that was coming to power in France. They

[139] *S.M.*, November 1877, p. 268.

[140] Carnes, *op. cit.*, p. 158.

[141] Archives de la Préfecture de la Police de Paris (E. a/1166, Dossier
100,000 "MacMahon"), Report of July 4, 1877.

may have sorely resented the fact that the most eminent soldier in the country had to knuckle under to these *"pékins,"* [142] but the army was incapable of making a move on his behalf, except at his command.

Impelled by a sense of duty and serving against his deepest inclinations, MacMahon had come to the presidency in the hope that the government would follow a truly conservative policy. The enactment of the constitutional laws of 1875, then the republican electoral triumph of 1876, and finally the victory of the Chamber in the *Seize-mai* crisis had inexorably sapped the bases for a conservative policy. Still the Marshal remained in office, but now with the more strictly limited aim of protecting the army and the military interests of the country. [143] In a sense, the army was the last conservative bastion that the republicans had left to him. In the general capitulation that had been forced upon MacMahon at the end of the *Seize-mai,* Dufaure had still managed to let him retain the nomination of the new Minister of War. The Marshal had named his former aide-de-camp, General Borel. [144] When Borel turned out to be unsuited for the political aspects of the job, which is to say he was too stiff and military in his dealings with parliament, the government thought it best that he be replaced. MacMahon was able to prevail upon the cabinet to name General Gresley, rather than General Farre, a man of the *Défense nationale* and a client of Gambetta. [145]

In the aftermath of the *Seize-mai* crisis, there was a veritable purge, in the upper echelons of the public administration and, to a lesser extent, the judiciary, of those considered to have been too zealous in championing the conservative cause. According to Freycinet, by the end of December 1877 all the prefects had been replaced, along with 280 subprefects. [146]

---

[142] *"Pékin"* is a civilian, in French military slang.
[143] Silvestre de Sacy, *op. cit.,* p. 368.
[144] *Ibid.,* p. 357.
[145] Freycinet, *op. cit.,* Vol. II, pp. 42–44.
[146] *Ibid.,* p. 6

Despite all of MacMahon's efforts to protect it, the army could not entirely escape this settling of accounts. In January 1878, at the behest of the republican majority in the Chamber, Mac-Mahon dismissed General Ducrot from his post as commander of the Eighth Army Corps. Although Ducrot was justified in his claim that he had done nothing that was, strictly speaking, in any way counter to military regulations,[147] he had certainly overstepped the bounds of discretion. Much as he proclaimed his distaste for the whole affair, MacMahon was probably not overly upset to see Ducrot depart.

Republican exigencies with regard to the army did not stop at the dismissal of Ducrot. The senatorial elections of January 5, 1879, resulted in a great victory for the republicans, who for the first time gained control of both chambers. That they intended immediately to profit by the situation was indicated by the ministerial statement of Marcère, Minister of the Interior, to the effect that the provisions of the 1873 law concerning the corps commanders would be scrupulously observed.[148] A vigorous debate in the Chamber over the ministerial declaration followed, and was climaxed by the passage of a resolution, in French parliamentary terminology an *ordre du jour,* or order of the day, which was authored by Jules Ferry and which called upon the government to pursue a firm policy toward the administrative and judicial personnel.[149] Under the circumstances, the government could not long delay in giving the republicans some satisfaction.

In the course of a cabinet meeting on January 28, General Gresley as Minister of War presented to the Marshal a proposition relieving five corps commanders of their duties: Bourbaki, du Barail, Bataille, Lartigue, and Montaudon. All had served at the head of their army corps since the original reorganization of the army in 1873, contrary to the specific provi-

---

[147] Chalvet-Nastrac, *op. cit.,* pp. 288 ff.
[148] *Le Temps,* January 18, 1879.
[149] *J.O.* (1879), p. 423.

sions of the law. More to the point, at least in the estimation of
République française, they were men who had been "politically compromised, whose . . . intentions were held in suspicion by the civilian population."[150] MacMahon, profoundly
shocked, refused to accede to Gresley's request. None of the
men in question had in fact committed any overt act such as
might require their summary dismissal. To abandon the military to the uncertain necessities of parliamentary politics in
this fashion would be harmful to the best interests of the army
and the country. Were he to do so, MacMahon declared, he
would consider himself dishonored, so much so that he would
not even dare embrace his children.[151] The government was
willing to compromise on the ways and means, but the
scruples of the Marshal would not permit him to see even one
or two of the generals retired for what he considered unjust
reasons. No compromise being possible, MacMahon resigned
as President of the Republic on January 30, 1879. In the eve-
ning of the same day, Jules Grévy was elected as his successor.

The matter of the five corps commanders was only a convenient incident, over which MacMahon could retire with dignity, as was pointed out in the *Revue des deux mondes.*[152]
With the Senate now dominated by the republicans, it would
no longer be able to brake the rampant radicalism that he saw
gaining ascendancy in the Chamber, and MacMahon felt his
position to be untenable. Fearing further indignities, he therefore sought the first favorable opportunity to retire.[153] It was
his good fortune that he could step down defending the best
interests of the army. In fact, the dismissal of Ducrot and of
the five corps commanders plus a few lesser figures was the
closest the republicans came in the decade of the 1870's to enacting a program of political reprisals against the military.
This is to be compared with republican actions toward the

[150] *République française,* January 31, 1879.
[151] Daudet, *op. cit.,* p. 218.
[152] *R.D.M.,* February 1, 1879, pp. 711–712.
[153] Silvestre de Sacy, *op. cit.,* p. 367.

other branches of the government and also with what had taken place in the wake of past revolutions with regard to the army.

The army admired the simple dignity with which Mac-Mahon relinquished a post for which he had never had any inclination. It regretted his departure. Beyond that, the military saw no reason to object to his more or less forced resignation. In his memoirs, General Millet, one of the leading soldiers of his day, notes that he was stationed in Algeria at the time and that the military authorities, fearing some kind of outbreak, alerted the troops and told them to maintain order at all costs. "Maintaining order was easy; no one made a move either in town or in the barracks." [154] The departure of Mac-Mahon and the advent of Jules Grévy signified that France was now a Republic in fact as well as in name. It was the duty of the officer corps to accept this situation and to be the loyal and obedient servants of the regime, no matter what their sentimental attachments were. The great political upheavals of the nineteenth century had well prepared the army for just such a role.

If the army was to serve the Republic without question, it in turn demanded that the government respect the private sentiments of the officers. A man whose loyalty to monarchist or Bonapartist political ideals did not interfere with the discharge of his professional duties or lead him to overt political acts should not be made to forswear these ideals or to be penalized for them. The military were thus happy not to be obliged to swear a particular oath of fidelity to the regime or to the chief of state. The Third Republic, contrary to the practice of all former regimes except the Republic of 1848, did not require such an oath, and in the estimation of the military this was both wise and just.[155]

In France political differences did not merely denote dis-

---

[154] Gen. C. Millet, unpublished memoirs, 2 vols., written in his own hand; now at the Service historique de l'Armée, Paris; Vol. II, p. 14.

[155] *S.M.,* February, 1879, p. 286.

agreements over policy within the generally accepted framework of a given regime but rather involved fundamental differences of opinion over the shape and spirit of the regime itself. The Republic had the right to expect obedience and professional competence from its servants; but, beyond this, to require a particular sign of loyalty or devotion would be to introduce political criteria into a sphere where they should be absent. Not only would this hinder the effective operation of the administrative machinery of the nation, but it would also, if taken seriously, deprive the Republic of the collaboration of a large number of competent functionaries, both civil and military.

Over the years, the political oath had shown itself to be an unsatisfactory means of assuring the stability of a given regime. One of the first acts of the Government of National Defense after the revolution of September 4 had been to abolish such an oath, in order to recruit all segments of the nation without political qualification for the great task of repelling the invader.[156] There was no real pressure for its reestablishment during the period of the National Assembly or in the first years of the Republic. By 1879 one could agree with *Spectateur militaire* that it was superfluous.

As long as the country is in favor of the present regime, no officer, no matter what his personal beliefs, would decline to be its loyal servant. If the day were to come when the Republic stood discredited before the country, no matter how vigorously it had governed, it would not be able to make the army defend it against the will of the nation.[157]

It should not be thought that the attitude of the officer corps toward the Republic was purely negative, a sentiment of distaste and distrust overcome only through an innate sense of discipline and an inherited tradition of absolute obedience. Despite all the supposedly basic incompatibility between a

---

[156] *J.O.* (1870), p. 1527.
[157] *S.M.,* July 1879, p. 123.

liberal republican regime and an authoritarian professional army, a number of high-ranking officers were nevertheless avowed partisans of the Republic. One of them, General Clinchant, was reported to have originally been a convinced Bonapartist, but he had become progressively disillusioned with the Empire during the Mexican campaign and the War of 1870. After escaping from the encirclement at Metz, he had joined Gambetta and had been given the command of one of the armies of the *Défense nationale*.[158] In 1876 he was considered to be the only corps commander in metropolitan France who was a republican.[159]

The most spectacular of the soldiers who rallied to the Republic was General de Galliffet. The *beau sabreur* of the Second Empire and the pampered favorite of the imperial couple, he had enjoyed a remarkably rapid promotion, rising from lieutenant to general within the space of seventeen years. Nevertheless, he did not feel that this gave the Bonapartists any special claims to his loyalty after 1870. He was supposed to have publicly declared: "It is true that the Emperor was very kind to me, but he is dead and I owe nothing to his son. I would only act on his behalf insofar as my chiefs gave me the order, for discipline alone is my watchword." [160] Although socially he moved in aristocratic and conservative circles, he was by 1878 in regular and intimate correspondence with Gambetta, advising him on military matters, particularly concerning personnel. The partisans of Galliffet would attribute this to his sincere admiration for the great tribune,[161] while his detractors would call it sheer opportunism.[162]

Of all these recent adherents to the republican cause, the

---

[158] Gheusi, *op. cit.*, 172–173.

[159] Bédarida, *op. cit.*, p. 141 n.

[160] Gheusi, *op. cit.*, p. 188.

[161] L. Thomas, *Le général de Galliffet* (2nd ed.; Paris: Aux Armes de France, 1941), pp. 84, 121–122.

[162] Castex, *op. cit.*, Vol. II, p. 303. See also Gen. Grandin, *Dix-huit ans de généralat dans la cavalerie* (Besançon: Bossane, 1901), pp. 171 ff.

noisiest in his new faith appears to have been General Carrey de Bellemare. In 1873 he created a considerable stir by publishing an open letter to the Minister of War in which he announced his unwillingness to serve a monarchical regime, even if it was restored by a vote of the National Assembly. The government responded to this distinctly provocative act by summarily dismissing him from his command.[163] In thus revealing to the world liberal and democratic opinions that had been "until that moment suspected by absolutely no one . . ." [164] Carrey de Bellemare quickly came to be looked upon within the army as one of the leading republican generals.[165] His republicanism may have had its origins in the decision of the Commission for the Revision of Officers' Ranks to deprive him of the rank of divisionary general obtained during the siege of Paris. Carrey de Bellemare had then prevailed upon Gambetta to plead his cause before the National Assembly,[166] but it was to no avail. As for General Billot, his political views before 1870 are not recorded, but after the *Défense nationale* he could hardly be anything but a republican. A very junior lieutenant colonel at the outbreak of the war, he was in command of the Army of the East at its conclusion some six months later and in possession of the permanent rank of brigadier general.

Whether they became republicans for selfish or disinterested reasons, all of these men were to enjoy over the next two decades brilliant careers. This was also to be true for those men whose republican sympathies were known even before 1870, such as Generals Saussier and Campenon.[167] Paradoxically enough, the greatest of the generals of the *Défense nationale,* Chanzy, although reputed to be "the chief of the

---

[163] Du Barail, *op. cit.,* Vol. III, pp. 430–434.
[164] Trochu, *op. cit.,* Vol. I, p. 361.
[165] See Bédarida, *op. cit.,* p. 135 n.
[166] *J.O.* (1873), pp. 2028–2029.
[167] Castex, *op. cit.,* pp. 252–253.

military party of M. Gambetta . . ."[168] and the acknowledged leader of the conservative republicans in the National
Assembly, the Center Left, grew progressively alienated from
Gambetta and his partisans during the 1870's. Distressed by
what he considered to be the radical program advocated by
the leader of the republicans, and in particular by his religious
policies, Chanzy resigned his post as Ambassador to Russia at
the moment of the formation of Gambetta's *Grand Ministère*
in 1881, rather than be the representative abroad of a France
led by such a government.[169] He was, at his own request,
named to the command of the Sixth Army Corps, where he
served until his untimely death early in 1883.

Along with the men of the old army who rallied to the Republic, there were after 1870 the men in the generations of officers graduating from Saint-Cyr and Polytechnique who came
from bourgeois republican backgrounds. To consider then
that the army of the Third Republic was, from the start, made
up of men who were essentially antirepublican would be
wrong. The opportunist Republic of the 1880's and the 1890's
showed great concern for the maintenance of social order,
public authority, and private property. The majority of the
officer corps found no trouble making their peace with it. But
if there were many good republicans in the army, there were
very few democrats. An army by its essence is undemocratic,
and to organize an army along lines of democratic theory or
practice would be to cripple it as an effective, functioning military machine. An officer had a necessary belief in an ordered
and established hierarchy according to whose rules he lived.
He had willingly sacrificed the constitutional liberties of
civilian life to bind himself to an ideal of strictly disciplined
service. The army, like the priesthood, is a calling with its own

---

[168] Quoted in Gheusi, *op. cit.,* p. 195.
[169] "La vie du Général Chanzy, 1823–1883: Lettres et documents," Vol. VI,
pp. 863–865; mimeographed volumes, privately prepared for Chanzy's de-
scendants; on file at the Archives Nationales, Paris.

rules and customs that may appear senseless to the outsider. As long as the Republic recognized this fact, there were very few antirepublican officers. It was only in the years after 1900, when the Republic in the name of democracy endeavored to interfere with these rules and customs, that one could consider the officer corps to be antirepublican.

CHAPTER THREE

The Army and Parliament:
1879-1897

The Chambers and the Unfinished Program of Reform

In the quarter century following the Franco-Prussian War, the army occupied an honored place in the affections of practically every Frenchman. All factions, on the left and on the right, shared in this sentiment of military patriotism, no matter how they differed with regard to social and political questions. "In a France conquered, humiliated, and divided by the Treaty of Frankfurt, the army was for Frenchmen the great common denominator." [1] Having been for half a century unknown and of little interest to most people, the army suddenly became in the aftermath of the war the center of attention. Certainly, this can be explained in part by the fact that military service was now in theory universal and in fact much more widespread than before 1870. The army touched millions of people, directly or indirectly, who before would have remained strangers to it.

Yet, there was something deeper than an increased familiarity with military things in this new patriotic fervor. The defeat and the loss of the two provinces had touched a vital nerve, and for at least a generation the army was looked upon as the instrument through which the great wrong would be

[1] R. Girardet, *La société militaire dans la France contemporaine, 1815–1939* (Paris: Plon, 1953), p. 171.

undone. As Girardet points out, the most astonishing thing is the unanimity of Frenchmen in this respect: "During almost twenty years there was not a discordant note to be heard." [2]

Naturally enough, the prestige of the soldier, in particular the officer, benefited tremendously from this patriotic revival. Before 1870 the officer was frequently looked upon as a great overgrown child, decent enough but still a little uncouth and backward. The high percentage of promoted N.C.O.'s in the old army, who possessed only the most rudimentary educational qualifications, contributed to this picture. In contrast was the elevated place now occupied by the officer in the social hierarchy. "Never it seems . . . was the social prestige of the officer raised to so high a point as in this period of two decades after the defeat." [3] There was a great influx of young men into the army as a career. The number of candidates for Saint-Cyr rose in spectacular fashion, while the intellectual level of the graduates of the great military school was much improved. An officer could no longer be promoted directly from the ranks. Special schools were set up after 1882 where an N.C.O. aspiring to a commission was obliged to study for a year before he could take an examination to qualify as an officer. Saint-Maixent was the school for the infantry, while N.C.O.'s from the cavalry studied at Saumur and from the artillery at Versailles.[4]

Although the institution of universal conscription and the sudden reawakening of the interest of Frenchmen in all things military contributed greatly to breaking down the barriers between the army and the rest of French society, the army retained its particularist tendencies. The military sought to remain self-sufficient, maintaining their own resources, their own social distractions, their own auxiliary services. The officer was still a man who had renounced his civilian rights and liberties in order to wear a uniform and to live according to a

[2] *Ibid.*, p. 178.
[3] *Ibid.*, p. 185.
[4] Col. Revol, *Histoire de l'armée française* (Paris: Larousse, 1929), p. 208.

different code. The military were not immune to the divisions so characteristic of French social and political life, but for a quarter of a century, at least, these divisions had no significant effect within the army. "Between Catholic officers, who were apt to be more or less disguised royalists . . . and republican officers in the manner of the devotees of Gambetta . . . there was a community of attitude which placed them apart from the regime." [5] The fact that they were soldiers, that they were a breed different from other Frenchmen, was of far more significance than any political loyalties they might have or any social connections that they might maintain in a specific civilian milieu. General Millet states that until he was assigned to duty in the Ministry of War in 1896, he was absolutely ignorant of such things. "With regard to politics, no one spoke . . . or even thought about it. Our profession and the war of 1870, these were our sole preoccupations. . . . In truth, I was a military monk living in the cloister of my single interest." [6]

Even if regiments were no longer transferred every twelve or eighteen months and even if it was no longer the avowed policy of the military authorities to prevent the soldiers from having any real contact with the civilian milieu, the army still continued to look upon it with a certain distrust and lack of comprehension. In its attitude toward the civilian world, the officer corps was governed by its sense of being an elite, protected by the uniform from the "contagious defects of civil society." [7] The interest and adulation showered on the army by the rest of the nation were not really reciprocated by the military.

As remarkable as was the reawakening of the enthusiasm of the French people for their army, it was ultimately of less import than the military renaissance that began in the immediate aftermath of the war and lasted until 1914. What was truly

[5] H. Contamine, *La Revanche* (Paris: Berger-Levrault, 1957), p. 19.

[6] Gen. C. Millet, unpublished memoirs, Vol. II, pp. 14-15.

[7] F. Bédarida, "L'armée et la République," *Revue historique,* Vol. 232 (July-September 1964), pp. 163-164.

extraordinary in this phenomenon was the fact that the generating impulse came from within the army itself. The war of 1870 would seem to have provided conclusive proof of the sterility and the irremediable decay of French military institutions. The army of the Second Empire had lost its intellectual and moral *élan*. Yet this same army, shattered in the summer of 1870, found within itself the necessary elements for a gigantic self-renovation. Most remarkable of all, the personnel who undertook this task were essentially the same as had filled the upper ranks of the army of Napoleon III. There was no radical infusion of new blood at the top, nor did the political transformation of France have much to do with it.

The Republic could, through legislative efforts, act to reinvigorate French military institutions by introducing universal conscription. It could also abolish some of the unsound practices of the old army, such as the purchase of substitutes. It could sponsor, on the advice of the military, a general reorganization of the army. Beyond that point, the government could not go. It could not awaken the French officer corps from its years of intellectual torpor, by inculcating habits of study and reflection where none had been evident before. It could not assure that men of character and intellectual vigor would now occupy positions of influence or that they would be heeded. The government could only vote the necessary funds and generally express its approval of what was being done.

There had been in the French army prior to 1870 men of high intellectual caliber. Colonel Ardant du Picq, who was mortally wounded leading his regiment near Metz in August 1870, was the author of one of the most penetrating works on warfare ever written, *Études sur le combat*. It was not published, however, until after the war.[8] To have shown himself to be the author of a book, or a savant, might have compromised his career in the old army. Colonel Lewal was another

---

[8] S. T. Possony and E. Mantoux, "Du Picq and Foch: The French School," *Makers of Modern Strategy*, E. M. Earle, ed. (Princeton: Princeton University Press, 1943), p. 206.

who was unknown before the war but whose book *La réforme de l'armée,* published in 1871, won him an immediate reputation. He became the first head of the École de Guerre and later served as Minister of War. General Trochu had risen to the highest echelons within the army, but his prophetic *L'armée française en 1867* was considered to be subversive and disregarded by all but a few officers. The great difference now was that such men were given a hearing and institutions were set up through which their talents could be utilized.

Within the officer corps, there could now be sensed a real intellectual ferment. A number of newspapers aimed specifically at a military audience appeared, while such periodicals as the *Revue militaire des armées étrangères* and the *Revue d'artillerie* were founded in the early 1870's to complement the older *Spectateur militaire*. The next four decades were to see a flood of books and pamphlets by military authors on every subject pertaining to the army.

The more intelligent soldiers came to realize that their conception of military virtue and military competence had been incomplete, that physical courage and bravura under fire were no longer enough. As General de Galliffet, the personification of these qualities, was reported to have declared during the critique of a cavalry maneuver, "Before the war none of us knew anything." [9] Typical of many of his generation, Galliffet set to work in middle age painfully to study and to master the basic intellectual elements of war as it was now being waged.

A further index of this military renaissance was the ceaseless introduction of new weapons and of innovations in standard items. Gone was the time when Napoleon III in the 1860's had had to exert his personal authority to force the generals in charge to adopt the chassepot rifle for the infantry or rifled cannon for the artillery. The chassepot was replaced shortly after the war by the Gras rifle, which in turn was replaced

[9] Millet, *op. cit.,* Vol. II, p. 51.

within comparatively few years and at great expense by the Lebel, a magazine-loading rifle with a high rate of fire. In the artillery, the decade of the 1870's saw the introduction of an excellent series of breech-loading guns.[10] French supremacy in the field of artillery was consecrated by the unveiling in 1896 of the seventy-five, whose recoil mechanism, perfected by Captain Sainte-Claire-Deville, allowed an effective rate of fire four or five times greater than any fieldpiece in the German army. As Girardet points out, all of these reforms and innovations conceived, undertaken, and brought to fruition by the men of the old army "clearly show that it had not been lacking in men either of real talents or real character. . . . The terrible shock of defeat seems to have liberated them." [11]

While the military themselves were undertaking a program of renovation on their own initiative, parliament still had an unfinished mandate of reform to fulfill. The conscription law and the laws on the organization of the army and on the cadres and effectives were passed before the National Assembly dissolved itself, but two other fundamental measures concerning the staff and the administration of the army had advanced no further than to be discussed in commission, while a new law governing promotion had not come even that far. The Chamber of Deputies and the Senate inherited the task of completing this basic program of reform for the army. From the beginning, however, there were indications that the two chambers lacked not only the means to deal with these rather technical military questions but also the interest. In 1879 *Spectateur militaire* commented: "It seems that the National Assembly exhausted the legislative verve of the French parliament in questions of military organization. . . ." [12] Still, the

[10] Gen. C. de Gaulle, *France and Her Army*, F. L. Dash, trans. (London: Hutchinson, 1945), p. 125.

[11] Girardet, *op. cit.*, p. 185.

[12] *Spectateur militaire* (hereafter cited as *S.M.*), January 1879, p. 14.

pending laws had to be voted, and the two newly constituted legislative bodies went doggedly about their job.

The main point in contention in enacting a law reforming the staff of the French army was whether to retain the old closed corps and to make the necessary innovations within its framework, or whether to introduce a new system, on the Prussian model, whereby staff officers would alternate between service with the troops and in the staff. In the simplest terms, they would then be members of an open service rather than a closed corps. The old Staff Corps had been instituted by Gouvion Saint-Cyr in 1818 to prevent the abuses of favoritism. By the nature of his duties, a staff officer is of necessity in much closer contact with the high command than is the man in the field. He is thus well placed for drawing attention to himself and for winning promotions and decorations. As a result, the staff has always been a fertile field for political influence and favoritism.

As Minister of War, Gouvion Saint-Cyr sought to minimize these abuses by obliging all staff officers to attend a special school, to which admission was obtained by competitive examination. An officer entered the Staff School upon graduation from Saint-Cyr, and after completing a two-year course of study, he was assigned to the Staff Corps. No one could serve on the staff of a unit who was not a member of this corps, and no one could enter the corps except through the school. This system effectively stifled favoritism in the choice of staff officers, but it also had certain disadvantages. Once admitted to the Staff Corps, an officer never commanded a body of troops, and there was nothing in his daily routine to prepare him for his wartime functions. The result was that the average staff officer became little more than a military bureaucrat, with the peculiar mentality of a bureaucrat and no conception of how he could best second his commanding officer in time of war.

There can be no doubt that the staff work in the French army in 1870 was very poor. Whether the fault lay with the staff officers themselves or with the men whom they were supposed to second, the generals commanding the army, is open to question. The function of a military staff being to prepare the orders of the commanding officer, to transmit them, and to assist in their execution, there is little even the best staff officer can do if the high command has no clear idea of what to do or if its orders are vacillating and contradictory. As one military commentator wrote in justification of the staff in 1870, "It is supremely unfair to say that the staff officers were not up to their mission. Rather they were given no mission to perform." [13]

Although two separate projects for the reorganization of the staff were presented to the National Assembly before it disbanded, one from the floor [14] and one from the government, [15] it was not until 1877 that the Army Commission of the Senate produced a bill that was actually debated. The commission that drafted the bill consisted primarily of military men, and most of those who participated in the debate had had military experience. All agreed on the general premise that the staff system of the French army should be reformed, but there was no consensus as to how it should be done. In the end, it was thought best to withdraw the bill. [16]

The Senate produced another bill in 1878, and this time it was voted and sent to the Chamber. There it languished in committee for the rest of the year despite the pleas of the Minister of War that it be quickly taken into consideration. [17] When the Chamber finally did act, it produced a measure differing from the Senate bill in several important particulars. In order to iron out the differences between the two chambers, a joint legislative commission was set up. By now it was 1880.

---

[13] Capt. Choppin, *L'armée française, 1870–1890* (Paris: Albert Savine, 1890), pp. 143–144.

[14] *Journal Officiel de la République française* (hereafter cited as *J.O.*), (1872), pp. 1031 ff.

[15] *J.O.* (1874), pp. 7949 ff.

[16] *J.O.* (1877), p. 8173.

[17] *J.O.* (1878), p. 5887.

A law on the staff had been in the works for six years, and the legislators were becoming weary of a subject most of whose details escaped them. When the joint commission finally did bring forth a plan more or less acceptable to both chambers, it was speedily voted upon. Nevertheless, at least one general in the Senate felt that the legislators had not yet grasped the full significance of the essential points under discussion. He wanted still more debate on the law.[18] The Chamber passed the law even more speedily than did the Senate, with no dissenting voices, although many abstained.[19] In the words of one senator, it was a law of "lassitude," enacted only when parliament could not face any further debates.[20]

The French staff system, as it was reorganized under the 1880 law, was based on the concept of a service whose members would not be set apart from the rest of the army. Admission to the service was to be chiefly through the École de Guerre, which had already been organized in rudimentary form and which replaced the old overtheoretical Staff School. Candidates for the École de Guerre would be eligible only after serving a number of years with the troops. The entrance examinations would be stiff and the curriculum demanding. Upon graduation, an officer would receive a *brevet* qualifying him for service on the staff of the larger military units. Frequent alternations between troop and staff assignments were meant to ensure that each staff officer had a constant awareness of the needs and problems of a unit commander. Provisions were also made for an officer to receive a *brevet* without going through the École de Guerre if he could pass the necessary examinations. The best of the *brevetés* would serve on the recently instituted General Staff, which was intended to perform a function similar to that of the Great German General Staff, that is, the careful, rational preparation of the army for war. In short, a system was set up whereby the intellectual

---

[18] *J.O.* (1880), p. 3199.
[19] *Ibid.*, pp. 3343–3345.
[20] *Ibid.*, p. 3199.

resources of the French officer corps could be most effectively utilized in time of peace as well as in time of war.

The other important part of the military reform undertaken by the National Assembly but not yet passed at the moment of its dissolution concerned the administration of the army. During the war the *intendance,* or quartermaster department, had failed even more miserably than had the staff. Like the rest of the French army, the administrative services were geared to peacetime conditions, with no provision made for the necessary transition to a wartime footing. They were completely outside the normal hierarchy of command, answerable only to the Intendant General of the army and through him to the Minister of War. At no point in the peacetime military hierarchy was a commanding officer responsible for the functioning of the administrative services pertaining to his command, nor was the officer in charge of supply and matériel in any way subordinate to him. Such a system gave the Minister of War more direct control over the management of the material resources of the army, but it denied the commanding officer all experience in overseeing the practical needs of his troops. In time of war, these matters became of the utmost importance, and the generals commanding the larger units were unequipped to cope with them. Nor could the men of the quartermaster department, accustomed to time-honored habits and regular methods of dealing with problems of supply, learn how to operate effectively in the gigantic improvisation that was the French war effort of 1870.

Shortly after the war the government instituted a mixed commission, made up of deputies to the National Assembly, eminent officers, and men from the quartermaster department, to consider what reforms were necessary in the methods of administration in the army. In 1874 this mixed commission produced a bill in the name of the government, the essential principle of which was the subordination of the administrative services to the high command. The authors of the project intended to assign to the commanding officer of a unit "in time of peace as in time of war, direction of the administrative services . . . to impose upon him the responsibility for everything concerning the well-being and the life of his troops."[21]

A special commission of the National Assembly took the government's proposal into consideration and, after studying the matter carefully, produced a bill of its own which was virtually the same except for a few modifications "of relatively secondary importance. . . ."[22] The National Assembly having expired before the bill could be brought to debate, the government then submitted it to the Senate. The Army Commission of the Senate, arguing that a new parliamentary body required a brand-new start, disregarded the two prior bills and undertook to restudy the whole question. The bill turned out to be practically the same as the other two. Freycinet, the reporter for the law, admitted: "We were led back, almost in spite of ourselves, to the principles first admitted by our predecessors."[23] The Senate passed the bill and sent it on to the Chamber. The military members of the Senate led the debate, and there were no significant dissenting motions or amendments produced from the other senators.

Five years were to pass before the Chamber acted on the Senate project. Even then the plan was amended only in a few minor details before it was sent back to the upper chamber. Both Senate and the Chamber reached an accord over these minor matters in 1881, and the law was ultimately enacted in 1882, eight years after its first presentation to the National Assembly.

In the general principles governing the law, there were no significant changes between the first bill produced by the mixed commission in 1874 and the one eventually passed in 1882. Although the advocates of the old system of a completely independent *intendance,* responsible only to the Minister of War, fought with skill and determination against the concept

[21] *J.O.* (1874), p. 5718.
[22] *J.O.* (1875), p. 9853.
[23] *J.O.* (1876), p. 6961.

of the subordination of the administrative services to the command, they managed only to delay the enactment of the law. They could not bring about any important revisions in it. Paradoxically enough, the Chamber, with a strong republican majority and few military members to defend the supposed vested interests of their comrades, became the center of opposition to any real reform in the administration of the army, while the Senate, where the military dominated the debate, voted for the reform with speed and dispatch.

The long-drawn-out efforts required to enact the laws on the staff and on the administration of the army were evidence of how difficult it was to regulate military reform by legislative means. In both the Senate and the Chamber, the men with military experience received free rein in the writing, amending, and discussion of the laws. The other deputies and senators, possessing little or no precise knowledge of these matters, could not do much more than vote blindly according to the advice of the experts. But, as General Trochu pointed out with regard to the law on the staff, the military experts had a propensity to get bogged down "in a contradictory debate, where affirmation and negation dispute each other with equal authority." [24] Thus these differences of opinion over fundamental matters of principle as well as over specific details resulted in an endless series of sterile discussions, punctuated by a periodic tabling of the bill under consideration.

Major questions such as reforms in the organization of the army, in military administration, and in the staff system seemed to require the sanction of something more stable and binding than an executive decree. Yet to give these reforms the sanction of law, duly weighed and voted upon, meant that a considered opinion had to be delivered by a body of men incompetent to judge. One method of mitigating this problem, which seems to be common to all legislative bodies, is to create a permanent standing committee made up of men who are expert in a given field; but this reform was not instituted in a

[24] Gen. Trochu, *L'armée française en 1879* (Paris: Hetzel, n.d.), p. 209.

French parliament until 1902.[25] To escape the dilemma by simply laying down the general principles in the law and leaving it up to the Minister of War to work out the details, as some would have advocated, would be to deny the rationale for writing a law in the first place. The office was held by a succession of different individuals, who could revise the details to suit themselves and, in the process, change the whole spirit of the law.

It was a problem that the Republic was never able to resolve in satisfactory fashion. Parliament was an inefficient instrument for effecting military reforms, yet the creed of a good republican demanded that all important questions be treated by the sovereign legislature. Eventually, the pragmatic military needs of the country began to take precedence over the imperatives of republican political theory. An increasingly large sector of military affairs came to be handled by means of executive decrees. If it was necessary to enact a law pertaining to the army or to amend some already existing law, it was generally done in the most perfunctory fashion. The Minister of War would introduce the measure and announce that it was needed. After a minimum of discussion, the vote would then take place. Under these circumstances, parliamentary action was little more than an official imprimatur to an initiative taken by the executive.

Where the government or the army considered a given law or a portion thereof to be militarily useless, it was not always necessary to undergo the inconvenience of bringing the matter to the attention of parliament. The law could simply be disregarded in calculated fashion. In theory, the chambers always had the right to interpellate the government if legislators believed a given law was being ignored, but this right was seldom exercised with regard to purely military matters unless there was also some vital political ramification.

[25] R. K. Gooch, *The French Parliamentary Committee System* (New York: Appleton, 1935), pp. 76–80.

The Conscription Law of 1889

As a whole, the program of reform that was undertaken by the National Assembly and brought to a close by the enactment of the law on the administration of the army was to regulate the functioning of French military institutions until 1914 and beyond. This fact would indicate that the laws adequately met the needs of the army. Even if some laws, considered individually, were open to criticism in many of their details and even if calls were periodically made for parliament to make the necessary corrections, the public tended to lose interest rather quickly in the whole subject of military reform. Along with the decline of public interest there went a decline in the interest of the legislators.[26] Only conscription proved able to excite the interest of parliament on any given occasion, and this was far more than a purely military question.

Although the conscription law of 1872 played an important part in the French military renaissance of the late nineteenth century, it must, paradoxically, be adjudged a failure. It did not lead to a resurrection of the old army, as Thiers had hoped, nor did it serve as an instrument of moral order. If it did accomplish its primary task of supplying more conscripts than heretofore, the 1872 law did not succeed in becoming integrated into the social fabric of France, as had the Soult law of 1832. With military service touching so much larger a proportion of the populace, and without any relatively easy means to escape it, as there had been before 1870, the inequalities of the law, especially the privileges accorded to wealth and education, became even more blatant. Militarily the 1872 conscription law worked well enough, but socially and politically it was impossible.

As early as 1876 a motion was introduced by the Radical deputy Édouard Laisant calling for the suppression of the one-year volunteers and the reduction in the term of service to

---

[26] "Le programme de 1880," *S.M.*, January 1880, p. 12.

three years.[27] Over a dozen similar propositions and projects were introduced within a few years, generally on the initiative of individual deputies. In the elections of 1881, there were some 275 candidates pledged to reform the five years' service.[28] Following the great republican victory of that year, the Chamber took positive measures. A commission was set up to consider the merits of the different propositions and to draft a bill for presentation to parliament.[29] It had taken only a decade for parliament to bring under discussion a major reform in conscription, evidence of its general unpopularity.

The fact that this essential military institution was to be challenged so quickly was not favorably received by the army. Although there had been, in the aftermath of the defeat, a strong current of opinion in the highest military circles in favor of a shortened term of service, it had died out when the 1872 law was enacted. *Spectateur militaire* noted in 1882 that the long term of service was defended by all the army corps commanders, except for possibly one or two, and by a majority of the members of the Conseil supérieur de la Guerre.[30] The military evidently preferred a workable, though imperfect, system to the inevitable confusion and dislocations that would result from the introduction of a plan that was only potentially better. General Chanzy, who, until his untimely death in 1883, was the man most likely to be designated as commander in chief of the French armies in case of war,[31] declared in an 1882 meeting of the Conseil supérieur de la Guerre that the present system provided adequate security for the nation. Considering the troubled foreign situation, he could not understand why anyone would want to tinker with conscription.[32]

[27] *J.O.* (1876), p. 4126.

[28] R. D. Challener, *The French Theory of the Nation in Arms* (New York: Columbia University Press, 1955), p. 46.

[29] Revol, *op. cit.,* p. 205.

[30] *S.M.,* April 1882, p. 122.

[31] Contamine, *op. cit.,* p. 32.

[32] Conseil supérieur de la Guerre, "Registre des délibérations" (hereafter cited as C.S.G., "Reg. dél."), No. 5 (1882), p. 41.

The military were not alone in not wishing to scrap the 1872 law before it had been given a proper trial. Even Gambetta hesitated. He had not voted for the five years' service in 1872, but he also believed that to question its value so soon would interfere with the functioning of the army and might even compromise its mobilization. In his own words: "We should touch the army only in an extremely prudent manner; indeed, we should be wary of doing so." [33] Gambetta prided himself on his nondoctrinaire attitude toward military questions. He was much like Thiers in this respect and in his willingness to deal with soldiers of all political complexions on strictly military business. If the generals did not want the three years' service, Gambetta was willing to defer to their professional opinion and to wait and see. Thus, when Laisant first proposed a reduction in the term of service in 1876, Gambetta was as resolute in opposing it as was the Minister of War, General de Cissey.[34] His conversion to a thoroughgoing advocacy of the shortened and equalized military service probably came about after the Tunisian expedition had revealed certain defects in the existing system, and when the smashing electoral victory of the republicans in 1881 made it politically expedient.[35]

The military had a more cogent reason for not wishing to reduce the term of service to three years than a simple unwillingness to try something new. They believed that until the French army had a solid core of N.C.O.'s, to introduce the three years service would be not only unwise but also dangerous. The N.C.O.'s provided the necessary cohesive element, without which the army would have no unity. Chanzy was willing to concede that the army might be more homogeneous if everyone served three years, but without enough N.C.O.'s it would be disastrous.[36] In his electoral manifesto in 1881,

[33] J. Reinach, *La vie politique de Léon Gambetta* (Paris: Alcan, 1918), p. 284.

[34] *J.O.* (1876), pp. 4126–4127.

[35] *S.M.,* April 1882, pp. 124–125.

[36] C.S.G., "Reg. dél." (1885), p. 42.

Gambetta too stressed the need for N.C.O.'s: "We favor the three years' service, if that period of time is compatible with the solidity of the army, if it allows the cadres to be formed. For us, that is an unalterable condition." [37]

The authors of the 1872 law had expected that a corps of N.C.O.'s would be recruited more or less automatically through conscription. The National Assembly had abolished the handsome reenlistment bounties instituted by Napoleon III in 1855 and financed in large part through the purchase of exemptions by the wealthy. Meant to attract and to retain a core of hardened veterans, the measure had worked too well. The noncommissioned ranks had become encumbered by a great number of old soldiers, many of whom were long past their prime and whose presence prevented many worthy younger men from being promoted. The National Assembly, looking upon the reenlistment bounties as but another example of the materialism so typical of the Second Empire, rather naïvely assumed that patriotic ardor combined with the natural benefits of a relatively long term of service would be enough to assure the recruitment of an adequate number of young and vigorous N.C.O.'s. In this assumption they were mistaken.

As early as 1874 a law was enacted providing that any soldier who reenlisted would be given a small increase in pay. Then by the law of June 22, 1878, the supposedly discredited practices of the Second Empire had to be resurrected, for now a bounty of 2,000 francs was to be paid to an N.C.O. when he reenlisted.[38] In an 1883 meeting of the Conseil supérieur de la Guerre, General Billot noted that over the past decade there had been six different measures enacted by parliament in an effort to increase the number of long-term N.C.O.'s. All had proved ineffective.[39]

In fact, for budgetary reasons no conscript ever served five full years during the period that the 1872 law was in effect.

[37] Reinach, *Gambetta*, p. 287.
[38] *J.O.* (1878), p. 5307.
[39] C.S.G., "Reg. dél.," No. 7 (1883–1885), p. 49.

The class of 1871, the first to be inducted under the law, was released in October 1876, at the end of forty-six months. The event provoked some ironical comments from *Avenir militaire* as to how Thiers had felt so strongly on the subject that he had been willing to provoke a governmental crisis if four rather than five years had been voted by the National Assembly.[40] By 1881 the government had been forced for financial reasons to reduce the service to forty months, which, with two long furloughs, was spread out over almost four years. This was a bastard compromise that satisfied no one. The conscripts and their families preferred their service to be completed in one single period, while the military complained that N.C.O.'s were sent home on furlough just when they were needed to train the new recruits.[41] When, in November 1881, General Campenon became Gambetta's Minister of War, he abolished the forty months' service as having been one of the things that contributed to the fall of the preceding government. Then, since the budgetary and political situation had not changed at all, he was obliged to reintroduce it on a slightly modified basis.[42]

Concurrent with this reduction in the length of time served by those who had drawn "bad" numbers, there was an effort made to increase the military service of those who had "good" numbers. In 1879 General Gresley, the Minister of War, announced his intention of holding as many as possible for three years, but his successor, General Farre, preferred to hold one portion of the contingent for forty months.[43] Finally in 1887 the Minister of War decreed that both portions of the contingent would serve for three years.[44] By then the three-years law was being discussed, and it was only a question of time before parliament enacted it.

[40] *Avenir militaire*, October 26, 1876.

[41] *S.M.*, January 1881, pp. 134–137.

[42] *S.M.*, January 1882, pp. 142–143.

[43] *J.O.* (1880), p. 5231.

[44] J. Monteilhet, *Les institutions militaires de la France* (Paris: Alcan, 1932), p. 282.

Whatever the difference of opinion, civilian and military, over the desirability of the three years' service, most people were in agreement that the one-year volunteers had been an unfortunate mistake. Whereas in Germany the system of one-year volunteers had been instituted specifically to meet the needs of the reserve officer corps, the number to be inducted in a given year being determined by the vacancies in that organization, in France anyone possessing sufficient financial means, plus the requisite diploma, could volunteer. Rather than being recruited to fill a specific military need, as under the German system, Frenchmen were exempted according to social and financial criteria. Writing in the *Revue des deux mondes* in 1874, Charles de Mazade considered that the institution had already gotten off to a bad start. There was no single over-all policy or program governing their training or their situation within the regiments; furthermore the level of instruction and the ability of the individual volunteers were extremely uneven. "The institution of the one-year volunteers has become something very elastic, something much akin to the old scheme of exoneration, a means to avoid five years of military service placed at the disposal of those who have 1500 francs to spend." [45]

In May 1883 a bill drafted by the special commission that had been set up to study the question of conscription was presented to the Chamber, but debate did not begin until the next year. The central feature of the project was the reduction of the term of service to three years. The commission did away with the one-year volunteers and abolished all exemptions except the usual ones for the eldest child in a family of orphans, the brother of a soldier killed while in service, the sole support of a family, etc. Young men aspiring to be schoolteachers or priests were to serve as conscripts just like everyone else. The only relief accorded to a person studying for an advanced diploma was a *sursis d'appel,* a postponement of his induction

[45] *Revue des deux mondes* (hereafter cited as *R.D.M.*), September 15, 1874, p. 464.

until his studies were completed.[46] It was the avowed intention of the commission "to erase down to the last vestige the division of the contingent into two sections serving unequal lengths of time." [47] The basic underlying principle of the bill as it was presented to the Chamber was thus absolute equality for all Frenchmen in the discharge of the military obligations. The bill passed its first reading in June 1884, after three months of debate. The second reading took place the following year, after which the bill was sent to the Senate. The Senate took no action on the measure during the remainder of the year 1885. Then on March 27, 1886, a presidential decree withdrew the conscription bill from the agenda of the Senate, thus killing it.[48] The reason for this action was directly connected with the arrival at the Ministry of War of General Georges Boulanger.

Boulanger was a protégé of Clemenceau. The chief of the Radicals saw in him a general of seemingly republican inclinations who would sponsor a number of necessary democratic reforms in the army.[49] Always a man with a taste for notoriety, Boulanger sought to make himself the personification of the spirit of vigorous republican renovation in the army. In withdrawing the bill just before a special Senate army commission was to take it into consideration, Boulanger was not postponing the measure indefinitely, as the opponents of the three years' service fondly hoped.[50] Rather, Boulanger was simply clearing away the debris of piecemeal attempts at reform in order to undertake a thoroughgoing program, in which conscription, the organization of the army and the cadres, promotion, and the institution of a colonial army

[46] *Journal Officiel de la Chambre des Députés: Documents* (hereafter cited as *J.O.C. Doc.*), (1883), pp. 736–737.

[47] *J.O.C. Doc.* (1884), p. 551.

[48] *Journal Officiel du Sénat: Débats* (hereafter cited as *J.O.S. Déb.*), (1886), p. 473.

[49] A. Dansette, *Le Boulangisme* (Paris: A. Fayard, 1946), pp. 30–31.

[50] *S.M.,* April 15, 1886, pp. 162–163.

would all be treated as parts of a single "organic" law. The project that he shortly presented to the Chamber contained 217 articles, and it purported to be a synthesis of the approximately fifty military laws that had been passed in the past decade and a half.[51] *Spectateur militaire,* long an advocate of a major program of military reform, was satisfied with the accomplishment of the Minister of War and lauded the singleness of purpose behind the bill and the way its different parts were coordinated one with the other.[52] Many conservatives, on the other hand, were less enchanted, looking on it as something of a suspicious tour de force that Boulanger and his republican coterie at the Ministry of War could produce so imposing a program of military reform only two months after the other conscription bill had been suppressed.[53]

Boulanger's grandiose scheme for reforming the whole of the French military edifice in one fell swoop soon had to be abandoned. Conscription was the only aspect of the "organic" reform having any electoral ramifications, and it seemed best not to have this aspect of the program bogged down in the arid quarrels that were sure to arise over the technical details of army organization. That particular section of the project dealing with conscription was thus detached from the rest of the bill and taken into consideration as a separate measure.[54] Basically the same in its provisions as the project first voted by the Chamber in 1884, the new measure came up for debate in June 1887. Once again the Chamber voted for it and sent it to the Senate. There the Army Commission, under the presidency of Freycinet, proceeded to make a number of significant amendments.

Although the Senate Army Commission agreed with the Chamber as to the desirability and the feasibility of a three-year term of military service, it did not believe that it should

[51] *J.O.C. Doc.* (1886), p. 587.
[52] *S.M.,* June 1, 1886, p. 450.
[53] *J.O.S. Déb.* (1887), p. 1134.
[54] *S.M.,* January 1, 1887, p. 87.

be equal for all. According to the Senate Army Commission, young men studying to enter the liberal professions and the priesthood should serve only one year instead of three. In their estimation, "The greatness of a people does not depend solely on the number of its soldiers or the strength of its military institutions but also on its degree of civilization and its advances in agriculture, industry, commerce, the sciences, and the arts." [55] To interrupt the studies of the future elite of the nation or to postpone the start of their careers for three full years would be a serious blow to the intellectual and scientific life of the country. The Commission further argued that as long as the state officially recognized organized religion and paid the salaries of the priests and pastors, it was only just that aspirants to sacerdotal functions should benefit from the same partial exemptions as the schoolteachers.[56] The Senate accepted the bill substantially as the Army Commission had presented it and sent it back to the Chamber.

With regard to the strictly military aspects of the question, the two chambers were in agreement: the maximum term of service for a conscript in the French army would now be three years. In the problem of how to apply the three years' service, however, where social factors came into play, there was a fundamental divergence between them. Before the project could become law, either the Senate would have to compromise on the exemptions or the Chamber of Deputies would have to forswear the principle of equality which it had made the basis for the law. The Chamber Army Commission examined the bill as it had come back from the Senate in "a broad spirit of conciliation" but felt obliged to stick to first principles, that is, absolute equality in military service. As the Commission professed to believe, "Stability is a formidable element in the strength of military institutions. We will achieve it by organizing the army to conform with the organization of society and

[55] *Journal Officiel du Sénat: Documents* (hereafter cited as *J.O.S. Doc.*), (1888), p. 135.
[56] *J.O.S. Doc.* (1888), p. 136.

not by any incomplete reform." [57] So the Army Commission reaffirmed the purity and vigor of the egalitarian sentiments of the Chamber by abolishing all the educational and religious exemptions in the Senate bill and by reinstating the *sursis d'appel* for those who wished to complete their studies.[58] The project was then brought up for debate before the Chamber of Deputies.

Since 1883 the republican majority in the Chamber had demanded that all conscripts serve an equal length of time. This had been the fundamental principle upon which republican military policy was based, and all efforts to dilute or attenuate it were rigorously spurned. Yet in a single afternoon the Chamber abandoned this principle with scarcely a murmur of protest. An amendment was introduced providing for the drawing of lots at the moment of the induction of the contingent. Those who drew "good" numbers would then be permitted to return home after serving only one year. Those who drew "bad" numbers would serve the full three.[59] Freycinet, at the time Minister of War, defended the amendment in the simplest terms. To incorporate three whole conscript classes for three years would result in an army with a peacetime effective strength of 580,000 men. The budget permitted 460,000; therefore, 120,000 men would have to be pared away. The Chamber had already recognized this problem and had written into its earlier bills a number of expedients to reduce the size of the army: long furloughs, anticipated release from service for needy cases, and so forth. All were theoretically consonant with the principle of equality, but Freycinet, in the name of the government, rejected them as being far too complex and clumsy. Only the release of a specified number of conscripts at the end of one year seemed to be an efficient and workable alternative. In Freycinet's own words: "We must not shrink in

<hr>

[57] *J.O.C. Doc.* (Session Extraordinaire, 1888), p. 348.

[58] *Ibid.*, pp. 350–351.

[59] *Journal Officiel de la Chambre des Députés: Débats* (hereafter cited as *J.O.C. Déb.*), (1889), pp. 11–12.

the face of words; we must not say that the second portion of the contingent is a monstrosity. We are obliged to create it. . . ." [60]

Freycinet, as president of the commission that had written the Senate bill, would probably have preferred to take care of the 120,000-man excess by means of the educational exemptions, but, always a consummate politician, he did not push the Chamber too far. A drawing of lots was at least more egalitarian than a system of exemptions based on educational criteria. It should be noted that this sudden denial of a principle that had been fundamental in Chamber military debates for five years aroused no storm of anger or disbelief. A few, including the reporter for the law, objected, but that was all. The amendment was passed by a solid majority of 396 to 130. [61]

When called upon to consider the amendments to the measure as accepted by the Chamber of Deputies, the Senate Army Commission was adamant. It was willing to accept a contingent that had been divided by a drawing of lots, but it also insisted that the educational exemptions be reinstated. [62] When the project once again came up before the Senate for debate, Tirard, President of the Council of Ministers, arose to demand that the senators not vote for so flagrant a violation of the French passion for equality, exempting the educated from two thirds of the military burden borne by the other groups in society. If the Senate rejected the educational exemptions, the government would endeavor to convince the Chamber that medical and ecclesiastical students should, in case of mobilization, be inducted into the medical service and not into combat units. [63] It was not much of a compromise offer, especially since the government could not even be sure that the Chamber would agree to it. The Senate rejected the pleas of the Presi-

[60] *Ibid.*, p. 22.
[61] *J.O.C. Déb.* (1889), p. 27.
[62] *J.O.S. Doc.* (1889), pp. 143 ff.
[63] *J.O.S. Déb.* (1889), pp. 404–405.

dent of the Council of Ministers and sent the bill back to the Chamber with the educational exemptions reinstated.

The Chamber Army Commission attempted to negotiate with its Senate counterpart in an effort to do away with the exemptions. It was of no use. As much as the Chamber wished to abolish them, the Senate was even more determined to see them maintained.[64] In this battle of wills, the Senate could be more stubborn. Elections were approaching, but the Senate on occasion could afford to disregard the electorate. The Chamber of Deputies, unfortunately, could not. "The three-years law was an electoral promise of too long standing to be decently repeated." [65] To send the bill back to the Senate once again would be to risk having no law at all before the end of the present session. In the estimation of the Commission,

All would have to be taken up again by the new legislature, and who knows how much longer the nation would have to wait for the three-years law. . . . The army during this whole time would remain in a state of uncertainty about its mode of conscription, and nothing would be more regrettable than a prolongation of this provisory condition, in which the constant expectation of change keeps the army. This would be a pitiable abortion.[66]

The Commission could not be sure whether the country would blame the Senate for thwarting the national will or the Chamber for not having been satisfied with the degree of reform already attained. In order to end this unpleasant state of uncertainty, the Chamber Army Commission finally decided to recommend that the Senate version of the law be accepted and to leave to "those who are to come the task of perfecting it." [67] The Chamber of Deputies thus accepted the inequalities against which it had fulminated for so long, and the three-years law was passed. Still, at the last moment in the final debate, it seemed as if the deputies might yet balk at it. Frey-

[64] *J.O.C. Doc.* (1889), p. 1343.
[65] Monteilhet, *op. cit.,* p. 224.
[66] *J.O.C. Doc.* (1889), p. 1343.
[67] *Ibid.,* p. 1344.

cinet, as Minister of War, was obliged once again to reiterate that, despite the educational exemptions, the law had to be voted upon as it stood. Otherwise, the fact that it had not been enacted in the present session would indicate that "the French parliament is, after a fashion, incapable of bringing into practice its ideas on military questions and that it has been unable to establish stability where stability is most necessary.[68] Adjuring the deputies to overlook the exemptions, he asked them to demonstrate their unwillingness to let politics stand in the way of the great task of national defense. It was a brilliant speech, for which the honors of *affichage* (to be published and posted on all official notice boards) were voted.[69] In the estimation of the *Revue des deux mondes,* the Chamber might still have rejected the law because of the exemptions, except for the timely intervention of the Minister of War, and Freycinet needed all his oratorical skill and flattery to override the partisan prejudices of the republican majority.[70]

The Senate was also able to defeat the Chamber on another aspect of the law, which, although primarily military, had social and political overtones. In the 1872 law the National Assembly had considered the possibility of imitating the German system of regional recruitment and had then decided against it. The undeniably efficient and less costly German method was rejected, and the old French system was perpetuated whereby each regiment was made up of recruits from all over the country. In his all-encompassing military reform bill, General Boulanger had provided for the units in each army corps to be recruited from the region in which the corps was stationed, with the proviso that men native to one military subdivision of the region should be stationed in another subdivision.[71] The Senate Army Commission objected to this provision, stressing the traditional arguments that the military education of a conscript and the instillation of the necessary

[68] *J.O.C. Déb.* (1889), p. 1883.
[69] *Ibid.,* p. 1884.
[70] *R.D.M.,* July 15, 1889, p. 467.
[71] *J.O.C. Doc.* (1886), p. 614.

discipline would take place more quickly and that the political unity of the nation would be better assured if he were stationed far from home. Then, too, losses in battle for a single army corps might be so severe that, in effect, a whole region would be depopulated. Possibly of more significance was the argument also advanced by the Commission that troops in garrison in their native region would be reluctant to repress local civil disturbances.[72]

From the time that the project underwent its first debate in the Chamber in 1884 until it was finally voted, five years had elapsed. In that period, the bill was discussed frequently and at length by both chambers, yet in the arguments advanced by both its proponents and its adversaries there was remarkably little substance. Each successive discussion of the bill was essentially a rehash of what had gone before. As *Spectateur militaire* commented wearily during the 1887 debate over the bill, "Few, very few, or, to state it more categorically, *no* new arguments."[73] Nor can the legislators be said to have gone about their task with any real sense of urgency, despite their often repeated declarations about the necessity of enacting a new law on conscription. The Chamber might well have stood its ground on the educational exemptions and have sent the bill back to the Senate once again if Freycinet had not in opportune fashion reminded the deputies of the approaching elections.[74] It is even debatable whether there was any strong electoral pressure for the legal enactment of the three years' service, or whether many deputies simply sensed that there was something ludicrous in making it a part of their electoral manifestos in 1889, as they had done twice before in 1881 and 1885.

The chief military argument of the parliamentary advocates of the law centered on the problem of numbers. According to

[72] *J.O.S. Doc.* (1888), p. 137.

[73] *S.M.,* Jan. 1. 1887, p. 87.

[74] E. Katzenbach, "Charles Louis de Saulces de Freycinet and the Army of Metropolitan France" (unpublished Ph.D. dissertation, Princeton University, 1953), p. 317.

Freycinet, the 1872 law was an admirable piece of legislation; its only defect was that it did not provide France with enough trained men to match the massive armies of other European powers.[75] This argument was questionable since in recent years the Ministers of War had been making a constant effort to shorten the term of service for the first portion of the contingent and to extend it for the second, thereby greatly increasing the number of adequately trained men in the country. Considering the time and effort required to replace the 1872 law, when so much could be accomplished within its framework, one might well agree with the military critic Captain Henri Choppin when he wrote: "Why bother devoting long sessions to the discussion of military laws if the Minister can effect the reforms more quickly and simply through administrative means?"[76]

In any case it was not the numerical insufficiency caused by the 1872 law which really generated the reforming ardor of the republican majority in the Chamber. As far as they were concerned, the two problems of numbers and the length of service were secondary to the matter of the one-year volunteers and the exemptions for the schoolteachers and priests. They looked upon the suppression of the 1872 law as, above all, a measure of social reform, but they were obliged by the patriotic proprieties of the era to stress the military aspects of the question.

Social and political considerations being dominant in their approach to conscription, the chief problem for the republicans in the Chamber was not one of obtaining adequate numbers of men but rather how to reduce the annual contingent in a manner consonant with the principle of equality. This problem would have evaporated if the term of service had been reduced to two years, but no one, apart from a few of the most radically inclined, would admit the feasibility of such a step, at least not until 1893 when the Germans took it. Unless parliament was willing to appropriate at least another 50,000,000

[75] *J.O.C. Déb.* (1889), p. 134.
[76] Choppin, *op. cit.*, pp. 45–46.

francs per year to finance the incorporation of three full conscript classes, it was necessary to dispose of some 40,000 men
out of each contingent in some fashion or other. The Chamber
Army Commission met the problem through a variety of in-
genious and complicated schemes,[77] the ultimate result of
which would have been a contingent where the majority of
conscripts actually served for two years although they were
enrolled for three.

The efforts of the Chamber of Deputies to reconcile the
principle of equality with both the three years' service and the
realities of public finance resulted in a measure that was overly
complex in its provisions and that would probably have been
highly unsatisfactory from the standpoint of military training.
Spectateur militaire, which almost as far back as 1872 had been
calling on parliament to undertake a program of basic military
reforms, starting with the three years' service, abruptly
changed its tune after watching the Chamber actually debate
the question in 1884. Considering the *status quo* to be preferable to any military reform likely to be produced by either the
Chamber elected in 1881 or the one that would probably be
elected in 1885, the journal writer sincerely hoped that the
deputies would in the future "pay as little attention as possible
to military matters." [78] The problem was that the Chamber, in
permitting social considerations to loom so large in the enactment of a military reform, was taking its cue from the more
radical elements within its midst, and that primarily for electoral purposes. "Absolute equality for all" had a splendidly republican ring to it at election time, but it is debatable whether
all the members of the republican majority in the Chamber
really believed in it. If the one-year volunteers were suppressed, some comparable educational exemption would have
to be instituted as a replacement in the interest of the French
bourgeoisie.[79]

Even if the principle of equality complicated unduly the

---

[77] *J.O.C. Doc.* (1886), p. 588.

[78] *S.M.,* December 15, 1884, p. 512.

[79] *S.M.,* November 1882, pp. 314–317.

military aspects of conscription, it was a convenient rationalization for the anticlerical sentiments of the republicans in the
Chamber. With the rigorous application of this principle,
there were no grounds for the Catholic deputies to seek special
concessions or exemptions for the clergy. *"Le curé sac au dos"*
was one of the standard republican rallying cries of the period.
For the more fervently anticlerical deputies, it was the essential feature of the law, even if it involved no more than 2,500
men per year.[80]

   In the name of equality, the republicans could righteously
counter all charges of anticlericalism or persecution, such as
were leveled by Msgr. Freppel, fiery archibishop of Augers.[81]
The reporter for the Chamber Army Commission noted that
the schoolteachers of the nation loudly and patriotically protested against the educational exemptions in the Senate bill
even though they benefited from them. As for the clergy, con-
scripting seminarians was in no way counter to the Concordat,
nor was it persecution. "Persecution," he declared, "implies exceptional and violent measures. We ask neither . . . with regard to the seminarians. We simply ask that they fulfill the
duty that has been imposed on every citizen." [82] On patriotic
grounds, the republican position was smugly irreproachable.

   The Senate was able to view the question of conscription in
more detached fashion than was the Chamber. In a sense, the
Senate inherited something of the nonpartisan attitude toward
military affairs of the National Assembly, as it also inherited
many of its members. Relatively immune to the Chamber's
electoral preoccupations, the Senate, then, could look upon
conscription as primarily a military matter, while in its deliberations it could also make use of the knowledge of the several
generals on active duty who were senators and who were pro-
hibited by law from sitting in the Chamber. Three of these

---

   [80] "La nouvelle loi militaire française," *Revue militaire suisse,* August 15,
1887, pp. 291–292.
   [81] *J.O.C. Déb.* (1884), p. 1197.
   [82] *J.O.C. Doc.* (1888, sess. ext.), p. 350.

generals, as of 1888, had been at one time or other Minister of War, which gave them a particularly acute appreciation of the issues involved. Freycinet, who was probably the most competent Minister of War of the Third Republic, also sat in the Senate continuously from 1876 until his retirement in 1920. As a result, the Senate debates on conscription were more sharply focused on the military aspects of the question and less apt to become digressive and irrelevant than the debates in the Chamber.

Certainly the Senate was not insensitive to social and political pressures when it insisted upon the educational exemptions. Even so, to divide the contingent into two portions, as in the Senate bill, was from a military standpoint simpler and more logical than splitting it some five or more ways, which was what the Chamber was trying to do. If it could be so arranged that the intellectual and scientific life of the nation benefited, so much the better. In the end the Senate prevailed over the Chamber not only because of the coming elections but also because its version of how the three years' service should be organized resulted in a better, more efficient law. This was, no doubt, recognized by a good many deputies.

Although the seemingly endless reiteration of the time-honored platitudes concerning the virtues or defects of equality was the most prominent feature of the debate over the conscription law, the technical aspects of the problem, involving the opinion of the military experts, also figured. Yet this technical advice was less decisive than it might have been. Having repeated the usual argument as to the need for more trained men and as to the impossibility of making a good soldier in less than three years, there was not much more that the advocates of the law could say. Indeed, those who opposed the measure on military grounds often seemed more persuasive. Basing their arguments on the recent military past, even if it was slightly tarnished, they gave the impression that they were dealing with facts. The proponents of the law, endeavoring to predict the shape of future conflicts, were at a disadvantage.

Technical military arguments, in fact, tended to amount to little more than educated or intuitive guesses. The advocate of a particular point of view could only rely on his long years of experience backed by a few vague historical analogies to indicate what was best. Essentially, it was the ideal of the "old soldier" with his "military spirit" embodied in the victorious army of the Crimean and Italian wars as opposed to a belief in the efficacy of mass armies, founded on the remote memories of the wars of the Revolution and the more recent experience of the Government of National Defense.

The opponents of the law raised the standard, though plausible, objection that a civilian parliament was incapable of dealing effectively with the problems of military reform.[83] The difficulty here lay in ascertaining what the soldiers believed to be the most adequate system of conscription. From the opinions expressed in the Conseil supérieur de la Guerre, the ranking generals were against any reduction in the term of service below four years.[84] Freycinet claimed, however, that during the debates over the law they had changed their minds. They had not believed the three years' service to be practicable a few years before, but with the general improvement in the quality of the cadres and with a more efficient program of training, they had come to see its virtues.[85] This argument was rebutted by a senator who said that the generals consulted by Freycinet, who was then the Minister of War, had had to hide their true beliefs when speaking to their hierarchical chief. Claiming to speak, not for the political generals, but for the officers who served in the field and who were purely military men, he said that they were all against reducing the term of service.[86]

The conscription law of 1889, despite all the legislative effort that its enactment had required, did not represent a significant

---

[83] *J.O.C. Déb.* (1888), p. 2863. See also *J.O.S. Déb.* (1888), p. 1178.
[84] C.S.G., "Reg. dél.," No. 7 (1883–1885), pp. 77–81.
[85] *J.O.S. Déb.* (1888), p. 597.
[86] *Ibid.*, p. 602.

or important new departure in French military affairs, as had the 1872 law. Throughout the 1880's there had been a steady evolution in the direction of the three years' service for reasons of sound finance and military necessity. The army had come tacitly to accept it as normal, regardless of all the official pronouncements in favor of a longer term of service. The version of the conscription law which the Senate forced upon the Chamber was thus an essentially pragmatic and empirical piece of legislation. The three years' service was already a *fait accompli,* while the educational exemptions were merely a reflection of the prevailing social conditions. It was very much a law that preserved the *status quo.* Had the Chamber prevailed with its version, the result would have represented, socially at least, a significant reform, although militarily it would probably have proved unworkable.

The Army Budget

From 1871 on, the prerogatives of parliament with regard to the army were never seriously questioned. Through the workings of the French political system and despite the intentions of the men who wrote the Constitution of 1875, the locus of sovereignty came to rest with the legislative rather than the executive branch of the government. Yet between the legal and constitutional authority of parliament in military affairs and the actual implementation of that authority there was a considerable gulf, at least in the first three decades of the history of the Third Republic. For one thing, the legislative process in France was relatively slow and often clumsy. It was hampered until 1902 by the lack of permanent standing committees staffed by those legislators considered to be expert in a particular field.[87] These committees might have facilitated the work of the legislators particularly with regard to technical questions, but it was the general belief that such bodies would detract from the sovereign powers residing in parliament as a

[87] *Vide supra,* pp. 94–95.

whole. Then, too, the lack of strong party lines or discipline often prevented the chambers from dealing quickly
and efficiently with most legislative matters.

Apart from the enactment of specific laws, the chief means
available to parliament for exercising its implicit power and
authority over the army in an effective manner was the budget. The fact that the funds necessary for the maintenance of
the army were appropriated annually gave to parliament an
instrument of great latent power. In Germany this possibility
was early recognized by the ruling military aristocracy. During the twenty years that he was Chancellor, Bismarck strove
mightily to keep questions of military finance from being discussed with any frequency in the Reichstag. Although he
never was able to win a permanent allocation of funds, he did
succeed in having the size of the army and of the military
budget discussed only at seven-year intervals. The traditional
Anglo-Saxon principle of redress of grievance before supply of
funds had no real historic weight in France; nevertheless, if
parliament wished to make use of its power to legislate funds
as a means for effecting desired modifications in the military
institutions of France, it had a perfect right to do so.

In France the army budget represented the estimate of needs
made by the Minister of War as modified by the parliamentary commissions for the budget. Under the Third Republic
there was no special budgetary branch of the government except the particular legislative commission. The Budget Commission in the pre–World War I era, although larger than the
other parliamentary commissions, was chosen in the same way
that they were. Its members were deputies or senators chosen
by lot in equal numbers from the eleven bureaus into which
the Chamber and the nine into which the Senate were periodically divided. It was only a temporary committee, and there
was no way to assure that those men who were most profes-
sionally competent to discuss budgetary matters might serve
on it. Stourm, the French budgetary expert, has asked: "How
can it be expected that a deputy could possibly acquire in a

few meetings of a temporary commission any degree of competency on a subject which he has never studied?" [88]

Once submitted to the Commission, the estimates of the Minister of War were then subjected to minute examination by the budgetary reporter for that department. The budget for each ministry had its own reporter. It was the task of the reporter to check the figures of the ministry and to bring them into line with the fiscal possibilities of that particular year. To be a reporter for one of the budgets was a golden opportunity for a deputy to make a name for himself as an expert in a given field. The aim of the reporter for the army budget, as for the others, was not so much to improve the condition of public finance as "to present the most imposing report possible." [89] It is probable that no one was meant to take these voluminous reports very seriously, except insofar as they signified that their author was a candidate for the post of undersecretary of state at the Ministry of War. Their value or importance, then, in the eyes of parliament was the same as "an essay in a competitive examination. . . ." [90]

To the Budget Commission fell the chief responsibility for controlling the funds requested by the Ministry of War and for riding herd on the extravagant tendencies that it shared with any government department. Although, in carrying out this task, the Commission scrutinized with care the anticipated financial needs of the army, it seldom withheld a really significant sum of money and only rarely questioned the validity of the ministerial estimates. Such an enlightened rapport as seems to have existed between them cannot have been entirely fortuitous. Marshal Joffre notes in his memoirs that the Minister of War, being an essentially ephemeral figure, was of little importance in drawing up the annual budget. The heads of the various departments produced their

[88] R. Stourm, *The Budget,* T. Plazinski, trans. (New York: Appleton, 1917), p. 288.

[89] Gooch, *op. cit.,* p. 190.

[90] *S.M.,* November 15, 1884, p. 333.

estimates with a minimum of ministerial interference. If there was any control and coordination of their requests, it was exercised by the chief of the auditing department. This role, which he came to assume over the years, was by no means in keeping with his normal, nominal functions. The auditing department modified and reshaped the requests of the other ministerial sections, reducing them to a "reasonable" level in such a way that in reality it prepared the budget. According to Joffre, "Its situation was relatively that much stronger in that it remained while the ministers passed on." [91]

In its efforts to keep the budgets within reasonable bounds, the auditing department was on occasion actually hurting the best interests of the army. According to Revol, the historian of the French army, many of the insufficient appropriations of the years before 1914 can be attributed to the reductions it imposed on the other ministerial departments, on the pretext of better ensuring a favorable vote in parliament. "This permitted parliament to claim, in its own justification, that it had never refused a single credit for national defense." [92] The work of the Budget Commission with regard to military appropriations was thus facilitated by the timidity of certain anonymous bureaucrats at the Ministry of War. [93]

Because it held the purse strings, the Budget Commission occupied a crucial position, for the whole business of government was eventually dependent on an appropriation of funds. In effect, the ultimate result of this fact was that the Commission's sphere of activities was extended to the point where it concerned itself "with practically everything." [94] But even though the Budget Commission had great implicit power, its full potentialities were seldom realized. Part of the reason for this lies in the nature of its composition. It was, after all, a temporary committee with an annually renewable mandate.

[91] J. Joffre, *Mémoires du Maréchal Joffre* (Paris: Plon, 1932), Vol. I, p. 59.
[92] Revol, *op. cit.,* p. 213.
[93] J. Bouchet, *Gouvernement et commandement* (Paris: Payot, 1930), pp. 197–198.
[94] Gooch, *op. cit.,* pp. 37–38.

Although some members might manage to sit on it for several years in a row, this was not the same thing as permanent membership, and the Commission could not develop that *esprit de corps* which comes from a group of men working together over an extended period of time at well-defined tasks. As a consequence the Budget Commission was ill-equipped to exercise any continuous, long-term influence in military affairs.

The Budget Commission never attempted to do much more than discharge its primary function of trying to reconcile the demands of the state with the interests of the French taxpayer. Nevertheless, within the bounds of this more strictly limited mission, the Commission went to considerable lengths to assert the prerogatives of parliament over the appropriation and, to a lesser degree, the spending of the public funds. The chief instrument here was the voting of money by chapter within the budget of each individual ministry.

The precedent for such parliamentary control in budgetary matters went back to the end of the Restoration and the beginning years of the July Monarchy. In that era parliament had established the practice of specifying by means of chapters within the budget for a given ministry how the money should be spent. This practice had ceased under the Second Empire, when the authority of parliament had all but disappeared, to be reintroduced in 1869 with the liberalization of the regime.[95] Under the Third Republic, the tendency was for increasingly detailed parliamentary scrutiny through a proliferation of chapters. Whereas the 1872 budget for the Ministry of War consisted of eighteen chapters for a total of 465,000,000 francs, with one of these alone, "Pay and Supplies," accounting for 320,000,000, by 1913 there were 142 chapters in a budget of some 983,000,000 francs.[96] In its efforts to control the allocation of funds, the Budget Commission did not merely accept the estimates of the Ministry of War for each chapter but rather

[95] P. Hautière, *Les dépenses du ministère de la guerre* (Paris: Jouve, 1914), pp. 73–74
[96] *Ibid.*, pp. 99–101.

broke them down in order to examine the various items in detail and often at great length. It was not, however, until several years after the defeat of 1870 that this came to be an accepted practice.

During the period of the National Assembly the budgets were treated in cavalier fashion, and the debates, like those in 1874, were so "precipitous as to preclude any detailed examination. . . ." [97] Until the disasters of the recent war had been in part repaired and the new laws on the organization of the army put into effect, parliament could do little more than vote in a lump the sums requested by the Ministry of War. Following their advent to power in 1876, the republicans quickly moved to show that the new budget would be "discussed more seriously than those of preceding years." [98] Then, too, there had also been reestablished some degree of order and stability within French military institutions.

This assertion by parliament of its right to deal with the minutiae of military life in the interest both of the taxpayer and of national defense was not appreciated by the military or by certain of their spokesmen within the Chamber. A Bonapartist deputy, Ernest Dréolle, considered it an affront to the dignity of the army that its expenditures were so carefully scrutinized by parliament. In his estimation, the army was above the other institutions of the state and therefore not amenable to such treatment.[99] Echoing these sentiments, *Spectateur militaire* wondered with regard to one item in the budget if parliament was not starting a discussion over a matter that was "absolutely foreign to it and about which no one could be found in France, except possibly within the Budget Commission itself, who would deny its incompetence. . . ." [100] As a result of such parliamentary zeal, it was to be expected that there would soon be not a single "gaiter

[97] *Année politique* (1874), p. 295.
[98] *Année politique* (1876), p. 126.
[99] *J.O.* (1876), p. 5905.
[100] *S.M.*, September 1876, p. 449.

button, cartridge, or grain of rice, whose origin, present location, and ultimate destination is not known to the whole of Europe." [101]

Speaking in the name of the newly triumphant republicans, Gambetta would not accept the thesis that the particulars of military finance were either beneath the dignity or beyond the ability of the legislators. Rather it was their obligation to discuss these matters especially when it was a question of the military budget. Parliament was not, in his words, made up of "great lords who disdain these little points and these many details." [102] Gambetta baited the Bonapartists with the memory of a recent era "when no one descended into details. . . . We had then a sumptuous military décor, but as experience has so terribly demonstrated, behind that décor were chaos and waste." [103]

Despite the confident declaration of Gambetta as to the responsibility and the competence of parliament in military matters, republican legislators during the next quarter of a century never really used their fiscal powers either to effect significant reforms in the army or even to influence its evolution in a particular direction. Over the years, as successive reporters for the army budget set about their work, they purported to uncover numerous defects in the functioning of the military machine and abuses demanding immediate correction. By the turn of the century this catalogue of errors filled over thirty pages of fine print in the *Journal Officiel*. Yet having discovered and analyzed the multitudinous deficiencies, both major and minor, of the army, the reporter never went any further. Not until after 1900 did the Commission implement its discontent over some wasteful practice or superfluous office and take the seemingly logical step of reducing the appropriation. Even then these reductions were announced as being "symbolic," that is to say, the Commission would cut the funds for some

[101] *S.M.,* August 1877, p. 276.
[102] *J.O.* (1876), p. 5905.
[103] *Année politique* (1876), pp. 256–257.

item in the budget by a few thousand francs as an indication of its displeasure.

The Budget Commission, upon receiving the estimates of the Ministry of War, examined them with care in an effort to trim a few francs wherever possible. Though the figures submitted by the Minister were seldom cut in any very drastic fashion, there was still a great deal which could be done through a close attention to detail. Then, having drawn up the budget, the Commission presented it to the Chamber, where it was usually accepted with little or no change. Economy and a balanced budget were the watchwords rather than military reform. The viligance of succeeding Commissions was responsible for the achievement of considerable economies. Thus, the reporter for the 1891 budget could point out that the cost of provisioning a French infantryman had fallen from 447 francs in 1878 to 394 francs in 1890. At the same time, his meat ration had been increased, and he now received rations of sugar and coffee not allotted before.[104]

There were limits, however, to what could be accomplished through the simple method of shaving francs from each individual item. The reporter for the 1889 budget stated that the point had now been reached where any further reductions would soon disrupt the functioning of the army.[105] If significant economies were to be made, it could be only through a major reorganization of French military institutions. As early as 1880 the reporter suggested that it might be advisable to restudy the composition of the army from the point of view of both military and fiscal efficiency, but he hastened to add that it was not the task of the Commission to initiate such a reform.[106] This manner of asserting the need for imminent, radical reform of the army, followed by an immediate disclaimer of competence or responsibility, was to become an almost yearly litany for succeeding reporters.

[104] *J.O.C. Doc.* (1890), p. 1203.
[105] *J.O.C. Doc.* (1888, sess. ext.), p. 281.
[106] *J.O.* (1880), p. 5729.

Being either unwilling or unable to take any positive steps
to correct the numerous shortcomings they unearthed, the reporters' only recourse was to call upon the enlightened patriotism of the Minister of War and indeed of the whole military
administration to remedy them. It seems not to have been a
very effective method, for the same abuses tended to reappear
in subsequent reports. In the budget of 1885 the reporter noted
the disproportionately large number of generals residing in
Paris and collecting the rather handsome special allowances
for the extra expenses of life in the capital. Some of them,
members of the special technical committees at the Ministry of
War, had gone so far as to refuse command assignments in the
provinces "in order to preserve their sweet sinecures. . . ."[107]
According to the report on the budget of 1892, there were
still far too many generals living in Paris and drawing special
allotments,[108] while in 1900 the technical committees had not
yet been modified in any way, to the disgust of the reporter for
the budget of that year.[109]

Another defect repeatedly emphasized by the reporters for
the budget was the chronic overloading in the auxiliary and
staff services of the French army. The size of this military
bureaucracy was noted every time a comparison was made
with the German army, which seemed to be able to function
effectively with about half the number of clerks, staff officers,
and consultative generals found to be necessary by the French.
Such a superabundance of office-bound, noncombatant soldiers
formed a dead weight, burdening the budget "without being
of any use for the defensive strength of the nation."[110] This
refrain was reiterated in budgetary reports, echoed by the Left,
the Right, and the Center in parliament, and lamented in
numerous articles in the military reviews, all to no avail. In the
opinion of the reporter for the 1890 budget, the only person in

[107] *J.O.C. Doc.* (1884), p. 1761.
[108] *J.O.C. Doc.* (1891), pp. 2221–2222.
[109] *J.O.C. Doc.* (1900), p. 293.
[110] *J.O.C. Déb.* (1883), p. 2681.

a position to do anything about it was the Minister of War. As for the Budget Commission, its role was limited to indicating to the Minister the abuses to be corrected and insisting "that he act in accordance with these indications." [111]

As may be imagined, the soldiers did not appreciate the off-hand way in which the members of the Budget Commission took it upon themselves to be the permanent, semiofficial spokesmen for military reform, albeit somewhat harmless and ineffectual ones. If there were defects in the army, it was up to the government or the legislators to present the competent parliamentary commission with a specific project of reform. But for the Budget Commission to set itself up as a "veritable committee for the direction of military affairs" would lead, in the estimation of *Spectateur militaire,* to a confusion of powers, at the very least.[112] That it was the task of the Budget Commission to approve or to reject for good reason the specific ministerial requests for funds was evident, but the military had difficulty in understanding how such matters as promotion, the organization of the army, or the structure and functioning of the high command had any place in the debate over a financial law.[113]

Because of the somewhat antipathetic attitude of the army toward its endeavors, the Budget Commission might well doubt that it always received frank and loyal cooperation from the military authorities. Any request for funds made by the Ministry of War was accompanied by a mass of corroborative figures, which were usually impossible to verify.[114] In drawing up the 1897 budget, the reporter, having noticed two different figures given for the effective strength of the army in successive tables supplied by the Ministry of War, prevailed upon the responsible officials in that department to reproduce

[111] *J.O.C. Doc.* (1889), p. 1035.

[112] *S.M.,* November 15, 1884, pp. 332–334.

[113] Gen. Lamiraux, "Rapports sur le budget," *France militaire* (hereafter referred to as *F.M.*), February 20, 1902.

[114] *J.O.C. Doc.* (1888, sess. ext.), p. 281.

the method for calculating the effective strength. This demonstration resulted in a third figure, different from the other two.[115] It would seem almost as if it were a point of honor among soldiers assigned to the task of preparing the army budget to confuse the reporter, to evade his inquiries, and, if necessary, to lie to him in a discreet fashion.[116]

The need for stability in the subordinate units had been part of the rationale for enacting a detailed law on the cadres and effectives in 1875. Such a law would keep the size of these units from fluctuating annually according to the demands of the budget.[117] That the law had little relevance for the military authorities seems evident from the account given by Godefroy Cavaignac, reporter for the 1896 budget. He contended that the Minister of War, although provided with funds to maintain a group of Algerian regiments at a level of 4,000 men in excess of their total legal strength, was still not satisfied. So he proceeded to take another 3,000 men from the perpetually undermanned companies of Metropolitan France, contrary to the law on the cadres and the provisions of the Budget Commission.[118] Having duly noted the irregularity of the Minister's actions in this and similar cases and having made a plea that the military authorities utilize more efficiently the men they already had, the Commission still did not refuse the funds necessary for the maintenance of the additional men to be incorporated.[119]

The justification for any sudden increase in the number of men under arms was military necessity as perceived either by the Minister of War or by the Conseil supérieur de la Guerre. This led the reporter for the 1897 budget to note somewhat ironically that in a country like Germany, where parliamentary democracy was less well developed than in France, similar

---

[115] *J.O.C. Doc.* (1896), pp. 1129–1130.

[116] E. Manceau, *Notre armée* (Paris: Charpentier, 1901), pp. 170–171.

[117] *Vide supra,* p. 57.

[118] *J.O.C. Doc.* (1895), p. 1174.

[119] *Ibid.,* p. 1175.

increases in the number of effectives would have been undertaken "only after profound debate over a specific bill." [120] Because parliament was unable to compel the military to heed its objurgations and the soldiers were determined to manage their own affairs with only minimal governmental interference, the budget was an ineffective instrument of civilian control. Despite their occasional discontent, the chambers could only continue to appropriate "considerable sums of money through a sense of patriotism, but without really being in possession of all the supporting proofs one might want. . . ." [121] It need hardly be added that as far as the army was concerned, this was not such a bad system so long as "patriotism" remained a dominant factor in parliament.

The remarkable willingness of parliament to appropriate huge and steadily increasing sums of money for the army was only one aspect of French financial patriotism in the decades after 1870. The ordinary budget, voted on an annual basis, covered the day-to-day repetitive expenditures of the army; it was paid by the usual means of tax receipts. However, in the aftermath of the Franco-Prussian War, a task presented itself that was far beyond the capacity of the ordinary budget: the repair of war damage and the replacement and renovation of whole war matériel of France, her weapons and her fortresses. It involved too huge a sum to be extracted from the taxpayer over a short period of time. The only feasible way to raise money on such a scale was through government borrowing. The funds thus appropriated were carried in an extraordinary budget.

To a degree, a financial policy that was predicated on the resort to extraordinary budgets smacked of fiscal irresponsibility. The fiscally conservative governments of the Restoration and the July Monarchy therefore turned to this expedient only on rare occasions, but under the Second Empire extraordinary

[120] *J.O.C. Doc.* (1896), p. 1030.
[121] *J.O.C. Doc.* (1882), p. 1932.

budgets became a regular practice. The rationale for this policy was given by Magne, probably the most able Minister of Finance during the reign of Napoleon III. He considered extraordinary budgets a legitimate means of financing those projects, such as railroads, "which consolidate themselves with and become part of the soil and thus increase the wealth of the state." [122] Hence, future beneficiaries should share in paying for them.

Although the Third Republic looked upon extraordinary budgets as but another unseemly trapping of the Empire, it was very early in its history obliged to resort to similar methods.[123] A bill was first introduced in March 1872 which suggested that there were expenses resulting from the recent war that "by their exceptional character, not being of a kind to be renewed annually . . . ," should be treated apart from the regular budget. The government advised grouping all these various charges in a "liquidation account" and providing certain extraordinary resources to pay for them.[124] There was, in the beginning, an obvious desire on the part of the conservative deputies to the National Assembly not to contract loans heedlessly, in the manner of former financial regimes, or to exceed the level of resources available. These resources originally included, among others, surplus revenues from the budget of 1869, as well as a loan from the Bank of France. When some 51,000,000 francs were realized from the conversion of the Morgan Loan and some 100,000,000 from the liquidation of the army endowment fund, the account was expanded to include this money.[125]

It was the original intention of the National Assembly not to engage in projects that might stretch out endlessly. The deputies also planned to maintain strict control over the handling of the hundreds of millions of francs then being ap-

---

[122] Quoted in Stourm, *op. cit.*, p. 242.
[123] *Ibid.*, pp. 236–242.
[124] *J.O.* (1872), p. 2526.
[125] *J.O.* (1875), p. 4052.

propriated, but this soon proved to be difficult, if not impossible. Blaming "contrary habits and traditions," one of the reporters for the liquidation account confessed that the Budget Commission had been unable to obtain an accurate accounting from the various branches of the Ministry of War or to impress them with the difference between money appropriated and money spent. Some members of the Commission were angry enough to contemplate cutting off the account and going no further than the 773,000,000 francs that had been voted as of March 1874, but the impossibility of taking this step was soon realized. The reconstitution of France's war matériel was under way; too much had been started already which could not be completed using only the resources to be tapped by the ordinary budgets.[126]

In response to the misgivings of parliament over the handling of such large sums of money by the government, efforts were made to introduce the usual method of control, the vote by chapter. The Minister of War by way of reply asserted that he, and not parliament, had to remain judge of the conditions necessary for the most efficacious and equitable spending of the money. It was his view that prevailed. In 1875 some 250,000,000 francs were appropriated in two large chapters, supplemented by a number of articles that were indicative of the wishes of the Assembly but that were by no means binding.[127] One deputy regretted not finding in the liquidation account "any trace of a resolution taken by the government to follow a plan for the ensemble; but this regret cannot go so far as to prevent me from voting in confidence and without explanation the credits accorded by the Commission. . . ."[128] Parliament as a whole seems to have echoed these sentiments, for practically all sums appropriated to the first liquidation account, and later to the second, were voted unanimously. Lauding the patriotism of the deputies in this matter, the reporter

[126] *J.O.* (1876), pp. 6762–6763.
[127] *Ibid.*
[128] *J.O.* (1874), p. 2146.

announced that in 1877, on the eve of the day when the Chamber was to be sent before the electors, "it did not hesitate to open a credit of 209,181,808 francs to the Department of War." [129]

The first liquidation account received 914,675,000 francs, of which 625,100,000 went to the Ministry of War. It was closed merely as a point of order in 1875, and the second liquidation account was immediately opened with an appropriation of 150,000,000 francs for works to be undertaken in the first months of 1876.[130] The second account was also meant to avoid the most obvious defects of an extraordinary budget. It was to be financed by six-year bonds. Financial engagements taken on so short a time could be expected not to get out of hand, for the day of reckoning was not too far in the distant future. By 1878 it was realized, however, that the work that had been undertaken and further planned was simply too extensive to be financed by so limited a means as six-year bonds. The government was forced to return to the practice of extraordinary budgets pure and simple based on long-term loans.[131] From 1879 through 1886 the first budget of extraordinary resources was employed, financed by 3 per cent bonds. It was followed by a second budget of an identical nature, which lasted until 1890.

The many expenditures that had seemed unique, and hence were carried in an extraordinary budget, were constantly having to be repeated. Science was making rapid strides, and the French had to keep their military machine "constantly on a level with this incessant progress." [132] Hence, by 1890 the government had decided to do away with the extraordinary budget and to place all appropriations of an extraordinary nature in a special section at the end of the annual budget. They would henceforth be considered as part of the ordinary budget

[129] J.O. (1878), p. 3329.
[130] J.O. (1876), pp. 4051–4052.
[131] J.O.C. Doc. (1880), p. 3458.
[132] J.O.C. Doc. (1890), p. 1252.

of the Ministry of War, payable from the yearly tax revenues of the treasury. This decision came at a time when France had completed the greatest part of her military reconstruction. The sums required were diminishing every year. There was also a realization on the part of the government that the huge sums raised under the various kinds of extraordinary budget required an impressive yearly carrying charge. Almost three billion francs had been raised between 1872 and 1890. According to the reporter for the budget of 1892, the service charge on this sum averaged out at 4 per cent, or some 110,000,000 francs annually.[133]

The notable thing about the various schemes originated for the extraordinary budgets was the willingness of parliament to relinquish all control over them once they were under way. In the first liquidation account, obvious efforts were made to regulate the appropriation, expenditure, and accounting of the hundreds of millions that were so easily voted. When such attempts at control were seen to be of little avail and the "obligation to give account was purely and simply ignored . . . ,"[134] parliament seemed unable to do anything but give more money. After the program of reconstruction began, the factor determining the appropriations became the individual projects themselves, and not the wishes of parliament. What had begun as an earnest attempt to control and, if necessary, to limit the spending of the Minister of War ended as little more than an automatic parliamentary rubber stamp on the expenditure of a sum whose yearly average was 150,000,000 francs.

The budgets for the Ministry of War, both ordinary and extraordinary, generally received a minimum of debate in parliament. *Spectateur militaire* noted, concerning the 1884 budget,

The Chamber, which has a precise sense of its own incompetence in military questions, let the debate as usual follow its course, without paying the least attention to it. The discussion thus be-

[133] *J.O.C. Doc.* (1891), p. 2190.
[134] *J.O.* (1876), p. 6762.

came a sort of private conversation between the Minister of War and the seven or eight deputies who, by virtue of their status as former officers, have set themselves up as a military areopagus.[135]

To the degree that the other legislators participated, they usually confined themselves to pleading some special local interest vis-à-vis the army or to making general observations about some aspect of the military establishment. Although the attitude of parlimament as a whole could be characterized as one of patriotic unity, still there was always some opposition, first from the Right, and in the later years of the century from the extreme Left, as Socialist deputies began to appear in the Chamber. The contribution of the Right to the budgetary debates seldom amounted to much more than nagging at the republicans. Their proffered amendments were invariably rejected, while their complaints in general were merely echoes of the ideas to be found in the budgetary reports, that is, a reiterated demand for more economy in the management of military finances or a call for a reduction in the overloaded administrative branches of the army. Essentially, the tactics of the Right were well summed up by Georges Cochery, who was several times the reporter for the army budget, with the statement that they consisted in "demanding economies in a block during the general discussion, and, when we attempt them, rejecting them in detail." [136]

If there were to be any solid, fundamentally novel criticism of French military policies, it would have to come from the Socialists. The ideas of Jean Jaurès concerning *l'armée nouvelle* were not to have much influence until after 1900 and, even then, not within military circles. As Challener points out in his study of the French theory of the nation in arms, "Socialist military thinking remained essentially negative throughout the nineteenth century." [137] Nevertheless, the Socialists were beginning to use the yearly debate over the budget

[135] *S.M.*, December 15, 1883, p. 511.
[136] *J.O.C. Déb.* (1892), p. 2067.
[137] Challener, *op. cit.*, p. 69.

as an occasion to put forth their theories in a rudimentary form. In 1894 Jaurès questioned the wisdom of spending so much on the regular army and so little on the reserves and reminded the deputies that no matter what military theorists said about the necessity of a large, well-trained standing army, it would be the reserves who would always form the majority of the fighting forces of the nation in time of war.[138] Two years later Jaurès scored the republican majority for preventing serious discussion of any defects or projected reforms in the army by their habitual tactic of pointing "toward the frontier with a tragic gesture even before we have been able to indicate what objections we want to raise. . . ." He suggested that before the Minister of War was granted additional funds for more recruits, he should endeavor to make better use of the men he had.[139] To go so far as actually to withhold funds from the Minister of War until he managed military affairs more efficiently was an idea that was too radical for anyone but an avowed Socialist to contemplate.

In seeking the real basis for what one must consider the naïveté and ineffectiveness of parliament in questions of military finance, one is forced to the conclusion that most of the legislators believed in the patriotic sentiments that they periodically affected. The Vicomte de Montfort, who was through the years a rather consistent critic of republican military policy, nevertheless made a specific point of quoting with approval the statement of a recent budget reporter, the noted Radical Camille Pelletan: "The budget for the Ministry of War is the sacred treasure of the country; we must not touch it."[140] This feeling of parliamentary solidarity over the welfare of the army was well expressed by Georges Cochery when he declared that "for the last twenty years, the French chambers have become united every time its strength and interests are brought into question."[141] If anyone except the Socialists

---

[138] *J.O.C. Déb.* (1894), pp. 768–771.
[139] *J.O.C. Déb.* (1896), pp. 2288–2289.
[140] *J.O.C. Déb.* (1891), p. 2068.
[141] *J.O.C. Déb.* (1890), p. 1913.

disagreed with these expressed sentiments, they did not speak for publication in the *Journal Officiel.*

As was to be expected, one of the most important underlying themes in all discussions of military questions in parliament was Germany. It was because of Germany that France hastened to reconstitute her army in the 1870's and 1880's, and that she burdened her public debt by constructing a great barrier of fortresses on her eastern frontier. When, in the years after 1890, the major part of the task of reorganization and reconstruction was completed, it was against the German standard of excellence that the French measured themselves. In examining the many tables of comparison between the two countries and in noting the many warnings of doom to be found in the *Journal Officiel,* one is almost led to believe that the Germans dictated French military policy and also decided the sums of money to be appropriated annually. Any major German innovation was the cause for immediate soul-searching in France and a reexamination of their own practices.

For the thirty-year period between 1871 and 1900, the tables of comparison show a remarkable similarity between the French and German armies. Both countries spent about the same amount of money on their military establishments during these three decades, and both armies were of about the same size at the turn of the century. Any increase in the number of men under the colors was usually initiated by Germany, to be followed within a year by a similar increase in France.[142] If France lagged a little in the 1890's in matching the German growth in military manpower, the reason is less likely to be found in the declining French birth rate than in the comforting thought of the Russian hordes on the eastern frontier of Germany. After the signing of the Franco-Russian Alliance in 1894, there was not quite the same compulsion to keep step with Germany, man for man, franc for franc. Military service already weighed more heavily in France than in any other European country. In 1895, out of every one thousand in the pop-

[142] *Ibid.,* pp. 1912–1913.

ulation, France had fourteen under arms as compared to eleven for Germany. The figure was ten for Russia, eight for Italy, and seven for Austria-Hungary.[143] With her rapidly rising population, Germany could continue to increase the size of her army without any great change in the ratio of soldiers to civilians, but France, with a stationary or even slightly declining population, could not without risking the creation of serious social and economic strains. It was a risk that the French preferred not to run until, by 1913, the discrepancy was so great between the size of the two military establishments that emergency measures were necessary. The result was the three-years law, which once again placed the French and German armies on an almost equal footing with regard to size.

France reached the height of her military spending in the late 1870's and early 1880's. While her extraordinary budgets remained high until 1890, the Budget Commissions may be credited with a major economy in reducing the size of the ordinary budget from 600,000,000 francs in 1882 to 550,000,000 francs in 1888. The ordinary budget began to mount again after 1890, but this may be explained in large part by the steady increases in the effective strength of the army. Germany, on the other hand, starting with an ordinary budget only three quarters as large as that of France in the early 1880's, continually augmented her spending until, in 1896, the two countries were all but equal in the size of their regular annual appropriations. The extraordinary budgets in Germany, which after the war had been very high, steadily diminished until they hovered around 40,000,000 francs in the mid-1880's. They took a tremendous leap to some 210,000,000 francs in 1887 and remained high until the end of the century.[144] In the decade and a half preceding the outbreak of war, German spending on those items which had originally been carried on the extraordinary budget in France, new war matériel and fortresses, surpassed French appropriations for the same items

[143] *J.O.C. Déb.* (1895), p. 747.
[144] *J.O.C. Doc.* (1896), pp. 1018–1020.

by figures that were on the order of two to one.[145] It was only in the year before the war that the French parliament took cognizance of how far behind Germany the country had permitted itself to fall. When war came, a spending program of some one billion francs was under discussion to catch up with Germany.

Whether the French received full value for the money that parliament appropriated with such apparent willingness is impossible to say. An army is never a very economical investment. It is, however, pertinent to ask if parliament might not have exercised its prerogatives more forcefully and have made an attempt to correct the abuses that the Budget Commission became so expert in analyzing. Such matters as the overloaded administrative branches and the technical committees with their array of superannuated generals, to mention two, would all seem to have been legitimate fields for parliamentary initiative. Since persuasion was an inadequate weapon, a simple reduction in the funds appropriated would have shaken things up, but nothing was ever attempted.

In summarizing the relationship that existed between parliament and the army in the decades following 1870, one is confronted with a paradox. No one seriously disputed the authority or the power of parliament over the army. The great quantity of military legislation that was voted in these years is witness to it. Yet, at the same time, one is obliged to note the curious impotence of parliament in military matters. Fundamental pieces of military legislation, after the great laws of the period 1872–1875, required years of sterile debate before being enacted, while, in spite of all the concern displayed by parliament over the abuses in the army as they were recorded in the reports on the budget, the legislators never seemed able to cope with them.

The essential explanation of this paradox would seem to be that the army of the Third Republic was a dual organism. On

[145] *J.O.C. Doc.* (1914), pp. 461–462.

one side, there were the troops, the men from the annual conscript classes, who were temporary soldiers; on the other, the permanent cadre of professional officers and N.C.O.'s. Under earlier regimes, both the men in the ranks and their chiefs had shared a similar point of view about military life and their function as soldiers. It had been one of the aims of Thiers and the other authors of the 1872 conscription law to perpetuate this aspect of the old professional army, when they insisted on the term of service being set at five years. Budgetary and social pressures were to thwart them from the beginning; thus no conscript ever served the full five years. The great majority of conscripts never came to accept military service as a way of life or to look on soldiering as a worth-while trade. Rather, it was no more than a temporary interlude in their civilian lives. The prospect of becoming an N.C.O. had lost its appeal.

The officer corps carried on the traditions and ideals of the old army, while a whole set of military institutions also came into existence through the enactment of universal conscription. It was in terms of these institutions that parliament could act to implement a "republican" military policy. Thus, over a period of thirty-five years, there was a gradual reduction in the length of military service, along with its equalization, and the abolition of practically all exemptions. In this sense, one could speak of a democratization of the French army. With regard to the institutions inherited from the old army as embodied in the officer corps, parliament was less effective. Here it was a question of tampering with the functioning and practices of a tradition-bound, hierarchical organism that was both bureaucratic and authoritarian in nature. Much of the waste and inefficiency singled out by the budget reporters stemmed from the need of the permanent cadre of officers to protect their institutional interests. For example, it was necessary that there be a sufficient number of billets available in the upper echelons, above the rank of captain, so that as many officers as possible might expect a reasonable rate of promotion, even if it meant maintaining many superfluous jobs.

That the existence of such vested institutional interests contributed to the inefficiency of the French military machine is
certain. It is equally certain that for the government to have
attempted to do away with them would have resulted in the
destruction of the army as that institution was understood by
the majority of Frenchmen. Until the republicans could con-
ceive of and create some substitute for a strong, permanently
organized standing army as the instrument of national defense, the government was obliged to respect these institutional interests and to allow the military considerable latitude,
not to say autonomy, in the management of their own affairs.

As a consequence of this situation, when publicists and politicians referred to the army, there was always a certain
ambiguity in their use of the word. The French army had indeed become more democratic in that the term of service had
been reduced and conscription was soon to fall equally on
every male citizen of a certain age. In this respect, the Republic could take a rather proprietary view of French military
institutions. At the same time, because the army still continued
to have an existence apart as a hierarchical, bureaucratic structure within the state, functioning according to its own particular code of ideals, republican politicians could never quite dismiss it as a potential source of danger to the regime.

CHAPTER FOUR

The Problem of the High Command: 1871-1897

The Prussian Model and the French Copy

In the great program of military reform and renovation undertaken in the two decades following the defeat of 1870, the army and the state had complementary roles to play. The government sponsored those measures where the needs of the army impinged upon the civilian life of the country, such as conscription, while the soldiers attended to more specifically technical matters. In general, there was remarkably little friction between them over the enactment and implementation of this program of reform. Both the army and the regime had their particular spheres of competence, which were respected by the other. The fact that they were constituted according to different principles and motivated by different ideals had little bearing on the solution of most of the military problems of the era. The essential political interests of the regime were not involved in the organization or the functioning of the army, while the military were seldom obliged to take specific cognizance of political developments under the Republic, at least not before the turn of the century.

Only one technical military problem had any significant political and constitutional ramifications: the organization of a permanent high command. A matter of the greatest importance for the French army, it also portended a conflict between

the necessities of national defense, as understood by the soldiers, and what the politicians considered to be their vital interests. The conduct of war, as had been so forcefully demonstrated by the Prussians, had now become a science, demanding long years of training and preparation. No longer could
the French, relying on their traditional qualities of courage
and bravura, afford to ignore such matters as tactics, strategy,
and logistics, nor was it now possible to wait until the moment of mobilization before considering how the armies
should be constituted and who would lead them in battle.

The new Prussian concept of a military science, predicated
on the rational analysis of warfare, was embodied in the
Kriegsakademie and the General Staff. It was through these
two institutions that a military elite was trained in the fundamental principles of this science and prepared for its practical
application in time of war. More than anyone else, the father
of the intellectual traditions of the Prussian army was Clausewitz, philosopher of war and, after 1815, head of the Kriegsakademie, but it was through the achievements of Moltke,
appointed to the post of Chief of the General Staff in 1857,
that this rational approach to warfare reached its full fruition,
its efficacy proved on the field of battle in 1864, 1866, and 1870.

As the French followed the example of their conquerors
with regard to conscription and the organization of the army,
so too they found themselves obliged to study the Prussian system of command. The problem was that republican sensibilities were ruffled at the prospect of anything analogous to the
Prussian system, where the men designated to lead the army
in time of war enjoyed a high degree of independent authority
over its peacetime functioning, and where the army, as a consequence, occupied a position of virtual autonomy within the
state. However well founded were the arguments of the soldiers as to the necessity of a powerful and independent high
command, organized on a permanent basis, the politicians
were understandably dubious about the existence of a large
standing army, free from all effective civilian control. The

resolution of this problem was possibly the crowning achievement in the French military renaissance of the years 1871–1914.

In the French army prior to the War of 1870, there had existed nothing like the Prussian General Staff, that is to say, a single centralized organ with the assigned peacetime mission of working to prepare the army for war.[1] To the degree that specific preparations for war were to be made, this task was understood as part of the larger operations of the different *directions* at the Ministry of War. Each *direction* stood at the head of one of the branches of the army—infantry, artillery, or cavalry—or was charged with some specific military function, such as pay and subsistence. Bureaucratic in operation and outlook, the *directions* were staffed by civilians up to and often including the director himself. As a result, there had been a fundamental lack of rapport between the military and the personnel of the Ministry as to the needs of the army. The functionaries at the Ministry of War "only knew the army by correspondence."[2] The *directions* were characterized in their operations by a high degree of autonomy.

Each *direction* followed a course which had been established by routine, while memoranda, often contradictory, circulated from one *direction* to another. . . . Each one carefully guarded its own secrets, obscured its particular methods of operation, in order that no one could penetrate them, and thus sought to render itself indispensable.[3]

The *directions* were effective enough organs of peacetime administration, but as the Crimean and Italian wars indicated and as the Franco-Prussian War proved, they were woefully inadequate for the preparation and conduct of large-scale military operations. It would almost seem that, in the French

[1] Cmdt. Avon, *Notice sur le Ministère de la Guerre* (Paris: J. Dumaine, 1879), pp. 76–77.

[2] Col. Lewal, *La réforme de l'armée* (Paris: J. Dumaine, 1871), p. 465.

[3] *Ibid.*, pp. 461–462.

army, war was not something that one prepared for but rather something that one fought when it came along.

There did exist in the Ministry of War a department, the Dépôt de Guerre, performing certain of the tasks of a general staff in the Prussian style, but it was never put to any effective use before 1870. The function of the Dépôt was to draw up topographical, statistical, and historical studies, most of which were, upon completion, filed away and forgotten. During the two and a half years between 1866 and 1869 that he was Minister of War, Marshal Niel tried to make some more effective application of the talents of the staff officers assigned to the Dépôt, but he was unable to overcome the inertial resistance that greeted his efforts.[4] The studies and operational plans undertaken by the men of the Dépôt were of a purely consultative nature. When war broke out, the men who commanded the army ignored them, preferring to evolve their own haphazard plans.

The campaign of the Army of Versailles against the Commune was hardly over when the government made its first move toward creating a high command on the Prussian model. By an executive order dated June 8, 1871, the administration of the Ministry of War was reorganized. In place of the ten *directions* that existed on the eve of the war, there were now only three: personnel, matériel, and accounting. There was also a general staff. The General Staff of the Minister, as the new organ was called, comprised two bureaus, one having charge of general correspondence, troop movements, decorations, and the drafting of decrees, while the other, the Second Bureau, concerned itself with historical studies, military statistics, topographical and geodesic surveys, and the general collection of plans and maps.[5] The Second Bureau incorporated the functions and even the personnel of the old Dépôt de Guerre.

---

[4] Avon, *op. cit.*, pp. 70–71.

[5] *Journal Officiel de la République française* (hereafter cited as *J.O.*), (1871), p. 1299.

The General Staff, as it was first created in 1871, was little more than the private cabinet of the Minister. The Chief of Staff, who in Germany exercised *de facto* authority over the whole military machine, was in France only a brigadier general. His role was essentially that of secretary-general to the Minister with no authority or power of command over the directors, who were his seniors in rank.[6] No mention was made in the 1871 executive order concerning the study and preparation of large-scale military operations, the main functions of a general staff. Following the collapse of French military power no one seemed to envision the possibility of such an undertaking.[7] The result was that, lacking any specific assignment, the officers of the Second Bureau went about their work just as they had in the Dépôt de Guerre, in disparate fashion with no unity of purpose, their primary function being to deliver opinions on the questions submitted to them in random fashion. Three years after the defeat, no one on the General Staff had drawn up any operational studies for an eventual war. In effect, the General Staff had been constituted before anyone had considered what its mission was to be. If war broke out, the French army would still be obliged to improvise from the very start, organizing its whole high command and drafting a plan of operations "at the very moment when the Prussian General Staff, already in the saddle, with the aplomb that comes from long practice and constant preparation, would be taking charge of the army in the field."[8]

In a period when the rest of the French army was undergoing a profound reorganization, the Ministry of War remained relatively untouched. The real authority over the functioning of the army continued to rest in the hands of the *directions,* and the great bureaucrats at the Ministry of War persisted in their traditional ways, serene in a sense of their

[6] *Spectateur militaire* (hereafter cited as *S.M.*), July 1871, p. 131.

[7] Anon. (Gen. Vanson), "Deux documents concernant la réorganisation de l'armée," *Sabretache,* 1896, p. 339.

[8] *Ibid.,* pp. 345–346.

own exclusive competence. "Having grown accustomed under the Second Empire to an all-powerful situation, they were in no way disposed to become once again mere agents as they were originally intended to be." [9]

By 1874 a number of important persons, including Marshal MacMahon and General du Barail, the Minister of War, had become concerned at the increasingly apparent inability of the Ministry of War, as it was now constituted, to meet the military requirements of a new epoch. All were agreed that what was needed was an organ for the planning and execution of military maneuvers and operations, a veritable general staff on the Prussian model. The creation of such an organ would result in a significant shift in the center of gravity within the Ministry, lessening the responsibility and authority of the *directions*. Thus the scheme for the creation of a general staff, when first propounded by du Barail, met with a great deal of resistance from those who had a vested interest in the traditional ways of doing things. Finally du Barail in his usual forthright manner settled the question. Summoning the chief supporters and adversaries of the scheme to his office at Versailles, du Barail announced that since both he and the President of the Republic agreed as to the need for an effective, responsible general staff, it would be set up. [10]

The General Staff of the Minister of War, as it was reconstituted by the decree of March 12, 1874, comprised a ministerial cabinet and six bureaus. [11] Over the next few years it underwent a number of changes and reorganizations until, in 1887, it was given its final form with the four traditional bureaus: personnel, intelligence, operations and training, and logistics. [12] During the first years of existence of the General Staff,

---

[9] Col. Fix, *Souvenirs d'un officer d'État-major* (Paris: Juven, n.d.), Vol. II, p. 107.

[10] Vanson, *op. cit.*, pp. 346–350.

[11] *J.O.* (1874), pp. 2410–2411.

[12] Abbé Hénin, *Le Ministère de la Guerre* (Paris: L. Fournier, 1937), pp. 75, 77, 84.

while the army was still engaged in the gigantic task of reorganization and the divisions and army corps were being formed, the operations of the First Bureau, personnel, were of primary importance. Then with the initial reorganization completed, the army could begin to contemplate the eventuality of a war and to prepare for it, all of which brought into prominence the Third Bureau as the center from which were disseminated the orders and instructions covering military training, and where plans were drawn up for the mobilization and concentration of the army.[13]

The General Staff of the Minister of War was an organ of tremendous latent power in the hands of a man of skill and determination, such as Moltke. This possibility was recognized by General Ducrot, for one. He ardently wanted to be named Chief of Staff, but MacMahon was wary of his rather authoritarian character and certain of his military views. He also disapproved of Ducrot's too open advocacy of the Legitimist cause.[14] Du Barail had an even more cogent reason for not wanting to see Ducrot in the post. As Minister of War, du Barail was chief of the army, but Ducrot was his senior and enjoyed greater prestige among their fellow officers. As Chief of Staff, Ducrot would therefore be able to exert such influence within the army that the result could be the eventual "annihilation" of the Minister of War. Du Barail saw himself being reduced to serving as a buffer between the Chief of Staff and the President of the Republic, and he did not relish the prospect.[15]

Many other military men had similar reservations about the creation of a strong general staff under a vigorous chief. Such a body would interfere with the traditional notions of military hierarchy, where the Minister of War was the unique head of

[13] Vanson, op. cit., p. 352.

[14] J. Silvestre de Sacy, Le Maréchal de MacMahon (Paris: Internationales, 1960), p. 320.

[15] Gen. du Barail, Mes souvenirs (3 vols.; Paris: Plon, 1894–1896), Vol. III, pp. 472–473.

the army after the chief of the state. In Germany, Moltke, although nominally subordinate to the Minister of War, was in fact responsible directly to the King-Emperor. He thus had the authority to galvanize the staff functioning of the whole army, to coordinate military operations, and to ensure unity of military doctrine and method. To give an analogous role to the Chief of Staff of the French army would be to institute a kind of independent power within the Ministry, making him, in the words of General Chareton, a "veritable mayor of the palace." [16] In the Senate discussion of the law on the staff, General Billot, as one of the authors of the measure, declared that it was intended that a general staff be set up functioning under the authority of the Minister and responsible only to him. It was not to be invested with autonomous authority "which might make it an institution rivaling the Minister of War." [17] The commission that drafted the law took particular care to retain the title of Chief of the General Staff of the Minister, rather than Chief of the General Staff of the Army, in order to affirm "beyond qestion the principle of hierarchical subordination, to which the Chief of Staff must be subject, as much as any other officer. . . ." [18]

In considering the position of the Chief of Staff with regard to the other staff officers in the army, the Army Commission of the Senate would have preferred to assign him the direction of the staff service, giving him in effect a great deal of authority and control over the staffs of the subordinate units. Recognizing that the "institutions of our country" would not permit the Chief of Staff to be invested with such power, the Commission decided to leave over-all supervision of the staff officers in the hands of the old staff committee, of which he would be the chairman.[19] It was, no doubt, assumed that such executive authority as a committee possessed was likely to be

[16] *J.O.* (1877), p. 7614.
[17] *Ibid.*, p. 7676.
[18] *Ibid.*, pp. 4581–4582.
[19] *Ibid.*, p. 2834.

dispersed and that it would not act as an independent power within the Ministrty.

Although the Chief of Staff was immediately responsible for drawing up war plans in time of peace, he was not responsible for their execution in time of war. Indeed, the role of the Chief of Staff in time of war was not really specified. In drafting the decree that reorganized the General Staff, du Barail did not emphasize its eventual situation in the event of war. In the 1870's it was generally assumed that if war were to break out, MacMahon would take command of the French army while the Minister of War would become his major general or Chief of Staff. The General Staff of the Minister would then become the General Staff of the army in the field.[20] It was not clear what could be the wartime mission of the peacetime Chief of Staff.

As long as MacMahon was President of the Republic, there was no real doubt as to the structure of the French high command. Article 3 of the constitutional law of February 25, 1875, stated that the President of the Republic "disposed of the armed forces of the state." This meant implicitly that he commanded the army, for an amendment forbidding him to assume personal command was rejected by the National Assembly.[21] MacMahon, who, in the eyes of the constitution makers of 1875, was to be a monarch in all but name, would be a military monarch to boot. MacMahon looked on the army as his special preserve and jealously guarded his prerogative of naming the Ministers of War and the Navy. The resignation of MacMahon and·the election of Jules Grévy changed the elements in the situation. Grévy might still "dispose of the army," but he really could not be considered its commander in chief. He was not even suited to act as a figurehead, to assume fictional command in the manner of such thoroughly nonmili-

---

[20] Vanson, *op. cit.,* p. 353.

[21] R. d'Ornano, *Gouvernement et haut commandement sous régime parlementaire français* (Aix-en-Provence: Pensée universitaire, 1958), pp. 100–101.

tary monarchs as Louis XVI, Louis XVIII, or Louis Philippe. Under these circumstances, the prerogatives of the Minister of War tended to increase. He might act as the mandatory of the President of the Republic when the latter was a Marshal of France and possibly the nation's most eminent living soldier; he could hardly regard Grévy in the same light. Naturally, the Minister of War paid Grévy and his successors the respect due to the constitutional head of the state, but with regard to the army he was much more of a chief in his own right than he had been under MacMahon. He, and not the President of the Republic, was the real head of the army.

The constitutional laws of 1875 were silent as to the precise nature of the relationship between the Minister and the army. Only in the decree of October 20, 1883, regulating the internal service and discipline of the army was it specifically stated for the first time that the Minister of War was "chief of the army." [22] That the military looked on him not only as "chief" but also as commander of the army may be gathered from the courses taught at the École de Guerre in the late 1870's.

> By special delegation of the chief of state, a minister of war is charged with command of the army and with its administration; he disposes of its personnel, prescribes its movements, assures its instruction and discipline, and sees to it that all the moral and material needs of the army are satisfied.[23]

It was further noted, however, that his role was more likely to be one of administration than command. In any case, he was never as Minister of War to take direct command of troops.[24]

The duality of the role of the Minister with regard to the army had always existed, but prior to 1870 his command functions had been of a very tenuous nature, his primary duties being administrative. After 1870, while his administrative

[22] Anon., *L'armée sous le régime civil* (Paris: H. C. Lavauzelle, 1894), pp. 16–17.

[23] École militaire supérieure, "Cours du service d'état-major" (1879), p. 260.

[24] *Ibid.*, p. 291.

functions continued, the command of the army assumed a totally new significance, and the Minister was responsible for it. Whereas the administration of military affairs is a matter of accepting and observing time-honored routines, the command of an army is an affair of initiative, a constant directing impulse imposed from above. As in any other department of state, an army could be administered through the action of its permanent bureaucratic element alone, but a military bureaucracy could not command. This would be especially true in a period of intense military reform and renovation.

In the aftermath of the defeat, students of military questions saw the problem of endowing the French army with an effective high command almost completely in terms of the role of the Minister of War. It was he who would supply the motive force necessary for the activation of the military machine. Thus a true general staff was instituted in 1874 so that the Minister could exert more forcefully his necessary prerogatives of command. Those who objected to the General Staff did so because they feared that, rather than reinforcing and facilitating the exercise of his command authority, this new organ under an ambitious chief might actually detract from it. Another factor that was thought to lessen the effectiveness of the Minister in the command of the army was to be found in the "bureaus," the conservative functionaries in the military administration who quietly and tenaciously resisted any innovations or progressive ideas that might interfere with their traditional prerogatives. It was not at first realized that, because the Minister of War was obliged to operate in a political as well as a military milieu, he might be seriously hampered in exerting the full theoretical authority of his office.

In addition to commanding and administering the army, the Minister of War was also a participant in a governing cabinet whose members were individually and collectively responsible to the sovereign legislature. The political complexion of the cabinet was dictated by the composition of the two chambers, and although the Minister of War as a soldier was barred from politics to the point of being denied the right to vote, he could not entirely escape this fact. During his tenure as President, MacMahon had insisted on naming his own Ministers of War and the Navy, irrespective of the political color of the cabinet, but once he was gone, the two chiefs of the armed forces were obliged to take cognizance of the day-to-day political realities.

As a soldier the Minister of War may in theory have had no political opinions, but as a member of a government responsible to a republican majority in parliament he was expected to be loyal to the Republic, and it was hoped that this loyalty extended beyond the perfunctory allegiance of any nineteenth-century French soldier to the regime of the moment. Many of the future Ministers of War of the 1880's and 1890's—Generals Campenon, Logerot, Loizillon, and Mercier [25]—had already in the 1870's been noted as being good republicans, even though they were relatively junior officers. Another future Minister, General Billot, was an assiduous member of Mme. Juliette Adam's republican circle [26] and, from the tone of his correspondence, on intimate terms with Gambetta.[27] As for Boulanger, his fervent republicanism may have been relatively late blooming. The chief thing to be said of him in a report dating from the 1870's was that he was "above all ambitious. . . ." [28] There were thus a sufficient number of avowedly republican officers in the army to provide the government with Ministers of War. Because of the rate of attrition of cabinets under the Third Republic, this was a distinct advantage.

Ministerial instability was to become one of the salient

[25] See P. B. Gheusi, *La vie et la mort singulière de Gambetta* (Paris: Albin Michel, 1932), pp. 174, 191–196.

[26] Mme. J. Adam, *Après l'abandon de la Revanche* (Paris: Lemerre, 1910), p. 159.

[27] Letters from Billot to Gambetta, dated June 26, 1880; December 9, 1880; January 22, 1881; January 31, 1882. Bibliothèque Nationale, N.a.f. 24,900.

[28] See Gheusi, *op. cit.,* p. 186.

characteristics of government in republican France, and it was to have a significant effect on the army's peacetime command structure. In the twenty-five years or so between the end of the National Assembly and the advent of the Radicals at the turn of the century, France had thirty-two governments and twenty-six Ministers of War. The fourteen occasions on which the Minister of War was retained at his post by the incoming government were, to a degree, offset by the fact that on seven occasions he was replaced before a government had fallen. The average tenure then was just under one year, and only ten managed to serve twelve months or longer.

Since the Minister of War was the *de facto* commander in chief of the army, the brevity of tenure and the frequency of replacement meant that this command was exercised in a rather uncertain fashion. An army whose chief changed so frequently could hardly be considered to be commanded at all. Looking back into the French military past, writers could point to Louvois remaining twenty-nine years as Minister of War, or his father, Michel Le Tellier, serving nineteen years, or d'Argenson fourteen years, or Choiseul ten.[29] On the other hand, under the constitutional monarchies and the Second Empire things had not been much better than under the Third Republic. In the fifteen years that the Second Restoration lasted, there were ten different Ministers of War, while the July Monarchy had thirteen during its eighteen-year span. The Republic of 1848 lasted almost four years and produced eight, or nine if one counts Saint-Arnaud, who was both the last Minister of War of the Republic and the first under the Second Empire. Napoleon III had only five down until the outbreak of war in 1870.[30] Compared to what had gone before and what was to come, the Second Empire represented real stability, although one may legitimately wonder if the quality of the French army improved very much because of it. The

[29] Anon., "L'instabilité des ministres de la Guerre," *S.M.*, November 15, 1883, pp. 281–283.

[30] Avon, *op. cit.*, pp. 90–93.

evidence seems to indicate that under a parliamentary system, the tenure of a Minister of War was apt to be short. As long as he was the chief of a government department, responsible in any way to a parliamentary body, and not simply the agent of an absolute monarch, he could not insulate himself from the workings of politics.

By the principle of ministerial solidarity, the Minister of War was responsible in the same way as the other members of a cabinet for the policy of a particular government. An adverse vote in the Chamber or the Senate obliged him to resign along with his colleagues even if the issue did not concern the army. At the same time, he was responsible in his own right as chief of the army for his own acts and for those of his subordinates. Thus an important part of the duties of a Minister of War, in addition to overseeing the administration of the army, was to defend before parliament both his own actions and the best interests of the army, as he understood them. A general who had spent his whole professional life in the army was ill-equipped to face the brutal give-and-take of French parliamentary life. Although members of parliament were apt to be indulgent with a general whose oratorical abilities were nil either because he represented *la grande muette* or because the army was supposed to be above party, at least in the eyes of the opposition he was still a member of the government. Sooner or later he would exhaust his parliamentary credit by some indiscreet political remark or the clumsy handling of a parliamentary interpellation.

It was generally agreed that the Minister of War should be a technician rather than a politician. By its very size and complexity and by the specialized nature of its operations, the department of war differed from the other branches of the state. Whereas a politician could act as nominal head of the Ministry of Education or the Ministry of Public Works, leaving the real administrative work in the hands of the great senior functionaries, the army and the navy seemed to demand experts as their chiefs. The facts that he was expected personally to administer his department, that he was considered the commander in chief of the army, and that he had to fulfill a political function before the chambers for which he had no prior training, all combined to make the task of a Minister of War a crushing one. When a government fell, many of its leading members, who were usually important politicians, simply changed offices, while a few new faces appeared, but the Minister of War in most cases returned to the ranks of the army worn-out by the burdens of office.

The Minister of War, though legal chief of the army, found that his real situation with regard to his fellow generals was ambiguous. Between 1875 and 1900 the generals who in their comrades' estimation were the most eminent, the natural chiefs of the army, and its probable leaders in time of war shunned the post. This could be explained in part by the fact that certain of them could not or would not display the requisite degree of fervor for republican institutions and ideals, but the main reason was that a good soldier found the job of Minister of War, with its ill-defined demands, half military, half political, to be most unappealing. Many generals would have agreed with the publicist Joseph Reinach that for a soldier there was something dangerous and unsettling about parliamentary life, with its pervasive sense of intrigue and its easy and artificial oratorical successes. "In the same way that the fresh invigorating air of the mountains is deadly for certain lung conditions," Reinach wrote, "so is the hot and heavy atmosphere of parliament fatal to the spirit of a soldier." [31] It was therefore not surprising to find that generals of real worth were not "overly anxious for ministerial grandeur." [32]

The best soldiers, then, preferred not to step out of the purely military sphere. In their eyes, the climax to a successful military career was not a term as Minister of War, chief of the whole French army, but rather an appointment to command one of the more important army corps, the Sixth at Châlons-

---

[31] J. Reinach, *La politique opportuniste* (Paris: Charpentier, 1890), p. 229.
[32] J. Richard, *L'armée et la guerre* (Paris: Librairie Illustrée, 1896), p. 8.

sur-Marne, the Seventh at Besançon, or the Fourteenth at Lyon, and ultimately to be designated to lead one of the armies in time of war. Chanzy, the Duc d'Aumale, Clinchant, Février, Wolff, Miribel, Négrier, Jamont, Baron Berge, and Davout d'Auerstadt were among the leading generals of the first thirty years of the Republic who never served as Minister. Lewal and Billot were about the only eminent generals who were willing to enter Rue Saint-Dominique. Galliffet did accept the post, but under unusual circumstances in the Waldeck-Rousseau government of 1899 and only after he had been retired from active service. Saussier, who was probably the first soldier of his generation and also a good republican, never accepted the portfolio though he was asked on numerous occasions.

With the more eminent and senior generals, the men who possessed a natural authority within the army, holding themselves aloof, the post of Minister of War went by default to lesser and more junior men. Although Billot ranked first in the seniority list of divisionary generals at the time of his second term as Minister, 1896 to 1898, none of the others, excepting Rochebouet, stood any higher than number twenty, and most were considerably farther down the list, nine being below forty. Of the seventeen different generals who were at one time or other Ministers of War between 1875 and 1899, eight had not commanded an army corps before their elevation, while at least two of them, Zurlinden and Mercier, commanded their respective army corps for so short a time before being named to the post that the fact was not noted in the *Annuaire officiel de l'armée française*. This unwillingness of the senior generals to accept the highest position in the army may be contrasted with the situation under the Second Empire, where all five of the Ministers of War were Marshals of France or were promoted to that dignity during their term of office. This did not mean that the army of Napoleon III was any better or more forcefully commanded, but it did indicate that the post had been one to which great prestige had been attached, implying as it did the supreme command of the whole army.[33]

For those generals who could not aspire to the command of the Sixth or Seventh Army Corps, a term at Rue Saint-Dominique might be the fitting climax to a military career or at least accelerate their nomination to some other, less prestigious army corps. In a letter written in the late 1880's to solicit the assistance of Joseph Reinach, General Ferron did not even presume to think of himself as a candidate for the approaching vacancy in the command of the Sixth Army Corps, although he had already served both as Assistant Chief of Staff and as Minister of War. His more modest hope was that the government would give him the army corps of whoever was to be named to the Sixth.[34]

The unwillingness of the best men to serve as Minister of War simply added to the weakness in the high command which had been caused by the phenomenon of ministerial instability and by the ambiguous dual nature of the post. In most cases the Minister too often found himself "without moral authority over the older generals commanding the army corps, who in any case had need of a healthy sense of discipline, in order to maintain at least the appearance of respect vis-à-vis a chief imposed upon them for political reasons." [35]

While the general who was Minister of War exercised command over the whole army by virtue of his position, he did not possess the added authority of rank. In the French army the highest rank was that of divisionary general. The authority vested in a general commanding an army corps or in the Minister came from the positions themselves, and not from any increase in rank pertaining to them. Nevertheless, the command of an army corps quickly became equivalent to an extra

---

[33] Gen. Thoumas, *Les transformations de l'armée française* (Paris: Berger-Levrault, 1887), Vol. II, p. 644.

[34] Letter of July 23, 1889. Bibliothèque Nationale, N.a.f. 13538.

[35] Anon., "Après les maneuvres," *Revue des deux mondes* (hereafter cited as *R.D.M.*), November 15, 1888, p. 438.

rank. It was traditional in the French army that between two officers of equal rank precedence went to the one who had been promoted first. Thus the general commanding an army corps usually had seniority over his two division commanders, whether by design or by the natural functioning of the military hierarchy. Only very seldom did one find a corps commander who was junior to both his subordinates. Discipline improved when the authority of a superior was reinforced wherever possible.

Because of this situation, a Minister of War who was usually junior to the majority of his corps commanders, and on occasion junior to all of them, was in an anomalous position. By military regulations he had authority over them, but he might well be hesitant in exerting that authority to the fullest. As the reporter for the 1885 budget noted:

> If because of his age and his relative lack of seniority, the Minister is obliged to reenter the ranks of the active army, the prospect of becoming once again from one day to the next the comrade and on occasion the subordinate of those generals who only recently owed him absolute obedience is not a situation made to facilitate the exercise of his authority.[36]

General de Galliffet, writing to Gambetta in the late 1870's, bewailed "the absolute lack of both character and real independence" in the generals who served as Minister of War.[37]

With regard to the actual command of the army, the most important of the Minister's immediate subordinates was the Chief of Staff. Being especially charged with the task of preparing the army for eventual military operations, he, more than anyone else, was supposed to add weight to the role of the Minister as commander in chief of the army; but, with the possible exception of General de Miribel, all those who served as Chiefs of Staff in the 1870's and 1880's were ordinary men.

---

[36] *Journal Officiel de la Chambre des Députés: Documents* (hereafter cited as *J.O.C. Doc.*), (1884), p. 1758.

[37] Letter of December 18, 1878, reprinted in *Le Jour,* October 9, 1895.

"For what are unfortunately the most natural of motives, the Ministers cared little for the prospect of being eclipsed by too eminent a figure." [38] A Minister of War who already felt inferior in prestige and authority to many of his corps commanders would not wish to compound his problems with a Chief of Staff who also overshadowed him in the estimation of his comrades. Each new Minister almost invariably brought with him a new Chief of Staff who was junior to him. Technically, they might be quite able men, but none of them remained long enough or had the natural authority to take advantage of the potentialities of the office. In a situation in which he had to deal directly with the senior generals of the army, such as during the annual maneuvers where he was the sole referee, the Chief of Staff, like the Minister of War, sensing his own lack of authority, was reluctant "to permit himself to criticize the heads of the army corps." [39] As a result, the maneuvers were often run in a slipshod way with little over-all control or firm direction.

Since the mission of the Chief of Staff was exclusively technical, his political opinions, unlike those of the Minister of War, were of no ostensible significance. Nevertheless, they could not be utterly disregarded, as was demonstrated at the time of the *Grand Ministère* of November 1881. In constituting his government, Gambetta designated a republican officer of long standing, General Campenon, to be his Minister of War; Campenon, in turn, chose as his Chief of Staff General de Miribel. This nomination created a furor with the extreme Left, for Miribel, a protégé of General Ducrot, had been Chief of Staff once before, having been named to the post by General de Rochebouet during the *Seize-mai* crisis. In his report on the parliamentary inquiry into the actions of the government in this crisis, Henri Brisson accused Miribel as

---

[38] X.Y.Z., "Aperçu sur notre situation militaire," *S.M.*, January 15, 1888, p. 129.

[39] Anon., "Après les maneuvres," *R.D.M.*, November 15, 1888, pp. 436–437.

having been tacitly involved in the supposed plot against the popular will, although there were no specific charges to be made against him.[40] Under the circumstances, Miribel seemed out of place in a republican government. Even *Spectateur militaire* questioned the wisdom of this particular nomination and speculated whether, because of his reputation and his antecedents, Miribel might not provide a ready-made occasion for the Radicals to mount an attack on the army.[41]

Whatever his political opinions, Miribel was considered by his comrades to be a superbly able officer, perhaps the best tactician in the army. It was because of his military talents that Campenon, with the assent of Gambetta, chose him. In so doing, Campenon hoped to demonstrate to those officers who in the aftermath of the *Seize-mai* had abruptly ceased to be devotees of Marshal MacMahon, and who were now assiduously courting the Republic, that the criterion for military preferment was now their technical ability, and not their political opinions.[42]

More than anything else, the nomination of Miribel as Chief of Staff was significant of the self-confidence of the republicans in the wake of their electoral triumph of 1881. Gambetta and his cohorts welcomed the chance to demonstrate that the republicans as the "party of government" were now secure enough to overlook purely political considerations in their choice of subordinates if the national interest was at stake. In the estimation of *République française,* Campenon would have committed an "unpardonable error" if he had not availed himself of the remarkable abilities of Miribel as a military planner.[43] Even so, the government would seem to have found it expedient to provide a political counterweight to Miribel, by naming as Assistant Chief of Staff General Ferron,

[40] *J.O.* (1879), pp. 2558 ff.

[41] *S.M.,* January 1882, p. 145.

[42] Letter from Campenon to Joseph Reinach, dated July 19, 1883. Bibliothèque Nationale, N.a.f. 13532.

[43] *République française,* December 15, 1881.

"an officer much favored by the men of the extreme Left." [44]
When the *Grand Ministère* fell at the end of January 1882,
Gambetta was said to have strongly urged the President of the
Republic, Grèvy, that his successor as premier keep Miribel in
office. "I bore all the inconveniences of this nomination; in the
name of both France and the army, you should maintain all the
benefits of it." [45] Miribel was, however, forced to quit his post,
"a necessary sacrifice to political susceptibilities which are both
touchy and dangerous." [46]

The full ramifications of the problem of the high command
were not at first realized in military circles. Until the army
was reorganized, or perhaps even reconstructed, matters pertaining to the weakness of the high command had little relevance. In the years immediately following the war, many people concerned with military affairs recognized that the resignation of one Minister of War and his replacement by another
was inconvenient, but mainly because it interrupted the tempo
of reform and reorganization.[47] Then, too, there was in the
1870's somewhat more stability in the Ministry of War. General de Cissey served two terms of two years each, while four
of his five successors lasted for at least one year or more. They
were all considered to be the personally chosen agents of
Marshal MacMahon and were thus outside the workings of
politics. Moreover, as long as MacMahon was in office, the
command of the army was assumed to be ultimately vested in
him, and not the Minister of War. Ministerial instability thus
had less apparent effect on the functioning of the high command than it was to have after his resignation.

General Farre, Minister of War in the Freycinet government of 1879, was the first truly "republican" general to accept
the post. He had led an army corps in the *Défense nationale*

[44] Quoted in the souvenirs of Galliffet, *Journal des débats,* August 1, 1902.
[45] Quoted in Reinach, *Politique opportuniste,* p. 233.
[46] *S.M.,* February 1882, p. 294.
[47] *Ibid.,* July 1874, pp. 128–129.

and was a protégé of Gambetta, and according to the memoirs of Mme. Juliette Adam, he owed his nomination to this fact alone. Since his fellow generals had only a very mediocre opinion of Farre's abilities, Gambetta was obliged to expend considerable energy pleading his cause.[48] Farre managed to survive as Minister for almost two years before a combination of difficulties brought him down, the climax to which was the faulty preparations for the Tunisian expedition of 1881. Though Farre held the post for some two years, only three of the nine men who followed him lasted as long as twelve months. It was this fact that drew people's attention to the problem of the high command.

As usual, the German army provided the standard of comparison. Although the French measured up in terms of manpower and matériel, there was still one category in which French inferiority still seemed evident. From 1857 until 1888 Moltke had been Chief of the General Staff, certainly irremovable and apparently indestructible. When he finally retired, he was eighty-eight years of age. Moltke summarized better than anyone else the French deficiency in a series of remarks made before a meeting of officers in Berlin, who had come to celebrate his eighty-seventh birthday. The great Prussian warned his colleagues:

The next war . . . will above all be a war where a knowledge of strategy and science will play a most important role. Our campaigns and our victories have taught our enemies, who, like us, have numbers, arms, and courage.

Our strength will be in the direction of the war, in the high command, in a word, in the Great General Staff, to which I have consecrated the last days of my life. This strength our enemies may envy us, but they do not possess it.[49]

Moltke had been appointed Chief of Staff in 1857, when William I became regent of Prussia. At that time the General

---

[48] Adam, *op. cit.,* pp. 292, 311–312, 364, 371, 456.

[49] Quoted in E. Boulanger, "La prochaine guerre d'après le Maréchal de Moltke," *Nouvelle revue,* August 15, 1888, p. 805.

Staff was a semiautonomous body attached to the Ministry of War. The Chief of Staff was not even permitted to communi-cate directly with the Minister, being obliged to go through the General War Office of the Ministry. It was the achieve-ment of Moltke to have transformed this important but still subordinate body into an instrument for the over-all command of the Prussian and then the German army. The planning and the conduct of the Danish War of 1864 first demonstrated his abilities. During the war he was Chief of Staff to Field Mar-shal von Wrangel and then later to Crown Prince Frederick Charles. On the eve of the Austro-Prussian War, the General Staff was released from subordination to the Minister of War for the duration of hostilities and given the right to communi-cate directly with the unit commanders in the field.[50] Even though Moltke was the first military adviser to the King after 1866, the General Staff was once again made subordinate to the Ministry of War. It was only in 1883 that the General Staff won its full independence in a kind of internal *coup d'état*.[51] Even so, after 1870 Moltke had occupied a position apart as the effective commander in chief of the army. Moltke's achieve-ment was always before the eyes of the French as they wrestled with the problem of how best to organize their own high command.

In bringing about a fundamental reorganization of the command structure of the Prussian army, Moltke had been able to take advantage of the peculiar constitutional arrange-ments of the Prussian state. The King of Prussia was the com-mander in chief of the army and, in the person of William I, a man whose passionate first interest lay in military affairs. Though the Minister of War was constitutionally responsible for his acts to the Prussian parliament, the army as such was still free from parliamentary control. This had been the chief issue in the constitutional crisis of 1862-1866, and parliament

[50] G. Craig, *The Politics of the Prussian Army* (London: Oxford University Press, 1955), pp. 193–195.
[51] *Ibid.*, p. 224.

had lost that struggle. Moltke was able to operate in a sphere where he was responsible only to the King, and to increase the importance of the General Staff at the expense of the Ministry of War. As long as Moltke enjoyed the confidence of his sovereign, his position was absolutely secure, and the high command of the German army was therefore stable.

Military Necessity and Political Reality

Even if the French army had possessed a general of Moltke's caliber, there seemed to be no way in which he might have been given a position of effective authority without either violating the spirit of the constitution or arousing the fears of republican politicians. By the terms of the Constitution, the President of the Republic disposed of the armed forces, but he was, in fact, neither the real sovereign nor anything more than the nominal commander in chief. Sovereignty was vested in parliament, to whom the Minister of War, the actual chief of the army, was responsible. To have copied the German example and to have erected a command structure where in the interests of stability the Chief of Staff, as the person charged with preparing the army for war and with leading it in battle, enjoyed a position of statutory permanence would have, in effect, removed him from parliamentary control. He would have been responsible to no one except a figurehead chief of state. Such a solution was permissible in a monarchy but not in the Third Republic during the first uncertain decades of its existence. Those who approached the problem of the high command found themselves obliged, therefore, by political and constitutional realities to focus first on ways of strengthening the position of the Minister of War and of making his situation more stable. Then, too, the position of the Minister at the apex of the military hierarchy had come to be considered as both normal and necessary in French eyes, and there was at first little inclination to set up the Chief of Staff as a coequal or even superior power.

Because of ministerial instability, the simplest solution to the problem of the high command was to shelter the Minister of War from the necessity of resigning every time a government fell. It seemed a particular absurdity of the French parliamentary regime that a good Minister of War had to quit the functions that he had exercised to the satisfaction of all just because the Minister of Finance did not intend to make certain economies demanded by the country or because the Minister of the Interior had taken measures displeasing to the majority of deputies.[52]

The principle of ministerial solidarity was founded on primarily political considerations, while the Minister of War was meant to be, above all, a military technician. Thus, it appeared logical that he should not be subject to precisely the same rules as the other members of the government. If the advent of a new government represented a radical reorientation in policy, the Minister of War could be expected to resign, along with the rest of his colleagues, but if the change in cabinets was merely a matter of a political nuance, absolute homogeneity might well be sacrificed to the "imperious necessity of giving to military affairs that unity of direction which is indispensable."[53] The Ministers of War and the Navy and possibly the Minister of Foreign Affairs would thus be responsible before the chambers for their own actions and policies alone, but not for those of the other members of the government.[54]

The drawback here was essentially a pragmatic one: how to make a legal or constitutional provision that would precisely define the circumstances under which parliament would or would not be obliged to retain the Minister of War from one government to the next. Such a measure would also require that parliament accept a diminution of its prerogatives, for to place the Minister of War outside the principle of ministerial solidarity would also place him, to a certain degree, outside the

[52] *S.M.*, February 1, 1888, p. 269.
[53] *Ibid.*, August 1882, pp. 266–267.
[54] *Ibid.*, January 15, 1888, pp. 178–179.

government and make him irresponsible. It was the opinion of
the newspaper *République française* that, although it was
best to keep the armed forces as far removed as possible from
politics, it was only through an intelligent evolution in parliamentary opinion that the "supreme command can finally be
guaranteed against too frequent changes." [55] Once parliament
and the President of the Republic were convinced of this imperious necessity, stability in the high command would occur
of its own accord, without the need for a specific law and
without any political complications. Any argument of this
nature, based on the assumption that the Minister of War was
simply a military expert sitting in the government for technical reasons, tended to ignore that there were occasions when
political considerations would dictate not only who was to be
chief of the French army but also his behavior while in office.
One such occasion occurred in 1883.

The Prince Napoleon, with an unfortunate lack of judgment,
had a manifesto posted on January 15, 1883, attacking the
chambers and the constitution and calling for a plebiscite. The
government arrested him and had the posters removed. The
Radicals, using this as a pretext, urged that the government
move against both of the former reigning houses, Orléans as
well as Bonaparte. A law in this sense giving to the government the right to expel the members of the two deposed dy-
nasties, whose presence "would compromise the security of the
State," was passed by the Chamber but rejected by the Senate.
The discussion of this proposal in parliament provoked the
resignation of Duclerc, the President of the Council, and
General Billot, Minister of War, along with the Minister of
the Navy.[56] The inability of the Senate and the Chamber to
work out a compromise project brought about the fall of the
new ministry under Fallières three weeks later. A more stable

[55] Quoted in *Avenir militaire*, November 1, 1883, p. 3.
[56] Ch. Seignobos, *L'évolution de la Troisième République*, Vol. VIII of
Histoire de la France contemporaine, E. Lavisse, ed. (10 vols., Paris: Hachette,
1920–1922), pp. 96–97.

government under Jules Ferry followed. Ferry found a compromise solution by simply removing the Orléans princes
from active duty in the army by executive decree. Although
this was an arbitrary measure, Ferry favored it as a means of
eliminating one source of Radical agitation. By expelling the
Dukes of Aumale, Chartres, and Alençon from the army he
gave partial satisfaction to the Chamber, while deftly making
them temporarily forget the more stringent law that would
have exiled all members of the houses of Orléans and Bonaparte from French soil.[57]

The difficulty lay in finding a Minister of War who was
willing to carry out any of the measures against the
Orléans princes contemplated by the government. To remove
them from the army was an act of political reprisal, in which
the military abilities of the men involved counted for nothing.
Beyond that, the conduct of the Orléans princes vis-à-vis the
Republic had been absolutely correct. After the resignation of
Billot, the post of Minister was offered to at least two other
generals, Campenon and Thoumas, both of whom declined it.
Finally a very junior general, Thibaudin, indicated he was
willing to act at the behest of the government.[58] Thibaudin
was actually junior to nine tenths of the divisionary generals.
His only credentials for the post of Minister of War were his
republican opinions of the most advanced sort and his willingness to execute what was essentially an arbitrary political sentence. As the *Revue des deux mondes* noted, where other
Ministers of War in deciding upon the premature retirement
of an officer had always excluded politics as a reason, Thibaudin refused to take into consideration any factor but politics.[59]

Within the army, Thibaudin was held in very low esteem

[57] Ch. de Freycinet, *Souvenirs, 1878–1893* (Paris: Delagrave, 1913), Vol.
II, p. 272.
[58] Capt. Choppin, *Souvenirs d'un capitaine de cavalerie, 1851–1881* (Paris:
Berger-Levrault, 1909), p. 179.
[59] *R.D.M.*, March 1, 1883, p. 231.

by his fellow officers for having violated the military code of honor during the war. According to a story that appeared in *Figaro* on January 29, 1883, Thibaudin, after pledging his word of honor to his German captors that he would not try to escape, fled back to France and took a commission from the Government of National Defense under a false name. He had risen to the position of general commanding the Fourteenth Corps before the end of the war. The Commission for the Revision of Ranks reduced him to colonel.[60]

Despite his supposedly dishonorable conduct during the *Défense nationale,* the Radicals seem, nevertheless, to have been enchanted with the new Minister of War, who did not hesitate in parliament to prove himself a partisan of the most progressive ideas. *Avenir militaire* sadly commented that in his first two speeches before parliament Thibaudin spoke "as the head of a party and not as the head of the army." [61] Lacking the prestige or the authority to play the role of chief of the army, he proceeded to act within the Ferry cabinet as "the personification of a governmental system inclining toward radical ideas. . . . The extreme Left looked upon him as their man, representing true republican principles in the midst of a suspect entourage." [62] It was indeed a novel situation for a Minister of War and one which the strong-willed Ferry did not appreciate.

On one occasion, after it had been decided in the Council of Ministers that General de Galliffet should preside over the coming cavalry maneuvers, Thibaudin, apparently under pressure from his Radical cronies, rescinded the government decision on his own initiative. That an individual minister could revoke a decision reached by the whole Council of Ministers sitting as a body was an unusual theory of government, and

[60] Archives de la Préfecture de la Police de Paris (E a/57), "Thibaudin" (file of newspaper clippings).

[61] *Avenir militaire,* February 11, 1883, p. 1.

[62] "Chronique politique," *Nouvelle revue,* October 15, 1883, p. 911.

there resulted a heated confrontation between Thibaudin and Ferry. The incident ended with Galliffet being reinstated as the general presiding but with the elimination of the spectacular climax to the maneuvers, a large-scale cavalry ride along the eastern frontier. Just in case Galliffet had any objections about being treated in this fashion, Thibaudin let him know that he could consider himself fortunate not to have lost the command of his army corps as well.[63]

Having had need of Thibaudin only to dispose of the question of the Orléans princes, Ferry was now anxious to relieve himself of his rather vexatious Minister of War. A suitable incident finally presented itself when the King of Spain passed through France in September 1883. After paying a visit to the German Emperor, Alfonso XII stopped over in Paris on his return journey. The King of Spain was an honorary colonel in the uhlans and had attended a military review at Strasbourg dressed in the appropriate uniform. This was enough to enrage certain of the superpatriotic Radicals, and his visit to Paris was greeted with jeers and boos from the crowd of demonstrators. The Radical opponents of the government were behind the demonstrations. More to the point, when the President of the Republic and the Council of Ministers went to the railroad station to greet the King on his arrival in Paris, Thibaudin was conspicuously absent, having pleaded a convenient illness. Although Ferry was able to smooth over the incident, he was justifiably angry at the participation of his Minister of War in an affair that might have proved highly embarrassing to the French government. He demanded and received Thibaudin's resignation.[64] The newspaper *Intransigeant* of October 12, 1883, reported the discontent of the various republican groups in Paris, who held a "punch" in honor of the fallen Minister of War. "All the orators rendered homage to the energetic behavior and the truly republican attitude of General Thibaudin . . . who did not want to lower

[63] *R.D.M.*, April 15, 1883, pp. 947–949.
[64] Seignobos, *op. cit.*, Vol. VIII, p. 100.

the dignity of the nation by going to greet a colonel in the uhlans. . . ." [65] Upon his resignation, Thibaudin did not even receive the command of a division, let alone an army corps, and remained in *disponibilité* for some two years. The only assignments he obtained before his retirement from the army were a position on one of the consultative committees in the Ministry of War and finally command of the defensive fortifications of Paris.

The other general of the period whose term as Minister of War had profound political repercussions was Georges Ernest Jean Marie Boulanger. Named to the post in the Freycinet government of January 1886, Boulanger was looked upon as a protégé of Clemenceau, but the chief of the Radicals did not sponsor him out of any ulterior motive or with the aim of using him for some special political end. Rather, Clemenceau simply wanted to have the three-years law accepted, and possibly to promote a more "republican" attitude within the army. "He thought he had a general at his disposal, so he made use of him." [66] Like Thibaudin, Boulanger had the reputation of being an avowed republican, and, like Thibaudin, he was junior to the great majority of divisionary generals. Unlike his predecessor, however, Boulanger was held in high esteem by his fellow officers, for his career to date had been brilliant. In Algeria, in Italy, in Indochina, and finally during the siege of Paris, he had won his promotions under fire, receiving in the process at least six wounds, one of them serious.

In the years since the war he had managed to add to his already splendid military reputation a certain celebrity as an outspoken patriot. On at least two occasions, once as a member of the official French delegation at the centennial of the Battle of Yorktown and then some years later while he was head of the French expeditionary force at Tunis, Boulanger had in a noisy and ostentatious way been able to defend the national honor against some seeming slight. Both incidents attracted a

---

[65] Clipping in Arch. de Pref. de Pol. (E/a 57), "Thibaudin."

[66] A. Dansette, *Le Boulangisme* (Paris: A. Fayard, 1946), pp. 30–31.

great deal of publicity and contributed to his renown among the more nationalistic elements within the country, the Radicals in particular. The result was that Boulanger was already something of a public figure when he was named to the Ministry of War.

Once in office, Boulanger proceeded to sponsor a number of reforms that reinforced his reputation as a vigorous and forward-looking soldier. In addition to presenting parliament with a bill portending nothing less than the total reorganization of the army,[67] he was also the author of several more modest measures, all aimed at bettering the living conditions and the morale of both the conscripts and the N.C.O.'s. These had widespread repercussions throughout the army and the country. Boulanger was also instrumental in introducing the Lebel, the army's first repeating rifle. By no means limiting himself to these purely military measures, he took the opportunity to speak before civilian audiences as often as the occasion presented itself, constantly seeking to appear as a republican soldier in the best Jacobin tradition. Within six months of his entry into the government, Boulanger had become the cynosure of all good patriotic eyes and the most talked-of figure in France, completely outshining his ministerial colleagues. The triumphant review of July 14, 1886, was the apotheosis of his popularity.

Boulanger quickly came to enjoy a kind of independent political support both in parliament and the country at large, such as no Minister of War before him and very few politicians had ever had. This fact, combined with an innate flair for the spectacular and a confidence in his own star, meant that he suffered from none of the inhibitions that usually affected the occupants of Rue Saint-Dominique. The Minister of War was the chief of the French army, and Boulanger intended to exercise the prerogatives of the office to the fullest extent possible. When General Schmitz, one of the more senior officers and the commander of the Ninth Army Corps at

[67] *Vide supra,* pp. 102–103.

Tours, merely gave the appearance of disapproving of one of the Minister's actions, Boulanger dismissed him without further ado.[68]

Boulanger did not even hesitate to challenge General Saussier, Military Governor of Paris and the probable Commander in Chief of the French armies in time of war. Annoyed by an article about him published in the antirepublican newspaper *Gaulois,* Saussier sent a letter of protest to the editor without first receiving permission from his hierarchical superior, the Minister of War. This was contrary to military regulations, and Boulanger reprimanded him for it. By way of indicating who was in charge of the army, he also transferred Saussier's chief of staff. According to Jules Ferry, Boulanger even went so far as to propose that Saussier be removed from his post.[69] The prestige of Saussier was too great for him to have to suffer such treatment. When Saussier requested to be relieved of his duties as Military Governor, the outcry was such that Boulanger realized he would have to back down. This he did with as much aplomb as he could muster.[70]

Though Boulanger was forced to retreat from a confrontation with Saussier, he was more successful in his dealings with the members of the former ruling houses. In an excess of republican fervor, he deprived of their ranks in the army five members of the Orléans family, including the Duc d'Aumale, along with two Bonapartes, an act contrary to the 1834 law on the status of an officer. Having been attacked in the Chamber because of it, Boulanger made a vigorous speech defending his quasi-illegal action, which was voted the honors of an *affichage* by the republican majority. For a moment it seemed as if this personal triumph would be marred by the publication of a rather obsequious letter from Boulanger to the Duc d'Aumale, written some six years earlier, in which he thanked the prince for having proposed him for promotion

---

[68] Dansette, *op. cit.,* pp. 34-35.
[69] J. Ferry, *Lettres de Jules Ferry* (Paris: Calmann-Lévy, 1914), p. 409.
[70] Dansette, *op. cit.,* p. 37.

to the rank of brigadier general. This did no more than to temporarily interrupt his soaring popularity.[71]

By the time he had been in office for a year, Boulanger was a political force of the first magnitude in France. His stoutly patriotic speeches and his bellicose attitude in the face of foreign enemies answered a very real longing in the hearts of many Frenchmen. At the same time, his irresponsibly chauvinistic conduct toward matters of state needlessly complicated the task of French statesmen and diplomats. On several occasions Boulanger, in response to a seemingly provocative act by the Germans, would have taken measures that might have precipitated a conflict for which France was neither diplomatically nor psychologically prepared; but his more prudent colleagues in the government restrained him. Boulanger was beginning to play the role of "General Revanche," having far overstepped the conventional limits placed on the authority of a Minister of War under the Republic. It thus became a matter of the greatest urgency for the more moderate and realistic elements in the government to get rid of him.

Since it was impossible to drop Boulanger when the Freycinet government fell in December 1886, he was retained in the Goblet ministry; but the occasion did present itself with the fall of the latter in May 1887. Even so, it was still extremely difficult to keep him out of a new ministerial combination. He had the firm backing of the Radicals, who made it a condition of their parliamentary support that he be included in the new government. The ministerial crisis lasted for almost two weeks and was resolved only by the formation of a government under Rouvier which looked much farther to the right than usual for its majority in the Chamber. Boulanger was named to the command of the Thirteenth Army Corps at Clermont-Ferrand. His departure from Paris was the signal for a tumultuous demonstration at the Gare de Lyon. Eight months later he was removed from the active list of the army for hav-

---

[71] *Ibid.*, pp. 45–49, 53–56.

ing secretly permitted his candidature to be proposed in five different by-elections.

The advent of Boulanger as Minister of War had been hailed by those who saw him as an apostle of military progress, and from a strictly military point of view his ministry could be considered to be of real significance. This was true not only because of the reforms that he initiated but above all for the improvement in morale for which he, more than anyone else, was responsible. If his gifts as a strategist and a leader of armies in battle were somewhat suspect in the eyes of his more eminent colleagues, it did not really matter.

Thanks to the somewhat haphazard vigor of the Minister, there emanated from Rue Saint-Dominique a sense of optimism that spread throughout the army. . . . The army found again the joyousness that had been lost at Sedan; it had confidence in its chiefs, and gained confidence in itself. "He taught us once again to wear our *képis* cocked over our ears," was the way old Canrobert expressed it.[72]

When Boulanger left the Ministry of War, the event was noted with real regret by *Spectateur militaire*,[73] and ten months later that journal regarded it as a tragedy when he was removed from the active list for his political maneuvers. "What a splendid role he had to play! . . . What a name he would have left in history if only he had known how to protect himself from that disease so deadly for men of war, politics." [74] Whatever his personal ascendancy over the army while he was its chief, it declined very quickly once he had departed. The military may have affected a certain disdain for civilians in general and for politicians in particular; they cared even less for one of their number using his uniform to political ends, even if he claimed to speak for those principles of patriotism and authority to which the army was devoted.

None of the chiefs of the Boulangist movement ever seri-

---

[72] *Ibid.*, pp. 43–44.
[73] *S.M.*, June 15, 1887, p. 531.
[74] *Ibid.*, April 1, 1888, p. 79.

ously entertained the idea of using the army against the regime for the very good reason that they knew the military would never have lent their support to such a plan. Boulanger realized this as much as anyone else.[75] The aim of those in charge of the movement was to bring the General to power legally, through a great electoral victory. To the degree that they directed their propaganda at the army, it was the conscripts they sought to win over. Being only temporary soldiers, they would soon regain the right to vote, but the officers, not possessing any electoral rights, could do little for the movement.

The voluminous police reports dealing with the Boulangist movement contain only the flimsiest rumors or a few unverified statements concerning the pro-Boulangist sentiments within the army or among ex-officers. The sole indication of some kind of conspiratorial activity in the army on behalf of the General is a dispatch of November 1888 noting the transfer from Paris of several officers who were suspected of harboring Boulangist sympathies.[76] Among the Boulangist candidates who stood for the Department of the Seine in the 1889 elections was an ex-Minister of War, the ostentatiously republican General Thibaudin, now retired.[77] He was not elected. The phenomenon of Boulangism was born and ran its course as a movement of political discontent, whose protagonists were all civilians. It involved the army only in that its hero, or perhaps its figurehead, had once worn with some distinction the uniform of a French officer.

If the Boulangist adventure demonstrated anything about the danger to the regime that the army might present, the lesson lay in the unreliability of political soldiers. A general who made a special point of loudly announcing his fervent

[75] Guy Chapman, "France: The French Army and Politics," in *Soldiers and Governments,* Michael Howard, ed. (London: Eyre & Spottiswoode, 1957), pp. 59–60.

[76] Archives Nationales, "Police générale" (F7. 12445), "Agissements Boulangistes," Report of November 17 and 18, 1888.

[77] Arch. Pref. de Pol. (E a/60), "Boulanger."

devotion to republican ideals and institutions was not only violating certain military proprieties but also acting in a highly opportunistic way. Such men were not likely to prove either the most competent or the most reliable soldiers. Both Thibaudin and Boulanger were particularly ardent and outspoken in their republican sentiments, and both ended by participating in an antirepublican movement. The army as a whole, then, passed this test of civic loyalty. Doubts that may have been lingering in the minds of some politicians over the equivocations of certain officers at the time of the crisis of May 16 were dissipated.

The Thibaudin and Boulanger episodes indicated among other things that the Minister of War could not always be treated as simply a military technician, whose presence in a cabinet had no political significance and who thus was not to be associated with its political acts. Under these circumstances, it was impossible to define just how one could avoid the full implications of ministerial solidarity and responsibility. Since it was difficult to achieve stability in the high command through some modification in the political situation of the Minister, another possibility was to shelter certain of his more important subordinates, in particular the Chief of Staff, from the fluctuations of parliamentary opinion, if it could be done without too overtly violating the principle of ministerial responsibility. As early as 1874, on the occasion of General du Barail's resignation as Minister, *Spectateur militaire* lamented the subsequent departure of his Chief of Staff, "a person who should be immutable as destiny. . . ."[78] During his first term as Chief of Staff in 1878, General de Miribel published a note on the necessity of the post being a permanent one. Coming as it did in the wake of the crisis of *Seize-mai* and in view of the known political opinions of its author, the note appears to have created a stir in republican circles.[79]

---

[78] *S.M.*, July 1874, p. 129.
[79] *République française*, January 18, 1879.

Hindered in the effective performance of his duties by the impermanence of his situation, the Chief of Staff in the 1880's also suffered from a lack of any precise definition of his functions. According to Miribel, it was as much a matter of words as anything else. Because his official title was that of Chief of Staff of the Minister of War, people within the army as well as civilians tended to look upon this personage as the Minister's alter ego. Instead of being able to occupy himself exclusively with the business of preparing the army for war, he was saddled with any number of auxiliary tasks, involving the ordinary affairs of the Ministry. This situation could be attributed mainly to a persistence of the old habits of mind in the mass of the officer corps, dating back to the days when the day-to-day life of the army rather than the planning of military operations was the real function of a staff officer. As a result, there was not a father "who wishes his son to be nominated as a lieutenant, or a general who wants one captain rather than another, who does not address himself to the Chief of Staff of the Minister." [80] The solution to this state of affairs in Miribel's estimation was simply to change the title of the office to Chief of Staff of the Army, thus ending the preconceived idea that he somehow depended directly on the Minister and was therefore obliged to resign along with him when a government fell.[81]

Although the Chief of Staff was supposed to oversee the preparations of the French army for war, he would not, in fact, preside over their execution in the event of hostilities. That task was reserved for the "Major General," the officer designated to be the Chief of Staff to the Commander in Chief of the Principal Group of Armies in the Eastern Theater, or as he was popularly called, the "Generalissimo." Like the Generalissimo, the Major General was not an explicit office in the

[80] Handwritten note by Gen. de Miribel, probably written in 1883. To be found in État-major de l'Armée, "Campagne contre l'Allemagne: 1914–1918" (hereafter cited as E.M.A.), Premier Bureau, carton No. 5.

[81] Handwritten note by Miribel, written in the late 1880's, *ibid.*

peacetime hierarchy, and the person designated to occupy this post in the event of war exercised no official function by right of it. Throughout the 1880's the Major General was Miribel. After the fall of the *Grand Ministère,* Miribel served as a member of the Consultative Committee for the Artillery. Membership on a consultative committee, if it was their sole assignment, was usually reserved for those generals who were too superannuated, lazy, or incompetent to command a division and who wanted a quiet sinecure while waiting out the years until their retirement. It was hardly the place where one would expect to find a general with the reputation for being one of the best tacticians in the army, and it may be assumed that other things were found for him to do around the Ministry. This would seem to be confirmed by Miribel's being made a member of the Conseil supérieur de le Guerre in 1885. During the Boulanger ministry, when it momentarily seemed as if the Schnaebelé incident might lead to a war with Germany, Miribel supposedly took over from Boulanger's incompetent Chief of Staff, overseeing the necessary preparations and drawing up the orders for the army.[82] In short, Miribel was able to act as an éminence grise at the Ministry of War and to exercise "a kind of occult influence over the task of preparing the army for war." [83]

Since the ministerial system of command kept those who, by their seniority, their prestige, and their authority over their comrades, were the real chiefs from occupying the top posts, there grew up a parallel, implicit command structure, where these important men could play the roles for which they were suited. By the terms of the 1883 decree, the Minister of War was the peacetime chief of the army, but in time of war the command of the army in the field would pass to one or several commanders in chief, depending on the number of theaters of operation, who would have the most extensive political, ad-

[82] E. du Saussois, *De Miribel* (Lyon: J. Gallet, 1894), pp. 48–49.

[83] Capt. Gilbert, *Lois et institutions militaires: six études organiques* (Paris: Nouvelle revue, 1895), p. 89.

ministrative, and military powers.[84] Although the Minister would not in time of war be obliged to efface himself completely, his importance with regard to the army would be considerably diminished. These eminent generals had no explicit place in the peacetime command structure except at the head of their army corps, a post that, paradoxically enough, they would have to leave at the moment of mobilization.

It was in order to give the leading generals a more effective role in the peacetime functioning of the army that General Campenon, during his short term as Minister of War in the Gambetta cabinet, reorganized the Conseil supérieur de la Guerre. The C.S.G. had originally been set up by Thiers in 1872. It brought together a large number of the more eminent generals and marshals with the ostensible purpose of rendering expert opinions on various military questions but more probably, in the words of du Barail, to listen to Thiers talk.[85] It met rather frequently in the course of the years 1872–1874 while the laws on the organization of the army and on the cadres were being drafted and discussed. Then it fell into disuse, being too unwieldy in size and too vague in its attributes and purpose.[86] Campenon endeavored to revivify the organ by drastically reducing its size. He hoped that it would become a permanent consultative body that would, upon the request of the Minister of War, aid him by giving an opinion on whatever measures he might contemplate. Thus reorganized, the C.S.G. would assure the army of the maintenance of those traditions which were "its glory and its strength" while at the same time acting as "a precious guarantee against precipitous and ill-considered innovations." Campenon also considered assigning special inspectoral missions to the members

---

[84] École militaire supérieure, "Cours de service d'état-major" (1879), p. 291.

[85] Du Barail, *op. cit.,* Vol. III, pp. 491–492.

[86] D'Ornano, *op. cit.,* pp. 138–139.

of the C.S.G., in order that they might assist the Minister in the task of controlling and overseeing the army.[87]

In endeavoring to give the real chiefs of the army a more explicit role, even if only a consultative one, Campenon was running the risk of reducing the already precarious authority of the Minister of War. The general opinion in the army according to *Spectateur militaire* was that the Minister, through the creation of the C.S.G., which was possessed of such weight and prestige that it was capable of checking his projects, had placed himself in "a position of veritable subordination vis-à-vis this Areopagus. . . ." [88] As the author of the decree, Campenon sought to answer such objections in advance: "Far from seeing his authority shackled or weakened, the Minister, backed by the opinions of the most eminent officers in the army, will see his decisions clothed with an absolutely indisputable moral authority." [89]

Any fears concerning the dangers of the C.S.G. lessening ministerial authority proved to be groundless, simply because that body continued to lead a rather fitful existence. Although constituted on a permanent basis, it was consulted only occasionally, a year sometimes going by without a single meeting. Nevertheless, membership on the C.S.G. did give a certain number of generals a special position in the army even if it was, for the moment, chiefly honorary, with only tangential influence. Just what their wartime commands would be was not meant to be public knowledge, nor was the identity of the future commanders in chief officially announced. Still, these matters were common knowledge within both higher military circles and the government, and the views of the men undoubtedly influenced the decisions of the Minister of War.

Although the French army did not possess the effective in-

---

[87] *J.O.* (1881), pp. 6571–6572.

[88] *S.M.*, November 1881, pp. 404–405. Similar fears are also expressed in *Avenir militaire*, December 1 and 6, 1881.

[89] *J.O.* (1881), p. 6571.

struments of command to be found in Germany, the situation was not quite so bad as it might at first appear. The French army was not, as one German critic put it, "acephalous." [90] Still, a system whereby the generals who would constitute the wartime high command could exert only an indirect and "occult" influence over the peacetime preparations of the army was not without its inconveniences. In the words of the brilliant military expert of the *Nouvelle revue,* Captain Georges Gilbert, the French army, because of its unstable command structure, was "in a perpetually provisional state, a never-ending period of transition." [91] This was a problem that excited an increasing amount of interest within both the army and civilian circles in the late 1880's.

Since the Minister of War could not escape the hazards of parliamentary life, the desirability of providing more stability for his chief military subordinate was becoming ever more evident. It was even admitted that the Chief of Staff should be given greater effective authority over the peacetime functioning of the army. There were numerous versions as to what the precise nature of the relationship between the Minister and his Chief of Staff might be and as to how the principle of ministerial responsibility could be preserved in a manner compatible with republican sensibilities. Some such solution, by increasing the authority of the Chief of Staff or perhaps of the Generalissimo, both of whom were primarily military technicians, automatically lessened the necessity for the Minister of War to be a general. Indeed, as the Minister could now devote his energies to the more purely political tasks of defending the army before parliament and of overseeing the operations of the administrative bureaucracy, there were even undeniable advantages to having a civilian in the post. Such was the opinion of both Gilbert [92] and Joseph Reinach.[93]

---

[90] Un officier prussien, *La France, est-elle prête?* (Paris: Henicksen, 1884).

[91] Gilbert, *op. cit.,* p. 82.

[92] *Ibid.,* p. 105.

[93] Reinach, *Politique opportuniste,* pp. 234–238.

In advocating a civilian Minister of War, Gilbert and Reinach were echoing an idea that had been current in recent years. In 1881, at the time of the formation of the *Grand Ministère,* there was a strong possibility that Gambetta would nominate Freycinet, his chief lieutenant during the *Défense nationale,* as Minister of War. Freycinet appears to have expected the post, and when Gambetta offered him the Quai d'Orsay instead, he declined to join the government.[94] Gambetta claimed to believe that neither the army nor the public was as yet prepared to accept a politician as head of the army.[95] *Avenir militaire,* while admitting that there was much to be said for having a civilian as Minister of War, and particularly Freycinet, still could not quite bring itself to believe that the army would be better off under a civilian than under a soldier, and it expressed the relief supposedly felt by the military when General Campenon was named to the post.[96]

As the procession of undistinguished generals continued on through the 1880's, people began to wonder if another approach might not be more satisfactory. One author, writing in 1885, speculated that since the search for a general who could, by his ability and sheer force of character, impose himself upon both the army and the government had so far been in vain, it might be worth while to place a civilian at the head of the department of war. Such a move would have the advantage, among others, of keeping a large number of generals out of politics, since no general could hope to hold himself completely aloof from participation in political affairs if he was a member of a responsible government. It would also put an end to the scandalous and unwarranted promotions bestowed on the military entourage of a retiring general.[97] A civilian

---

[94] Freycinet, *Souvenirs,* Vol. II, pp. 193–194.

[95] E. Katzenbach, "Charles Louis de Saulces de Freycinet and the Army of Metropolitan France" (unpublished Ph.D. dissertation, Princeton University, 1953), p. 275.

[96] *Avenir militaire,* October 26, 1881, and November 16, 1881.

[97] Anon., *Pourquoi la France n'est pas prête* (Paris: Flammarion, 1885), pp. 64–66.

head of the army was expected to be immune to the spirt of camaraderie that naturally exerted its influence over a general who had spent forty years in the ranks of the officer corps.[98]

General Boulanger was as responsible as anyone else for clearing the way for a civilian Minister of War. If a politician could not be, for the army, a chief "towards whom each soldier lifts his eyes with enthusiasm . . . ," [99] neither would he be a spectacular uniformed figure who might use the prestige attached to his office and to his uniform to threaten the regime. For a short while Boulanger had seemed to be the vigorous, progressive leader that people had so long demanded, until it became apparent that his concept of his role extended far beyond the mere peacetime direction of the French army. After the Boulanger experience it was no longer so certain in both civilian and military circles that a general had to be Minister of War. The ground was thus prepared for the innovation, as it had not been in 1881. Katzenbach, in his study of Freycinet, notes that there was an extensive campaign during late 1887 in certain of the more respectable papers of the Left advocating the nomination of a civilian as Minister of War, which indicates that the Radicals were willing to support the idea.[100] As a result, Freycinet was named Minister of War in the Floquet government of April 1888.

The Freycinet Solution

Charles de Freycinet is generally recognized as having been the most able Minister of War in the history of the Third Republic. The almost unqualified success of his five-year ministry may be explained by his wide knowledge of military affairs, but it also depended on his political ability. Possessing an exquisite sense of tact and a lucid mind, Freycinet was also

[98] X.Y.Z., "Aperçu sur notre situation militaire," *S.M.*, January 1, 1888, pp. 131–132.

[99] Un officier prussien, *op. cit.*, p. 130.

[100] Katzenbach, *op. cit.*, pp. 275–279.

an excellent speaker. This combination of talents made him a politician of rare and consummate skill, as his four terms as President of the Council of Ministers attest. Some would say that his abilities as a compromiser and conciliator were carried to excess, to a point where they actually constituted weakness of character.[101] Still, Freycinet could always patch together a parliamentary coalition, thus allowing the business of state to continue. Sinuous and supple, the "little white mouse," as he was called, threaded his way through the intricacies of French parliamentary life for fifty years, the living embodiment of the Opportunist Republic.

Less striking than his gifts as a politician, but possibly of greater significance, was his ability as an administrator. For some two decades before he entered politics, he had served in the Department of Roads and Bridges. He thus had a first-hand knowledge of the realities of public administration unequaled by any but a few of his political contemporaries. The particular talents of Freycinet with regard to the administrative aspects of government were well summarized by General Millet, who as Director of the Infantry served under at least six Ministers of War in the years 1896–1900. He has left this incisive portrait of Freycinet at the time of his second term as chief of the army:

He was certainly not an overwhelming personality, this pale, thin little man with a mild voice and a calm manner of speaking, steady eyes and restrained gestures; but he studied, he worked, he understood with an intelligence that was keen and lucid. At first glance, he appeared more like a notary for widowed ladies, strictly in black from head to foot, than a chief of the army. But all questions were familiar to him, their solutions were readily apparent, and he could explain them as clearly as he understood them. . . .[102]

Freycinet had a wide and profound knowledge of military affairs. He had won his spurs as Gambetta's closest associate at

---

[101] J. Caillaux, *Mes mémoires* (Paris: Plon, 1943), Vol. II, pp. 47–48.

[102] Gen. Millet, unpublished memoirs, Vol. II, p. 77.

the time of the *Défense nationale*. Although the generals who led the mass levies that made up the armies of Gambetta accused Freycinet of being overtheoretical in his conceptions and overrigorous in his directions for carrying them out, no one could deny the verve and the vigor he had shown.[103] After the war Freycinet served as military specialist for Gambetta's paper, *République française*. Upon his election to the Senate he sat on the Army Committee of that chamber, which gave him the opportunity further to increase his knowledge of military questions. Freycinet thus entered the Ministry of War thoroughly familiar with the workings of the military establishment and possessing a clear conception of what was needed for its improvement. His gifts as a politician not only facilitated his relations with parliament, and so permitted him to remain in office long enough to put his ideas into effect, but they also enabled him, unlike preceding Ministers of War, to gauge what measures were feasible, according to the temper of parliament, and which were not.

Like many others, Freycinet had drawn up a program of military reform after the war. It was presented in the concluding chapter of his book *La guerre en province pendant le siège de Paris*.[104] There was nothing startling or original in the measures he proposed, and most of them were enacted in the two decades following 1870. Freycinet particularly emphasized the need for a general staff such as the Prussian army possessed.[105] Although the creation of the General Staff of the Minister represented a step in the right direction, more obviously had to be done. As early as 1872 the future Minister of War published a series of articles calling for the institution of such an organ, whose chief would be the peacetime commander of the army. Freycinet recognized the potential politi-

---

[103] Col. J. Revol, *Histoire de l'armée française* (Paris: Larousse, 1929), p. 202.

[104] Ch. de Freycinet, *La guerre en province pendant le siège de Paris* (Paris: M. Lévy, 1871), pp. 356–366.

[105] *Ibid.*, p. 336.

cal dangers inherent in so great a concentration of power in the hands of a single general, but he "avoided the problem rather than met it with the suggestion that inasmuch as 'the army had never had anything to do with revolt,' it presumably never would." [106] At the same time he recognized that, groundless though their fears might be, republican politicians were still too apprehensive of the shadowy possibility of some *pronunciamiento* to give to any French general the same kind of prerogatives enjoyed by Moltke. In moving to effect what he considered to be necessary improvements in the General Staff, Freycinet was particularly careful not to arouse republican fears on this point.

Freycinet envisioned less a reorganization or a reconstitution of the General Staff than a heightening of its prestige and an increase in its authority. In effect, his reform involved little more than a change in the name of the organ, from General Staff of the Minister of War to General Staff of the Army, plus the specific statement that the Chief of Staff would henceforth be the Major General of the French armies in time of war and that there would be greater stability in the post than heretofore. In changing the name of the General Staff, Freycinet was trying to accustom people to think of it less as something of a "secretariat-general" and more as a "specific, autonomous service, essentially technical, which must remain sheltered from ministerial instability. . . ."

I do not mean that the Chief of Staff is to be assured complete permanence, which is incompatible with ministerial responsibility; but we should at least do away with the idea that he must resign along with the Minister. This has taken place continually between 1874 and 1888, and it has given us twelve Chiefs of Staff in fourteen years.[107]

Freycinet had planned this reform from the time he became Minister of War. Because of republican sensibilities, however, he did not put it into effect until after he had been in office for

---

[106] Katzenbach, *op. cit.,* pp. 187–188.

[107] *J.O.* (1890), pp. 2233–2234.

two years, since General de Miribel was his candidate for the post.

Freycinet recognized that public opinion would have to be prepared in advance for the elevation of Miribel to Chief of Staff of the Army, with all the power over the army that the title implied. Hence, Freycinet first named him to the command of the Sixth Army Corps. By commanding a corps that was considered to be made up of the best troops in metropolitan France, Miribel automatically rose in the estimation of the public. The triumphant review that he staged at Saint-Mihiel in 1890 was a kind of climax.[108] According to Freycinet, "People had grown accustomed to looking upon him as one of our most able chiefs. We could then, without offending public opinion, call him to the side of the Minister of War." [109] By the decree of May 6, 1890, the General Staff of the Army was created, and Miribel was made its Chief. In the wording of the decree, Freycinet took almost exaggerated care to show that the Chief of the General Staff of the Army would not occupy an irresponsible, independent position. As in the past, he would continue to work under the authority of the Minister of War and to be responsible to him. The signature of the Minister was necessary for the validation of all his directives and commands.[110]

Although Miribel was now in a position of greater effective influence over the French army in time of peace than any general before him, his situation was still only partially analogous to that of Moltke. In time of war Miribel would become the Major General of the French army, Chief of Staff to the general commanding the principal group of armies in the eastern theater. This post was commonly referred to as the "Generalissimo" of the French army. Miribel would thus occupy the second-ranking position in the army, and not the first, as did Moltke.

[108] Freycinet, *Souvenirs,* Vol. II, p. 404.
[109] *Ibid.,* p. 444.
[110] *J.O.* (1890), p. 2234.

Freycinet further strengthened the high command by reorganizing the Conseil supérieur de la Guerre. As with the General Staff, it was not a question of instituting anything new but rather of more sharply defining the attributes and powers of an already existent body. Freycinet proposed that the C.S.G. be required to meet at least once a month and that the Minister of War be obliged to consult with it before taking action on all the more important military questions, such as the essential dispositions for mobilization, the initial concentration of the armies in war, general methods of training, the creation or suppression of fortified places, etc. The C.S.G. was to consist of twelve members, four by virtue of their offices: the Minister of War as its president, the Chief of Staff, who would be permanent reporter for its meetings, and the Presidents of the Consultative Committees for the Artillery and the Engineers. Eight other members would be chosen from among those divisionary generals whose talent and experience designated them to exercise "the important commands in time of war." [111]

Another decree, promulgated two weeks later, gave a more precise definition of the peacetime situation of those generals who were designated to command the larger wartime units. Although it had for some time been a standard practice to bestow upon a certain number of generals a "letter of service," informing them of the commands they would exercise in case of war, Freycinet felt that it would be wise to issue a decree concerning these letters which specifically stated the attributes and duties of those who received them. In bestowing them by virtue of a definite presidential decree, he believed that the authority of the men who would command the wartime armies would be increased vis-à-vis the corps commanders, who would someday be under their orders. It would thus facilitate the task of overseeing the state of preparation of the various army corps. Freycinet also advocated giving to those members of the C.S.G. destined for the highest command posts the job

[111] *J.O.* (1888), p. 1964.

of directing several army corps at once during the annual maneuvers.[112]

The two decrees carefully specified that the letters of service were revocable at any time and that they did not confer any real, present prerogatives of command. Although they might supervise and criticize the measures taken by the corps commanders with regard to the training of their troops and their general preparation for war, they had no right to interfere in the internal affairs of an army corps, that is to say, in its discipline, its administration, or matters of promotion. Nor was any member of the C.S.G. to undertake a tour of inspection without specific orders from the Minister of War.[113] Here Freycinet was discreetly exercising his acute political sense, creating what was, in effect, another rank in the military hierarchy while trying to appear not to do so. In drafting the decrees and in citing the different precedents for the reorganization and the strengthening of the C.S.G., Freycinet made no reference to the 1873 law on the organization of the army. Since what he was doing was a violation, in spirit at least, of the 1873 law, he probably thought it wise not to draw anyone's attention to it. The experience of his immediate predecessor as Minister of War, General Logerot, certainly provided grounds for such caution.

Logerot had tried to create just such a system of inspections by purely budgetary means, quietly inserting a credit to pay for them into the budget of 1888. A deputy of the Left, Édouard Lockroy, objected to this violation of the 1873 law. He claimed that so important a measure deserved to be fully discussed and not handled in so offhand a manner.[114] It is highly probable that the Minister of War did indeed wish to avoid bringing up for full parliamentary discussion a question with so many inflammatory implications as the need for a

---

[112] *Ibid.*, pp. 2177–2178.

[113] *Ibid.*, p. 2178.

[114] *Journal Officiel de la Chambre des Députés: Débats* (hereafter cited as *J.O.C. Déb.*), (1888), p. 789.

stronger high command. Thus, it was very conveniently "slipped into the budget." [115] Once it had come to the attention of the Chamber, Logerot had no choice but to withdraw the credit in question and to send the whole matter to the Army Commission of the Chamber for consideration. [116] Two months later, the new Minister of War arranged things by means of an executive decree. Parliament raised no objections.

The Minister was to preside at the regular meetings of the C.S.G., but if the President of the Republic saw fit, he might call a meeting. In that case he would preside. The decree reorganizing the C.S.G. further provided for a vice-president, who would be designated by the Minister on an annual basis and who would preside if he were absent. [117] It was nowhere so stated in the decree, but the Vice-President was the general who was designated to command the principal group of armies in case of war, the "Generalissimo." For a period of ten years, until 1898, the post was occupied by General Saussier.

Saussier was the leading soldier of his generation. A republican since 1848, when he had been at Saint-Cyr, Saussier had for that reason refused the post of aide-de-camp to the Emperor. [118] Even so, he had enjoyed an outstanding career, participating in almost all of the campaigns of the Second Empire. Following his capture at Metz in 1870, Saussier, then a colonel, refused to pledge his word not to try to escape. Rather than undergoing the comfortable "table d'hôte captivity" [119] along with the rest of the officer corps, he had been confined to a fortress in eastern Germany, from which he was later able to get away. His subsequent career under the Republic had included a term as deputy to the National Assembly and the command of both the Nineteenth Army Corps in Algeria and the Sixth at Châlons before he was named in 1884 Military

---

[115] *Ibid.,* p. 790.

[116] *Ibid.,* p. 791.

[117] *J.O.* (1888), p. 1964.

[118] Millet, *op. cit.,* Vol. I, p. 81.

[119] H. Contamine, *La Revanche* (Paris: Berger-Levrault, 1957), p. 58.

Governor of Paris. Soon thereafter he was also designated Commander in Chief of the French armies in time of war.

In Saussier was to be found the unlikely combination of real military ability and a highly developed political sense. That Saussier possessed a precise appreciation of the political realities of a given moment and also a perception of the best interests of the army in its dealings with the regime was evident from an incident that took place during his term of command in Algeria. Until 1879, the officer commanding the Nineteenth Army Corps was also Governor General of the colony, but in that year the two functions were split, with the latter one being conferred upon a civilian, Albert Grévy, brother of the President of the Republic. According to Millet, who was at that time stationed in the colony, the news that the army was to be deprived of its mission of governing Algeria created much discontent among the troops. Saussier quieted all murmurs with a display of his astute sense of political realism. When Grévy disembarked, Saussier greeted him with the words: "I salute you, Monsieur civil governor, my chief." [120]

Freycinet and Saussier appear to have worked very closely together. Between the politician, with his profound knowledge of military affairs, and the general, with his acute understanding of political realities, there was a real and intimate friendship, a mutual appreciation for the talents of the other. As for Freycinet and Miribel, on the other hand, no such closeness existed. "Freycinet left the General alone to do his work and there seems to have been neither friction nor friendship between them." [121]

The extent of the authority and the effective attributes of the newly reorganized instruments of command, as well as the nature of their relationship to the Minister of War, were not immediately clear in the minds of either the public or the army. The Conseil supérieur de la Guerre as an organ reflected the prestige of its eminent members, and the Minister

[120] Millet, *op. cit.,* Vol. II, p. 25.
[121] Katzenbach, *op. cit.,* pp. 322–325.

of War might well be somewhat awed in his dealings with it. General Zurlinden, who was named Minister of War in January 1895, recounts in his memoirs how delicate a task he found it to preside for the first time at a meeting of the C.S.G., whose members had all a short time before been his chiefs. There were, however, no problems, "thanks to the spirit of discipline and of deference to my position which was inherent in the army." [122] Zurlinden announced to the assembled generals that he considered it his duty as Minister of War to mitigate the drawbacks of ministerial instability by giving as much influence as possible to the "stable elements of the army. . . ." [123]

Where Zurlinden appeared to be advocating a conscious abdication by the Minister of some of his authority vis-à-vis the C.S.G., his immediate successor, Godefroy Cavaignac, evidently went to some lengths to assert ministerial prerogatives. The son of the illustrious republican general of 1848 and a former reporter for the army budget, Cavaignac was confident of his mastery of military affairs. On two separate occasions he refused to consult the C.S.G. on matters of some importance, and on another he submitted a decree to the President of the Republic for promulgation, despite its unanimous disapproval.[124] Although his actions attracted unfavorable comment within military circles, Cavaignac was acting fully within his rights when, on the basis of his authority as Minister of War, he refused "not only to cover himself with the opinion of the C.S.G. but even to ascertain that opinion." [125] As *France militaire* noted in 1895, it was not yet certain whether the C.S.G. was simply a consultative body, or if it

[122] Gen. Zurlinden, *Mes souvenirs depuis la guerre* (Paris: Perrin, 1913), pp. 47–48.

[123] Conseil supérieur de la Guerre, "Registre des délibérations" (hereafter cited as C.S.G., "Reg. dél."), No. 6 (1895–1896), pp. 208–209.

[124] Maréchal-de-Camp, "L'État-major de l'armée," *France militaire* (hereafter cited as *F.M.*), May 13, 1895.

[125] Comte de Villebois-Mareuil, "Organisation du haut-commandement dans l'armée française," *Correspondant*, May 5, 1896, p. 546.

possessed the right to initiate measures and the power of veto, that is to say, "an effective responsibility in the organization of national defense." [126]

The prerogatives of the Chief of Staff, in the wake of the Freycinet reforms, were also uncertain, although Miribel tended to act as if they were quite extensive. A man with an extremely authoritarian temper, Miribel had long admired the Prussian system of command built around an autonomous general staff and had advocated the introduction of something like it into the French army.[127] The 1890 decree on the General Staff could well be taken as at least partial vindication of his views on the subject. In any case, Miribel considered that the General Staff, in the discharge of its special mission of preparing the army for war, took precedence over the other bureaus and *directions* at the Ministry of War and in fact enjoyed broad authority over them. Naturally enough, this annoyed the men in charge, always jealous of their bureaucratic prerogatives, and there were during Miribel's tenure as Chief of Staff a number of conflicts between the bureaus and the General Staff.[128]

The lack of clarity in the new organization of the high command also extended to the relationship between the C.S.G. and the General Staff. The General Staff, the organ of preparation, functioned independently of the C.S.G., which, by bringing together the designated chiefs of the wartime armies, could be considered as the organ of command. Despite the heavy responsibilities that at the outbreak of war would fall to the members of the C.S.G. for the execution of the General Staff's plans, they had no direct influence over their elaboration in time of peace. At best, the C.S.G. had only a consultative role, being on occasion asked to pass judgment on the

[126] *F.M.,* December 3, 1895.

[127] "Notes sur l'organisation de l'État-major de l'armée," handwritten note by Miribel, dated 1880; E.M.A., Premier Bureau, Carton No. 5.

[128] Gen. Tricoche, "Les chefs d'État-major généraux," *F.M.,* July 20–21, 1899.

work of the General Staff at various stages. The two bodies "would enter into contact with each other only at the moment of mobilization, at the very instant when they should already be in full collaboration." [129] In actual fact, some kind of accommodation was usually worked out between the interested parties, with the Chief of Staff working closely with the Generalissimo, his wartime commander.[130] The only difficulty in such an arrangement was that for it to be effective, there had to be a gracious entente between the people involved, an entente that might not always exist.[131]

With such a degree of fluidity in the attributes and the actual functioning of the various branches of the high command, much depended on the personality of Saussier, on the one hand, and Miribel, on the other. Both men enjoyed great authority and prestige within the army, but whereas the Generalissimo was of a prudent and easygoing temperament, possibly a bit indolent,[132] the Chief of Staff was energetic, hard-working, and authoritarian by nature. He was, on occasion, reported to have treated the C.S.G. in dictatorial fashion, calling upon that body purely and simply to record his decisions as Chief of Staff rather than to examine and discuss them.[133] Following the sudden death of Miribel in 1893, he was succeeded by his principal assistant, General de Boisdeffre. Lacking the seniority and the prestige of his predecessor, and being suave and diplomatic, Boisdeffre seems to have deferred more readily to Saussier.[134]

For all that Freycinet did to strengthen the high command

---

[129] Ministère de la Guerre, "Historique de l'organisation et du fonctionnement de l'État-major et du Conseil supérieur de la Guerre," *Travaux d'études,* No. 23, March 14, 1923 (typewritten M.S., no author), pp. 4–5.

[130] Gen. Boucher, *L'oeuvre du général de Miribel* (Paris: Berger-Levrault, 1924), p. 38–40.

[131] "Note sur le haut commandement," E.M.A., Premier Bureau, Carton No. 4, Dossier No. 5, handwritten statement, no author, no date.

[132] Millet, *op. cit.,* Vol. I, p. 81.

[133] Gen. Tricoche, "État-major général," *F.M.,* April 20–21, 1895.

[134] Boucher, *op. cit.,* p. 38.

and to increase its stability, the unity of command which would be necessary in case of war was still not adequately prefigured in time of peace. To that degree, there was something incomplete in his program of reforms, although it represented a great advance over the ambiguous situation existing before. That Freycinet did not go further in this direction is understandable, for an independent and virtually irresponsible high command on the German model was too much for a French government to accept in 1890, even if it were sponsored by a civilian politician of unimpeachably republican sentiments. Any explicit evidence of republican distrust of the army in this period is difficult to find. Yet all the writers for the military press, in considering how better to strengthen the command structure of the army, had a tendency to attribute the government's unwillingness to create for some French general a situation analogous to that of Moltke to the vague fear of some kind of *pronunciamiento*.

In so far as it presented no danger to republican political institutions, the army could thus, in terms of men, matériel, and training, be as strong as possible. All the basic elements of a potent military machine were there, but the ultimate cohesive factor that would permit it to be set in motion, an organized high command, was held in abeyance. The General Staff would function, but the future commander in chief would have no authority over it. The generals who would lead the armies and groups of armies were designated and were to prepare themselves for their future tasks, but they were not permitted to exercise any effective command over their troops in time of peace. One might characterize the attitude of the republican politicians of the period as a combination of an outward generalized military patriotism and an inward fear and distrust of the professional soldier in particular.

It was in the light of this peculiar amalgam of sentiments that Freycinet had to operate in bringing about the reforms he felt to be necessary. Probably no one but a politician of Freycinet's skill and tact could have successfully taken the first step toward removing the high command from the enervating effects of ministerial instability. Had a military Minister of War attempted such a thing, the suspicions of parliament would have immediately been aroused, as when General Logerot tried to increase the effectiveness of the generals designated to command the wartime armies. That Freycinet could go as far as he did in the years 1888 to 1893 was a tribute to the disciplined behavior of the army since 1871, and especially during the Boulangist episode, which, in a sense, cleared the way for an era when relations between the army and the Republic were characterized by real mutual confidence and trust.

The efforts of Freycinet to strengthen the high command by giving a greater measure of permanence to the Chief of Staff and through more precisely and explicitly defining the powers and attributes of the C.S.G. were generally well received in the army.[135] Still, just as there were politicians whose distrust of the military obliged the Minister of War to be discreet in drawing up his reforms, there were also officers who disliked them because they went against the traditional forms of military hierarchy. Freycinet was careful to stress in the text of the decrees that both the C.S.G. and the General Staff were still responsible to the Minister of War; nevertheless, both organs now had greater authority over the army than before, while the Minister had less. In objecting to this state of affairs, one military spokesman declared that in France the Minister of War was the single chief of the army. "There can be no other one sharing the command of the army with him, since there is no higher authority to whom they may refer in case of a divergence or conflict of views." [136]

Possibly it was because his reforms in the high command ran counter to orthodox military tradition that the departure of Freycinet from the Ministry of War and his replacement by

[135] Katzenbach, *op. cit.*, pp. 332–333.
[136] F. Th. de Guymarais, "La stabilité au Ministère de la guerre," *S.M.*, March 15, 1894, p. 452.

a soldier, General Loizillon, in January 1893 were by no means universally regretted. For many it simply seemed more fitting that the chief of the French army should be a soldier. The spectacle of the Minister of War appearing before his troops dressed as a notary was somehow absurd in an era when the troops expected their chiefs to have a certain *panache,* a quality that Freycinet most obviously lacked.[137]

Through the Freycinet reforms the autonomy of the army within the state was augmented, and moreover this was tacitly acknowledged by the government. Despite the assurances given in the relevant decrees that the prerogatives of the Minister and his responsibility were in no way to be diminished, it was evident that, through the greater effective stability of the high command and its increased explicit authority, a larger sector of military affairs now escaped the control of the responsible minister. What could be considered as the "real" military hierarchy, made up of the natural chiefs of the army, was now, through the C.S.G. and the General Staff, to play a more obviously influential role in the military affairs of France. This hierarchy had always existed in a nebulous fashion, parallel to the hierarchy at the top of which stood the Minister of War, and it had been able to exercise considerable influence over his actions. Now, however, the Minister, unless he consciously asserted his authority and his rights, tended to become merely the advocate of the great military chiefs before parliament and before the country. It was for this reason that the Freycinet reforms were to a degree unconstitutional. They were also illegal, in that they ignored those parts of the 1873 law on the organization of the army pertaining to high command, which specifically stated that there was to be no echelon of command higher than the army corps. That other portions of the 1873 law had already been consistently disregarded may, however, have facilitated Freycinet's efforts here.

The intention of the authors of the law had originally been

[137] Gen. Tricoche, "Les réformes militaires," *F.M.,* December 15–16, 1895.

that a general commanding an army corps should serve no more than three years, but the occasions on which this actually happened were so rare as to excite comment.[138] This almost constant violation of the spirit, if not the precise letter, of the 1873 law did not give rise to a parliamentary interpellation until 1912. Apparently, the republicans were agreed that it was militarily unsound, not to say unrealistic, to make the command of an army corps a temporary, limited function. Such objections as were raised to the continual violation of the law were found not in parliament but in the military press. There the argument was that nothing was more harmful to discipline than systematic disobedience to the law. The government, they argued, should either enforce this portion of the 1873 law or revise it.[139]

As a result of the effective removal of this statutory limit, an officer commanding an army corps, although still wearing the three stars of a divisionary general on his sleeve, was considered to possess a higher rank, simply by virtue of his office. To accept the command of a division after having served at the head of an army corps was therefore the equivalent of agreeing to a demotion in rank. Rather than do that, a corps commander preferred to retire from the army. As long as the 1873 law could in this fashion be circumvented legally, there was little pressure for the repeal of the provisions in question, particularly since the army believed the legislators to be quite incompetent in military matters. In strengthening and defining the attributes of those generals designated to command the wartime armies, Freycinet may have been violating the spirit of the 1873 law, but a solid precedent for such an act had already been established.

Just as a general commanding an army was on an echelon above a general at the head of a division, and in effect held a higher rank, so too did the men designated to command the

[138] *Vide supra,* pp. 54–55.
[139] *S.M.,* May 15, 1884, p. 340.

four or five wartime armies outrank the corps commanders, although they themselves still headed a corps. Even if the wording of the 1888 and 1890 decrees forbade the members of the C.S.G. to interfere in the internal affairs of the army corps under their jurisdiction and limited their prerogatives to matters pertaining to military preparedness, and even if their situation vis-à-vis the corps commanders was on occasion equivocal, the fact was that their authority over the rest of the army was nevertheless very real. By sheer force of necessity, a functioning military hierarchy above the rank of divisionary general was coming into existence. Many felt that this *de facto* extension in the table of rank should be sanctioned by law despite the inconveniences of a debate on the subject. Their primary reason for so thinking was to be found in the succinct statement of the great general of the Revolutionary and Napoleonic period, Jourdan: "Orders given to subordinates are orders, but orders given to equals in rank are negotiations." A number of incidents over the years, reported in circumspect fashion in the military press, provided further justification for such a reform.[140]

Freycinet evidently considered it expedient to create at least one rank in the hierarchy above that of divisionary general. He and the other members of the C.S.G., the presumed beneficiaries of such a measure, devoted a large part of one meeting to discussing what would be a more suitable title for the new rank: "general" plain and unadorned or "general of the army."[141] General Billot, in a report on an inspection tour of the troops designated to be under his command in time of war, stressed the need for more rank among the generals. He noted that he had been treated with all possible deference and respect, but he believed that this was due primarily to his seniority and to the important positions he had already held. To expect the same deference to be given to any general,

[140] Gen. Paris, "Le quatrième étoile," *F.M.,* July 3, 1896.
[141] C.S.G., "Reg. dél.," No. 4 (1891–1892), pp. 216–217, 225.

merely on the basis of an always revocable letter of service, would be "too much to ask of human nature, which has its innate susceptibilities and weaknesses, with which one must always reckon." [142]

As a result of this flurry of interest in the problem of the high command, a number of bills were submitted to parliament in the years 1890–1897. All purported in some way or other to strengthen the command structure of the army. That it was a nonpartisan question may be seen from one of the bills originating in the Chamber; its list of sponsors ranged all the way from the conservative Eugène Melchior de Vogué to the Socialist Clovis Hugues.[143] Freycinet, in the name of the government, also prepared a bill on the high command, but it was never brought up for discussion before parliament. The only measure to reach the floor of the Chamber was one authored by General Billot in 1896, during his second term as Minister of War. Billot sought to do little more than give legal confirmation to the existence of the C.S.G. and to add an extra rank to the hierarchy.[144]

The proposal submitted by Billot to the Chamber Army Commission emerged virtually intact, except for a few minor revisions,[145] to await the debate on the floor. Despite the supposedly urgent need for its enactment, the bill did not reach the floor for several months. It was then debated on three separate occasions, with a delay of a week or more between them, before the Chamber departed for the holidays. In fixing its agenda for the reentry of parliament, the Chamber indefinitely postponed the further discussion of the bill on the organization of the high command.[146] It was reported that the

[142] Report dated December 8, 1888, E.M.A., Troisième Bureau, Carton No. 94.

[143] *J.O.C.* Doc. (1896), p. 300.

[144] *J.O.C.* Doc. (1897), pp. 458 ff.

[145] *J.O.C.* Doc. (1896), pp. 1321–1322.

[146] *R.D.M.*, April 15, 1897, p. 947.

Chamber Army Commission had set to work to revise the bill,[147] but nothing apparently came of its efforts. Until 1914, therefore, the high command of the French army continued to be regulated by a series of decrees, and not by a specific law.

That parliament was either unable or unwilling to enact a law on the high command would indicate that it was a matter in which the public had little real interest. Despite its fundamental importance for the army, the question of the high command was one only indirectly affecting the average Frenchman. There was therefore no real pressure on parliament to do something to provide a legal organization for the high command.

In the decade that followed the Freycinet reforms in the high command, none of his successors tried to undo his work or to return to the Minister any of the prerogatives that Freycinet had so skillfully abdicated. Rather, there were a number of decrees tending to confirm what Freycinet had begun. In a decree of November 1895, Cavaignac placed the directions under the authority of the Chief of Staff in all matters pertaining to "the organization and training of the troops, mobilization, armament, defense of the territory, and the gathering of provisions for war." [148] This simply specified and defined certain powers that the Chief of Staff implicitly possessed by virtue of the 1890 decree and that Miribel had already asserted. In 1899, Freycinet, serving his second term as Minister of War, moved to reinforce the position of the members of the C.S.G. by issuing a decree publicly announcing for the first time that they would inspect those army corps which were to make up their wartime armies. The decree also stated that these inspections were permanent assignments, even though the letter of service was to be annually renewable. Nevertheless, in the interests of legality and good form, Freycinet felt obliged to remind the commanders-designate of the armies that their peacetime mission was to control and

---

[147] N. Desmaysons, "Le Haut Commandement," S.M., June 1, 1897, p. 392.
[148] J.O. (1895), p. 6478.

"not to supplant the authority of the generals commanding the army corps. . . ."[149] It all represented a steady, unobtrusive strengthening of the structure of command.

The first two decades after the defeat of 1870 may be looked upon as a period of intense reform and renovation. It was an essentially anonymous undertaking, the result of the ardent and humble abnegation of all. No single person could be considered as the leading animator of the endeavor, unless perhaps it was Moltke. By the time Freycinet arrived at the Ministry of War, the main tasks of reorganization and reconstruction had been accomplished. All that remained to be done was to give a coherent organization to the high command and to arrange things in such a way that those men who were the real military leaders of the country could play a more effective role in preparing the army for war. This meant placing them in a position where they could more openly exert their influence and even their authority over the army and where they would be relatively immune to the fluctuations of politics. It involved both a calculated violation of the Constitution and a considerable change in the traditional French military organization.

As of 1890, the French army was commanded in time of peace to a degree that it had never been before. Although the Minister of War did not completely efface himself, the situation of the Generalissimo and of the Chief of Staff was much reinforced. Miribel and his successor, Boisdeffre, were no longer obliged to operate in "occult" fashion behind the scenes, while Saussier presided over the army with matchless aplomb. By allowing this increase in the authority of the Chief of Staff and the Generalissimo, the Republic was also, in effect, allowing the military a far higher degree of control over their own concerns than had any prior regime in the nineteenth century. That the politicians would acquiesce in this was indicative of their growing sense of confidence in themselves and also in the discipline and loyalty of the military.

[149] J.O. (1899), p. 1487.

How deep rooted was this sense of confidence was soon to be revealed by the Dreyfus Affair. Relations between the army and the state were to be severely strained by the Affair, as republican politicians became confused and finally disillusioned by the behavior of the military. In the process, the newly constituted structure of command broke down. That it could be rebuilt within a decade and on a stronger and therefore more independent basis was most significant of the manner in which the republican politicians were able to recognize the fundamental demands of national defense and to disregard their past anxieties in meeting them.

PART III

THE BREAKDOWN OF THE ENTENTE

CHAPTER FIVE

The Dreyfus Affair: 1897-1900

The Army and the Affair

The Dreyfus Affair momentarily ended the entente between the army and the Republic, as it had evolved over the years since 1871. Based on a sense of mutual confidence and a respect for the terrain on which the other operated, this pragmatic accommodation had permitted the civil and the military elements within the French state to coexist with a minimum of friction. If neither really comprehended the codes and customs of the other or sympathized with its ideals, it did not matter, so long as the defense of the nation was assured and so long as a period of relative calm and political stability was thereby possible. Because of the Dreyfus Affair, this sense of mutual confidence disappeared, and the Republic was forced once again to consider the old problem of whether an army founded on authoritarian principles could function within the framework of a fundamentally democratic state without endangering it.

It all began as a case of common espionage. On October 15, 1894, Captain Alfred Dreyfus, a *stagiaire,* or probationer, on the General Staff, was arrested on the charge of having sold military secrets to Germany. Two months later, he was convicted by a court-martial and sentenced to life imprisonment. After being deprived of his insignia of rank and discharged from the army in a humiliating public ceremony, he was sent to Devil's Island in February 1895 to begin his incarceration.

Although there were, over the next two years, occasional articles appearing in the French press on the subject of Dreyfus,
including one suggesting that his court-martial had not been
conducted in a strictly regular fashion, the matter was, to all
intents and purposes, forgotten by the French people and by
the army.

From the beginning of the case, a small group of men had
been dubious as to the guilt of Dreyfus. Some of them, in particular Mathieu Dreyfus, the brother of the condemned man, had
worked indefatigably to bring about an official review of the
case. Although they made little headway against the authorities, they had nevertheless slowly been winning converts to
their cause, including several men prominent in public life.
The most important of these was Auguste Scheurer-Kestner,
an old collaborator of Gambetta, life Senator from Alsace, and
Vice-President of the upper chamber. In July 1897 he was presented with convincing evidence of the innocence of Dreyfus
and the guilt of another party, Major Esterhazy. Unfortunately, the conditions of secrecy under which the information
was revealed to Scheurer-Kestner severely hampered him in
his efforts during the fall of 1897 to convince those in authority that the case of Captain Dreyfus should be reopened.

It was also at this time that a number of journalists, having learned of the probable irregularities in the court-martial,
began to take a public interest in the case. The leading
figure here was Georges Clemenceau. He had seen his political
career come to halt in 1893 as a result of the Panama scandal,
and had turned to journalism as a means of making a living.
Clemenceau was now associated with the recently founded
Aurore. Although *Aurore* became the most ardent and determined advocate of the cause of Dreyfus, the most prestigious
newspaper involved was *Figaro*. The preliminary results of
this first press campaign were disappointing. The vast majority of the public were solidly anti-Dreyfusard, their belief upheld by the great mass-circulation dailies, which hurled
invective at anyone so presumptuous as to believe that a court-

martial, or for that matter anyone in a uniform, could err. Even so, this press campaign did lead to Esterhazy being brought before a military tribunal. Since Dreyfus had already been convicted of the crime for which he was, in effect, being tried, Esterhazy was unanimously acquitted in January 1898.

Up until the time of the Esterhazy court-martial, the efforts of those doubting the guilt of Dreyfus had been directed at convincing the men in power, both the politicians and the soldiers, of the wisdom of reopening the case. Forswearing demogogic methods, the revisionists, as they came to be called, tried, in a rational, straightforward way, to show that there were a number of questionable points in the whole affair and that the original court-martial may have been marred by certain procedural irregularities, in itself adequate grounds for a review of the case. Before all such assertions the attitude of the military authorities was one of apparently serene certainty. In reply to an interpellation on the subject, the Minister of War, General Billot, declared that there had been nothing wrong with the 1894 court-martial and that in his "soul and conscience" he believed the verdict to have been just and Dreyfus guilty.[1] If there were any doubts lingering in the mind of such a person as Scheurer-Kestner, they were meant to be stilled by references to further conclusive documentary evidence that had come to light after the court-martial.[2]

Reassured by the responsible minister, the government saw no reason to reconsider what was, after all, *res judicata,* a closed case. As Jules Méline, President of the Council of Ministers, declared before the Chamber on December 4, 1897, "At this moment there is not and cannot be a Dreyfus case."[3] The evidence in the hands of the various members of the revisionist camp was too disconnected, too tenuous at that point to permit them to contradict this official view of the matter. Not only did the revisionists fail to make any impression on either

[1] M. Thomas, *L'affaire sans Dreyfus* (Paris: Fayard, 1961), p. 496.
[2] *Ibid.,* pp. 443-444.
[3] G. Chapman, *The Dreyfus Case* (London: R. Hart-Davis, 1955), p. 167.

the public or the government, but they found their efforts greeted with real hostility. *Figaro,* which published a number of letters written by Esterhazy filled with virulent comments on the French army and its chiefs, was made the object of a systematic campaign to persuade its readers to cancel their subscriptions. Citing *raison d'état* as its motive, *Figaro* quit the field.[4] Seemingly at a dead end in their efforts, the revisionists had their hopes revived and their campaign placed on an entirely new terrain by the audacious action of the novelist Émile Zola, who on January 13, 1898, two days after the acquittal of Esterhazy, published in *Aurore* his scathing open letter to the President of the Republic, *"J'accuse. . . ."*

Zola hoped that his polemic would create as great a scandal as possible, thereby obliging the government in one way or another to take official cognizance of the Dreyfus Affair. He savagely attacked all those who had been involved in the case since its origin, including General Mercier, Minister of War at the time of the arrest and the trial of Dreyfus, General de Boisdeffre, Chief of the General Staff, General Gonse, Assistant Chief of Staff, and General Billot. This represented a marked change from the heretofore prudent tactics of the revisionists and indicated how their campaign would henceforth have to be carried on. Reasonable and measured arguments having failed to shake the stubborn refusal of the military authorities to reconsider *res judicata,* other tactics became necessary.

The most outspoken and virulent of the polemicists were to be found in the socialist press. As Joseph Reinach, one of the leading Dreyfusards, sardonically noted, "Diatribes against capitalism had grown stale; those against the army . . . had all the savor of novelty."[5] These extremists soon ceased to concern themselves solely with the plight of Captain Dreyfus and began to attack first the French army and then "armies in

---

[4] J. Reinach, *Histoire de l'affaire Dreyfus* (7 vols; Paris: Revue Blanche, 1901–1911), Vol. III, pp. 157–158.

[5] *Ibid.,* Vol. III, p. 257.

general as institutions. . . ."[6] Among those who prided themselves on drawing from the Dreyfus Affair "arguments of a general order" was the former monarchist Urbain Gohier. His antimilitarism was so scurrilous that Clemenceau resigned from *Aurore* rather than appear on the same pages with him.[7] Starting in early 1898, this new phase of the Dreyfusard campaign quickly reached a high degree of violence.

Caught unawares by this sudden assault, the military reacted in a predictable way. As far as they were concerned, a court-martial made up of officers of honor and probity had by a unanimous verdict condemned Dreyfus. This in itself was sufficient evidence of his guilt. The categorical statements, emanating periodically from the chiefs of the army, as to the conclusive nature of the proofs against Dreyfus dispelled any possible passing doubt. Considering who were the men leading the Dreyfusard agitation, the military by their lights had plausible reasons to doubt their reliability and their disinterested motives. For one thing, they were all civilians, a sufficient reason in itself for them to be suspect in the eyes of a soldier. Then, too, Dreyfus was a Jew, and two of the early Dreyfusards had had connections with the more unsavory elements of "Jewish" finance. Clemenceau had been involved with Cornelius Herz, the villain of the still-recent Panama scandal and had lost his seat in the Chamber because of it, while Joseph Reinach was himself a Jew and the nephew of another prominent *Panamiste,* Baron Jacques Reinach, whom the blackmailing Herz had driven to suicide. The role of anti-Semitism in the case is exceedingly difficult to measure, but it was not a negligible factor. When Zola, with the publication of *"J'accuse . . . ,"* noisily joined the ranks of the Dreyfusards, nothing further was needed to convince the soldiers of the essential wrongheadedness of the revisionist cause. In 1892 Zola had published *Le débâcle,* a novel of the Franco-Prussian War, in which the French army was depicted in a

[6] Chapman, *op. cit.,* p. 3222.
[7] Reinach, *Dreyfus,* Vol. VI, pp. 68-70.

very unflattering way. He could hardly expect to receive a respectful hearing in military circles. The inflammatory tone of *"J'accuse . . ."* merely accentuated their distrust of him.

Though the soldiers could almost expect a Gohier, a Zola, a Reinach, or a Clemenceau to behave in irresponsible fashion, they were frankly bewildered when in the course of the year 1898 a growing number of people who came to call themselves "intellectuals" joined the ranks of the Dreyfusards. The fact that men of intelligence, occupying positions of great responsibility, authors, judges, university professors, were so quick to credit vague hearsay rumors about the innocence of Dreyfus, in the face of the solemn assertions of the most eminent chiefs of the army, was incomprehensible. Writing in *France militaire,* General Tricoche asked the "intellectuals" if, in taking this title, they presumed that they had a monopoly over the intelligence of the country.[8]

As the assault kept up through the spring and summer of 1898 and as increasingly disturbing indications began to appear that the Dreyfusard agitation might be grounded in fact, the more intelligent soldiers found themselves in a perplexing situation. The arguments of the revisionists could not easily be dismissed, yet their chiefs, evidently in a position to know more than anyone else about the details of the case, continued to affirm the guilt of the traitor. Unwilling to renounce their fundamental, instinctive trust in their fellow soldiers, the military had no choice but "to place themselves in the hands of their comrades and chiefs, who, be they judges, witnesses, Ministers, or Chiefs of Staff, have said again and again: 'For us Dreyfus is an abominable traitor.' "[9] Still, the revisionist campaign went relentlessly on, as the attitude of the army changed from one of confusion and bewilderment at this civilian meddling to a feeling of anger and exasperation.

The highest military authorities, including the Minister of

[8] Gen. Tricoche, "Les intellectuels," *France militaire* (hereafter cited as F.M.), February 22, 1898.

[9] Anon., "L'affaire Dreyfus," *F.M.,* September 9, 1898.

War and the Chief of the General Staff, had very sound reasons for not wishing the case of Captain Dreyfus to be reopened. They knew that the court-martial had indeed been
conducted in irregular fashion and that a tremendous scandal
would probably result if the matter were to be submitted to a
court of appeals, one that would be disastrous for their reputations and very harmful to the army. No matter what evidence
was produced by the revisionists and no matter how persuasive were their arguments, the chiefs of the army could not
voluntarily abandon their stand that the case was *res judicata.*

That Dreyfus was suspected in the first place of selling military secrets to the Germans was the consequence of some extremely sloppy detective work by the counterespionage bureau of the General Staff. Wrongly assuming that the author
of a certain piece of evidence, the famous *bordereau,* which
had been stolen from a wastebasket at the German Embassy,
could only be an officer assigned to the Ministry of War, the
counterespionage bureau, or, as it was called, the Statistical
Section, limited its investigations from the very beginning.
The thought that there was a traitor at work within the Ministry of War or, worse yet, the General Staff, was hardly a
pleasant one, and the Statistical Section was under considerable pressure to uncover him as quickly as possible. The investigation was thus conducted with precipitous haste. By the
time Dreyfus came under suspicion, because of a superficial
resemblance between his handwriting and that of the real
author of the *bordereau,* Major Esterhazy, everyone with any
knowledge of the case was so anxious for the traitor to be
found that this inconclusive evidence, backed by an extremely
tenuous series of deductions, was taken as definitive proof of
his guilt.

If anyone within the Ministry of War had to be a traitor,
people were relieved that it was Dreyfus. For one thing, he
was of a cold and unsympathetic character, unpopular with
both his comrades and his chiefs. He was also a Jew, the first

one ever to serve on the General Staff. Anti-Semitism was to be of considerable importance in the later evolution of the Affair, but at this point its effect was merely to accentuate the certainty of the officers involved in the investigation that the traitor had been found and to prevent Dreyfus from being given the benefit of the doubt.[10] The rapid apprehension of the traitor was a triumph for all concerned, but for none more than the Minister of War, General Mercier.

Mercier had a reputation as an intelligent, hard-working officer. A nominal Catholic, he was nevertheless considered to be rather liberal in his personal beliefs, and as long ago as the 1870's he had been noted as sympathetic to the Republic.[11] In appearance, he was a soldier to the core, tall, thin, and erect in carriage. Although Mercier was polite and endowed with no small amount of tact, underneath there was a kind of obstinacy that forcibly impressed many observers. General Millet, who served under him in the command of a division, noted that once an idea was set in his mind, "he could neither withdraw nor undo it." [12] In the estimation of Marcel Thomas, the author of a recent and probably the definitive study of the Affair, Mercier was obviously not a stupid man, but he allowed himself to be carried away by first impressions and then apparently made it "a point of honor never to seem to change his mind." [13] From the moment he first saw the available evidence against Dreyfus, Mercier was convinced of his guilt, and nothing was ever able to budge him.

Aside from a natural desire to protect the national interest, Mercier had another probable reason for wishing to see the traitor apprehended and convicted. Like many other generals suddenly elevated to the post of Minister of War, Mercier enjoyed being at the summit of the military hierarchy and would willingly have remained in office for as long as possible. Un-

---

[10] Chapman, *op. cit.,* pp. 64–66. Also Thomas, *op. cit.,* pp. 130–131.
[11] *Vide supra,* p. 149.
[12] Gen. Millet, unpublished memoirs, Vol. II, pp. 67–68.
[13] Thomas, *op. cit.,* p. 135.

fortunately, a number of ill-calculated statements and actions on his part had placed him in bad odor with his ministerial colleagues and with many in parliament.[14] Mercier sorely needed some spectacular exploit to reestablish his political situation. The discovery of treason at the Ministry of War and the speedy unmasking of the culprit could hardly have come at a more opportune time. Mercier was thus somewhat taken aback by the counsels of caution he received from certain of his fellow ministers, in particular Charles Dupuy, the premier, and Gabriel Hanotaux, the Minister of Foreign Affairs.

Unlike the soldiers privy to the affair, the men in the government were struck by how flimsy the evidence was against Dreyfus. Since the matter was one involving the German ambassador, or in any case one of his subordinates, they urged Mercier to be exceedingly discreet. This advice was echoed by at least one high-ranking officer, General Saussier, still the Military Governor of Paris and the designated commander of the main group of French armies in case of war, although he was now approaching the age of his retirement. Prudent and skeptical where Mercier was coldly determined, Saussier was of the opinion that the investigation should be dropped and Dreyfus sent to Indochina. There he could get himself decently killed.[15] Mercier was temperamentally incapable of heeding such advice. Fortified by his own certainty and that of his subordinates on the General Staff and confirmed in his views by the criminologist Bertillon, Mercier ordered that Dreyfus be arrested on October 15, 1894, and held in the strictest secrecy. One of the most promising young officers on the General Staff, Major du Paty de Clam, was assigned the task of building a presentable case against him. The only difficulty was that Dreyfus, despite the rigors of solitary confinement and the incessant questioning, refused to confess, while during the next two weeks the most thorough investigation failed to uncover any further evidence of his treasonable activities.

[14] Chapman, *op. cit.,* pp. 45–46.
[15] Thomas, *op. cit.,* pp. 133–138.

Mercier was now in a most perplexing situation. The only piece of positive evidence against Dreyfus was the similarity between his handwriting and that of the *bordereau,* and even here there was no unanimity among the experts consulted. With no more of a case than that against him, Dreyfus would in all likelihood be acquitted by any court-martial. For Mercier to be obliged to release Dreyfus now after having so patently disregarded the advice of his colleagues in the government would certainly lead to his imminent retirement as Minister of War. His subsequent expectations of some important command were not likely to receive much consideration from those in authority. On the other hand, if he released Dreyfus, he knew what he might expect at the hands of the anti-Semitic press, in the forefront of which stood *Libre Parole,* edited by the brilliant polemicist Édouard Drumont. Mercier had already, on a number of occasions, been the object of attacks by Drumont for his supposedly excessive solicitude toward a Jewish officer and for other acts as Minister of War.[16] While he contemplated these two equally distasteful alternatives, *Libre Parole* made up his mind for him.

In the November 1 edition of *Libre Parole,* banner headlines announced that Dreyfus had been arrested and was being held on suspicion of treason. Mercier seemed to have no alternative but to proceed with a court-martial, but as the month of November progressed without the prosecution being able to dredge up any more evidence, he grew increasingly distressed. One may imagine that this distress was not permitted to pass unnoticed by his subordinates at the Ministry of War. No doubt impressed by the sense of the anxiety of their chiefs, the Statistical Section endeavored to supply something more conclusive against Dreyfus. Under the direction of Colonel Sandherr, the head of the section, a number of documents that might possibly be understood as implicating Dreyfus were brought out of the files and, along with an "interpretive" commentary by du Paty, were given to Mercier.[17] This was the

[16] *Ibid.,* pp. 136, 146–147.
[17] *Ibid.,* pp. 158–168.

secret dossier that, unknown to the defense at the Dreyfus court-martial, was submitted to the military tribunal just before it was to render its verdict. As impressive as they might have seemed at first glance, the "proofs" in the dossier, some of them probably forgeries, would have been easily refuted by the defense, hence the necessity for the dossier not to be introduced in open court. The secret dossier contributed in no small way to the unanimous verdict against Dreyfus.

The communication of evidence to the judges without its having been seen by the defense constituted a flagrant irregularity in judicial procedure. If Mercier and his subordinates had any qualms about the legal or ethical implications of such an act, these were overruled by their certainty that Dreyfus was a traitor. What did a few legal technicalities matter when justice had been done? For those who had doubts on this point, the testimony of Major Henry of the Statistical Section was most reassuring. Henry, a promoted N.C.O. of peasant stock, who somehow seemed out of place in an organization devoted to the delicate work of counterespionage, played from the start a crucial role in the Dreyfus Affair. A man with a total loyalty to his superiors and a blind respect for discipline, Henry had in excess the virtues of an old N.C.O. in the French army. "Throughout the affair, his conduct, reprehensible as it may have been, was most often motivated by his desire not only to carry out orders that were no more than hints, but even to anticipate the wishes that he, rightly or wrongly, attributed to his chiefs." [18]

Sensing that the case for the prosecution against Dreyfus was not very strong and realizing that his superiors wanted and needed a conviction, Henry on his own initiative asked as a qualified member of the Statistical Section to be allowed to take the stand. "In his thirty years' service he had seen much of the peculiarities of military justice. It was no matter to him who was condemned, so long as someone was. He was unscrupulous and he was bold." [19] Henry swore that he had

[18] *Ibid.*, pp. 73-74.
[19] Chapman, *op. cit.*, p. 94.

learned from a trusted informer as long ago as February 1894 that there was a traitor in the Ministry of War and that it was Dreyfus. He refused to name his informant on grounds of military secrecy, stating bluntly that there were things in an officer's head "that his cap should not know." [20] The apparent conviction with which this rugged son of the French soil made his affirmation was calculated to impress the judges deeply. In effect, it was a confrontation between two officers, one of whom was a true Frenchman and the other a *métèque*. There could be little doubt as to which one of the two the court-martial was more likely to believe.

Once the conviction of Dreyfus had been obtained, all those most deeply involved had a mutual vested interest in his guilt. Under no circumstances could they permit the case to be re-opened, lest the tenuousness of the proofs against him be revealed, along with the irregularities in judicial procedure which had led to his being condemned. The task of defending the verdict of the court-martial fell mainly on the shoulders of Boisdeffre, the Chief of the General Staff. Within a month of the successful conclusion of the court-martial, which Mercier had hoped would reestablish his ministerial prestige, the Dupuy cabinet resigned. Mercier was not maintained in the new government of Alexandre Ribot. With his departure, Boisdeffre was the highest-ranking person at the Ministry of War who had been privy to the affair from its start.

Boisdeffre was the successor to the already legendary Miribel, having been his immediate subordinate on the General Staff and before that his Chief of Staff at the Sixth Army Corps. His brilliant career had also included service on three different occasions as aide-de-camp to General Chanzy, as well as the post of military attaché at Saint Petersburg during the latter's mission as Ambassador to Russia. With his tall, aristocratic figure, his worldly air, and the experience gained as protégé of two of the most eminent soldiers of his generation, Boisdeffre had been ideally suited to carry out the delicate ne-

[20] Thomas, *op. cit.,* pp. 174–175.

gotiations leading up to the 1892 military convention with Russia and eventually the alliance of 1894. Upon the sudden death of Miribel in September 1893, he had been made Chief of Staff, although he was still a relatively junior general. Reinach feels that the republicans, in their ignorance of military matters, let Boisdeffre assume "this awesome office . . . to the scandal of the real soldiers, who were aware of his incapacity, except for intrigue. . . ."[21] This is, no doubt, unduly harsh on Boisdeffre, but he did appear to lack certain attributes that one might have expected to find in so eminent a personage as the Chief of the General Staff, in particular force of character and industriousness.

An intelligent, cultivated man, Boisdeffre did not have Mercier's implacable fervor. He was as much committed as the former Minister of War to the thesis that the verdict of the court-martial was now beyond question; but, unlike Mercier, who never wavered in his serene, almost monomaniacal certainty that Dreyfus was a traitor, Boisdeffre craved further proofs. For him, at least, this certainty required an act of faith, and a difficult one. As a reopening of the case began to be inevitable, the two men reacted in opposite ways. Whereas Boisdeffre faltered at the prospect, the former Minister of War seemed in indomitable fashion to take on strength. By the time of the second court-martial in 1899, Boisdeffre was obviously a broken man, while Mercier, in complete control of himself, was practically able to direct the course of the trial.

The Dreyfus Affair would have been ended in 1895 with the incarceration of the supposed traitor, had it not been for the inconvenient discoveries of Lieutenant Colonel Picquart. Picquart was made chief of the Statistical Section in July 1895, succeeding Sandherr, who was forced to retire because of his badly deteriorating health. In the course of an investigation of the possibly treasonable activities of one Major Esterhazy, Picquart discovered that he was almost certainly the author of the *bordereau,* the one substantial piece of evidence against

[21] Reinach, *Dreyfus,* Vol. I, pp. 270–271.

Dreyfus. Further study revealed the inconsequential nature of the "proofs" in the secret dossier. Having reported his findings to his superiors, Gonse and Boisdeffre, Picquart was shocked to discover that he could not convince them of the evident fact that Dreyfus was innocent. Picquart believed that it was to the best interests of the army to take the initiative and to undo the judicial error before others found out the truth and obliged the army to act. Having no suspicion as to just how deeply committed was the General Staff to the guilt of Dreyfus, he could not understand why neither Boisdeffre nor Gonse responded to his explanation of who the real traitor was.

Though Picquart did not see the facts of the situation, Major Henry did. As the second-ranking officer in the Statistical Section, Henry was aware that Picquart now doubted that Dreyfus was guilty, and he knew that if his chief continued to pry into the Affair, it was very likely that irreparable damage would be done to what he believed to be the best interests of the Statistical Section and the General Staff, not to mention his own career and the reputations of Boisdeffre and Mercier. After a short conversation with Picquart in which Henry tried to explain to him as an experienced old soldier that one should not make trouble for one's superior officers, he saw that Picquart was in no way aware of this essential military truth. He, therefore, set about arranging the removal of this dangerous person from the Statistical Section.

Boisdeffre and Gonse were both coming to realize that Picquart represented a real peril to them by his presence at the Ministry of War and were seeking a convenient excuse to have him transferred far away from Paris at the earliest possible occasion. They were very receptive to the reports of Henry that Picquart was now neglecting his regular duties as chief of the Statistical Section in his single-minded obsession about the guilt of Esterhazy and the innocence of Dreyfus. General Billot, who had been made Minister of War in April 1896 and who was not yet aware just how important it was that the Dreyfus Affair not be reopened, was nevertheless reluctant to have so obviously fine an officer sent in quasi disgrace to Indochina or Algeria without more evidence of his incompetence.

In fact, when Picquart had first informed him of his well-grounded suspicion that Esterhazy was a traitor and that Dreyfus was innocent, Billot was willing to authorize him to follow this line of investigation further. Apparently, Boisdeffre was able to dissuade the Minister of War by hinting that the reputation of his old friend Saussier might inadvertently be compromised if one went too far into the Dreyfus Affair. In any case, with the great ceremonial visit of the Czar in the immediate offing, Billot did not want to raise an unnecessary scandal.[22]

In order to supply his obviously worried chiefs with the evidence they needed as to the incompetence of Picquart, Henry set to work to manufacture the conclusive proof, hitherto lacking, that Dreyfus was the traitor. Before he was finished, he had created a massive dossier of forged pieces. The keystone to the whole elaborate structure was a note suppoedly written in September 1896 by the Italian military attaché at Paris to his German colleague, in which Dreyfus was specifically named as having formerly been in contact with them.[23] This piece has come to be known as the *faux Henry*. In embarking on this series of forgeries, it appears fairly certain that Henry was acting on his own initiative, but Thomas is of the opinion that Gonse had told Henry that something had to be done about Picquart.[24] An old soldier as devoted to his superiors as was Henry hardly needed more explicit orders. On November 2, 1896, Henry showed the note, which had supposedly been obtained by the Statistical Section in the manner usual for such documents, to Gonse, who immediately passed it on to Boisdeffre. Boisdeffre took it to Billot, and the Minister of War needed no further convincing that Picquart had made a

[22] Thomas, *op. cit.*, pp. 302–303.
[23] *Ibid.*, pp. 333–335. This account of how Picquart came to be involved in the Dreyfus Affair is drawn primarily from Chapman, *op. cit.*, pp. 116–137.
[24] Thomas, *op. cit.*, pp. 330–332.

serious error in judgment. Billot agreed that he should be un-obtrusively eased out of the Statistical Section.

We may surmise that Billot was very much relieved when the *faux Henry,* ostensibly proving the guilt of Dreyfus, was shown to him. He may well have been aware of the relatively fragile nature of the original "proofs" concerning Dreyfus. The Minister of War was an astute enough person to recognize the scandal that would develop and the harm that would be done to the prestige of the army if it was later shown that the man on Devil's Island was innocent. At the same time, Billot was not necessarily the man to connive at so monstrous a thing as was implied in keeping Dreyfus in prison while the real traitor was still at liberty. Unlike the men of the General Staff, he had had until now no personal stake in the guilt of Dreyfus. The *faux Henry* thus rescued Billot from an unpleasant moral dilemma. Whatever critical faculties he may have possessed were certainly kept in rein as he examined this most reassuring piece of evidence that so conclusively established that Picquart had been mistaken about Dreyfus. Billot was probably not yet aware of the fact that by accepting the *faux Henry* he too was now committed to the official thesis of the General Staff concerning the inviolability of *res judicata.*

Thomas has convincingly shown that the other members of the Statistical Section were not the active accomplices of Henry in the drafting of this vital document. They were, nevertheless, probably aware of what he was doing. In any case, they all acted to keep Picquart, still their nominal chief, from learning about a piece whose authenticity he could easily have refuted. Gonse was personally involved in the conspiracy, and it is likely that Boisdeffre knew and approved of it.[25] With the *faux Henry,* the point of no return in the Dreyfus Affair had been passed.

From the moment in 1894 when the chief actors in the Affair had concluded that Dreyfus was the guilty party until the presentation of the *faux Henry* in October 1896, they had

[25] *Ibid.,* pp. 337–343.

almost inevitably been led to adopt a course of action which became progressively more irregular and then dishonorable. Now at last they were all to some degree implicated in an overtly criminal act. Henceforth, each effort made by Boisdeffre and his subordinates to extricate themselves from the dilemma they had created only mired them more deeply in a morass of misrepresentations, falsehoods, and forgeries. Before it was over, they were to find themselves in the absurd position of having to champion the real traitor, Esterhazy.

Their rationalization for committing the original error in judicial procedure lay in their certainty that Dreyfus was guilty. They believed, after all, that justice was being done. When Picquart demonstrated that, in fact, justice had not been done, the people most deeply involved could only, against all common sense, deny the validity of his evidence or finally argue that to reveal the truth now would be to destroy the confidence of the French people in their army, thereby seriously endangering the welfare of the country. Guilty or not, Dreyfus would have to remain on Devil's Island. Even if they were probably quite right in their contention that to reopen the case now would result in people becoming dubious about the army, the longer they persisted, the more terrible was to be the eventual reckoning.

As the revisionist campaign continued through the spring and summer of 1898, there began to be indications that the allegations of the Dreyfusards were founded on facts. In particular, the discovery of the *faux Henry,* followed by the suicide of its author, was a damaging blow to the army. With the legal bases for the defense of *res judicata* being undermined, the military had to take their stand on increasingly emotional grounds. Their most powerful argument here, one probably provoked by the more scurrilous attacks in the Dreyfusard press, was that the "honor of the army" had now become involved. Whether Dreyfus was guilty or not was now immaterial. General du Barail, former Minister of War, spoke for the soldiers when he declared that a misfortune befalling a single individual, no matter how poignant, could not be compared with "the national calamity which would result from a slur cast on the honor of the army." [26]

Cooler heads among the officer corps recognized the dangers of taking so emotional a stand,[27] but the great majority seemed instinctively to close ranks at this slogan. A future Minister of War, Adolphe Messimy, at the time a captain in the Chasseurs Alpins, having been converted to a revisionist view by the suicide of Henry and having been unable to convince any of his comrades, found it expedient to quit the army, so great was the enmity in his regiment against any soldier unwilling to accept the majority view.[28]

By the time Henry committed suicide, the officer corps had no choice but to believe in such phantoms as his "patriotic forgery," intended to be a substitute for another document that irrefutably proved Dreyfus guilty but whose revelation would have resulted in a war between France and Germany.[29] Any more rational hypothesis led to what must be for an officer a most distasteful conclusion. If the chiefs of the army, the men who would in time of war be responsible for the fate of the nation, could be so wrongheaded in the face of conclusive evidence—and the suicide of Henry would appear to be conclusive evidence—France was most certainly in a perilous situation. If they were not merely stupid but also dishonorable, sending an innocent man to Devil's Island and then keeping him there in order to cover up their own mistakes, or perhaps even to disguise the guilt of someone else, then service in an army where such men occupied the highest posts was indeed a hollow mockery. Faced with the potential implications of the

---

[26] Quoted in Reinach, *Dreyfus,* Vol. IV, p. 423.

[27] See F.G., "La vérité et ses obligations," *F.M.,* December 13, 1898.

[28] A. Messimy, *Mes souvenirs* (Paris: Plon, 1937), pp. 13–14.

[29] This particular thesis, published in a royalist newspaper, was originated by Charles Maurras and represented his first real success in the field of polemical journalism.

innocence of Dreyfus, the officer corps as a whole preferred not even to admit the possibility.

Some officers could not, of course, so easily reject the demands of reason and common sense. By the end of 1898 these men were in an agonizing position. Louis Le Gall, Director of the Personal Staff of Félix Faure, President of the Republic, has depicted the intellectual and spiritual crisis that many of these officers underwent. One officer, General Hagron, also a member of Faure's personal staff, was ready at one moment to admit the necessity of reopening the case, whatever the consequences, only to reverse himself a few hours later after discussing the subject with a more intransigent comrade. He would end by cursing the revisionists and declaring that Dreyfus was being used systematically to weaken the army and endanger the country.[30] Another military member of the staff of the Élysée, General Legrand-Girarde, in the privacy of his diary, deplored the outrageous tactics of the Dreyfusards but also bitterly condemned the underhanded actions of the General Staff.[31]

Angered and confused as they were by the seemingly gratuitous attacks of the Dreyfusard press, they were equally annoyed at the inability or the unwillingness of the government to take some action against the worst offenders. Although the Chamber of Deputies voted a motion censuring the perpetrators of the "odious campaign undertaken to disturb the public conscience," [32] it was not translated into judicial action against any of the leading Dreyfusard journalists. Finally when, in early 1899, the government did move to prosecute Urbain Gohier on the charge of defaming the army, he was acquitted. During the trial a large number of witnesses testified to the brutality of individual officers and N.C.O.'s

---

[30] Ch. Braibant, *Félix Faure à l'Élysée: Souvenirs de Louis Le Gall* (Paris: Hachette, 1963), pp. 181–183.

[31] Gen. Legrand-Girarde, *Un quart de siècle au service de la France* (Paris: Presses Littéraires de France, 1954), pp. 133, 170, 198.

[32] Chapman, *op. cit.*, pp. 169–170.

they had known. For the military it was sadly indicative of the nation's new attitude toward the army that such stories were sufficient to convince the jury that there was a modicum of truth in the allegations of Gohier.[33]

In the unwillingness of the government to take more vigorous measures in defense of the army, the military tended to see a latent fear of the soldier, supposedly present in the hearts of all republican politicians. The military were pleased when, in November 1898, the Chamber voted a motion declaring its confidence in the army, "faithful observer of the laws of the Republic," and inviting the government to put an end to the "campaign of insults against the army"; but they were wounded that the same motion also reaffirmed the "supremacy of civilian authority," and discouraged that it was passed by a majority of only fifty. The military saw no need to reaffirm civilian authority since no one in the army had ever questioned it. The real question in their minds was whether the politicians would know, when the time came, how to use, "bravely and nobly, the irreproachable sword offered to them."[34]

At no time during the Dreyfus Affair did the officer corps as a group or in any numerically significant minority contemplate an overt act against the government. For all their exasperation at the Republic, indirectly reinforced perhaps by their anger at their chiefs, the soldiers did no more than grumble menacingly. They might assure certain members of the antirepublican opposition, self-appointed defenders of the army, that "their swords trembled and sought only to be drawn from their scabbards, but in the end they kept them sheathed."[35] Jaurès could proclaim in the Chamber that the Republic had never run so great a danger as it did now and that a military *coup d'état* was now a distinct possibility.[36]

[33] "L'armée et le jury," *F.M.*, March 18, 1899.

[34] Col. X, "L'armée," *La nouvelle revue*, November 15, 1898, p. 358.

[35] Reinach, *Dreyfus*, Vol. IV, p. 306.

[36] Chapman, *op. cit.*, p. 199.

On precisely what evidence he based this warning, it is difficult to know.

Had there been a general of the Boulanger stamp ready to make a spectacular gesture in defense of the honor of the army, some soldiers might possibly have rallied behind him. No such person existed in 1898 or 1899. At least one observer, much more familiar than Jaurès with the state of mind of the army, Édouard Drumont, had no illusions about finding a general to lead an assault on the regime.[37] The military were naturally gratified that some elements within the nation still showered them with adulation and accepted their thesis that the Affair was *res judicata*. "As isolated as monks from the main currents of civilian society the generals did not know enough to decline the help of political charlatans who hoped to use them for their own purposes." [38]

The different groups in the antirepublican political spectrum, still in disarray after the collapse of Boulangism, all followed the evolution of the Affair with great interest. Each group nursed a sanguine hope that it might yet be able to profit from the discontent of the military for the promotion of its particular cause. The police reports of the period are filled with rumors to the effect that a certain general or generals met in a royalist salon where "they talked seriously about a *coup d'état*" [39] or that all the nationalist and anti-Semitic forces were coalescing into a common front but that they would attempt a coup only "after being assured of the support of various high-ranking officers." [40] Almost every general of any importance was mentioned somewhere in a police report as being considered to be heart and soul in some conspiracy or other.

More indicative of the actual sentiments of the leading men

[37] R. Girardet, *La société militaire dans la France contemporaine, 1815–1939* (Paris: Plon, 1953), p. 253.

[38] Chapman, *op. cit.*, pp. 199–200.

[39] Archives, Préfecture de la Police de Paris (B/a 1310, Doss. 72136), "Zurlinden," Report of February 25, 1899.

[40] Archives Nationales, "Police générale: Surveillance des nationalistes" (F7.12458), Report of June 3, 1899.

in the army was a series of reports concerning the activities of the Duc d'Orléans. Kept under close surveillance even though he was in exile, the Orleanist pretender frequently made extended visits to Brussels, where he would receive royalist delegations from Paris and northern France. According to one report, he had made a number of discreet overtures to certain generals whom he believed to be sympathetic to his aspirations. The results were disillusioning. "He did not find a single high-ranking officer who was willing to forswear his duty in order to promote a restoration."[41] This is corroborated by another report, where the Duc d'Orléans was quoted as saying, with regard to recent events in Spain and the possibility of his cousin the Carlist pretender using the army for his own political ends, "Tell my cousin not to trust generals. . . . Explain it to him, emphasize it, that I give him this advice from experience, not to trust generals."[42] Whether or not there was a serious military conspiracy during the Dreyfus Affair, no traces of it have been found in contemporary police reports, nor was the government ever led to prosecute any soldiers for crimes against the state. The one attempt to involve the army in an overt attack against the regime was more a farce than a real source of danger to the Republic. Its instigator was Paul Déroulède, one of the founders of the League of Patriots and a perennial advocate of *la Revanche*.

Déroulède was convinced that vigorous action, taken at the right psychological moment, would crystallize all the latent disgust felt by the French people for the Republic. The result would be a spontaneous uprising, which he would lead to the Élysée or the Palais Bourbon, and the French nation would at last have a regime worthy of its aspirations. But he needed a soldier, or everything would collapse. "His whole system, which he had long proclaimed, was based on an alliance of the people with the army."[43] He had been deprived of one such

---

[41] Arch. Nat., "Police générale: Agissements royalistes" (F7.12434), Report of December 9, 1898.

[42] *Ibid.* (F7.12439), Report of February 27, 1899.

[43] Reinach, *Dreyfus,* Vol. IV, p. 574.

opportunity on the night of January 27, 1889, when Boulanger in the wake of his triumph ·in the Paris by-election had been unwilling to use illegal means to obtain power. Déroulède saw the funeral of Félix Faure, who had died suddenly on February 16, 1899, under somewhat compromising circumstances, as providing another opportunity.

Faure had been very popular with the army, "which he had literally conquered by the numerous instances of his sympathy and his interest." [44] One possible consequence of this fondness for the army was that Faure was reputed to be against reopening the Affair, although Le Gall argues that the President was restrained from taking a more forceful and open stand in favor of revision by his constitutional scruples. [45] His successor as President of the Republic, Émile Loubet, was known to favor reopening the case. Counting on the disgruntlement of the military at the election of a revisionist and on the fervent nationalism of the people of Paris, Déroulède believed that the funeral, bringing together crowds of onlookers, as well as a large number of troops and high-ranking generals, would provide the vital elements for his undertaking. Following some dramatic gesture from him, these would coalesce in an irresistible surge toward the Élysée, and France would be saved.

Just how much prior planning went into the projected *coup d'état* is a matter of conjecture. It would appear from the police reports of the period that it was common knowledge in nationalist and antirepublican circles that Déroulède was up to something, but as to precisely what it was, no one seemed to be sure. He may well have made discreet overtures to General de Pellieux, who was to lead a detachment of troops in the funeral procession. [46] According to Paul-Boncour, then just beginning his political career, several members of parliament and a number of generals met at the home of a former magistrate named Grosjean a few days before the funeral to organ-

---

[44] "Le Président et l'armée," *F.M.*, February 21, 1899.

[45] Braibant, *op. cit.*, pp. 222–223, 287–288.

[46] Chapman, *op. cit.*, p. 255.

ize a provisional government in case Déroulède succeeded. Since they never went beyond these rather conjectural discussions, the government did not feel obliged to prosecute.[47]

In the afternoon of February 23, the day of the funeral, Déroulède had his followers drawn up at Place de la Nation, where the troops would have to pass on their way back to their barracks from the interment. For some reason Pellieux, whom Déroulède expected to see at the head of the troops, was not there. Undaunted and apparently believing that any general would do, he ran out of the crowd and grabbed the bridle of the horse being ridden by General Roget, although he was completely unknown to Déroulède. Crying "Follow us, General, for the sake of France," Déroulède tried to lead him and his troops in the direction of the center of Paris. Completely flabbergasted that this hysterical man wanted to make a Bonaparte of him, Roget spurred his horse and dragged Déroulède, still holding the bridle, and a small band of his followers into the courtyard of the barracks. He then informed the authorities. They were at first a little unwilling to arrest a man who was a deputy to the Chamber, but they finally took Déroulède into custody. He wished to be charged with trying to overthrow the Republic, but the government arrested him on the demeaning grounds that he had trespassed on military property and had refused to leave.[48]

The Army versus the Republic

The Dreyfus Affair was an event of pivotal importance in the history of the relations between the army and the state. It also exercised a profound influence on the political evolution of the Republic and on the development of the French public spirit.[49] Before it was over, the Affair had led to a polarization

[47] J. Paul-Boncour, *Entre deux guerres* (Paris: Plon, 1945), Vol. I, pp. 110-111.

[48] Chapman, *op. cit.*, pp. 255-257.

[49] F. Goguel, *La politique des partis sous la troisième République* (3rd ed.; Paris: Éditions du Seuil, 1958), p. 86.

of all the active political elements in France: those who believed in the Republic as it had evolved since 1871 against
those who wished to see it replaced by a more conservative or
authoritarian regime. Although the great majority of republicans eventually came to understand the necessity of reopening
the case, it still must be remembered how long they prudently
avoided taking any stand on the issue. Throughout the evolution of the Affair, republican politicians played a highly opportunistic game, aiming first at keeping the issue out of the
political arena and then, once that became impossible, endeavoring to minimize the damage it might do to their
partisan interests. In the process, the Affair was unnecessarily
prolonged and the French public needlessly subjected to an
abrasive clash of ideologies.

Part of the reason for this opportunistic course of action can
be found in the traditional attitude of most Frenchmen toward the army. The typical civilian automatically assumed
honor to be the wellspring of a soldier's existence. Even if
there were perhaps a few irregularities in the conduct of the
Dreyfus court-martial, it did not occur to most people, politicians included, that there were high-ranking officers dishonorable enough to keep a man on Devil's Island when there
was some question as to his guilt. The chief reason, however,
why the leading political figures of the period would try to
avoid this potentially dangerous and extremely complex matter lay in the recent evolution of the Republic.

Since the real founding of the regime in 1875, the dominant
faction had been the great Republican Party. A loosely organized, amorphous body, it appeared to function as a unit only
in times of peril for the Republic or under certain electoral
conditions. This party could roughly be divided into two
wings, the Moderates, or Opportunists, on one side and the
Radicals on the other. The Moderates, the stronger of the two
wings, would willingly have governed without the support of
the Radicals and the compromises in policy this entailed, but
the strength of the antirepublican minority in parliament

made this impossible throughout most of the 1880's. But with the ludicrous failure of the Boulangist movement discrediting many of this last group, followed by the directives of Leo XIII in the early 1890's that Catholics forswear their traditional but futile monarchist ideals and rally to the Republic, it seemed as if the goal of the Moderates might yet be achieved. In the elections of 1893 a large number of Catholics, heeding the wishes of the Holy Father, deserted the monarchist camp and supported Moderate candidates. The Moderates were returned 311 strong, compared to 140 Radicals, while the old monarchist parties barely won 60 seats.[50] The Casimir-Périer and Charles Dupuy governments of November 1893 and May 1894 both excluded the Radicals, as did also the Méline government of April 1896. This particular cabinet was to last twenty-six months, longer than any since the founding of the regime.

Between the Moderates and the Catholic *ralliés,* as they were called, there was a basic similarity of outlook with regard to social and fiscal problems. In the hopes of founding a relatively homogeneous parliamentary coalition, the Moderates were willing to let the clerical issue rest. Méline specifically condemned anticlericalism as a fraudulent policy, by which the Radicals sought to mislead "the hunger of the electors." [51] A cabinet based on such a bloc of legislators would be able to govern in accordance with the sound conservative principles that, socially at least, probably represented the real wishes of the French people. Méline considered it "a great victory for the Republic" to have won to his policy "a large number of conservatives, until now allied with the revolutionary parties . . . against the regime. . . ." [52]

Since the policy of the Méline government was one of union of all forces of social conservatism, based on a general identity of economic interests "with no doctrinal questions

---

[50] *Ibid.,* pp. 71–72.
[51] *Ibid.,* p. 75.
[52] Braibant, *op. cit.,* p. 122.

raised or answered," [53] any matter of principle or ideology threatened to upset his majority. Herein lay the danger of the Dreyfus Affair. It touched too many sensitive points, especially among the Catholics, for any Moderate politician to wish to approach it head on. For one thing it involved a Jew, and the government did not wish to alienate "those Catholics who had been affected by the anti-Semitic campaigns of Drumont." [54] It also involved the military in an era when the soldier was idolized and the republican politician merely tolerated.[55] The French public was not likely to react very favorably if the government, in making trouble over a mere procedural irregularity, gave the appearance of doubting the word of the most eminent military chiefs. More to the point, by making any move that could be interpreted as an attack on the army, the government would also estrange the same Catholic elements it was trying to placate, thereby endangering its own existence.

For a Catholic of strongly conservative beliefs, the army was about the only career left wherein he might serve the state. As Girardet has pointed out:

The army alone . . . was still protected, had escaped more or less completely all attempts at "republicanization" and would continue to escape them, until the beginning of the twentieth century, thus continuing to provide an official outlet for the traditionalist families that was that much more precious, because all the others were becoming more and more hermetically sealed.[56]

Access to the civil service, the diplomatic corps, and the magistrature had been made systematically more difficult for them. If the army seemed to contemporary observers to be a stronghold of monarchist or Catholic sentiment, there were solid reasons for it.

From a political point of view, therefore, the Dreyfus Affair

[53] D. Brogan, *The Development of Modern France* (London: Hamish Hamilton, 1940), pp. 336–337.

[54] Goguel, *op. cit.*, p. 89.

[55] Brogan, *op. cit.*, p. 310.

[56] Girardet, *op. cit.*, p. 199.

was for Méline a most inopportune matter. Relying on the assurances of his Minister of War, General Billot, he found it prudent to accept the sanctity of *res judicata*. In reality, until the discovery of the *faux Henry* provided the "new fact" required by law for the reopening of a case, the evidence in the hands of the Dreyfusards was not strong enough to make any other course of action imperative. In declaring before parliament that there was no Dreyfus Affair, Méline was stating what was at the time a legal truth. To ignore the Affair was for him the judicious thing to do.

Méline would have been in a serious dilemma if the cause of Captain Dreyfus had been really popular in the country, but it manifestly was not, at least up until the very end. The comparative figures for the circulation of the Dreyfusard and anti-Dreyfusard papers indicate the degree to which the revisionists were in a small minority. Except for the Socialist papers, only *Aurore* was wholeheartedly committed to the Dreyfusard cause, *Figaro* having discreetly quit the field. Against *Aurore,* for which the 200,000 copies sold on the day *"J'accuse . . ."* appeared were an exception, were massed *Libre Parole,* with a circulation of 500,000, *Petit Journal,* whose 1,500,000 made it the most widely read Parisian daily, along with numerous others, of which *Intransigeant, Gaulois, Petit Parisien, Éclair,* and *Echo de Paris* were the most important. This does not take into account the tremendous circulation of the different publications of the Assumptionist fathers, both in Paris and in the provinces. *La Croix,* published daily in Paris, was the most important of these.[57] In general, the provincial press was either anti-Dreyfusard or studiedly neutral. The prestigious organ of French Radicalism, *Dépêche de Toulouse,* maintained a prudent reserve about the Affair, declaring as late as February 1899 that the facts were still too obscure to permit it to take a stand.[58] There was not the slightest hint of

[57] P. Miquel, *L'affaire Dreyfus* (Paris: Presses Universitaires de France, 1959), p. 52.
[58] *Ibid.,* p. 53.

any real ground swell of opinion in favor of Dreyfus that might have forced Méline to desert his discreetly noncommittal position and thus endanger the delicate political operation in which the Moderates were engaged.

The polarization of public opinion began to take place only as it became apparent that a reopening of the case was probable. Until the discovery of the *faux Henry,* responsibility for the agitation in the press had lain with the Dreyfusards, desperately endeavoring to keep the Affair alive and before the public eye. Now the initiative passed to the anti-Dreyfusards.

Until then they had defended the *res judicata,* and the revisionists had attacked it. Now the situation was reversed. The latter group would now have to bear the blows, and it would be the Nationalists who would launch the greatest campaign of opinion of the Affair, mobilizing all their forces, using the most brutal methods and the most subtle, in order first to prevent a reopening of the case and then later rehabilitation.[59]

In the face of the extremely violent campaign undertaken by the Nationalists and the other anti-Dreyfusards against a review of the case, the Moderates saw that their alliance with the moderate conservatives, in defense of the social *status quo,* was now being superseded by the need for a renewed understanding with the Radicals in defense of the regime. Yet it was not until June 1899 and the formation of the Waldeck-Rousseau government that the Moderates made their decision final. Here the precipitant was the great Nationalist demonstration of June 4 at Auteuil, during which a young royalist aristocrat came up to Loubet and struck him over the hat with his cane. Dupuy, who had been premier since the previous November, was taxed with having made insufficient security arrangements, and his government fell a week later. The Auteuil incident permitted the politicians to raise the cry that the Republic was in danger, and it was on this basis that the Waldeck-

[59] *Ibid.,* p. 77.

Rousseau government was finally formed, some two weeks after the fall of Dupuy.

That the Republic was never menaced by anything more dangerous than the opportunism of its leading politicians, their confusion, and their inability to act decisively would appear to be evident. Nevertheless, the myth of the "Republic in danger" was sufficiently strong to lead to the formation of a government whose parliamentary backing stretched all the way from the Moderates in the center to the Socialists on the extreme left. For the first time there was a government all of whose supporters recognized the necessity of a revision of the case. This meant that the government had taken its stand against the official thesis of the military, that the honor of the army did not permit the verdict of the 1894 court-martial to be questioned. The army thus found itself supported by a coalition of all the antirepublican forces in France and opposed by the government. Herein lay the larger tragedy of the Dreyfus Affair.

Once the army had been an institution considered to be above faction. By equating national security and the honor of the army with the need to cover up their own mistaken and even criminal actions, the highest military authorities sought to make of *res judicata* an impregnable fortress. The rest of the army and a large sector of the French public were, either through a sense of hierarchical obedience or out of a natural sympathy for the soldiers, committed to the defense of this ultimately untenable point of view. Before the case could be reopened, there would have to be a public debate of unprecedented violence centering on the army, and it would be dragged off the pedestal it had occupied above the sordid strife of party. In the process, the soldiers found themselves becoming alienated from the regime, while the fears of republican politicians as to the dangers inherent in a strong military establishment, more or less stilled since 1877, were reawakened.

As a reopening of the case of Captain Dreyfus became inevitable and the government was forced to take sides against the army, enormous strains were placed on the structure of the high command as it had evolved during the past quarter of a century. This was evident in the situations of both the Minister of War and the Chief of the General Staff. By the 1890 decree, the latter personage was meant to enjoy a degree of relative stability compensating for the unavoidable instability in the office of Minister of War, but in the two years following the resignation of Boisdeffre, three different men served at the head of the General Staff. Only in 1900 with the nomination of General Pendezec to the post was some measure of permanence restored. As for the Ministry of War, it was occupied by five different men between the fall of the Méline cabinet in June 1898 and the formation of the Waldeck-Rousseau government one year later. Only one of these men did not quit the post either in disagreement with the policy of the government of which he was a member or in the wake of an attack in parliament.

In contrast to what was to come, General Billot, Minister of War in the Méline cabinet, enjoyed real permanence, remaining in office for the two full years that the government lasted. In many ways, Billot was ideally suited for the job. By the time he took office, he was the senior general in the French army, having been promoted to divisionary rank as long before as 1878. Unlike most other generals, Billot, a life Senator, was thoroughly at home in the parliamentary milieu, being endowed with real oratorical ability and a fine sense of political tact. To these gifts were added a soldierly figure, even if he was getting a bit portly, and enough of a military reputation so that he could act as more than the nominal chief of the French army.[60] Billot had the misfortune to hold the office of Minister of War at a moment when a solution to the problems created by the Dreyfus Affair required more than his merely political qualities. He was "too intelligent not to admit in his heart of hearts that Picquart was right, but not intelligent enough to take up the cause offered to him, whatever the

[60] "Chronique française," *Revue militaire suisse,* June 1898, p. 45. See also *ibid.,* July 1898, p. 417.

cost." [61] With a man of moral courage and force of character as Minister of War, the whole unfortunate business might have been resolved before the honor of the army was involved. Boisdeffre, Mercier, and a few others would have been discredited, but the army itself would not have been implicated. As it was, by his ability to evade and temporize, Billot contributed in no small way to prolonging the Affair and to making the ultimate debacle that much more terrible.

Billot left the Ministry of War with the fall of the Méline government. His successor in the Brisson cabinet of June 1898 was the rising republican politician Godefroy Cavaignac, who had already served a six-month term in the post two years before. As the son of the victorious general in the Bloody June Days of 1848, Cavaignac was the bearer of an illustrious republican name. Taught from childhood to look upon himself as the "future Cromwell of the Republic, the reincarnation of the purest pures of 1793," [62] he represented that brand of Radical virtue embodied in an advocacy of the income tax. Cavaignac was profoundly ambitious, probably aiming at the Presidency of the Republic. A considerable step in that direction would be taken if he was able to resolve the Dreyfus Affair once and for all, by conclusively demonstrating the guilt of the traitor and by moving decisively to stop the agitation in the Dreyfusard press and to expose the machinations of the "Jewish syndicate" that was behind it all. [63] He abhorred the continual disorder being created by the Dreyfusards, and with a few bold, vigorous moves he sought to end it once and for all. Knowing nothing of the seamier underside of the Affair, he could not realize that such a tactic would lead him straight to disaster.

In answer to all public questions about the guilt of Dreyfus, Billot and his predecessors had always referred prudently to the irrefutable but necessarily secret proofs that existed. Cavaignac, incapable of appreciating the reason for so timid a

[61] Reinach, *Dreyfus*, Vol. II, p. 335.
[62] Chapman, *op. cit.*, pp. 210–211.
[63] Thomas, *op. cit.*, p. 513.

policy, boldly read the *faux Henry* before the whole Chamber on July 7, 1898. His discourse received a spontaneous standing ovation and was voted the honors of *affichage*. Meanwhile, Cavaignac had instructed one of his subordinates, Captain Cuignet, to make a detailed inquiry into the whole Dreyfus Affair, to reconstruct the case against Dreyfus from the ground up. In the course of this investigation, Cuignet made the disconcerting discovery that the *faux Henry* was indeed a forgery. On the following day, August 14, 1898, the letter was laid before Cavaignac, who, in Chapman's words, "suffered the exquisite horror of seeing that the document which was placarded outside every one of the thirty-five thousand Mairies, and which he had guaranteed, was false." [64]

The revelation of the *faux Henry* resulted in the resignation of Boisdeffre as Chief of Staff and the suicide of Henry. It did not convince Cavaignac that Dreyfus had been wrongly condemned or that there were now grounds for reopening the case. Arguing that the forgery had been committed long after Dreyfus had been convicted, Cavaignac felt that it had no bearing on the verdict of the original court-martial. When someone declared that a revision of the Affair was now inevitable, Cavaignac replied, "Less than ever." [65] Unable to convince Cavaignac that he should now move for a judicial review of the case, Brisson was obliged to request his resignation.

An official review of the Affair could hardly be avoided, but it was certain to be badly received by the army and an important sector of public opinion. Under the circumstances, the government believed that it should be openly advocated by the Minister of War and that "only a soldier could undertake the task without stirring up trouble in the army." [66] Brisson turned first to General Saussier as the most likely candidate. Some seventy years of age and approaching the date of his re-

[64] Chapman, *op. cit.*, p. 221.

[65] Thomas, *op. cit.*, pp. 520–522.

[66] Chapman, *op. cit.*, p. 230.

tirement, Saussier had no stomach for the coming fight. He declined to accept the portfolio offered to him.

The refusal of Saussier at this crucial juncture was unfortunate. He, more than anyone else, had the authority and the prestige to bring the army to a realization of the necessity for reopening the Affair. Having been from the start dubious about the guilt of Dreyfus, he had maintained a detached attitude toward the whole case and was in no way implicated in any of the machinations of the General Staff. More than that, the Republic had bestowed numerous honors and dignities upon him over his long career. In the words of one author, Saussier was the *"enfant gâté"* of the regime.[67] Whatever it might have cost him in terms of attacks in the nationalist press, he owed this one last service to the army and to the state. Here again is to be seen the lack of moral courage so often evidenced by the French generals during the course of the Affair. As far as can be surmised, Saussier's real reason for refusing the post was a simple one. Like so many other figures of the period, he was profoundly afraid of the vitriolic pen of Drumont, and on particularly good grounds. His former aide-de-camp, Maurice Weil, was Jewish and a man with a somewhat tarnished past. Saussier, it was reported, kept this dubious and compromising personage in his entourage primarily because of a romantic interest in his wife. Needless to say, Drumont and his cohorts would have been able to make spectacular journalistic capital out of these assorted bits of scandal.

Following the refusal of Saussier, Brisson, on the advice of the President of the Republic, turned to General Zurlinden, Military Governor of Paris. Along with many of the more clearheaded soldiers, Zurlinden appears to have recognized the necessity of submitting the case to the Court of Appeals, in the aftermath of Henry's suicide. According to both Le Gall and Brisson, the new Minister of War was an avowed partisan of

[67] Braibant, *op. cit.,* p. 49.

revision at the moment of his entering the government.[68] Nevertheless, Zurlinden felt duty bound to examine the Dreyfus dossier for himself, and naturally enough he turned to the men in the Ministry of War who were the experts on the subject. Within two weeks they had convinced him that there were still inadequate grounds for reopening the case.[69] Zurlinden believed that the *faux Henry* did not indicate that Dreyfus was innocent, and he noted that in this view he was sustained by the Court of Appeals, which later did not cite it in its verdict.[70] He resigned on September 17, and Brisson had to find another general.

The successor to Zurlinden was General Chanoine. Chanoine does not appear to have been held in very high esteem by his comrades. Legrand-Girarde considered him to be "a man of no character who has sought to become Minister of War by all possible means. . . ."[71] A rather mediocre person, he had on several occasions been considered for the command of an army corps but had never made it.[72] Now he was suddenly made chief of the army, probably because no other general would accept the post under the present circumstances. Although he had close connections with the Radical Party and had declared himself to be "the fiercest advocate" of revision,[73] Chanoine was, within a few weeks, to succumb to the atmosphere of the Ministry of War and the persuasive arguments of his fellow officers. On October 25, during an interpellation by Déroulède relative to the Affair, Chanoine suddenly rushed to the tribune to announce that his view of the guilt of Dreyfus was the same as that of his predecessors and that he, therefore, was returning to the representatives of the

[68] *Ibid.*, pp. 161–162. Also H. Brisson, *Souvenirs* (Paris: Cornély, 1908), pp. 84–85.

[69] Chapman, *op. cit.*, pp. 230–231.

[70] Gen. Zurlinden, *Mes souvenirs depuis la guerre* (Paris: Perrin, 1913), pp. 185–187.

[71] Legrand-Girarde, *op. cit.*, p. 186.

[72] "Chronique française," *Revue militaire suisse*, October 1898, p. 631.

[73] Braibant, *op. cit.*, p. 171.

nation the sacred trust that had been confided to him, "the interests and the honor of the army." [74] He thereupon resigned his portfolio. Chanoine had given his ministerial colleagues no hint of his change of mind, and the government, already in a shaky situation through Brisson's lack of forceful leadership and the successive resignations of Cavaignac and Zurlinden, fell as a result.

Charles Dupuy, formerly premier at the time of the 1894 court-martial, was named to succeed Brisson. The most difficult post to fill in the new cabinet was that of Minister of War. Relations between the army and the Republic were becoming so strained that it was all but impossible to find a general willing to enter a government consisting of men ready to attack the "honor of the army," while the politicians, after the perfidy of Chanoine, were dubious about any other general. What was required was a civilian minister, familiar with military matters and possessing enough authority to be able to impose his wishes on the chiefs of the army, but also a man who "offered every guarantee of impartiality to the supporters of revision. . . ." [75] Only one man, Freycinet, had this combination of qualities.

Vaguely implicated in certain aspects of the great Panama scandal, Freycinet had gone into temporary political eclipse, although he still retained his seat in the Senate. For him as for another politician compromised by Panama, Clemenceau, the Dreyfus Affair offered a second chance. [76] Freycinet had no particularly strong beliefs about the rights and wrongs of the case. He was of the opinion that it was possible to arrive at "a logical and legal solution to the Dreyfus Affair, and as a corollary, that once solved it could be forgotten." [77] He recog-

---

[74] *Journal Officiel de la Chambre des Députés: Débats* (1898), p. 2110.

[75] Braibant, *op. cit.,* p. 202.

[76] E. Katzenbach, "Charles Louis de Saulces de Freycinet and the Army of Metropolitan France" (unpublished Ph.D. dissertation, Princeton University, 1953), p. 468.

[77] *Ibid.,* pp. 471–472.

nized that if it was not settled with dispatch, the uproar and agitation that it was ⸢creating would seriously damage the army, as always the ultimate guarantor of France's place in Europe and of her national existence. Whether Dreyfus was guilty or not was of comparatively minor importance. That was for the courts to decide. His mission was to take things firmly in hand at the Ministry of War and, in unobtrusive fashion, to reestablish the authority of the government over the army, while at the same time doing his utmost to soothe the ruffled feelings of the military. Thus Freycinet did not block the court-martial of Picquart, although he must have realized that it was primarily a vendetta undertaken by the military authorities in which he was acquiescing.[78] He also persuaded the government to begin legal action against Urbain Gohier for his violent attacks on the army.[79]

Had the atmosphere been a little calmer, Freycinet might have succeeded in his endeavor. Once the case was submitted to the Court of Appeals, people were justified in arguing that there was thus no further cause for the exacerbating assaults on the Dreyfusards. The anti-Dreyfusards would not permit any such truce. As the avowed defenders of the army, the anti-Dreyfusards, in their hysterical determination not to let the case be reopened, prevented the restoration of the reasonable, calm atmosphere in which Freycinet could operate. Then, too, as an intelligent man able to judge the situation in an objective fashion, Freycinet had to recognize that Dreyfus was probably innocent and that a number of high-ranking officers had conducted themselves in a highly questionable manner. He knew that a revision of the case, by now bound to come, would seriously harm the careers of many officers to whom he was closely attached.[80] In a matter where both sides had chosen to stand uncompromisingly on opposed principles, the honor of the army versus the demands of justice, a man like

---

[78] Chapman, *op. cit.*, p. 241.
[79] Katzenbach, *op. cit.*, pp. 480-481.
[80] *Ibid.*, p. 495.

Freycinet, for whom principles were generally of secondary importance, could accomplish very little. After six months in office he resigned. The incident that led to his departure was quite trivial but nevertheless indicative of the problems he had to face.

A young history teacher at the École Polytechnique, Georges Duruy, having written a number of Dreyfusard articles, was shouted down in class by the cadets. Duruy had done nothing wrong, but the Minister of War, seeking in all possible ways to restore some measure of calm within military circles, removed him from his post. During an interpellation on the subject in the May 5, 1899, session of the Chamber, Freycinet attempted to justify his actions in the case, but to no avail, for his words were drowned out in the clamor coming from the Radical and Socialist benches.[81] Supposedly thunderstruck that a man of his age and eminence should have to suffer such treatment, he abruptly left the Chamber and submitted his resignation to the President of the Republic, claiming that he had lost all authority vis-à-vis the parliament.[82] In Reinach's opinion, Freycinet could have forestalled the whole matter by simply restoring Duruy to his post; but, annoyed at certain of his ministerial colleagues, harassed by the leading generals, and worried about the imminent reopening of the case, he was glad to have the occasion to quit.[83]

The precipitous departure of Freycinet upset the government, and the possibility of giving his portfolio to Dupuy was briefly considered. Dupuy refused on the grounds that he had been premier at the time of the 1894 court-martial and thus might seem to be unduly prejudiced.[84] The post finally went to a deputy named Camille Krantz. Millet wryly notes that Krantz was an amiable fellow who found "that there was lit-

[81] Chapman, *op. cit.,* p. 261.

[82] A. Combarieu, *Sept ans à l'Élysée avec le Président Loubet* (Paris: Hachette, 1932), pp. 11–12.

[83] Reinach, *Dreyfus,* Vol. V, pp. 81–82.

[84] Combarieu, *op. cit.,* p. 12.

tle similarity between the Ministry of Commerce, which he was leaving, and the Ministry of War, which he was taking over." [85] He lasted seven weeks, until the fall of the Dupuy cabinet.

In the long and difficult ministerial crisis that followed the departure of Dupuy, the usual efforts to patch together a Moderate center coalition failed. Some kind of new departure was needed. Forswearing their allies to the right, a solid block of Moderates turned decisively to the left. Under the bold and vigorous leadership of René Waldeck-Rousseau, they formed a coalition embracing all republican groups from the Socialists to those Moderates who placed the preservation of the regime before the defense of the social *status quo*. Waldeck-Rousseau's cabinet consisted of men of vigor and determination. Collectively they represented that most unusual phenomenon under the French parliamentary system, a strong government. The announced policy of the new premier was to "put an end to the agitation," "make the decisions of justice respected," and "defend the discipline necessary for the army." [86] This last task was assigned to the new Minister of War and perhaps the most striking figure in the cabinet, General de Galliffet. He was at the time almost seventy years of age and had been retired from active service for over four years.

In naming Galliffet, Waldeck-Rousseau hoped to restore a measure of health and sanity to the seemingly disoriented army. Among the soldiers dissension was rife, and discipline appeared to be in real danger of breaking down. Stubbornly clinging to an untenable and increasingly nonsensical position, the military were becoming confused as to where their allegiance lay. Was it to the government, which attacked the honor of the army, or was it to their hierarchical chiefs, who steadfastly affirmed that Dreyfus was a traitor? As Galliffet scornfully noted, "Little subalterns say they won't obey such and such a general because he has submitted to the orders of

[85] Millet, *op. cit.*, Vol. II, p. 77.
[86] Goguel, *op. cit.*, p. 97.

the Minister of War." [87] While declaring that it was urgently necessary to reestablish order and discipline in the ranks, the new premier also recognized the danger inherent in any further decline in the morale of the army and in its alienation from the Republic. Waldeck-Rousseau was no antimilitarist. He had a profound respect for the real sources of power within the state, and he saw that a program of systematic reprisals against the army would certainly destroy its effectiveness as a fighting force and as an instrument of state policy. In addition to being one of the few men capable of bringing the army back to its traditional sense of discipline, Galliffet by his presence at the Ministry of War also went far in reassuring the military that they would be protected against the more extreme elements in Waldeck-Rousseau's parliamentary majority. For the army, Galliffet as Minister of War was a "pledge of its security." [88]

A brigadier general at the age of forty and a divisionary general at forty-five, Galliffet had been near the summit of the military hierarchy for two decades. Despite his advancing years, he had maintained his vigor, his upright military bearing, and his own unique style, a combination of "bandit chief, afraid of nothing, and great lord, who made fun of everything." [89] By family tradition, birth, and social predilection, he was a royalist, but this background had no effect on his loyalty to the present regime. A fervent admirer of Gambetta, for whom he was reported to have acted as a kind of informal military councilor on matters of personnel and promotion,[90] Galliffet had served the Republic devotedly and unreservedly in the belief that he thereby served the best interests of the army.

Despite the impression he gave of being a soldier and noth-

[87] Chapman, *op. cit.*, p. 308.

[88] Col. X, "L'armée," *Nouvelle revue*, July 15, 1899, p. 349.

[89] Reinach, *Dreyfus*, Vol. V, p. 168.

[90] Paul-Boncour, *op. cit.*, Vol. I, p. 101. Also see the letters published in *Le Jour*, October 1895, and in *Journal des débats*, August 1902.

ing more, Galliffet had a well-developed political sense. He was not a politician in the style of a Billot, but he nevertheless enjoyed no small amount of influence in parliamentary circles, at least with regard to military matters. Galliffet was ambitious in the extreme, and his career, already brilliant under Napoleon III, would certainly have been less so under the Republic if there had not been an acute political awareness artfully concealed behind his remarkable qualities as a soldier and a warrior. He had nothing but scorn for those in his circle who passed their time cursing the Republic and who, if they bestirred themselves to action, ended by being compromised in such fatuous undertakings as Boulangism.

Personally, Galliffet thought that Dreyfus was in all probability guilty, but he also recognized that there were no serious proofs of his guilt.[91] Too intelligent and too independent a person not to see the blunders committed by the military authorities, "he declared himself to be an opponent of both the Dreyfusards and the anti-Dreyfusards." [92] The only reasonable course was to liquidate the Affair as quickly as possible while endeavoring to protect the best interests of the army. "He was displeased at the actions of the bureaucrats of the General Staff, as he irreverently called them, the 'Senators' of the army, stubbornly persisting in a despicable operation. He returned to active duty to put them in their place." [93]

The type of French general usually called upon to be Minister of War would in the present situation be excessively prudent, cowed by the prospect of angering his more eminent comrades and thereby compromising his future career. Galliffet, for whom *"je m'en foutisme"* was a way of life, had no career to worry about, while the thought that he might offend his fellow generals caused him no concern at all. He was a better man than they, and he knew it. Galliffet did not

[91] H. de Rolland, *Galliffet* (Paris: Éditions de la Nouvelle France, 1945), p. 182.

[92] Combarieu, *op. cit.,* pp. 26–27.

[93] Paul-Boncour, *op. cit.,* Vol. I, p. 102

trouble to hide his scorn for most of them. He characterized Zurlinden as an "imbecile," [94] while he accused Billot of duplicity and Boisdeffre of weakness and of being afraid of what the newspapers would say.[95] As for Mercier, whom he had originally recommended as Minister of War, Galliffet now called him "this raving lunatic." [96]

To reestablish at least nominal order and discipline within the army did not require any harsh or spectacular punishments. A number of officers who had compromised themselves in the Affair or who had spoken their minds too candidly to the press were tranferred to new posts. At worst, they were placed temporarily in *disponibilité*. The measures taken by Galliffet were, all things considered, rather mild. In 1886 General Boulanger had in summary fashion removed from the command of an army corps General Schmitz, one of the leading soldiers of the day, for even appearing to question one of his decisions as Minister of War. In 1899 Galliffet, although enjoying far greater prestige within the army than had Boulanger, thought it prudent to do more than transfer Hartschmidt, a relatively junior general who had publicly insulted the President of the Republic, calling him a *Panamiste*.[97] In effect, the transfer amounted to a promotion, for Hartschmidt went from Angers, a military and social backwater, to Reims, a city only two hours from Paris, and the command of what was considered to be one of the two best divisions in France.[98]

The only overt disciplinary measure involving one of the more eminent officers was the removal of General de Négrier from the C.S.G. In July 1899, while on an inspection tour in eastern France, Négrier was reported to have told an informal gathering of officers that if the government did not put a stop

---

[94] Rolland, *op. cit.,* p. 213.

[95] J. Clarétie, *Souvenirs du dîner Bixio* (Paris: Charpentier, 1924), p. 91.

[96] Chapman, *op. cit.,* p. 309.

[97] Col. X, "L'armée," *Nouvelle revue,* July 15, 1899, p. 350.

[98] "Un colonel," *La nation et l'armée* (Paris: A. Colin, 1900), pp. 10–11.

to the outrageous attacks being directed against the army, the military should look to the C.S.G.[99] Precisely what he meant to imply by his statement and whether he was being insubordinate or merely indiscreet are not certain, but the incident created a furor in the press. Even though the military admitted the necessity for disciplining Négrier, they were bitter that the situation had reached a point where a general of his eminence should feel himself obliged to speak in such a fashion.[100] Négrier was placed in *disponibilité* but was returned to his position in the C.S.G. the following year by Galliffet's successor, General André.[101]

The government did not move to open proceedings against either Mercier or Boisdeffre, although both men had been guilty of conduct dishonorable in the extreme. Galliffet had made this one condition of his entry into the Ministry of War.[102] To bring legal action against them would only prolong the Affair and add to the agitated and feverish state of the nation, not to mention that of the army. Since peace and quiet were, above all, what the French people needed, Waldeck-Rousseau found it wise to forgo the demands of justice in the interests of expediency. In November 1899, Waldeck-Rousseau presented an amnesty bill to the Senate which covered all crimes and misdemeanors connected with the Dreyfus Affair, with the exception of the Déroulède episode. Although the Dreyfusards objected violently to the manifest injustice of the bill, it was finally passed on December 20, 1900, after a fourteen-hour session during which Waldeck-Rousseau was obliged to exert his full authority over the Socialists and other Dreyfusards to obtain their consent.[103]

---

[99] As reported in various newspapers. Clippings in Arch. Pref. de Pol. (B/a 1209, Doss. 275,450).

[100] Gen. Tricoche, "Un peril," *F.M.*, August 2, 1899.

[101] Gen. André, *Cinq ans de ministère* (Paris: L. Michaud, 1907), pp. 51–55.

[102] Chapman, *op. cit.*, p. 275.

[103] Combarieu, *op. cit.*, p. 102.

The retrial of Dreyfus, following the favorable verdict of the Court of Appeals, was another example of the willingness of the Waldeck-Rousseau government to connive at injustice in the higher interests of the state. In the court-martial that opened at Rennes on August 7, 1899, and lasted for about a month, the government was careful to maintain a scrupulous neutrality, exerting no pressure and letting the military decide for themselves whether they considered Dreyfus to be guilty or not. By that late date, however, things had gone too far for the case to be decided merely on the basis of what the available evidence did or did not prove. As was noted in *La Croix,* "People no longer ask themselves: Is Dreyfus innocent or guilty? They ask: Who will get the better of it, the enemies of the army or its friends?"[104] In an interview printed in *Intransigeant* on August 3, Mercier put it most succinctly: "Dreyfus will certainly be condemned again, for in this case there is someone certainly guilty. And that guilty party is either he or myself."[105]

At Rennes the chief personage was not the defendant, the prematurely aged, bent, still fever-wracked Dreyfus. The furies that had been brought into existence and that swarmed about his cause seemed to pass him by. Dreyfus had been too long absent from France to understand what was happening. Mercier dominated the trial, and at times he actually appeared to be conducting it. Having given his main evidence on August 12, he remained in court thereafter, intervening in the discussion whenever he saw fit to do so, ready to defend each one of his actions from the start of the case.

In this trial the army made a last stand in defense of its honor, and Mercier directed the operation with reckless determination. "Fertile in invention, resourceful, *rusé,* he continually widened the battle-front, staging ambushes, mounting counter-attacks, always in the breach."[106] As Mercier had

---

[104] P. Boussel, *L'affaire Dreyfus et la presse* (Paris: A. Colin, 1960), p. 211.
[105] Miquel, *op. cit.,* p. 107.
[106] Chapman, *op. cit.,* pp. 293–294.

said, the verdict would have to be either for him or for Dreyfus, and the seven officers sitting in judgment could not be expected to condemn the former chief of the army. To do so would have been to admit implicitly that the Dreyfusards had been right in their charges, and this would have been tantamount to denying the principles upon which their whole professional code was based. Yet, the court did not quite make Dreyfus a traitor. "That is why, having to pronounce the truth with a 'yes' or a 'no', it said neither. . . ." [107] Dreyfus was found guilty, "with extenuating circumstances," by a vote of five to two and sentenced to ten years' imprisonment, five of which had already passed. The honor of the army, such as it was, had been saved.

The more ardent Dreyfusards wanted to appeal this patently absurd verdict, although Galliffet predicted that, given the state of mind of the army, "a third court-martial would condemn him by a vote of six to one, a fourth one unanimously." [108] The only course that would satisfy both the demands of humanity and the self-respect of the army was for Dreyfus to receive a presidential pardon. On September 19, Loubet remitted the remainder of his sentence, and Dreyfus was a free man. The demands of justice would have to wait until 1906, when the Court of Appeals made a final and painstaking review of the case and declared that Dreyfus was completely innocent of all the charges brought against him. On September 21, Galliffet, acting on his own, promulgated a memorandum to all corps commanders:

The incident is closed. The military judges, surrounded by the respect of all, have given their verdict in complete independence. Unreservedly we defer to their judgment. Equally we defer to the action which a sentiment of deep pity has dictated to the President of the Republic. There should be no question of reprisals whatever.

[107] "Chronique française," *Revue militaire suisse,* October 1899, p. 684.
[108] Princess Radziwill, *Lettres de la Princesse Radziwill au Général di Robilant* (Bologna: Zanichelli, 1933), Vol. II, p. 220.

Therefore, I repeat, the incident is closed. I ask you, and if it were necessary I should order you, to forget the past so that you may think only of the future. With all my comrades I heartily cry, "Vive l'armée," which belongs to no party, but to France alone.[109]

For all his prestige and authority, Galliffet could not bring the incident to a close so easily. "The whole officer corps had been too severely shaken for two years, too violently hurled into politics, to stop suddenly." [110] A long period of convalescence would be necessary before the military regained their former state of mind and their unreflective, automatic loyalty to the regime. Instead of closing ranks and rallying behind him, the officer corps execrated Galliffet as an agent of the enemies of the army. At the same time, the more extreme elements in Waldeck-Rousseau's parliamentary coalition were impatient at the moderate policy of the government toward the army and eager to undertake a thorough "republicanization" of the military institutions of France. Galliffet admitted to being disturbed by the exigencies of the Socialists.[111] Under the circumstances, he could do little but, in somewhat frivolous fashion, shrug his shoulders and depart.

Galliffet resigned his portfolio over a trivial matter. During an interpellation on an incident touching the Dreyfus Affair, Waldeck-Rousseau had used the phrase "felonious officer" to characterize the conduct of a certain individual. Galliffet immediately stalked out of the Chamber and submitted his resignation, declaring that he could not permit himself to hear a civilian so qualify an officer without protesting. All efforts by Waldeck-Rousseau to bring him to reconsider his decision were to no avail. The opposition was quick to profit by his unforeseen action, which they considered a gesture of protest against the policy of the government and evidence of the difficulties he was having in defending his department "against

[109] Chapman, op. cit., p. 304.
[110] Reinach, Dreyfus, Vol. V, p. 247.
[111] Radziwill, op. cit., Vol. II, p. 345.

the intrusion of politics. . . ." [112] Because of the brutal demands of the Ministry of War at that particular moment,
Galliffet himself may have come closer than anyone to a succinct summary of his motives in a letter to his young colleague
in the Waldeck-Rousseau government, Joseph Caillaux: "I
was too old. . . ." [113]

In trying to prevent a reopening of the case of Captain
Dreyfus, the soldiers were not, as was unthinkingly announced by so many of them, defending the honor of the
army. Rather, they were fighting for something far more vital,
its effective autonomy within the state. This was the real stake
in the Dreyfus Affair. Even if the officers as a group were perhaps not consciously able to define the real issue, they reacted
instinctively at any incursion by the civil government onto
hitherto sacred terrain:

> Lawful or not, judicial error or justified punishment, the con-
> demnation of Captain Dreyfus was, according to their customary
> point of view, a strictly military affair, affecting military security,
> coming within the sphere of military justice, involving the larger
> interest of the army, and something in which the civil authorities
> had absolutely no business.[114]

Mercier, Boisdeffre, Gonse, Billot, *et al.* may have been striving
to save their own reputations, but they were also thinking of
the larger institutional interests of the army as these had come
to be understood down through the nineteenth century.

By placing what they considered to be the interests of the
army above a concern for the unjust sufferings of one man,
they were acting in an inhumane fashion. The dilemma, of
course, is that any social institution must on occasion require
its faithful servants to act this way, or it cannot function. The

---

[112] *Revue des deux mondes,* July 15, 1900
[113] J. Caillaux, *Mes mémoires* (Paris: Plon, 1942), Vol. I, p. 144.
[114] Girardet, *op. cit.,* p. 256.

invasion by the Republic of this traditional area of military autonomy was justified in the name of a universal principle of justice so imperious in its demands regarding the rights of the individual that the great interests of the state should be subordinated to them. How many of the republican politicians really believed in this ideal is a debatable point, but no soldier could. In any army, the rights of the individual must of necessity be subordinated to the collective interests of the whole. All of the military men most deeply involved in the conspiracy to keep the Dreyfus case *res judicata* would have agreed with Goethe that injustice may be preferable to disorder. As Thomas notes in his splendid study of the Affair, this is, above all, a matter of temperament.[115]

To the degree that an army or any other institution allows or encourages one of its members to evade the problem of personal responsibility, it is morally reprehensible. When a person realizes that the institution can be saddled with the responsibility for a given act of his, whatever its consequences, his own moral sense atrophies. The perfect example here is Major Henry, who was certainly unaware of any of the ethical implications of his actions. His conduct was motivated at all times by a sense of absolute loyalty to his superiors and to the army. By his lights, and by the lights of any good soldier, it required no further justification.

Once the military sensed that their institutional interests were involved in the fate of Captain Dreyfus and therefore endeavored to keep the case from being reopened, a confrontation between the army and the Republic could hardly be avoided. Nor could its outcome be doubted. For the army to have made its thesis prevail and to have thereby retained its autonomous situation within the state, it would have to have participated in the overthrow of the regime. The time was long past, or had not yet come, when the French soldier would think of taking arms against the powers that be, no matter how sorely tried he was by their policies. The military

[115] Thomas, *op. cit.,* p. 278.

would not and could not be reconciled to the republican point of view in the Dreyfus Affair, while the politicians, alarmed at the unsuspected implications of military autonomy, set about breaking it down. For that reason, the entente between the army and the Republic, one of the cardinal features in the political development of France since 1871 was, temporarily at least, ended.

CHAPTER SIX

The Crisis in Civil-Military Relations: 1900-1910

The Origins of the Crisis and "L'Affaire des Fiches"

In the history of the French army and of its relations with the state, the years between 1900 and 1910 present a striking contrast to the period immediately preceding. Whereas the 1890's seemed in retrospect to have been a kind of golden age, when the soldiers, aware of their technical proficiency and allied to the Russian colossus, felt no sense of inferiority vis-à-vis the Germans, the next decade saw the army wracked by a grave crisis in morale, which seriously impaired its military effectiveness. Although it was decisive in bringing about this sudden reversal, the Dreyfus Affair alone could not have shaken the army so profoundly if there had not already been other forces at work undermining its confidence in itself.

Evidence of a preexistent malaise within military circles was to be found in the almost pathological sensitivity displayed by the officer corps in the face of the journalistic attacks of such men as Urbain Gohier.[1] As one anonymous military author noted:

Except for two or three dailies, the newspapers at present certainly carry less criticism, particularly of an offensive nature, than did the press of the period 1873–1877, for example. But all that is needed is for a few crude attacks to be published in some paper or

[1] *Vide supra,* p. 207.

other without circulation and the nationalist dailies pick them up to show that a good half of France persists in a stubborn and unjust enmity toward the officer corps.[2]

That the military would not ignore these attacks and would not recognize that the army was still held in admiration by the great majority of Frenchmen indicated that their state of mind was none too healthy.

The fundamental element in this moral crisis was the fact that by the turn of the century the French army had not been at war for some thirty years. There existed for the army of the Third Republic nothing comparable to the long pacification of Algeria, which had supplied, at a relatively low cost in men killed and wounded, an outlet for the warlike energies of the soldiers of Louis Philippe and Napoleon III. The colonial campaigns of the Third Republic were of short duration, involving a small number of men. Many fine soldiers refused to participate in these overseas endeavors, for they believed that precious energies were thus diverted from the true mission of the French army: preparing itself for the war of revenge against Germany.[3]

This is not to argue that frequent wars are necessary for the well-being of an army. Men are attracted to military life less by the expectation of war and slaughter than through a sense of calling and by the prospect of devoting their lives to the disciplined pursuit of an ideal. The peculiar combination of qualities to be found in a good soldier are not necessarily those manifested by the born warrior. Nevertheless, the expectation of imminent war did play a vital role in the life of the French army over the years 1871–1914. The vision of *la Revanche* had inspired a generation of soldiers to two decades of unremitting labor and had also attracted to a military career a disproportionately large number of young men from the educated

---

[2] Un colonel, *La nation et l'armée* (Paris: A. Colin, 1900), p. 12.

[3] R. Girardet, *La société militaire dans la France contemporaine, 1815–1939* (Paris: Plon, 1953), p. 304.

classes who might otherwise have entered different professions.

The number of candidates for Saint-Cyr rose steadily from year to year, while the best graduates of Polytechnique embraced military rather than civil careers. Even with the increase in the size of the annual promotions, caused by the constant growth in the size of the army, it was still possible to be much more selective than in the years before 1870. The result was a marked improvement in the intellectual level of the officer corps. Whereas in 1881 there had been 217 graduates of Saint-Cyr entering the infantry, by 1891 there were 320 and in 1896 over 440. This gives some indication of the power of attraction that the French army was able to exert over an important segment of the youth of the nation. At the same time, as the number of graduates of Saint-Cyr rose, the number of promoted N.C.O.'s declined. In the 1880's the annual contingent of infantry officers promoted directly from the ranks, and after 1885 from Saint-Maixent, outnumbered the Saint-Cyriens by a proportion of three to two and occasionally even two to one. After 1891 the proportions changed in favor of the latter.[4]

The number of men coming from the great military schools in the subaltern ranks began to rise just at a time when promotion to the higher echelons was slowing down because of the long years of peace. Officers were spending increasingly longer periods of time in the lower ranks, while their chances of reaching positions of real importance or responsibility were diminishing.

In order to keep promotion from being even slower than it was, the army had to resort to a number of expedients. According to the reporter for the budget of 1901, the army maintained as a "complementary cadre" at least 1,172 officers, above the rank of lieutenant, who were in excess of its real peacetime requirements. The jobs to which they were assigned were not

[4] *Journal Officiel de la Chambre des Députés: Documents* (hereafter cited as *J.O.C. Doc.*), (1901), pp. 1491-1492.

really necessary, while the cadre itself fulfilled no actual need. "Rather, the job has been created or maintained in order to justify the utilization of the cadre in time of peace." [5] But even the existence of a complementary cadre could do little to alleviate the more or less constant promotion crisis.

In the years before 1870 a man coming from one of the two great military schools could reasonably expect to retire as a major or a lieutenant colonel. The old long-term N.C.O.'s who were made officers late in life, and who filled from one half to two thirds of the lieutenant's billets, wanted little more than to retire as captains. With their more humble ambitions, they did not compete with the young men from the schools. After 1870, with the all but complete disappearance of the old N.C.O.'s from the officer corps, the elements of the problem changed. There was a relatively higher percentage of officers from Saint-Cyr and Polytechnique, while the N.C.O.'s seeking commissions via Saint-Maixent, Saumur, or Versailles were generally only a few years older than their comrades from the great schools. Unlike their forebears in the old army, they now aspired to something more than a captain's pension and perhaps the cross of a *chevalier* in the Legion of Honor. By instituting stricter requirements for the promoted N.C.O.'s, the army undeniably raised the intellectual level of the officer corps and increased its homogeneity, but there were also some less desirable consequences. Rather than complementing the men from Saint-Cyr and Polytechnique, they were now their rivals. According to one authority, "By lessening the differences which formerly existed between these two categories of officers, we have ended by increasing the reasons for dissension." [6] In the competition for promotion to the higher ranks and for entrance into the École de Guerre, the men from Saint-Cyr generally won over the men from Saint-Maixent, but even the Saint-Cyriens found that there were too few billets above the rank of captain to satisfy their legitimate ambitions.

[5] *J.O.C. Doc.* (1900), p. 2105.
[6] E. Manceau, *Notre armée* (Paris: Charpentier, 1901), pp. 137–138.

By the end of the century a lieutenant was obliged to wait ten or twelve years before being promoted to captain. A captain had to spend a comparable length of time before becoming a major somewhere in his mid-forties. The young graduates of the great military schools entering the army in the late 1890's could look forward to an even grimmer prospect, the majority of them being destined to "cruel disappointment, without perhaps being aware of it, for they do not have the elements of information necessary to find out. . . ."[7] All who contemplated the problem of officer promotion were agreed that the situation had reached crisis proportions and that something would have to be done. Almost all agreed that the 1832 law on promotion should either be drastically amended or replaced by a new law. Actually, a revision of the 1832 law had been one of the cardinal features in the program of military reform of the National Assembly. Through the years there were flurries of interest in the subject whenever it was announced that the Minister of War of the moment was about to address himself to a reform in the system of promotion, but no measure had yet been seriously debated in parliament by the time war broke out in 1914.

With officers of talent vegetating for long years as lieutenants and captains in some provincial garrison, the ideal that had prompted their original choice of career faded. After the initial excitement of the postwar years, and their vision of impending battle, the officer corps settled down. The great reforms of the 1870's went into effect, and the army began to function with the precision of a machine. As one commentator noted, "Everything is carried out with regularity and monotony, without enthusiasm, but also without lassitude."[8] An officer lulled into the routine of military life and eventually of marriage soon came to lack the intellectual or physical vigor necessary either to try for the École de Guerre or to enlist in the colonial army, the only two sure paths to reasonably rapid

[7] *J.O.C. Doc.* (1901), p. 1492.

[8] P. d'Ameugny, *L'âme de l'armée* (Paris: Nouvelle revue, 1898), p. 9.

promotion. Although it was a peaceful, pleasant life, not without its satisfactions, it was also a life that was closely restricted
by custom, by a different code of law, and, perhaps most important, by a low scale of pay. Reporters for the army budget
occasionally lauded the Republic for all it had done to improve the conditions of an officer's existence, particularly by
raising his pay scale, but for a man with a family to support
and children to educate, life was a matter of rigid *économies*.
In the words of the Socialist Gustave Hervé, speculating on
the possibility of winning the army over to the ideal of the
class war, "Oh! the life of a poor officer, earning until the age
of forty the same salary as a very minor functionary, but still
required, because he is an officer, to maintain a social position." [9]

That many officers grew discouraged at the condition of
military life was nothing new. As long before as 1886, *Spectateur militaire,* in reporting that eighty-nine officers had resigned their commissions over the past year, noted that this
was evidence of a sense of discouragement "all too justified
by the inadequate pay and the disheartening slowness of promotion. . . ." [10] Only toward the turn of the century, however, did the malaise reach crisis proportions. The disillusion-
ment that so many officers had come to feel with regard to
their chosen profession would not have been so serious if there
had not been a concurrent and discernible cooling of the nation's affection for the army.

The fervent, almost naïve military patriotism that characterized French life during the decades after the defeat was by the
1890's starting to decline, at least in certain social and intellectual milieux. Born of an unparalleled national humiliation and
maintained by the hope of an imminent *Revanche,* this military patriotism began to fade as the memory of the terrible
year receded and as a new generation came of age that knew

[9] G. Hervé, *La conquête de l'armée* (Paris: "La guerre sociale," 1913), p.
131.
[10] *Spectateur militaire,* August 1, 1886, p. 249.

of the defeat only by hearsay. In one sense, it was the reaction of one generation against the ideals of their parents. Its most evident manifestation was literary, where a whole group of authors and critics made a fetish of their antipatriotic opinions and of their rejection of the whole corpus of ideals and sentiments embodied in the army.[11]

More striking than the rather aloof distaste of the *fin-de-siècle* aesthetes and intellectuals for things patriotic was the appearance in the late 1880's and early 1890's of a number of novels whose theme was the brutality and senselessness of army life. The first of these was *Cavalier Miserey* by Abel Hermant, published in 1887. The story of the systematic corruption of a young conscript during his stay in the army, it was shortly followed by Henri Favre's *Au port d'armes,* Lucien Descaves's *Sous-offs,* and Georges Darrien's *Biribi.* All purported to depict military life as it really was, in brutal, naturalistic style. According to Girardet, it became the usual thing for several years that a young author make his literary debut with a novel of this genre.[12]

In itself, the publication of such novels as *Cavalier Miserey* and *Sous-offs* did not necessarily indicate a sudden, widespread disaffection for the army on the part of the French people. But the fact that several such novels did appear showed that they at least had a market and that they struck a responsive chord. They represented at first only a minor countercurrent in the still strong patriotic tide, but they were nevertheless a portent, indicating that one vocal element among the middle classes was rejecting the military ideal.

In the same period other groups in society were also beginning to question the need for an army and the principles upon which it was founded. Prior to the decade of the 1890's the Socialists had constituted only a small faction-ridden seg-

---

[11] Girardet, *op. cit.,* p. 221.

[12] *Ibid.,* pp. 214–217. Also see W. C. Buthman, *The Rise of Integral Nationalism in France* (New York: Columbia University Press, 1939), pp. 89–90, for a synopsis of the novels of Hermant and Descaves.

ment in the French political spectrum, their ideals and their programs being of little immediate importance. The year 1893 saw their first significant electoral gain as some forty-eight Socialists of varying descriptions were returned to the Chamber.[13] With the appearance of the Socialists, there was a resurrection of the old republican ideals of pacifism and internationalism as stated in the Belleville Program of 1869, when Gambetta had called for the suppression of permanent standing armies, "source of hatred between peoples."[14] In the aftermath of the defeat the republicans, with Gambetta at their head, had renounced this humanitarian idealism to take up a fierce Jacobin patriotism,[15] and it was not until the advent of the Socialists that the great dream of universal brotherhood once again found its spokesmen.[16] Socialist antimilitarism was not a strong enough force to have any immediate political effect, but it did signify a fissure in the patriotic solidarity of the Left.

Within the French educational system, there appears to have been a sharp reaction against the principles of the preceding generation. At that time the school had been looked upon as a means for the inculcation of patriotic ideals and for the training of good citizens. Here the youth of the nation would be given the spiritual and moral preparation to make them better appreciate why they were to be obliged to undergo military service. Now a number of notable figures in the *Université* began to stress the need for a more universal ideal than mere patriotism and to expound on the antithesis between the goals of education, which aims at the development of the individual, and those of military life, in which the individual is submerged in a common body for a common good.

[13] Ch. Seignobos, *L'évolution de la Troisième République,* Vol. VIII of *Histoire de la France contemporaine* (10 vols.; Paris: Hachette, 1920–1922), p. 172.

[14] Ch. Seignobos, *Le déclin de l'Empire et l'établissement de la Troisième République,* Vol. VII of *ibid.,* p. 75.

[15] Girardet, *op. cit.,* pp. 166–167.

[16] *Ibid.,* pp. 222–223.

All of this represented a noticeable evolution in the French social and intellectual milieu, and the army could not help but be aware of it. The military certainly overestimated the extent of this new antimilitarism among Frenchmen in general, because the young littérateurs and authors who found army life distasteful wrote books about it, the Socialists were assiduous propagandists, and the schoolteachers were well placed to disseminate their views. The older partiotic themes had had all the strength of novelty when first enunciated, but they had now over a thirty-year period become somewhat banal. The army thus sensed that an important and influential segment of public opinion was turning away from it, while there was little to be said in its favor that had not come to sound hackneyed and stereotyped.

It was against this growing sense of alienation from a vital and articulate sector of French society that the Dreyfus Affair must be understood. In itself, the Affair certainly contributed to the malaise, but it was, above all, a catalyst for the other, already existent currents of discontent, focusing and accentuating them. When, in the aftermath, the government moved to exercise what it considered to be its legitimate prerogatives over an army that had become accustomed to managing its own concerns, the military looked upon this control as a gratuitous and unwarranted assault. The result was a serious crisis in morale, in which the internal cohesion and solidarity of the officer corps were strained almost to the breaking point.

The man most intimately associated with the efforts by the Republic to assert its control over the army and thereby to lessen its autonomy within the state was General Louis André, Galliffet's successor as Minister of War. Supposedly sponsored by the Radical notables Henri Brisson and Léon Bourgeois,[17] André was a very junior divisionary general at the moment of his entering the Ministry. He was known

[17] J. Reinach, *Histoire de l'Affaire Dreyfus* (7 vols.; Paris: Revue Blanche, 1901–1911), Vol. VI, pp. 121–122.

chiefly as the author of a number of technical treatises on the artillery and for having forbidden in 1899 the circulation in the barracks of his division of any newspapers too vociferously hostile to the government.[18] A firm believer in the doctrines of positivism and a former collaborator of Littré during the Second Empire, he was, in the words of Seignobos, "the only divisionary general who was looked on as being republican. . . ." [19] If this statement implied that all the other generals, to a man, were Bonapartists or monarchists, it would certainly be misleading; but it was probably true that André was the only general whose fervent republicanism satisfied the Radicals and who sympathized wholeheartedly with the Republic in its handling of the Dreyfus Affair. Despite his rigidly doctrinaire and narrow-minded adherence to the ideals of positivism and his generally dry and stiff manner, André had enjoyed a successful military career, although it was possible that he owed his promotion to the rank of general to his lifelong friendship with his classmate at Polytechnique, Sadi Carnot.[20]

André contended that the program he was to carry out with regard to the army had been agreed upon by himself and Waldeck-Rousseau the first time they met, on which occasion he was offered the Ministry of War. Both concurred that a gradual, prudent, although energetic, effort should be made at "purification." Included in this purification was a change in the personnel of the General Staff. They also agreed that it was necessary to reestablish a healthy sense of discipline among the chiefs of the army and again to impress upon the army the idea that it should serve the Republic.[21] André summed up his goals in the phrase "To adapt the army to modern ideas, customs, and institutions." [22]

[18] A. Combarieu, *Sept ans à l'Elysée avec le Président Loubet* (Paris: Hachette, 1932), p. 66.

[19] Seignobos, *op. cit.,* Vol. VIII, p. 218.

[20] É. Mayer, *Nos chefs de 1914* (Paris: Stock, 1930), pp. 128–129.

[21] Gen. André, *Cinq ans de ministère* (Paris: L. Michaud, 1907), pp. 15–16.

[22] *Ibid.,* p. 24.

Through the years since 1875, French military institutions had been obliged to suffer periodic bouts of "republicanization." Precisely what was intended by this vague and sonorous term varied according to the circumstances. In 1879 it had involved nothing more than the retirement of a certain number of corps commanders who were too evidently loyal to monarchist or Bonapartist ideals, while under General Boulanger it had meant an effort to improve the living conditions of the conscripts and the enactment of the three years' service. André saw the term as signifying something far more profound and revolutionary, for he intended to attempt something that had never before been undertaken by a Minister of War of the Third Republic: a fundamental change in the attitudes and ideals of the office corps. Many republican politicians believed that the Dreyfus Affair had been permitted to go on as long as it did, seriously endangering the stability of the regime, because the army was governed according to concepts that were antithetical to those upon which the Republic was founded. It was therefore necessary that it cease to be an autonomous body within the state led by men whose social and political outlook was not in keeping with the spirit of the times.

André approached his new assignment with grim tenacity of purpose and the fanatical determination of a true believer. That he envisioned his term of office in a somewhat different light from the usual Minister of War could be seen from a speech delivered soon after he entered the government.

The task which I have taken upon myself I will carry out against all comers. I will go to the very end. I will swallow whatever will be necessary in the way of insults or injuries. I will never, so long as I am Minister, stoop to demanding satisfaction from those slanderers who snap at my footsteps. I will remain at my post, and I will never be removed from the Ministry except as a corpse.[23]

By his own account, André expected to be condemned by everyone, but he declared himself not afraid. As he said to one

[23] E. Simond, *Histoire de la IIIe République: Présidence de M. Loubet* (Paris: H.-C. Lavauzelle, 1922), p. 135.

military commentator, Émile Mayer, "I shall have opened the way. I shall have demonstrated that with a little courage one can accomplish something." [24]

In effecting a republicanization of the army, and in particular of the officer corps, the problem was one of method. The Minister of War intended to transform not so much the structure of French military institutions but rather their spirit. The standing army, built around a large cadre of professional officers and N.C.O.'s, was not to be abolished in favor of a militia on the Swiss model. Rather, the officer corps would be imbued with an understanding and appreciation of those democratic values believed by the Radicals to be personified in themselves. André proposed to accomplish this necessary lesson in the virtues of democracy and republicanism by means of officer promotion. It was an article of faith for republican politicians of the era that during the past quarter of a century officers who were hostile to the Republic had been systematically favored in the promotion tables. André intended that political and ideological factors should continue to play an important role in determining who was to be promoted but that now they should operate in favor of republican officers. His first aim then was to find among the "silent and anonymous" mass of officers those who could be singled out for his "solicitude because of their republican sentiments." [25]

From the very beginning of his term as Minister of War, André endeavored to gain as much information as he could about the political and social sentiments of the officer corps. Many officers were known to him personally as good republicans, while others, no doubt sensing in which direction the political wind was blowing, came to the Ministry of War to make a profession of faith. Still others were singled out by friends or comrades whose republicanism was certain. In the process, André and his ministerial aids were able to compile a list of some 700 or 800 officers known to be either good republicans or ferocious reactionaries. Since there were over 25,000

[24] Mayer, op. cit., p. 129.
[25] André, op. cit., pp. 24–25.

officers in the French army, this was only a beginning.[26] In order to get the information he desired about the rest, the Ministry of War turned to other sources.

The French government had long used the prefectorial administration as a means of obtaining information about the loyalty of its functionaries, both civilian and military. Although André availed himself of the prefects and subprefects to ascertain the political sentiments of many officers, there were limits to what could be accomplished here. The prefects could be expected to know of the actions and opinions of the higher-ranking officers in a given area, but their intelligence networks were too rudimentary or uncertain to be very satisfactory concerning the great mass of officers in the lower echelons. So André called upon "all good republicans" to enlighten him. "I authorized my collaborators to request and receive information from all republican associations, the Freemasons as much as any others." [27]

The Freemasons occupied a special position vis-à-vis the Republic. In a regime that implicitly denied the validity of revealed religion, Freemasonry provided a secular equivalent, preaching the lay ideals of brotherhood and charity to be found in Christianity, without its trappings of antirationalism and superstition. Then, too, a large number of republican politicians, particularly among the Radicals, were adherents to one or the other of the masonic rites. With their numerous lodges scattered throughout the country, the Freemasons were in an excellent situation to gather information of the kind wanted by the Minister of War. The justification used by the Radicals for this somewhat questionable practice was that the Catholic religious orders had been used in exactly the same way by the enemies of the Republic. There may indeed have even been a republican precedent for it. It is the opinion of one scholar that the detailed information gathered in the 1870's for

[26] Capt. Mollin, *La vérité sur l'affaire des fiches* (Paris: Librairie universelle, 1905), pp. 51–55.

[27] André, *op. cit.,* p. 306.

the compilation of Gambetta's dossiers on the political opinions of the officer corps was obtained through the Freemasons.[28] From a practical point of view, the Grand Orient was the most suitable of the rites established in France to assist the government in obtaining information. It was by far the largest in terms of membership, and it had a widespread, well-organized network throughout France, which was centered on the Paris lodge on Rue Cadet.

The only Freemason in the entourage of the Minister of War was an aide-de-camp, Captain Mollin, who was the son-in-law of Anatole France. Acting on the instructions of Colonel and later General Percin, *chef de cabinet* for General André, Mollin put himself in touch with the Paris lodge of the Grand Orient, which was, in effect, the national headquarters of the rite.[29] Every time information was required concerning the political or religious views of an officer, Mollin would pass on the name to the Secretary-General of the Grand Orient, a man named Vadécard. Vadécard would then write to the provincial lodge in the town where the officer was stationed. Having obtained the desired particulars, he would transmit them to Mollin. On the basis of the information gained from the Grand Orient, as well as from a variety of other sources, the Ministry of War hoped to accumulate a complete file on the "correctness" of the political attitudes of the officer corps. One could then try systematically to favor the good republicans with prompt promotions and with assignments to the more desirable garrisons. In order to use this information in any effective fashion, however, the Minister of War had to be in full control of the machinery of officer promotion, and this was something that had been obtained only very recently, through two decrees promulgated by Galliffet during his term as Minister.

Before the advent of Galliffet, promotion by choice had been

---

[28] See F. Bédarida, "L'armée et la République," *Revue historique,* Vol. 232 (July–September 1964), p. 129.

[29] Mayer, *op. cit.,* p. 139.

regulated exclusively by the classification commissions. Composed of the leading generals in the army, the classification commissions operated as virtually autonomous, irresponsible organs, drawing up the annual promotion tables and submitting them to the Minister of War for his approval. The Minister, acting in the name of the government, did no more than give his assent to the choices made by the commissions. In effect, promotion was governed by the military solely in accordance with their own canons and their own estimation as to who the best men were. The government could influence the process only in an indirect fashion. This abandonment by the Minister of his lawful rights and prerogatives over promotion was something that had been taking place over the years prior to 1870, but it reached its apogee in the first decade of the Republic.[30] That is to say, whereas the Minister of War under other regimes had to a small degree participated in the process of drawing up the promotion tables, under the Republic he became a rubber stamp, his only function being to indicate the number of vacancies that existed each year in the different ranks.

The fact that the Minister of War had so little influence in deciding who should be promoted appeared to be of no great consequence as long as the army and the Republic maintained their entente. In the immediate aftermath of the Dreyfus Affair it suddenly became somewhat sinister and even a little absurd. According to Galliffet, as he explained the matter in the preface to the decree drastically reducing the powers of the classification commissions:

For the government, it means an absolute abdication of its rightful powers. It is no longer anything but the bound agent for the wishes of a commission composed of general officers who are not responsible before parliament. In the eyes of those officers, who wish, understandably, to reach the highest posts in the army, the government and the Minister of War count for nothing. The

---

[30] L. Thile, *Pouvoir civil et pouvoir militaire* (Paris: Rousseau, 1914), p. 250.

classification commissions are everything. This is the inversion of all rules of logic or of wisdom. One will find an example of similar practices in no other country and in no other French governmental department.[31]

By the terms of the decrees of September 29, 1899, and January 9, 1900, the classification commissions were not completely abolished. Rather, they were reduced to a consultative function, submitting their recommendations to the Minister of War, who would then on his own responsibility draw up the definitive promotion tables for the year.[32] Nevertheless, by so limiting the authority of the commissions and at the same time increasing that of the Minister, Galliffet had effectively done away with them. In the eyes of many soldiers, Galliffet was therefore to be severely criticized. The old system had had its drawbacks. Each general had his protégés whose careers he sought to advance, but in the extensive bargaining back and forth between the generals for places in the promotion tables, more often than not the good soldiers were chosen, and the best interests of the army were served. In that way, according to *France militaire,* the old system had contained "incontestable advantages, precious guarantees. . . . Henceforth, based on the appraisement of a single man, professed to be responsible, the system will be only as good as the man who operates it."[33] Galliffet had, in effect, promulgated a revolutionary measure without thinking of its future consequences. As one general put it, "He wanted to be completely in control of promotion, as if he were assured of being eternal."[34]

General André finished the task begun by Galliffet. By the decrees of February 27 and March 15, 1901, the commissions were abolished, the Minister assuming sole responsibility for setting up the promotion tables. The fitness report of each offi-

---

[31] Quoted in *ibid.,* pp. 257–258.

[32] *Ibid.,* p. 259.

[33] D——, "Nos généraux," *France militaire* (hereafter cited as *F.M.*), October 14, 1899.

[34] Gen. P. Cherfils, *Pour l'armée* (Paris: Berger-Levrault, 1913), p. 58.

cer, which was made periodically by his hierarchical superior, was transmitted to the Minister, along with the nominations for promotion of the various commanding officers. Working on the basis of these elements of information alone, the Minister then proceeded to draw up the promotion tables.[35] His authority over promotion was thus absolute and untrammeled by the influence of any "lateral power" within the military hierarchy, such as the C.S.G. As General André declared in 1902 before the Chamber, he and Galliffet had replaced the irresponsible commissions with the responsible Minister, which meant that officer promotion was now, according to him, "in the hands of parliament." [36] This bland admission as to the powers of the politician in officer promotion created an uproar, and André was forced to qualify his statement slightly to the effect that rather than actually directing promotion, the deputies and senators were now in a better position to demand an accounting from the Minister.[37]

Theoretically, the system was meant to operate with rigid mathematical impartiality. The fitness report of each officer was given a numerical equivalent and then subjected to a mathematical formula. On the basis of the result of these calculations, the promotion tables were drawn up. The difficulty that now arose, as Mollin pointed out, was that some twenty officers were likely to be at the head of the list, with all but identical scores, when there might only be three or four vacancies in the rank above.[38] Because the military abilities of the individual officers, as far as they could be ascertained in time of peace, were inadequate grounds for deciding who should or should not be promoted, the Minister of War felt justified in seeking others. It was here that information concerning the political and religious views of the officers in question was of value. All other things being equal between two officers, the

---

[35] Thile, *op. cit.,* p. 259.
[36] Quoted in *Le Temps,* January 19, 1902.
[37] Reinach, *Dreyfus,* Vol. VI, p. 394.
[38] Mollin, *op. cit.,* pp. 35–37, 74–75.

one who was known to hold republican views was favored over the one who was either indifferent or hostile to the Republic. That André's efforts were soon bearing fruit was to be seen from a comment in the October 1902 issue of the *Revue militaire suisse*. The commentator on the French military scene noted that among the names of the twenty-five generals recently promoted, there was only one containing the prefix "de," indicating some degree of nobility, a situation which, in his words, "pleasantly titillates our democratic prejudices." [39]

The thing that brought an end to the system of promotion instituted by General André, and also to his ministerial career, was a leak in the intelligence network set up by the Freemasons. The Grand Orient kept a scrupulous record of all its transactions concerning the officer corps. Such bureaucratic habits were understandable, but they turned out to be extremely inconvenient. All the pieces of information garnered about the political views of the individual officers were noted on individual index cards, or *fiches,* and filed away at the Ministry of War and at the Grand Orient. A number of *fiches* were stolen from the Ministry of War during the course of 1902, but the most significant theft was accomplished by a certain Jean Bidegain, a clerical employee of the Grand Orient. By his own account, Bidegain inadvertently learned that the Grand Orient was the center of a vast intelligence network that concerned itself with the private opinions of the officer corps. Claiming to believe that this kind of thing "had absolutely nothing in common with the supposed aims of Freemasonry . . ." and revolted at the constant flow of *fiches* through the Paris lodge, he finally stole a large number of them. Through an intermediary, they were handed over to the Nationalist deputy, Guyot de Villeneuve.[40] According to one

---

[39] "Chronique française," *Revue militaire suisse,* October 1902, pp. 885–886.

[40] J. Bidegain, *Le Grand Orient de France* (Paris: Librairie Anti-Sémite, 1905), pp. 25–28.

source, Bidegain received 40,000 francs for his pains,[41] although the latter does not mention money in describing the incident.

Guyot de Villeneuve used his newly acquired ammunition carefully. On October 28, 1904, in the midst of an interpellaon that he was developing on the subject of Saint-Cyr, Guyot de Villeneuve suddenly introduced the question of promotion in the army and began to read a number of stolen *fiches* before the Chamber.[42] Although there had been stories in the press during recent weeks on the existence of the *fiches* and although *Le Matin* had, in the October 28 edition, announced that the subject of delation in the army would be discussed that day before the Chamber,[43] André had apparently prepared himself to answer an interpellation concerning Saint-Cyr and could offer only a weak and confused reply.[44] André disavowed the correspondence between Mollin and Vadécard in which the impression was given that the two of them practically directed officer promotion, but he did declare himself ready to defend his general policy with regard to the *fiches*. The cause of the government and of the Minister of War was better defended by the Socialists Gérault-Richard and Jaurès than it was by André. After Jaurès cautioned the Chamber not to let itself be overwhelmed in a temporary moment of emotion, an "order of the day" more or less favorable to the government was carried by four votes.[45]

André did not defend his policy of using nonofficial sources of information until a week later. In a rambling speech rendered almost inaudible by the insults and catcalls that came from the Right. André stated that his policy of republicanization had been undertaken with the full assent of Waldeck-Rousseau. Citing the numerous cases where republican or Jew-

---

[41] M. Paléologue, *Un grand tournant de la politique mondiale, 1904–1906* (Paris: Plon, 1934), p. 147.

[42] *Journal Officiel de la Chambre des Députés: Débats* (hereafter cited as *J.O.C. Déb.*), (1904, sess. ext.), pp. 2232 ff.

[43] *Le Matin*, October 28, 1904.

[44] *J.O.C. Déb.* (1904, sess. ext.), p. 2239.

[45] *Ibid.*, pp. 2239–2243.

ish officers had been made to suffer insults at the hands of
their comrades and recalling the overt antirepublicanism of
certain of the military, he declared that he considered it his
right as Minister of War to be informed about the political
opinions of the individual members of the officer corps as well
as about their behavior vis-à-vis the Republic. Since it had appeared to be impossible to obtain this information in sufficient
quantities through the usual hierarchical channels, he had
turned to whatever source was available, including the Freemasons. According to André, Captain Mollin had been authorized to request and to receive information from the Grand
Orient, but he did not have the right to engage in so intimate
and confidential a correspondence as had been revealed by
Guyot de Villeneuve. This André energetically condemned.[46]
Jaurès once again vigorously defended the government, but it
was still able to survive a motion on the order of the day by only
two votes.[47] A few minutes later, while he was seated at his
place arranging his papers, André was physically attacked by
a Nationalist deputy, Gabriel de Syveton, who hit him at least
twice with considerable force. Since the Minister of War was
seated at the time and thus taken by surprise, and since his
assailant was much younger than he, it was a particularly
brutal act. Another order of the day was immediately presented, which the government, profiting from the revulsion
felt by the Chamber for Syveton's attack, carried by a large
margin.[48]

The government was thus given a reprieve, although it was
only a short one. André resigned within ten days, declaring to
Émile Combes, the President of the Council of Ministers who
had succeeded Waldeck-Rousseau in 1902, that even if the
government were to give him its full support, he did not feel
that he could remain in office any longer, as he now lacked,
with regard to the army and the country, "the indispensable

[46] *Ibid.*, pp. 2275–2281.
[47] *Ibid.*, pp. 2284–2288, 2295.
[48] *Ibid.*, p. 2296.

moral authority. . . ." [49] After the revelations made by Guyot de Villeneuve, André could be nothing but a liability to the government, and it may be assumed that Combes was not too sincere in his protestations that André remain. The sacrifice of André prolonged the life of the Combes ministry by only two months. Having obviously lost its majority, the government resigned on January 19, 1905.

The great fault of General André was his lack of perspective in attempting to fulfill what appeared to him an explicit mandate for the republicanization of the army. The scandal provoked by the disclosure of the system of *fiches* has tended to obscure the fact that in other fields André was a vigorous and effective chief of the army, one who introduced a number of measures that placed France in a better posture to meet the exigencies of modern warfare. It was during his tenure as Minister of War that many outmoded regulations covering tactics were suppressed and more modern and flexible concepts were introduced. Paul-Boncour, who was a reserve officer in the early 1900's, was deeply impressed by the way the army had progressed in the years since he had done his military service. Training had become more realistic, with greater stress on the use of terrain in field maneuvers, while less emphasis was placed on close-order drill and the traditional spit-and-polish minutiae of military life.[50] According to Caillaux, "We owe to General André the 155 mm. cannons that we had in August 1914 and a corps of reserve officers who were prepared for their task. These are eminent services to have rendered the country." [51]

The general public reaction to the disclosures of Guyot de Villeneuve, as reflected in the press, was one of revulsion. The nationalist dailies were, of course, loudest in their denuncia-

[49] É. Combes, *Mon ministère: mémoires, 1902–1905* (Paris: Plon, 1956), p. 246.

[50] J. Paul-Boncour, *Entre deux guerres* (Paris: Plon, 1945), Vol. I, pp. 160–161.

[51] J. Caillaux, *Mes mémoires* (Paris: Plon, 1942), Vol. I, p. 151.

tions, but the more moderate organs, including many staunchly republican papers,[52] also condemned the actions of the Minister of War, even if in somewhat more measured tones. Only the Socialists were willing to defend André. Writing in *Humanité,* Jaurès recalled that the system of *fiches* had been instituted of necessity by the victims of the Nationalists and the "Jesuits," and he declared that it was therefore hypocritical to condemn these republicans for "the irregular means to which they had been reduced in order to defend themselves." [53]

Needless to say, all those in the government or in any other position of authority declared their ignorance as to the extent of the connection between the Grand Orient and the Ministry of War. Combes says he was greatly surprised at the revelations of Guyot de Villeneuve and found it incomprehensible "that an aide-de-camp could have conceived and set in motion a system of this nature on so large a scale without the Minister or his personal chief of staff having discovered or at least suspected its operations." [54] There is some evidence, however, that Combes had been very precisely informed concerning the system of *fiches.* In the journal of Waldeck-Rousseau there is an account of a meeting between himself and General Percin on December 24, 1902. According to Waldeck-Rousseau, who by then had retired as President of the Council of Ministers, Percin came to him to complain about certain practices at the Ministry of War, in particular, the use of the Freemasons as a source of information on the political opinions of the officers. The former premier agreed with Percin that such practices were blameworthy and inadmissible, but he felt that, rather than resigning in protest, Percin should remain to combat them. Waldeck-Rousseau noted that on December 30 he had informed Combes about the problem and warned him that there

---

[52] *Le Temps,* October 29, 1904. For a daily résumé of the Paris press, see *Le Matin* at the end of October and the beginning of November 1904.

[53] Quoted in *Le Matin,* November 2, 1904.

[54] Combes, *op. cit.,* pp. 242–243.

might be unpleasant consequences if word of these methods were to leak out.[55] In his memoirs, Combes makes no mention of having received any such advice from Waldeck-Rousseau. Combes, for his part, claims to have been told by Percin that there were some 3,000 *fiches* at the Ministry of War, most of which had accumulated under Waldeck-Rousseau. He was assured by General André that they were used in only a tangential and ancillary way in questions of promotion.

In revealing his apprehensions to Waldeck-Rousseau, Percin appears to have been covering himself in prudent fashion in case the system of *fiches* should ever come to light.[56] That he was acting in a disingenuous way was indicated by a number of letters that he sent to the Secretary-General of the Grand Orient, thanking him for the assistance he had already rendered in the great task of purification. These letters were reproduced by Mollin in his book on the affair.[57] Percin was also discomfited by a letter published in *Humanité* at the end of 1904, dated in March of that year, fifteen months after his conversation with Waldeck-Rousseau, in which he personally requested the Grand Orient for information about the political opinions of a certain officer.[58] Despite their vigorous efforts to deny any knowledge of the extent of Masonic influences in officer promotion, the Waldeck-Rousseau and, especially, the Combes governments could be ignorant of the situation only because they wanted to be. As was bitterly noted in *Le Temps,* the organization of a political police was an "integral part of the present system of government." [59]

Although admitting that he had used the Freemasons as a source of information, André denied having been under their control. He claimed that he personally weighed and verified all

[55] Mayer, *op. cit.,* pp. 138–139.
[56] *Ibid.,* p. 140.
[57] Mollin, *op. cit.,* pp. 82–89.
[58] Mayer, *op. cit.,* p. 142.
[59] *Le Temps,* November 1, 1904.

such information and that it was he who decided who should be promoted. In support of this contention, André quoted from the *fiches* of a number of colonels, all harboring strong Catholic and antirepublican sentiments, who were nevertheless promoted to the rank of brigadier general on his order.[60] The weak point in this argument, and indeed in the whole system of promotion introduced by Galliffet, was that the Minister of War and his entourage were not really very well equipped to judge both the needs of the army and the merits of some 25,000 officers. Though André himself could personally supervise the promotion of the relatively few men who rose as high as brigadier general, thus in theory guaranteeing that the rules of equity would be observed, it was not the same for the officers in the lower echelons. Here André was obliged to delegate the dask of drawing up the promotion tables to the members of his ministerial cabinet. The result was that the ministerial cabinet quickly concentrated great power and initiative in itself. It would have had to possess almost superhuman qualities of virtue and self-denial not to have taken advantage of its situation.[61]

No Minister of War could avoid being to some degree involved in political matters. As a member of a cabinet, he was constantly and of necessity subject to requests for favors from his ministerial colleagues and from the parliamentary supporters of the government. This was particularly true in the case of General André, whose evident intention was, from the beginning of his term of office, to be guided as much by political as by military considerations in leading the army, and it was even truer for some of the more fervent members of his own personal staff, such as Mollin, who in effect had the decisive word on promotion. What was distressing to supporters of the government, as to others, was the insolent tone of the correspondence between Mollin and the Grand Orient. No more than a captain, he was obviously conscious that his posi-

---

[60] André, *op. cit.*, pp. 316–318.
[61] "Chronique française," *Revue militaire suisse*, June 1902, p. 786.

tion as aide-de-camp to the minister of War gave him tremendous power over the careers of his fellow officers, even if he used that power in what by his lights was a disinterested fashion. André might declare and perhaps believe that the Grand Orient was merely a source of information, on a par with any other such source, but Mollin as a Freemason would be predisposed to give full credence to its reports. If, then, as was supposed to be the case in one garrison, the regimental cobbler was the man entrusted with the task of ascertaining the political opinions of the officers stationed there,[62] to all intents and purposes he, and not the Minister of War, decided which men in the regiment should be promoted.

Even if the Minister of War and the other members of the government were as ignorant as they claimed to be about the degree to which the Freemasons were influential in military affairs, the officers stationed in garrisons all over France were not. Mollin noted with some pride that a nucleus of republican officers had been formed in each unit and that "the spirit of the army was noticeably changed." [63] Republicanism was obviously in the ascendant, and no officer who cared for his career could afford to ignore this fact. This new enthusiasm seems to indicate a well-developed sense of the realities of the moment on the part of the soldiers rather than any sudden realization about the truth of republican social and political ideals. One officer, commenting on the alacrity with which many of his comrades were converted to these new ideals, wryly wrote: "The neophytes burned their former idols . . . crowded into the masonic lodges, courted the Republic." [64] The discomfiture that overtook these converts to republicanism when it was revealed just what role the Freemasons had played may be imagined. Indeed, any officer promoted during André's tenure as Minister of War found himself automati-

---

[62] *Revue des deux mondes* (hereafter cited as *R.D.M.*), November 1, 1904, p. 472.

[63] Mollin, *op cit.,* p. 183.

[64] Capt. d'Arbeux, quoted in Girardet, *op. cit.,* p. 265.

cally suspect in the eyes of his comrades once the truth about the *fiches* was revealed.[65]

More discouraging in the estimation of the military than the fact that the government had used the Freemasons to spy on the army was the willingness of certain officers to cooperate in the sordid business of delation. As Denis Brogan points out, the grocer in the garrison town was at best an uncertain source of information about the political opinions of his officer customers. On the other hand, a man who had access to the uninhibited conversation of the officers' mess was in a position to supply some very precise particulars on the subject.[66] Although it was by no means true of every garrison, there were still enough recorded cases of officers surreptitiously spying on their comrades to have created a real scandal in the officer corps. According to one writer, "As in the worst epochs of the history of the world, each person suspected that there were traitors everywhere, and was afraid lest his actions, his words, and even his silence be made to indict him." [67] That a number of officers were willing, with the tacit approval of the Minister of War, to act as informers against their comrades and against their superiors was symptomatic of a deep malaise within the army. The more rabid spokesmen for the Republic professed to see in the army a solid, monolithic organization that was drawn up against the regime. Much nearer to the truth would be the estimate of one military author who sensed that the officer corps was in the process of losing its traditional cohesion. "The officer draws no strength from the group to which he belongs, finds no support among his peers." [68]

Rather than closing ranks to defend its threatened institutional interests from the attacks by the government, the army

[65] *Ibid.*, p. 261.

[66] D. Brogan, *The Development of Modern France* (London: Hamish Hamilton, 1940), p. 383.

[67] Comte de Pimodan, *Simples souvenirs* (Paris: Plon, 1908), p. 350.

[68] Capt. d'Arbeux, *L'officier contemporain* (Paris: Grasset, 1911), pp. 24-25.

was in danger of falling apart. The officer corps appeared unable to respond to the degree of punishing and ostracizing those of its number who had, by acting as informers, gone against the principles of honor and camaraderie. "In the officers' mess where they would be seated, secretly envied for their good fortune, the cold disdain of the first days quickly gave way to an obsequious frankness towards the favorite who was the delegate of the powers that be." [69] One officer who resigned his commission at this time, the Comte de Pimodan, lamented the lack of civic or moral courage in most of the French military men. Although the officers were ready to give their lives on the battlefield without a moment's hesitation, they displayed a discouraging weakness of character in any matter pertaining to the "advancement of their careers." [70] All this evidence of a lack of corporate spirit among the military seems to confirm how slight a danger the army presented to republican institutions at the time of the Dreyfus Affair.

Always at the root of this profound crisis in the morale of the army lay the problem of promotion in time of peace. More than anything else, it explained the tenuous nature of the internal solidarity of the army, when after 1900 it found itself under attack. In seeking to be promoted, each officer was, after all, competing against every other officer of the same rank. This mania for promotion was something new under the Third Republic, although it had been one of the salient features in the military mores of the Second Empire.[71] Millet notes that in the aftermath of the Franco-Prussian War he and his comrades were not much interested in their chances for promotion, expecting that it would come in due course and that it would be bestowed according to the candidates' merits. No one would have ever thought to seek the backing of some-

---

[69] Cmdt. de Civrieux, *Du rêve à la réalité* (Paris: Belleville, 1908), p. 246.

[70] Pimodan, *op. cit.,* p. 359.

[71] Lt. Col. Chalmin, *L'officier français de 1815 à 1870* (Paris: Rivière, 1957), p. 34.

one outside the military hierarchy.[72] Then, too, in the first years after the defeat there was a considerable expansion in the size of the French military establishment which allowed those, such as Millet, who had already reached the rank of captain by 1870 to enjoy a relatively rapid series of promotions. As promotion began to slow down by the 1890's, officers came to realize that a deputy or a senator could bring considerable influence to bear on the army, even if only indirectly. Freycinet told Millet that between the time he was first Minister of War and his second term in that office, "the number of visits, solicitations, and requests had increased by a factor of five." [73]

With the suppression of the classification commissions and with the evident intention of General André to use ideological criteria in questions of promotion, the political connections of an officer became all-important. In the words of one commentator, "As long as the generals were omnipotent in the classification commissions, they were surrounded by courtiers; now that the Minister regulates promotion for the whole army, these same courtiers have turned to the journalists and politicians." [74] Charles Humbert, a deputy who was much interested in military affairs, tells of how one young officer solicited his assistance in obtaining promotion. Humbert looked into his dossier and found that the officer in question intended to be covered for all possible political circumstances. In it were letters of recommendation from two Socialist deputies, as well as letters obtained before the separation of church and state from a cardinal, an archbishop, and a noted priest.[75] Under the old system, simply because promotions were all arranged among the soldiers, some kind of solidarity and *esprit de corps*

---

[72] Gen. C. Millet, unpublished memoirs (Service historique de l'Armée, Château de Vincennes), Vol. II, p. 19.

[73] *Ibid.,* Vol. II, p. 77.

[74] D'Arbeux, *op. cit.,* p. 23.

[75] Ch. Humbert, *L'armée: sommes-nous défendus?* (Paris: Juven, 1907), pp. 18–19.

had been maintained. The new system automatically led to the introduction within the hitherto sheltered military milieu of the fierce partisan quarrels dividing French civil society. The effects of this change on the traditional ideals of camaraderie and mutual confidence were most unfortunate.

Almost all commentators on the contemporary military scene were unanimous in their regrets over the passing of the supposed golden age of a decade or two before. Then the officer corps had been united, and no one had paid any attention to the political and social antecedents of his fellows. Pimodan writes concerning his days at the École de Guerre in the 1890's that he was ignorant of the religious convictions of some of his most intimate comrades.[76] According to one military author, some officers were imbued with traditionalist political opinions as a result of their early education or because of some family atavism, but they never manifested them openly. As for the great majority, "they were, quite obviously, *je m'en moquiste*. . . ."[77]

Military Morale and Republican Policy.

The resignation of General André and the fall of the Combes ministry did not automatically end the crisis in morale. The new Minister of War, Maurice Berteaux, was one of the leading Radical deputies, and by virtue of having served as reporter both for the 1902 army budget and also for the new conscription law, he was considered to be quite conversant with military affairs. A genial, expansive type, unlike his predecessor, Berteaux plainly had the mission of restoring a measure of harmony and mutual confidence within the officer corps, but it is doubtful how much he or anybody else could accomplish in this direction. Although André had departed and the unsavory practices associated with his ministry had been stopped, the other fundamental conditions underlying the

[76] Pimodan, *op. cit.*, p. 251.
[77] M.P., "Les officiers et la politique," *F.M.*, May 13, 1903.

malaise in the army were still there. The rate of officer promotion remained slow, while a military career in an era when the
noble vision of *la Revanche* was fading had lost none of its
apparent futility. In fact, a number of other factors at this
moment contributed to prolonging and possibly even accentuating the crisis in morale.

In the decade after 1900 the army was, with increasing frequency, obliged to perform one of the more disagreeable tasks
traditionally assigned to it, that of assuring internal peace and
order. Though much of the unrest came from an expected
source, the working classes, much of it was also new, stem-
ming from the virulently anticlerical policy pursued by the
Combes government. Following the great electoral victory of
the *Bloc des Gauches* in 1902, Combes believed that he had a
mandate to apply the recently enacted law on the associations
in the most stringent fashion. The law had been written by
Waldeck-Rousseau with the aim of giving the government an
effective means of exercising surveillance and control over the
activities of the various religious congregations established in
France. Combes, however, exploiting certain ambiguities in
the law, set about mounting a full-scale attack on the congregations.[78]

The policy of the Combes government, leading to the closing of many religious houses, provoked manifestations and
scenes of disorder, particularly in the more traditionally Catholic rural areas. Bands of the faithful came together to interfere with and, if possible, to prevent the closing of the
condemned congregations. Army units were naturally called
upon to assist the local authorities in carrying out the decrees
of the government. Similar scenes took place in 1906, following the enactment of the law on the separation of the church
and state. By the terms of the law, religious associations were
to be organized for the administration of ecclesiastical property, formerly owned by the state. Before transferring this

---

[78] F. Goguel, *La politique des partis sous la troisième République* (Paris:
Éditions du Seuil, 1958), pp. 112–120.

property, the state had to make an inventory of it, and these official inventories were the cause of further disorders. The papacy having objected to the law, the clergy sometimes went so far as to barricade themselves in their churches to prevent the officials from performing their assigned task. Here, too, the army was obliged to help maintain order and to assure free access to the churches for the representatives of the state.[79]

Any Catholic officer assigned the duty presiding at the closing of an unauthorized religious house or of ordering the doors to church broken down was faced with an acute moral dilemma. The state was ordering him to perform a task that the Church condemned. Many officers found that, in this case at least, the traditional concepts of discipline and absolute obedience to all orders emanating from above could not provide an adequate rationale for an action running counter to their deepest personal convictions. Throughout the years after 1902 there were a number of incidents reported in the press of officers refusing to obey orders of this nature. Their treatment at the hands of a military tribunal was usually lenient.[80] Some officers took the more drastic step of resigning their commissions rather than carry out the orders of the government in this regard. Indeed, certain traditionalist families required this of an officer if he was engaged to one of their daughters.[81] It is also possible that there were many officers "who weary of their profession or exasperated by the slowness of their promotion made this religious controversy a pretext for quitting the army with éclat." [82]

[79] Girardet, *op. cit.*, pp. 262–263.

[80] See, for example, two cases recounted in *Le Temps* during August and September 1902. The generally unfortunate effects of such leniency on discipline, along with the inequity of government policy in obliging officers to act against their religious convictions, are treated in an editorial in *Le Temps,* May 30, 1904.

[81] F. Kuntz, *L'officier français dans la nation* (Paris: H.-C. Lavauzelle, 1960), p. 85.

[82] J. d'Epée, *L'officier français* (Paris: H.-C. Lavauzelle, 1907), p. 57.

The military, no doubt with some justification, speculated that the government, fully aware of the strong religious sentiments of many officers, was seeking to place them in a humiliating situation. Few chiefs of the era seem to have had the courage of Millet, who, as general commanding the Third Army Corps at Orléans, informed the local prefect that while he would permit his troops to be used for the maintenance of order in the streets, he did not believe it to be the mission of the army to break down the doors of churches. Consequently, Millet asked the prefect "to have that task performed by the voters, there being no lack of Radical-Socialists in Orléans." [83]

In addition to the disorders occasioned by the anticlerical policy of the government, the first decade of the twentieth century, especially the years 1907–1909, saw a great increase in working-class unrest. This ferment differed from what had taken place in the past, for the labor movement had now adopted an extremely militant syndicalist program, stressing violence as the most effective means of achieving real social progress. As a consequence, there were serious disturbances in the industrial and mining districts. The government, despite the fact that its majority was oriented to the left, still had the responsibility for maintaining order. Inevitably, it had to call upon the army.

The soldiers, who bore the onus of repressing, often with bloodshed, the more violent working-class outbreaks, felt an understandable repugnance at the task assigned to them. Having implicitly denied the validity of the military ideal and having apparently made it a policy to humiliate the officer corps, the government still had to turn to the army to do its dirty work. The labor unions, or syndicates, fought back with an intense and widespread campaign of antimilitarist propaganda aimed at wrecking discipline, particularly among the working-class conscripts.[84] Possibly as a result of such propaganda, and in any case symptomatic of the strong pacifist

---

[83] Millet, *op. cit.*, Vol. II, p. 93.

[84] Seignobos, *op. cit.*, VIII, p. 260.

currents of the era, the number of those who tried to escape induction or who deserted rose sharply, going from 5,000 in 1907 to 17,000 in 1909.[85]

The military were resentful that the government would take no measures to repress this propaganda. It seemed illogical to spend hundreds of millions of francs each year on the maintenance of an army, with the express mission of assuring the defense of the nation, while allowing to develop, in complete tranquillity, within that same army the seeds of decomposition that would "render it incapable of carrying out that task." [86] In the estimation of the soldiers, the government had by its slackness and its politically motivated tolerance permitted antimilitarism to become endemic within the ranks. The military might take a certain wry satisfaction at the plight of the Radical government under Clemenceau when it was faced with the predictable results of its policy.

In 1907, during the economic crisis besetting the wine growers of the Midi, there were a number of massive demonstrations on the part of the local populace, climaxed by the mutiny of the soldiers of the Seventeenth Infantry Regiment stationed at Agde. Rather than carry out their assigned mission of maintaining order at a mass meeting in nearby Béziers, these troops, all recruited locally, defied their officers, plundered the powder magazine, and attempted to join their compatriots in their protest demonstration.[87] Those military traditionalists who had always doubted the wisdom of inducting troops into units stationed in their native regions, a practice that had gradually been accepted over the past two decades for reasons of convenience and economy, were now momentarily vindicated. As they had always claimed, such troops would not be very trustworthy in suppressing local disorders when they broke out in a milieu "whose ideas, sentiments, and passions

---

[85] Gen. Weygand, *Histoire de l'armée française* (Paris: Flammarion, 1953), p. 309.

[86] B. H., "L'antimilitarisme," *F. M.,* April 23, 1907.

[87] Seignobos, *op. cit.,* Vol. VIII, pp. 261–262.

they share and which is made up of their relations and friends." [88]

Rightly or wrongly, the military saw in the policies of the government evidence that the Republic was consciously seeking ways to reduce the prestige of the army and to lessen the esteem in which it had formerly been held by the French people. The most explicit example of that policy was the decree of June 18, 1907, on official honors and ceremonial precedence. Among the declared aims of the decree was the confirmation of the supremacy of civil authority within the state, assigning to the representatives of the legislative branch "a rank corresponding to their importance; . . . preeminence over all the other authorities. . . ." [89] On ceremonial occasions a prefect was now to come before a general commanding an army corps, while the Ministers of War and the Navy, who had once received special honors, were to be treated no differently from any other member of the government. The soldiers were annoyed that at this particular moment the government should seek, "under the guise of democracy, to diminish the exterior marks of respect to which the more eminent military chiefs were until now entitled." [90] Questions of protocol were obviously childish, as was noted by one astute observer of military affairs, Captain d'Arbeux, yet the government, by taking the trouble to revise the Napoleonic decree covering such matters, showed that it attached some importance to them. In his words, "The Republic is thus considered saved when a colonel fifty years old defers to a subprefect who may be half his age." [91]

Less obvious in intent than the 1907 decree but still indicative of the unsympathetic attitude of those in power toward the army were the officially sponsored efforts of many prominent figures to define for the army a new role within the na-

[88] *R.D.M.,* July 1, 1907, p. 234.
[89] *Journal Officiel de la République française* (1907), pp. 4274 ff.
[90] "Honneurs et préséances," *F.M.,* August 9, 1907.
[91] D'Arbeux, *op. cit.,* p. 81.

tional community. In a way that was almost reminiscent of the Government of Moral Order three decades before, the Radicals hoped to use the army as an instrument of social betterment and moral uplift. The only difference was that, whereas in the 1870's the army by its very nature had complemented the ideals of the men of Moral Order, now the sociomilitary program of the Radicals presupposed a necessary evolution in the outlook of the military themselves to bring them into line with the most up-to-date democratic concepts. In the preface to the budget of 1902, Berteaux as reporter reflected this current of ideas: "The officer corps must become imbued with the same sentiments as the country, must live its life, and adapt itself to its social and political organization. Those who are at its head, who guide it, must educate it along these lines. . . ." [92]

The concept of the social mission of the officer in modern society was first given an explicit statement in a famous article that was published anonymously in the *Revue des deux mondes* in 1891, "Du rôle social de l'officier dans le service militaire universel." Its author was a young captain in a chic cavalry regiment, Hubert Lyautey. His thesis was that in a world where war had ceased to be a common occurrence and yet where the whole youth of the nation was obliged to pass through the army, it was becoming difficult to justify the situation of the officer unless his whole conception of his role and his mission were broadened. Lyautey argued that the state should use this incomparable opportunity provided by universal conscription not only to prepare its young men for the remote possibility of war but also to train them as responsible members of society, "to discipline their minds, to mold their characters, to temper their souls." [93] Lyautey was an intimate of Albert de Mun, and his program may be understood in terms of the ideals of social catholicism. As such, it had no immediate impact on the army or on its conception of what its mission was. For Lyautey, the hostile reception to his article in military circles meant the end of his career in France.[94] As a result he departed for Indochina, where, as assistant to Colonel Galliéni, he was given the chance in a notably different milieu to develop further his views on the social role of the officer.

Paradoxically enough, a program first enunciated by a devotee of Albert de Mun was put into effect by a Radical government. It was during the five-year ministry of General André that a number of decrees and circulars were promulgated which incorporated many of the concepts of Lyautey and which looked on the officer as more than a mere military technician. Courses were introduced at Saint-Cyr and Polytechnique on the social role of the officer, and some of the more eminent professors in the country assisted in preparing the curriculum. The reporter for the 1905 budget, Klotz, expatiated on the task of the officer of the future. It would be his mission to present to the men under his care a salutary example of character, to provide for them the necessary training in civics and morality, and to watch over their intellectual and spiritual welfare.[95] The army was to become a kind of continuation of the *Université,* while the officer would cease "to be a military leader in order to become an agent of social improvement."[96]

This new evolution in the conception of the officer's role was not necessarily to the taste of many of the military. Even though Lyautey might have been justified in his contention that too many of the officers of his generation had paid too little attention to the moral and intellectual needs of the men in their charge, the Radicals seemed to go too far in the opposite direction, insisting that the army now perform any number of missions, except that of being a fighting machine.[97] An

---

[94] *Ibid.,* p. 289.

[95] *J.O.C. Doc.* (1904), p. 2090.

[96] D'Arbeux, *op. cit.,* pp. 17–18.

[97] R. D. Challener, *The French Theory of the Nation in Arms* (New York: Columbia University Press, 1955), p. 66 note.

officer was now to be judged on how well he conducted a discussion group on current affairs or how effectively he explained to his men the workings of a mutual assistance plan. The old criteria, which had had to do with the smart appearance of his troops and his ability to handle them in field maneuvers, were in abeyance. Writing in *France militaire,* one anonymous author cursed all the schoolteachers and sociologists who sought to make of the army an institution for the propagation of civic ideas:

Thanks to . . . their mania for repeating to the soldiers that they are above all citizens, that is to say, free men, they no longer look upon themselves as soldiers, that is to say, bound by an oath of obedience, once and for all, and under all circumstances.[98]

In an army that had become uncertain of its mission and of its *raison d'être* and that believed itself to have been treated in an unjust and at times underhanded way by the government, a sense of malaise was widespread. This situation could not help but attract the attention of those who were concerned with military affairs. It was difficult to ignore the growing number of officers who resigned their commissions long before they had reached retirement age or the many long furloughs requested by officers anxious to try another profession before it was too late.[99] Concurrent with this sense of discouragement there was a marked decrease in the number of candidates for Saint-Cyr, from 1,920 of them in 1897 to 982 in 1907. In the artillery, close to 50 per cent of those in the classes of 1905 through 1907 who had entered the army upon graduation from Polytechnique had resigned their commissions by 1910.[100]

In the years after 1900, the peacetime organization of the high command, as it had been instituted by Freycinet, broke down. His achievement in giving to the army a command

---

[98] H., "Politique maudite," *F.M.,* July 25, 1907.
[99] Z., "La nouvelle Chambre," *F.M.,* June 23, 1906.
[100] Girardet, *op. cit.,* p. 274.

structure that in time of peace prefigured and corresponded closely to what it would be in time of war was predicated on there being a considerable degree of mutual confidence between the army and the government. A system whereby the responsible Minister of War effaced himself, while the Generalissimo and the Chief of Staff exercised real independent power over the army, could not function otherwise. Needless to say, by 1900 whatever confidence the Republic may have had in the chiefs of the army was seriously damaged, and with some reason. It was certainly open to question whether the General Staff had shown itself capable of the discreet and intelligent exercise of its independent powers. A reduction in the prestige and in the autonomy of the General Staff was an unavoidable result of the Dreyfus Affair.

General André took the first vital step toward a reestablishment of ministerial authority over the General Staff within a few weeks after he had assumed office in June 1900. He dismissed from their posts as bureau or section chiefs three officers whom he considered to be the most implicated by the recent events.[101] As soon as André had nominated three new officers as their replacements, General Delanne, the Chief of Staff, submitted his resignation on the grounds that as the man responsible for the functioning of the General Staff, he had to be able to choose subordinates in whom he had confidence. In reply, André cited the 1890 decree on the reorganization of the General Staff to the effect that the Chief of Staff was to act under the "authority" of the Minister of War. He interpreted this to mean that the Minister had the ultimate word in assigning officers to that organ. In any case, he refused to accept Delanne's resignation, it being his belief that military posts were not at the disposal of "those occupying them, but rather of the Minister of War."[102] André did, however, allow him to inform the officers being replaced that he had done his best to defend them. Delanne made a further

[101] André, *op. cit.*, pp. 26–27.
[102] *Ibid.*, p. 31.

effort to prevent ministerial intervention in the affairs of the General Staff, when he refused to receive one of the new men appointed by André, stating that his predecessor still occupied the post.[103]

The attempted resignation of Delanne was followed about two weeks later by that of General Jamont, successor to General Saussier as Vice-President of the C.S.G. Jamont contended that because of the instability within the General Staff, he was no longer able to shoulder the heavy responsibility of commanding the main group of French armies in the event of war. To prepare for this arduous mission, he needed collaborators who were known to him and in whom he had confidence.[104]

The appointment of a man such as André at this juncture had apparently angered many of the higher-ranking officers, and they used the incident in an effort to bring about his fall, or at least to cause him to lose face. According to one report, Jamont had a personal interview with Loubet, the President of the Republic, in which he painted a grim picture of the disorganized state of the army, in the hope of inducing the Chief of State "to overcome his constitutional scruples and to intervene in the matter." [105] A certain General Bailloud declared to Abel Combarieu, head of Loubet's personal staff, that Delanne's actions provided a troublesome example for the army and for the rest of Europe, but the conclusion he drew from this case of quasi insubordination was that the Minister of War, and not the Chief of Staff, should resign his post.[106] According to André, things even reached a point where the military attaché of a friendly power, presumably Russia, came to him to demand that in the best interests of the alliance he revoke the order transferring the three officers in question.[107]

---

[103] *Ibid.,* p. 27–32.

[104] *Ibid.,* p. 39.

[105] "Chronique française," *Revue militaire suisse,* July 1900, p. 530.

[106] Combarieu, *op. cit.,* p. 75.

[107] André, *op. cit.,* pp. 33–37.

Against all this pressure from the upper ranks of the army, the government held firm, accepting the resignations of both Jamont and Delanne. In reply to an interpellation on the subject of Jamont's resignation, André declared that the Generalissimo had in effect protested against one of the government's acts, and as a result he had been relieved of his functions.[108] Without further delay, the government then named General Brugère, long known for his republican opinions[109] and at the time Military Governor of Paris, to the post vacated by Jamont. Brugère, in turn, was allowed to pick his own candidate as Chief of Staff, since this person would have to serve directly under him in time of war. His choice was General Pendezec, who had been his Chief of Staff both when he commanded the Eighth Army Corps at Bourges and during his term as Military Governor of Paris.

By asserting his authority over the General Staff in this fashion, André may not have been acting in accordance with the letter of the 1890 decree, and he was certainly violating its spirit. The decree stated that the Chief of Staff was empowered to pick his own subordinates. It was assumed that there would be a general working agreement between him and the Minister of War. If such did not exist, the Minister might dismiss him. The decree did not, however, seem to allow the Minister to impose upon the Chief of Staff officers he did not want.[110] Whatever the precise legal niceties of the situation, André was undaunted by them. In his memoirs he states that only the first step was difficult and after that everyone readily admitted that the Minister of War had a perfect right to shift personnel in the General Staff as in any other branch of the army.[111]

At the time of his nomination as Chief of Staff, Pendezec was still a brigadier general and a relatively unknown person-

---

[108] *J.O.C. Déb.* (1900), p. 1797.
[109] Reinach, *Dreyfus,* Vol. V, p. 248.
[110] *Le Temps,* June 30, 1900.
[111] André, *op. cit.,* pp. 41–42.

age within the army. He thus stood below André in the seniority list once he was promoted to divisionary general the following year. Actually, as has been pointed out, André himself was a very junior divisionary general, ranking about ninetieth in a list of 110 at the moment of his nomination. Although Pendezec stood quite high on the list by the time he resigned in 1906, his successor as Chief of Staff, General Brun, ranked ninety-fifth. All this would indicate that the office of Chief of Staff was to be reduced in importance from what it had been under Miribel and Boisdeffre to something approximating its situation in the 1880's, before the Freycinet reforms. At the same time, the General Staff was to lose its position of virtual autonomy and to be once again subordinated to the Minister. General Revol, the distinguished historian of the French army, states in his memoirs that in the 1900's, when he was first appointed to the General Staff, it was answerable only to the Minister of War. The Generalissimo exercised no authority whatsoever over it.[112] This is especially noteworthy in the light of the fact that Pendezec had been the personal choice of Brugère.

None of the successors to General Saussier as Vice-President of the C.S.G. was of comparable eminence. Part of the reason for the tremendous prestige enjoyed by Saussier may have been the fact that for a decade he held two very important posts concurrently: Vice-President of the C.S.G. and Military Governor of Paris. The desire of the government to build up the stature of a general who was a lifelong republican no doubt had something to do with this cumulation of offices, but it was not without its inconvenient consequences for the effective functioning of the army, particularly in the later years. For one thing, Saussier's laziness was well known.[113] Having created such an eminent military personage with so great an aura of authority, the government was almost auto-

---

[112] Gen. J. Revol, unpublished memoirs, p. 98.
[113] Reinach, *Dreyfus*, Vol. IV, p. 239.

matically obliged to maintain him in office for another five years beyond the usual retirement age, even though he was past his prime. Jamont held no other position of command besides the vice-presidency of the C.S.G., while Brugère resigned the military governorship at the moment of his elevation to that office. The reason given was that the two offices involved too much work to be assigned to one man.[114]

Sound as these reasons may have been, the government had other motives as well. The title of Generalissimo had nothing official about it, but the post nevertheless had great implicit authority over the functioning of the army. Although the position could not be abolished, to reduce the stature and the prestige of the men occupying it would work to the benefit of the Minister of War, and indirectly lead to a lessening of the autonomy of the army within the state. That André himself was trying to accomplish something of this nature is apparent from his memoirs. He went to considerable pains to explain to his presumably unenlightened readers that there was really no such position as that of Generalissimo and that the person so called was really just the Vice-President of the C.S.G., "i.e., the possible substitute for the Minister in presiding over that consultative body. As he has no direct command over the troops, it is not of so much importance as people think whether he is kept in office or changed." [115] The publication of these views in 1906 led the editors of *France militaire* to shudder with alarm at the thought of what would have happened if the French army had had to go to war with the high command functioning according to this conception.[116]

The ideas of André concerning the importance and the authority of the Generalissimo appear to have had a favorable echo in parliament. In his report on the 1902 budget, Berteaux reminded the legislators that the Generalissimo was not the

---

[114] *Le Temps,* July 30, 1900.
[115] André, *op. cit.,* p. 44.
[116] "Le Généralissime," *F.M.,* June 24 and 25, 1906.

commander of the whole French army but rather the designated commander of a portion of it.[117] The Generalissimo, in the opinion of the reporter for the 1903 budget, was the Minister of War, since, as a member of the government, he was the real chief of the army.[118] This was, in effect, the negation of the underlying assumptions that had governed the functioning of the high command since 1890. Klotz, the reporter for the 1906 budget, went even further. He revived the old argument that the wartime high command should not even be organized in time of peace. To do so would be to limit the power of the government to decide who was best fitted to command the armies, given the actual situation at the outbreak of hostilities. He drew the conclusion that it was useless to maintain the post of Generalissimo.[119]

The reaction of the military to this effort to increase the effective power and authority of the Minister of War at the expense of the Generalissimo was not a favorable one. If the government, acting from political motives, returned "to the Minister of War an essential part of the role of Commander in Chief, we would end with a detestable conflict of powers." [120] In particular, General Brugère did not care for this diminution in the authority and prerogatives of the Generalissimo. In fact, he endeavored to increase them during his tenure. In the months after his nomination, Brugère constantly importuned the government with demands for numerous extra perquisites, which he believed were in keeping with the exalted post he occupied. Naturally enough, the overbearing attitude of Brugère created considerable friction between himself and the Minister of War. In December 1901, Brugère objected to the fact that André had, on his own authority and without consulting him, named General Langlois to the command of the vital Twentieth Army Corps at Nancy, when he would have

[117] J.O.C. Doc. (1901), p. 1528.
[118] J.O.C. Doc. (1902), p. 741.
[119] J.O.C. Doc. (1905, sess. ext.), p. 156.
[120] E., "L'État-major," F.M., February 15, 1902.

preferred to see another general in the post. He forthwith sent in his resignation to the President of the Republic. Even though the incident was eventually smoothed over, this problem and indeed all the difficulties created by the pretensions of Brugère were a source of profound concern for Waldeck-Rousseau as President of the Council of Ministers. He wished to avoid the unfortunate impression before the country that the government could not get along with any military chief, "not even a tried and tested republican, one who was hand-picked and a personal friend of the President of the Republic." [121]

Not only did André seek to reduce the authority of the Generalissimo, but he also systematically ignored the C.S.G. During his term of office that body met only infrequently. In 1903 there were but three meetings, while in 1904, up until the moment of André's departure in November, it had met only twice. Since the C.S.G. was, by presidential decree, supposed to meet at least once a month, the Minister of War was evidently seeking to give it as small a role as possible in the direction of the army. This led one military commentator to declare that under André the C.S.G. had been "little by little annihilated. . . ." [122] The efforts of André in this direction also appear to have been favorably received in parliament. In his report on the 1907 budget, Adolphe Messimy, at the time the unofficial military expert for the Radical Party, advocated a thoroughgoing reorganization of the whole French army, including a fundamental change in the attributes of the C.S.G. As now constituted, it was able to block necessary reforms and thus represented an "impairment and a limitation on the authority of the Minister." [123]

This reversion toward an essentially ministerial structure of command did not require any drastic revision in the decrees

[121] Combarieu, op. cit., pp. 170–171. See also pp. 103–104.
[122] Gen. Prudhomme, "L'apaisement et le C.S.G.," F.M., May 7 and 8, 1905.
[123] J.O.C. Déb. (1906), pp. 1316–1317.

governing the high command. Rather, the decrees in question were simply interpreted literally, with the accent placed on those clauses which stated that both the General Staff and the C.S.G. operated under the authority of the Minister of War. In fact, a reemphasis on the importance in the command structure of the French army of the Minister of War, as opposed to the Generalissimo or the Chief of Staff, was much more in keeping with the Constitution than was the system engineered by Freycinet.

None of the Ministers of War who over the next half-dozen years followed André was either a noteworthy or an outstanding figure. Two were civilians, the afore-mentioned Berteaux and his immediate successor, Eugène Étienne. Nor did the nomination of any of these men, civilian or military, as head of the French army appear to signify an attempt to initiate a particular social or political program with regard to the military. They were simply appointed to administer the department of war. The only possible exception here was the government of Georges Clemenceau, which assumed power in October 1906, for his choice as Minister of War was General Picquart.

Picquart had been dismissed from the army for the part he had played in the Dreyfus Affair. Along with Dreyfus, he was reinstated in 1906. Dreyfus was raised only one step to the rank of major, when, on the basis of his ability and his training, he might well have become a lieutenant colonel in the ordinary course of promotion. Picquart, on the other hand, was given the maximum promotion possible consonant with the rules governing time in rank. Having been dismissed from the army as a lieutenant colonel, he was reinstated as a brigadier general. With a Clemenceau cabinet in the offing and Picquart his nominee for the Ministry of War, the government made him a divisionary general with almost unseemly haste a month before the old Radical became premier. As a consequence, Picquart was, at the moment of his being named Minister of War, literally the most junior divisionary general in the army. Clemenceau was unperturbed at the objections of those who did not like Picquart becoming chief of the French army after so short a time in rank, and he sardonically declared: "To those who are of this opinion, I shall reply simply that a civilian Minister of War would have still less seniority." [124]

The nomination of Picquart was not well received in conservative circles. The argument was that with regard to the Dreyfus Affair, it was now most desirable that it be treated calmly and if possible covered with oblivion, but as the *Revue des deux mondes* pointed out, to make Picquart Minister of War would have just the opposite effect. It was not to be inferred that he would lend himself, directly or indirectly, to any of Clemenceau's schemes. "But his nomination in itself is an act of revenge against the great majority of the army and a good half of the nation." [125] There was in the army some fear that Picquart would use the occasion of his elevation to the summit of the military hierarchy to pay off a number of old scores. *France militaire* felt it necessary to remind its readers that Picquart was simply a soldier, a man of duty. "Let all be assured that the new Minister will never take into consideration anything but the military merit of his subordinates." [126]

Even though most of the officer corps looked upon the nomination of Picquart as a calculated affront, they accepted it without a murmur. A possibly apocryphal story, drawn from a police report of the time, quoted Galliffet to the effect that his house was always full of "officers of every rank, all of them known anti-Dreyfusards, who came to request that he recommend them to General Picquart." [127] If the workings of politics were now to make the once despised and execrated Picquart the Minister of War, the French officers were too well

---

[124] "La crise ministérielle," *F.M.*, October 24, 1906.

[125] *R.D.M.*, November 1, 1906, pp. 236–237.

[126] "Le général Picquart," *F.M.*, October 30, 1906.

[127] Archives de Préfecture de la Police de Paris (B a/1221, Doss. 262, 023), "Picquart," report of December 26, 1906.

disciplined and too resigned to do anything but accommodate themselves as best they could.

During his years of disgrace, Picquart had written at some length for the *Grande revue* on the necessity of introducing a certain number of fundamental reforms in the military institutions of France. His theories were generally in accordance with those advanced by the Radical Party, that is, a reduced term of service, greater stress placed on the reserves, and a breaking down of the wall separating the army from the rest of the state.[128] According to this prior statement of policy, it would seem that Clemenceau had made him Minister of War in order to initiate another bout of republicanization. In the seventeen-point program of democratic reforms that Clemenceau enunciated before the Chamber in November 1906, three points had to do with the army: a new law on the cadres and effectives, a law to reestablish "justice in the promotion of officers," and a law to reform military tribunals.[129] Not one of these measures had been enacted when the Clemenceau government fell two and a half years later.

As Minister of War, Picquart did not play the ferocious republican. Indeed, he went to great pains to be completely impartial in his dealings with the army, as when in 1907 he bestowed the command of the Sixth Army Corps, as always the most prestigious in France, upon a general reputed to have been seriously compromised in the Dreyfus Affair.[130] His term as Minister was characterized by no significant reforms, at least none of a "republican" nature. If considerable hopes had been placed in Picquart at the moment of his accession, they were disappointed. In the words of Paul-Boncour, "The gesture of Clemenceau was more spectacular than efficacious or useful."[131] Part of the reason certainly lay in one of the

[128] Col. Picquart, "Notes sur la situation militaire et sur les modifications qu'elle comporte," *Grande revue*, January 1, 1902, pp. 1 ff., and subsequent issues.

[129] Seignobos, *op. cit.*, Vol. VIII, p. 254.

[130] "Chronique française," *Revue militaire suisse*, August 1907, p. 656.

[131] Paul-Boncour, *op. cit.*, Vol. I, pp. 167–169.

essential traits in Picquart's character, his intellectual ability to see both sides of every question, accompanied by his consequent hesitancy to act decisively. He also had a well-founded, detached scorn for most of humanity. His sufferings and his rejection at the hands of his comrades had profoundly disillusioned him and sapped his force of will. "He did his best to do his duty conscientiously, but he also did it grudgingly and without enthusiasm." [132]

The man who succeeded Picquart as Minister of War, General Brun, had enjoyed an especially successful career before entering Rue Saint-Dominique. Having served for about four years as Chief of the General Staff and before that as head of the École de Guerre, he was possessed of either rare military ability or excellent connections. He was noted primarily for his profound skepticism. Messimy recounts how Brun once chided him for his vigorous interest in military affairs, calling him one of those enthusiasts who still believed in the possibility of war.[133] On the other hand, *Spectateur militaire* claimed that Brun, despite appearances, was an extremely prudent man with a circumspect force of character.[134] Whatever the truth, in the nineteen months that he was Minister, Brun did not exercise the prerogatives of his office in any very forceful way.

In reorganizing and strengthening the C.S.G. and the General Staff, Freycinet had originally intended to give to the peacetime structure of command a permanence and stability that for political reasons could not be obtained through the Minister of War. One of the paradoxical consequences of the Dreyfus Affair was that by bringing into existence a relatively cohesive parliamentary coalition, based on a large block of Radical deputies, it also provided a much higher degree of stability than usual for a Minister of War. André stayed in office for four and a half years, while Picquart held the post

[132] "Chronique française," *Revue militaire suisse,* August 1909, pp. 691–692.

[133] A. Messimy, *Mes souvenirs* (Paris: Plon, 1937), p. 71.

[134] *S.M.,* February 1, 1911, p. 320.

for almost three years. Of the five other men who served as Minister of War between 1900 and 1911, two had their terms of office cut short by death.

Political circumstances decreed that the Ministers of War of this period were to enjoy a comparatively high degree of stability, but they also brought almost chronic instability to the post of Generalissimo. Whereas Saussier held the job for over a decade, in the thirteen years that followed his retirement six different men served as Generalissimo. Three of them resigned as the result of differences of opinion with the government over military policy: Generals Jamont in 1900, Hagron in 1907, and Michel in 1911. Only Brugère served for any length of time, but, as has been seen, his relations with the government were often stormy. As for the post of Chief of Staff, two of the men who held the office, Generals Pendezec and Brun, served for a relatively long period of time, five and four years respectively. They were rigidly subordinated to the Minister of War, however, and their prerogatives with regard to the army were closely circumscribed.

The consequence of this lessening in the authority and prestige of the Chief of Staff and the Generalissimo was a weakening in the high command of the army. A forceful reassertion by the Minister of War of his prerogatives as constitutional chief of the army, as was done by General André, might to a degree compensate for it, except that André acted from political rather than military motives. None of the men who succeeded André had either the ability or the desire to play the role of Commander in Chief. With the Generalissimo and the Chief of Staff in eclipse and with no concurrent increase in the authority of the Minister of War, the French army was all but acephalous during the first decade of the twentieth century. This fact combined with the prolonged crisis in the morale of the officer corps meant that in the years after the Dreyfus Affair, France was in a very poor military posture vis-à-vis Germany. The military would, no doubt, claim that the government only made this already unfortunate situation worse by enacting a new conscription law in 1905 which reduced the term of service to two years.

The Two-Years Law

In sponsoring the two-years law the government was going against the apparently unanimous opinion of the soldiers. Contrary to what had taken place in the period before the enactment of the three-years law in 1889, when a very large portion of the officer corps had advocated the measure, it was very difficult to find any professional military man who did not believe that a reduction in the term of service would be harmful to the army. Every time it was discussed in the military press there was complete agreement on this point. One simply could not make a soldier in that short a period of time. As early as 1895 the C.S.G., representing the considered opinion of the most eminent generals in the army, declared itself opposed to the idea. In response to an inquiry made by General Zurlinden, at the moment Minister of War, General Saussier, speaking in the name of the members of that prestigious body, announced that he was against any further reduction in the term of service.[135]

The arguments advanced by the military against the two years' service had a curiously familiar ring. Essentially they were the same ones that had been used in the 1880's by those who opposed reducing the term of service to three years. As long as France lacked an adequate corps of N.C.O.'s, it was foolhardy to talk of the conscripts serving any less than three years. Even if the term of service in the German army was now two years, there they also had some 75,000 or 80,000 N.C.O.'s as well. France with her corps of 22,000 long-term N.C.O.'s was in no position to experiment.[136] In the opinion of one general, the introduction of new and more effective weapons had made

---

[135] Conseil supérieur de la Guerre, "Registre des déliberation," No. 6 (1893–1895), p. 209.

[136] "Service de Deux Ans," *F.M.*, July 5, 1902.

warfare more terrible than ever before. To withstand its demands now required an even greater degree of training, discipline, and moral stamina. He asked if this was really the moment to reduce further the length of military service.[137]

Innate military conservatism and the traditional distrust for any idea originating in civilian circles were the chief reasons why the army refused to admit the feasibility of the two years' service. Recent interventions by the state in military affairs certainly exacerbated this distrust. Actually, there were a number of perfectly valid military reasons for reducing and equalizing the term of service. Approximately two fifths of each conscript class managed to qualify for some kind of exemption, with the result that in many infantry regiments well over 50 per cent of the troops served no more than ten months. Since they were thrown into the same units as their less fortunate comrades who were obliged to serve the full three years, their effect on the morale and the solidity of these regiments was bad.[138] The constitution of an adequate cadre of reserve officers was also made difficult by the 1889 law because so large a proportion of the educated youth of the nation served only ten months.[139]

Even if every able-bodied young man in France now spent at least ten months in the army, thus greatly increasing the number of trained men in case of war, the most troublesome faults in the 1872 law, the privileges accorded to wealth, had not been erased. In one sense, the defects in the old law were even accentuated. Where the one-year volunteers had at least had to pay 1,500 francs for the privilege of having their military service reduced and had received a supposedly more difficult and intensive course of training, the new privileged classes, those seeking higher education, had to make no pecuniary sacrifices.[140] In effect, anyone who was not obliged

[137] Gen. Darrécagaix, *La guerre et l'armée* (Paris: Chapelot, 1901), pp. 36–39.
[138] Col. Revol, *Histoire de l'armée française* (Paris: Larousse, 1929), p. 206.
[139] H. Contamine, *La Revanche* (Paris: Berger-Levrault, 1957), pp. 94–95.
[140] Simond, *op. cit.,* pp. 551–552.

by financial reasons to quit school at an early age was certain to escape two years of military service. This provision of the 1889 law thus served less as a means to foster the cultural and scientific life of the nation than as a privilege for the sons of the bourgeoisie.[141] Although the 5,000 in every class who were candidates for a university degree were militarily of little importance when compared to the 60,000-odd exempted for some social or humanitarian reason,[142] their exemption more than anything else provided the grounds on which the 1889 law was condemned.

The educational exemptions also had an unforeseen effect on the schools and universities. Since the mere fact of being a candidate for certain diplomas was sufficient to qualify one for an exemption, the result was that the institutions of higher learning were, in the words of Messimy, flooded with "innumerable postulants, eager for studies without a future, and all aspiring for membership in that fortunate intellectual elite which will exempt them from two years in the barracks."[143] The number of young men who discovered vocations in the learned professions rose sharply in the decade after the enactment of the 1889 law. Whereas there were 591 doctorates in medicine awarded in 1891, a figure which had not changed substantially in over ten years, by 1897 there were 1,200, and the number was still rising. The increase in the number of doctorates in law was comparable: 100 in 1889, 250 by the turn of the century. The School of Oriental Languages showed the most striking spurt in enrollment, going from only 34 students in 1884 to 372 in 1898.[144]

In France during the 1890's there was considerable discussion of the feasibility of a two-year term of service. It may have been prompted by the introduction of a similar measure

[141] *R.D.M.*, July 15, 1902, pp. 475–476.

[142] *Le Temps*, May 24, 1901.

[143] *Journal Officiel du Sénat: Documents* (hereafter cited as *J.O.S. Doc.*), (1901), p. 511.

[144] Ch. Dupuy, "Le service de deux ans et les dispenses," *Revue politique et parlementaire*, February 1903, pp. 235–239.

in Germany in 1893. A number of bills to that effect were presented to the chambers, but the first one to be given serious scrutiny came from a relatively obscure Senator, Doctor Rolland, who confessed to being quite ignorant in matters pertaining to the army.[145] Originally presented in 1898, Rolland's proposition was then taken up by the Senate Army Commission. The bill emerged from the Commission in 1901, but another two years passed before the first reading of the bill in the Senate was completed. The chairman of the Commission was Freycinet, and he, more than anyone else, guided the bill through its various stages until its final passage into law. Since the contributions from the floor of the Senate and from the Chamber were minimal, this, in effect, made him the coauthor of the law.

In drawing up the bill, the Senate Army Commission unhesitatingly faced the full implications of a shortened term of service. There could now be no doubt that in any future war, the reserves, and not the men on active duty, would have the preponderant role. Most conscripts, it was frankly admitted, would not acquire military spirit in time of peace. Since the qualities to be found in a purely professional army could not be instilled, there was no longer any reason to keep a man in training for an extended length of time. In fact, this might even be harmful. Under the new military regime, a conscript would serve twenty-two or twenty-four months, in theory, just long enough to acquire and perhaps to retain the necessary fundamentals of military training. His service would end before he began to be bored by routine and while his sense of discipline was still fresh and vigorous.[146]

In the debates over the law the legislators, and in particular the deputies, showed themselves to be "more preoccupied by their electoral interests than by the interests of the army." [147]

---

[145] J. Monteilhet, *Les institutions militaires de la France* (Paris: Alcan, 1932), pp. 243–244.

[146] *J.O.S. Doc.* (1901), pp. 512–516.

[147] Simond, *op. cit.*, p. 549.

The emphasis was on the political and social desirability of the two-year service. Insofar as military considerations were weighed at all, the contention was simply that the army would not be harmed by it and might even be improved. As Freycinet declared, inequality had been the one significant defect in the 1889 law; the legislators now had a unique opportunity to consolidate French military institutions and to "give to the army a definitive law by causing the disappearance of that troublesome element." [148]

Any argument to the effect that the two years' service would not seriously impair the military efficiency of the army was strenuously refuted by the soldiers and by their spokesmen in parliament. General Billot, one of the leading adversaries of the law in the Senate, had been a member of the famous Commission of Forty-Five in 1872 and had opposed Thiers on the five years' service. He claimed as a good republican to be in sympathy with current social developments, but as a soldier he believed that "war is war. . . . In this matter, social evolution means nothing." Two years would simply not be long enough to give France the solid and well-trained army she needed.[149]

Aside from the reduction in the term of service to two years, the most significant feature in the bill was the abolition of all exemptions. No one who was physically able could now escape serving his full term under the colors. This included those who had formerly been exempted for humanitarian reasons, such as the sole support of a family and the eldest in a family of orphans. A provision was made in the law for the payment of a small stipend to needy families, for whom the departure of a son, father, or brother might cause undue hardship. For anyone wishing to complete his studies there was a *sursis d'appel,* or a postponement of induction.

The Senate first debated the bill in the late spring of 1902.

---

[148] *Journal Officiel du Sénat: Débats* (hereafter cited as *J.O.S. Déb.*), (1902), p. 885.

[149] *J.O.S. Déb.* (1905), p. 264.

Possibly chagrined that the initiative for so eminently egalitarian a measure had come from the upper chamber, the deputies actually anticipated the opening of the Senate debate by a few months, interjecting a lively discussion of the principle of the two years' service into the debate on the 1902 budget and expressing their approval of it in a vote on the order of the day.[150] The first reading of the bill in the Senate was interrupted for a period of about six months and was not finished until January 1903. The second reading took place later in the same year, after which it was sent to the Chamber.

The only important modification in the bill that was introduced and accepted in the course of the debate in the Senate was an amendment providing that candidates for Saint-Cyr or Polytechnique spend a year in the ranks before admission to either of the two schools.[151] When the Chamber Army Commission examined the bill, true to egalitarian principles, it raised the figure to two years in the ranks for future officers, declaring that one could learn to command only after first having obeyed and that officers who had lived the life of a soldier for two years "would know better what is proper for the nation under arms and what may be expected of it." [152] After debating and voting on this slightly altered version of the bill in the course of 1904, the Chamber sent it back to the Senate. There provision for the second year in the ranks for future officers was abolished. The Chamber did not insist on this point or on a number of other minor matters, accepting and voting on the Senate version in its entirety during one long session. Thirty-three years after it had been announced as the fundamental principle of French military institutions, equality in the discharge of a citizen's military obligations was finally achieved.

From the moment the Senate first took the measure into consideration, the enactment of the two-years law had a sense

---

[150] *J.O.C. Déb.* (1902), pp. 885–915.

[151] *J.O.S. Déb.* (1903), p. 906.

[152] *J.O.C. Doc.* (1904), p. 172.

of inevitability about it. The degree to which all but a few legislators had come to accept a reduced and equalized term of service as either desirable or politically expedient may be seen from the size of the majorities favoring its passage through both chambers. In the Senate the article concerning the length of service was passed 231 to 26,[153] while in the Chamber the majority was an absolutely overwhelming 510 to 3, with only 25 abstaining.[154] Many Nationalist and Conservative deputies opposed the law, but they were, by the electoral facts of life, obliged either to vote for it or to abstain. *Le Temps* noted that at the moment of the final vote in the Chamber, 22 of these deputies abstained, while 69 of them actually voted in favor of it, "faint with terror at the thought of angering their constituents." [155]

Few as they were, and although obviously defending a hopeless cause, the opponents of the two years' service were tireless debaters, often speaking cogently and always at length. Their most telling argument was built on the unanimous objections of the military to the measure. This they attempted to dramatize, quite effectively, by calling upon the Minister of War at least once during each reading of the bill to consult the C.S.G. in order to ascertain its opinion. He was unwilling to do so for obvious reasons. General André declared before the Senate that since he had already contacted each individual member of the C.S.G. and had learned his views on the subject, there was no need officially to call a meeting. In any case, neither the government nor the chambers were constitutionally obliged to consult the C.S.G. concerning conscription.[156] Every time this or a similar motion was presented, the two chambers invariably upheld the Minister of War and rejected it.

The lengths to which the adversaries of the law were willing to take their oratorical and rhetorical efforts was demonstrated by General Billot just before the final vote in the Senate. Declaring that since the Chamber still had to vote for the last time, the bill was not yet law. He therefore hoped that the President of the Republic, using the authority given him by the Constitution of 1875, would intervene and withdraw the bill from consideration in order that it could be resubmitted to parliament for further debate and more detailed scrutiny. The President of the Senate had to remind Billot that it was impossible for the Chief of State to act against the express will of parliament.[157]

In opposing the enactment of the two-years law, the conservative deputies and senators claimed that they were thinking above all of national defense and that they represented the views of the military on the subject. They could also pose as the defenders of the poor and humble. The abolition of all exemptions, both humanitarian and educational, could be interpreted as falling much more heavily on the lower than on the middle classes. A young man from a poor family, which had made great sacrifices for his education, would now see his start in life delayed for a full two years. As one senator declared to the authors of the bill: "You only inconvenience the young men from the wealthy classes . . . the sons of the poor you crush." [158] One general, writing in *France militaire,* said that he had made an impartial survey into the probable effects of the suppression of all social and humanitarian exemptions on rural families. He claimed to have found that people did not like the idea, particularly if it involved the family breadwinner. "Their vital interests are harmed." [159]

The Chamber, in its approach to the two years' service, tended more than the Senate to stress the fact that it represented an important social and military reform and that it

---

[157] *J.O.S. Déb.* (1905), p. 262.

[158] *Ibid.,* p. 61.

[159] Gen. Luzeux, "La vérité sur le service de deux ans," *F.M.,* August 6, 1902.

heralded the advent of the nation in arms. According to the report of the Chamber Army Commission on the bill, "The modern concept of the army is that by which it is identical with the nation, draws from it all its resources, and has no separate and distinct existence outside the nation." [160] Having posited the concept of the nation in arms in fine rhetorical fashion, the military theorists in the Chamber nevertheless displayed an inability or an unwillingness to follow the idea through to its logical conclusion. After stating that the necessary military training could be instilled in a citizen soldier within the space of one year, the Chamber Army Commission was obliged to justify holding the conscripts a second year by claiming that their training would be thus "confirmed." The Commission further pointed out that it would be impossible to maintain the army at its required legal effective strength of 575,000 without the second year of service. Otherwise, there would be needed some 200,000 long-term volunteers, coming at the rate of 40,000 per year, a number impossible to obtain in France.[161] Why, if it was to be little more than a school for the nation in arms, one needed to worry about its size as an organized standing army, was a question that the military theorists in the Chamber did not answer. It is, however, indicative of a certain fundamental ambiguity in their military thinking, even when they were at their most doctrinaire.

By the turn of the century, there were those in parliament for whom even a reduction in the term of service to two years represented an inadequate step. The Socialists, who first began to appear in the Chamber of Deputies in a sizable number during the 1890's, believed that the best solution to the problem of national defense lay in the introduction of a military system based solely on the reserves, a true nation in arms. Thus it was that during the debates in the Chamber, the Socialist deputy Édouard Vaillant introduced an amendment calling for the abolition of the standing army and the institu-

---

[160] *J.O.C. Doc.* (1904), pp. 148–150.
[161] *Ibid.*, p. 151.

tion of a militia organized along the same lines as in Switzerland. His amendment was voted down 505 to 68.[162]

The debate over the two-years law came at a time when relations between the Republic and the army were severely strained, the final discussion of the law in fact taking place only a few months after the revelations concerning the *fiches* and the consequent resignation of General André. Yet very little of this tension is reflected in the actual debates over the law. At one point, Vaillant did raise the subject of the persecution of Socialist conscripts and gave an account of various disloyal acts toward the Republic committed by officers of "Jesuitical tendencies."[163] General Billot, on the other hand, injected an impassioned plea that the government recognize the nonpolitical attitude of the army and the fact that it was now loyally serving the Republic as it had every other regime.[164] This was about as close as the troubled state of civil-military relations came to being introduced into the discussion, let alone influencing it.

Between the Dreyfus Affair and the enactment of the two-years law there is no clear-cut cause-and-effect relationship. The initiative for the law came from the Senate, always more immune than the Chamber to the currents of public opinion. The Senate Army Commission had already taken the original proposition of Doctor Rolland into consideration before the Affair began to have any serious political reverberations. There is evidence that the Waldeck-Rousseau government was not anxious to see the two-years law enacted. Galliffet told a parliamentary commission, in his capacity as Minister of War, that such a measure would be dangerous without an adequate corps of N.C.O.'s, and he contended that Waldeck-Rousseau was of the same opinion.[165] At most, the Dreyfus Affair may

---

[162] *J.O.C. Déb.* (1904), p. 1294.
[163] *Ibid.*
[164] *J.O.S. Déb.* (1905), pp. 137–138.
[165] Letter from Galliffet to *Journal des Débats,* June 20, 1902.

have hastened the coming of the two years' service by contributing to the general consolidation to the left of the republicans in the Chamber, followed by the victory of the *Bloc des Gauches*. The Combes government, unlike its predecessor, made the enactment of the law part of its official program, but by then the Senate was about to begin debate on it.

The two years' service would have come about eventually in any case. On one side was the current French passion for equality, coupled with the fact that Germany had reduced her military service to two years in 1893. According to Monteilhet, "It was henceforth impossible to persuade any Frenchman, by nature conceited, that he could not become a good soldier in the same period of time as the subjects of William II, who were represented as slow in mind and body." [166] On the other side was the unwillingness of the bourgeoisie to see their sons serve three years under the colors, as well as the financial impossiblity of keeping a whole conscript class for thirty-four or thirty-six months. The two years' service was the logical result of these two opposing pressures.

After the passage of the 1905 law, the professional soldiers recognized that a number of fundamental changes would have to be made in the methods and spirit of military training. Even if they disapproved of the law and doubted the motives of the parliament that enacted it, the military were still obliged to make the best of things. As General de Négrier wrote, "It is now solely a question of studying those arrangements which will permit this law to do the least possible harm." [167] The army would now have to give the conscripts a different kind of training, which would aim less at turning them into disciplined soldiers who were part of a large standing army than in making them capable of being quickly reintegrated as reservists. This in turn demanded an evolution

---

[166] Monteilhet, *op. cit.*, p. 245.
[167] Gen. de Négrier, "Le moral des troupes," *R.D.M.*, February 1, 1905, p. 502.

in the outlook of the officer corps. Writing in *France militaire,* one anonymous critic declared that the French officer had not yet prepared himself for his new task.

> We still concentrate on machine-like instruction and not enough on education. We demand too much of memory and not enough of the natural intelligence of a conscript. And it is very hard for it to be otherwise. We are an old army and therefore weighed down by traditions, left over from other periods when they were perfectly valid, but which are now nothing more than empty formalities and stifling routines.[168]

The years during which the new conscription law was being discussed and voted on coincided with an ominous phenomenon long forecast by demographers. France was beginning to lag far behind Germany in population. Even though France had a higher percentage of her people under arms than any other European country, she had been able to match each increase in the size of the German standing army without undue strain for a quarter of a century after the defeat of 1870. After about 1895, however, as the population of France remained stationary, with a fairly constant number of men reaching military age each year, Germany was able slowly to increase the size of her army in a way which was beyond French capabilities. This growing discrepancy between the two armies continued to bother French military theorists until 1914. The Russian hordes, which by the signature of the Alliance Treaty of 1894 would seem to have compensated for the French deficiency in manpower, appeared less reassuring after the Russo-Japanese War. Under these circumstances, the enactment of the two-years law seemed in the estimation of the soldiers to herald a slackening in the military effort of France at a moment when it should have been intensified.

In reply to such assertions, one could well argue that the two years' service, with all exemptions disallowed, actually weighed more heavily on French youth as a whole than had

---

[168] "Le service de deux ans, son application," *F.M.,* April 29, 1905.

the 1889 law. A larger percentage of each conscript class than formerly was to be enrolled, including many who would once have been rejected because of physical deficiencies or for some humanitarian reason. The weaker physical specimens were supposedly to be assigned to sedentary, auxiliary tasks, thus releasing the fit and able for service with the line companies. At the same time, the authors of the law intended that the army change its traditional attitude toward the troops in uniform. With the military authorities taking the second- and third-year men to act as orderlies and personal servants and to perform the multitude of other auxiliary tasks around the regiment, 90 per cent of the troops actually training with combat units under the 1889 law had been men either serving ten months or in their first year of training.[169] The legislators demanded that such practices cease forthwith and that all men inducted for military service spend their whole time under the colors learning how to be more effective fighting men.

The army, however, despite the reiterated declarations of parliament as to the more efficient use of its personnel, did not appear anxious to mend its ways. In his report on the 1907 budget, Messimy noted that there were still large numbers of troops employed, in one capacity or another, as officers' servants. The French army, in his words, would appear to have become an "immense employment office," through whose operations "some 75,000 or 80,000 men out of the 200,000 in each contingent spend almost half the time they owe their country in doing the dishes, walking children and dogs, or driving a horse and carriage."[170] Despite further evidence provided by the deputy Charles Humbert concerning the scandalous conditions in the garrison at Verdun, where troops were taken away from their primary mission of assuring the defense of the eastern frontiers of France and assigned to the upkeep of officers' tennis courts and skating rinks,[171] parliament, as usual, was

[169] *J.O.S. Doc.* (1901), p. 513.
[170] *J.O.C. Doc.* (1906), p. 1357.
[171] *J.O.C. Déb.* (1906), pp. 3027–3028.

unsure of how to implement its exhortations in any very forceful way.

As trivial as may have been the whole issue of the officer corps using conscripts as domestic servants, it was nevertheless indicative of a continuing duality in the French military establishment. For many the two-years law presaged a new military era. In the event of war the defense of France would be entrusted no longer to the standing army reinforced by a certain number of reserves but to the reserves themselves, the nation in arms. The standing army would thus become no more than a school for the training of the nation in arms in time of peace, losing its identity within it in time of war. But such a vision as to the significance of the two-years law implied the enactment of a considerable program of supplementary legislation, including a law on the organization of the reserves and one on the recruitment of officers and N.C.O.'s, not to mention a new law on the cadres, all aimed at placing the armed forces on a new footing vis-à-vis the nation.[172]

The ultimate effect of such a program would be the disappearance of the professional soldier as such, a man living under a special legal and social code. He would be replaced by a kind of military civil servant with a status and function analogous to those of a teacher in the *Université*. This was essentially the ideal proposed by Jaurès in his famous work *L'armée nouvelle*. Whatever the possible military benefits to be derived from such a system, it would have required a legislative effort comparable to that undertaken by the National Assembly in the 1870's, and this was beyond either the capabilities or the pretensions of the parliaments elected in 1902 and 1906.

The logical corollary of the two years' service was an intensified program of reserve training, but parliament in fact moved in the opposite direction. In 1907 the Clemenceau government introduced a bill calling for a reduction in the length of the two training periods that were mandatory for

---

[172] J. L. de Lanessan, *Nos forces militaires* (Paris: Alcan, 1913), pp. 74–75.

every reservist and member of the territorial army. The official justification for this measure was that the military authorities, always less interested in the reserves than in the men on active duty, did little to make these military refresher courses either interesting or worth while. Here General de Lacroix, the Vice-President of the C.S.G., had to admit that there might be good reason for the reservists to be discontented.[173] Although some opposed the measure, including Freycinet, who endeavored in a memorable speech before the Senate in January 1908 to prevent its enactment,[174] it was to no avail. Whatever authority the former Minister of War, who more than anyone else laid the foundations for an effective reserve program, may have had over his colleagues, it was offset by the electoral pressure on the left to lessen in any possible way the burden of military service.

Because parliament was unwilling to respond to the full implications of the nation in arms, the army continued to exist as an institution apart within the French state. Its autonomy was reduced, since the government, disturbed by the attitude of the officer corps during the Dreyfus Affair, found itself obliged to interfere more directly in its internal concerns than before. Yet even here the government did not attempt a direct frontal attack on the institutional interests of the military but rather limited itself to secretive and behind-the-scenes maneuvers. Certainly, many of the presuppositions upon which civil-military relations had been founded since 1871 broke down, but the fundamental structure of the army and its situation within the French state underwent no significant change. This fact was to be of considerable importance in the years just before the outbreak of World War I.

---

[173] Monteilhet, *op. cit.,* p. 258.
[174] *J.O.S. Déb.* (1908), pp. 68 ff.

PART IV

THE ENTENTE RESTORED

CHAPTER SEVEN

The Army and the
Réveil national: *1910-1914*

The Shadow of War and the Reorganization of the High Command

The *Réveil national,* of the years 1910–1914, was one of those nebulous but nevertheless real phenomena in history which can be neither wholly explained nor discounted. A movement in public opinion of great political significance, its underlying causes and the reason for its profound impact are difficult to assess. In effect, the *Réveil national* was a rediscovery by an important segment of the French political and intellectual elite of the patriotic ideals and the patriotic vocabulary apparently discredited and abandoned at the time of the Dreyfus Affair. If during the late 1890's and early 1900's an increasingly large and vital element in France had rejected the slightly stale patriotic themes dear to the generation of 1870 to seek a more universal and humanitarian ideal, this reaction did not last very long.

A necessary factor in any humanitarian vision of the world was a *détente* with Germany. Although for some years at the turn of the century German assertiveness on the international scene did not appear to touch the vital interests of France, the *coup de Tanger* of June 1905, opening the First Moroccan Crisis, ushered in a new era of tension. The First Moroccan Crisis reminded people once again that war was still a possibility. As each succeeding crisis in the coming decade served only to reaffirm this possibility, "there was to be seen within the milieux of the cultivated bourgeoisie, and especially among the students, a very powerful renewal in both the patriotic and military ideals." [1]

The increased tensions on the international scene were the dominant factor in this revival of the old enthusiasms, but there were also developments at home pointing in the same direction. A growing intransigence could be sensed among the working classes. Fearful of losing support from this sector of the electorate, the Socialists in parliament found themselves obliged to advocate a more uncompromising line than had been considered expedient in recent years. The result was a breakdown in the *Bloc des Gauches.* The specter of social revolution, which now seemed to hover about their erstwhile political allies, forced the Radicals to look toward the Center and the Right in their parliamentary combinations, "to accept ever more 'moderate' government and, increasingly, to adopt nationalist symbols." [2] In the process, their attitude toward the military necessarily changed. The army, after all, was the surest guarantee of the continuance of the established social order in which the Radicals too had a stake.

These developments, both domestic and international, reacted in an intellectual milieu already in the process of evolving toward new ideals and interests. If, in the words of Péguy, everything "begins as a *mystique* and ends as a *politique,"* the generation of ardent intellectuals who had rallied to the cause of Captain Dreyfus, and who had vigorously rejected the rationale offered by the army, had cause to be disillusioned by the antics of the triumphant Radicals. "The Radicals in power had been no different from any other government in power." [3]

---

[1] R. Girardet, *La société militaire dans la France contemporaine, 1815–1939* (Paris: Plon, 1953), p. 238.

[2] E. Weber, *The Nationalist Revival in France, 1905–1914* (Berkeley and Los Angeles: University of California Press, 1959), p. 39.

[3] *Ibid.,* p. 64.

They were no less arbitrary in their policies and no less prone to corruption than their Moderate or Opportunist predecessors. A reaction against the government policies of the Combes era was understandable for this reason. It was also a natural reflex on the part of the younger generation. Just as the young aesthetes and intellectuals of the 1890's had rejected the ideals and the vocabulary of their fathers, so too were their successors rejecting theirs. Whatever its ultimate explanation, the *Réveil national* was a vital force, profoundly moving public opinion and affecting the attitude of the politically dominant elements in France toward the army.

The Radicals had come into their political inheritance at the turn of the century, defending the regime against its internal enemies. In this category, some of the more doctrinaire members of the party were wont to place the army as well as their traditional foe, the Church. For this and a number of other reasons, an effort was made to transform the military institutions of France, but this transformation was hardly under way when the Radicals were forced to pause and wonder whether an army organized according to the precepts of the nation in arms that they were championing would be very effective. In the face of the outbreaks of violence led by the syndicates, the army had to be used as a police force, a mission certainly not in accordance with the usual theories about the nation in arms. Then, too, the First Moroccan Crisis led many to question whether the standing army should be weakened any further and whether the officer was likely to have only a social role to play in the near future. Political power naturally entailed responsibility for the Radicals just as for any of their predecessors. This sobering realization by the Radicals that France still had to be governed and defended provided the grounds for a new understanding between the army and the regime.

During the Clemenceau ministry, lasting from 1906 to 1909, there were already signs that this accommodation was beginning to take place. Despite the fact that Clemenceau, in his choice of Picquart as Minister of War and in the new decree

on honors and ceremonial precedence, made what appeared to
be calculated affronts to the military, the conservative *Revue
des deux mondes* did at least credit him with understanding,
"contrary to most of his political friends . . . the need for having an army." [4] By 1908, and perhaps before, Clemenceau had
come to believe that war with Germany was both certain and
near. [5] Under these circumstances he was not going to be doctrinaire or to be guided purely by political considerations in
his choice of military subordinates. In 1907 the man he wished
to have as head of the École de Guerre was Ferdinand Foch, at
the time a brigadier general. Foch was a practicing Catholic
and the brother of a Jesuit priest. [6] He had been passed over
for promotion during the André ministry because of his religious views. When Clemenceau was confronted with these
supposed drawbacks to Foch's nomination, he made it clear
that he had no interest in them at all. The military qualities of
the man who was to be the head of the École de Guerre were
now all that counted. The political and religious factor that a
few years before might have dictated who held the post were
to be disregarded.

This realization by the government that there might be
something to be said after all for the traditional organization
and attributes of the army was accompanied by a noticeable
evolution in the rhetoric of republican politicians on the subject of military affairs. In the years after 1905, and particularly
after 1910, patriotism was becoming "once more an honored
ingredient of the politician's vocabulary." [7] The process could
be seen in the annual reports on the army budget. Adolphe
Messimy, the reporter for the 1908 budget, still referred to the
army in terms that could be considered as normal for a good
Radical, calling upon the officer corps not to form a special

[4] *Revue des deux mondes,* August 1, 1907, p. 712.

[5] Weber, *op. cit.,* p. 50.

[6] G. Bruun, *Clemenceau* (Cambridge: Harvard University Press, 1944), p.
81.

[7] Weber, *op. cit.,* p. 50.

caste separate from the rest of the nation. Still, he did commend the military for beginning to demonstrate a willingness to understand the aspirations of their contemporaries and no longer to be "systematically ignorant of them. . . ." [8] The reporter for the 1909 budget, Gervais, displayed somewhat more sympathy for the point of view of the soldier than had his recent predecessors. After discussing at some length the social role of the officer, he nevertheless warned of the danger of making him into too much of a "schoolmaster." [9]

For the next three years, the preparation of the army budget was entrusted to Étienne Clémentel, a Radical in the original patriotic tradition of the party. Rather than stressing the duties of the soldier toward the Republic, he wondered what the government might do for the army, both materially, in terms of better pay, and morally, by making "every effort to raise to a higher level than ever the esteem in which those who devote their lives to the service of their country are deservedly held." [10] Two years later, he cited the recent Agadir crisis as conclusive evidence of both France's need for a strong army and of the insubstantial character of those comforting dreams "of universal brotherhood, which seemed to prove the impossibility of a European conflict." [11]

The degree to which blatant patriotism had come back into favor with the Radicals could be seen in Clémentel's advocacy of the red trousers for the French infantryman. In recent years a number of European armies, including the German and the British, had outfitted their troops for field service, at least, in uniforms of an unobtrusive color. The great virtue of such uniforms from a tactical point of view was their lessened visibility. When the French made similar experiments with a drab shade called *réséda* during the fall maneuvers of 1911, there

[8] *Journal Officiel de la Chambre des Députés: Documents* (hereafter cited as *J.O.C. Doc.*), (1907), p. 1427.

[9] *J.O.C. Doc.* (1908), pp. 2859–2860

[10] *J.O.C. Doc.* (1909), p. 1734.

[11] *J.O.C. Doc.* (1911), p. 1324.

was a tremendous outcry in the nationalist press. It was, apparently, all part of a Masonic conspiracy against the French officer "to reduce his already compromised prestige."[12] In his report on the 1912 budget, Clémentel was not that rabid in his defense of the red trousers, but he did question whether the transformation of the attire of France's "alert little troopers" into some dull shade would not lower their morale.[13]

Further evidence that military patriotism was again acceptable to the Left may be seen in the evolution of the attitude of certain politicians toward the army. Alexandre Millerand, who as a Socialist had been taken into the Waldeck-Rousseau cabinet as a counterweight to the presence there of General de Galliffet, had by 1912 progressed so far as to be an eminently suitable Minister of War in the first Poincaré government. Among his earliest actions as Minister of War was to order the destruction of all files at Rue Saint-Dominique relating to the political opinions of the officer corps.[14] By thus demonstrating that the government no longer took official cognizance of such matters, Millerand implicitly repudiated the policy of the Waldeck-Rousseau and the Combes governments.

This same evolution may also be seen in the case of Adolphe Messimy. Having quit the army as a consequence of his Dreyfusard beliefs, he entered politics with the avowed intention of working to "reconcile the army with the nation."[15] His first efforts in that direction included a proposition presented to the Chamber in 1903[16] and the report on the 1908 budget,[17] both of which advocated a complete reorganization of France's military institutions in order to render them more

----

[12] *Echo de Paris,* October 2, 1911. Quoted in A. Messimy, *Mes souvenirs* (Paris: Plon, 1937), p. 118.

[13] *J.O.C. Doc.* (1911), p. 1344.

[14] A. Millerand, *Pour la défense nationale* (Paris: Charpentier, 1913), p. 254.

[15] Messimy, *op. cit.,* pp. 14–15.

[16] *J.O.C. Doc.* (1903), pp. 873 ff.

[17] *J.O.C. Doc.* (1907), pp. 1425 ff.

efficient and to make them correspond more closely with the needs of the country and the spirit of the times. A few years later, in 1912, after he had been Minister of War for six months, Messimy was chided for having deserted the vigorous and original ideas of his earlier days. He replied that anyone bearing the heavy responsibilities of the department of war had no business trying to win a precarious notoriety through the novelty of his personal ideas. "Rather he must try to contribute something useful and truly effective to strengthening the nation's defense."[18] In itself this may be taken as a succinct statement of the maturity in military questions achieved by the Radicals.

This return to the old military patriotism of the 1870's and 1880's made possible a revival of the climate of confidence similar to what had existed in former days. Certainly, the Dreyfus Affair and all that had accompanied it were not forgotten by either the army or the state, but there did seem to be a mutual willingness on the part of both to ignore it. Throughout that trying period the military as a body had given the politicians no real cause to doubt their traditional disciplined obedience to the powers that be, while the Republic had to recognize that, when all was said and done, it still needed the army. No one in the government or in parliament had any feasible or coherent alternative to a standing army organized according to traditional precepts, or at least not one likely to win the adherence of the majority of legislators. The result was that, with regard to a number of the important military problems broached in this period, the government tended to favor the solutions advocated by the soldiers themselves, rather than trying to act in accordance with the dictates of recent republican military theory. This is evident in the most significant military reform of the period, the reorganization of the high command in 1911, and also in the enactment of the three-years law of 1913.

[18] *Journal Officiel de la Chambre des Députés: Débats* (hereafter cited as *J.O.C. Déb.*), (1912, sess. ext.), pp. 3079–3080.

One of the most unfortunate consequences of the break-down in the entente between the army and the Republic had been a serious weakening in the high command. Following the retirement of General Brugère in 1906, there was, as has been noted, chronic instability in the post of Generalissimo, with four different men holding the job over the next five years. Although the Chief of Staff enjoyed a greater degree of permanence, with only three incumbents over a period of ten years, he was so completely subordinated to the wishes of an ephemeral Minister of War that he no longer exercised a deci-sive influence over the army.

Whatever the military competence of the chiefs of the army in the first decade of the century, none of them could aspire to the natural ascendancy of a Saussier or a Miribel. Certain of them, such as Michel, elevated to the post of Generalissimo in 1910, or Laffon de Ladébat, named Chief of Staff in the same year, appeared to owe their good fortune as much to political intrigue or camaraderie as to any discernible military ability. Michel made much of his humble origins and his democratic views; these, in addition to being a protégé of General Billot, had resulted in an "almost scandalously successful military ca-reer." [19] In the estimation of Messimy, the army in this period was thus "a great body, hierarchically solid in organization, but at whose summit there was no one." [20] In his short sec-ond tenure as Minister of War, ended by a freak but fatal air-plane accident in May 1911, Berteaux made an effort to remedy this state of affairs by replacing Laffon de Ladébat with General Dubail, a vigorous and effective soldier, as he was to prove during the war.[21] This was only a palliative compared to the one basic defect in the high command which had persisted since the Freycinet reforms two decades before. Between the two essential organs, the C.S.G. and the General Staff, there was no continuing and effective contact. Each

---

[19] "Chronique française," *Revue militaire suisse,* August 1911, pp. 685–686.
[20] Messimy, *op. cit.,* p. 71.
[21] *Ibid.,* p. 72.

functioned independently of the other with no one in any real position of authority to coordinate their actions. The *Réveil national* provided a favorable atmosphere in which this ultimate lacuna in the military organization of France could be repaired.

The immediate train of events leading up to the promulgation of the decree on the reorganization of the high command was triggered by a question raised in the Senate on June 19, 1911. During the debate on the budget, the Comte de Tréveneuc, a former officer and over the years a rather consistent critic of the military policies of the Republic, asked how the high command would function in case of war. Was there to be one single chief of the army, responsible for directing the whole military effort of the country, or would there be a number of generals, each in charge of operations in a given theater? In the latter case, Tréveneuc wondered who would oversee and coordinate the military effort of the country in the different theaters, allocating men and supplies to each. If there was to be one over-all commander in chief, the problem arose of how he would be able to prepare himself and his subordinates for their future roles, since the Generalissimo possessed no specific authority over either the General Staff or the men designated to be under his orders in the event of war.[22]

The Minister of War, General Goiran, had succeeded to the office only three weeks before, after the tragic death of Berteaux. By his own admission, he was not yet familiar with all the questions pertaining to his new duties, and he was also not a very able speaker. He claimed that the government should maintain over-all control, coordinating military operations in several different theaters. In the field there would be a number of armies or groups of armies, and to the general in command of each the government, working through the Minister of War, seconded by the Chief of Staff, would assign a specific mission though leaving him full liberty as to how it should be

[22] *Journal Officiel du Sénat: Débats* (hereafter cited as *J.O.S. Déb.*), (1911), p. 797.

carried out. With regard to the mission of the Generalissimo, Goiran stated that there was no single person in command over the whole French army. He was, in fact, of the opinion that such a task "would be beyond human strength." [23] In responding to Tréveneuc's question and to a similar interpellation in the Chamber four days later, with this theory of the high command, Goiran created a very unfavorable impression, so much so that the government, already weakened by the death of Berteaux, its strongest member, fell after an adverse vote in the Chamber on the order of the day.[24]

Although the organization of the high command as it stood in 1911 had a number of serious defects, the incident also revealed a great deal of confusion on the part of the politicians concerning the question. This confusion was, above all, semantic, and Goiran contributed to it by his awkward handling of the interpellations. In speaking before the Senate, Goiran actually said that unity of command in time of war would be assured by "the Council of Ministers," which phrase was changed before it was published in the *Journal Officiel.* The *Revue des deux mondes* wryly commented that in the three weeks he had been Minister of War, Goiran apparently had been so filled with admiration at the competence of his colleagues in all matters that "he did not hesitate to entrust them with the over-all direction of military operations." [25] Goiran's remarks were thus interpreted to mean that he advocated governmental interference in the conduct of operations in the field. But, as Paul-Boncour, at the time a member of the cabinet, pointed out, all he was actually doing was to remind people that the government was ultimately responsible for directing the war. The thesis advanced by Goiran was "rigorously in line with the legislation of the moment." [26] According to the *Journal des sciences militaires,* that the government

[23] *Ibid.,* p. 798.
[24] *J.O.C. Déb.* (1911), p. 2520.
[25] *R.D.M.,* July 1, 1911, pp. 237–238.
[26] J. Paul-Boncour, *Entre deux guerres* (Paris: Plon, 1945), Vol. I, p. 217.

in time of war should give directions to the high command was "a very sound doctrine. . . ."[27]

Whatever the confusion in their minds on this question, the fact remained that the legislators, by rejecting Goiran's explanation, were also rejecting the legally correct and constitutionally orthodox theory on the organization of the high command. The Radical deputy André Hesse appears to have echoed the current sentiment in parliament when he declared: "When the guns begin to speak, it is best that the politicians keep quiet."[28] Both Hesse and General Pédoya, who were men of the Left, advocated giving to one single general the ultimate responsibility for the conduct and the coordination of operations in one or several theaters.[29] That parliament should now openly favor this theory was significant. All measures that previously had led to a stronger and more independent high command had been undertaken almost surreptitiously by the government, as if it were wary of offending the susceptibilities of republican legislators. By repudiating Goiran's thesis that the whole responsibility for preparing the army for war rested with the Minister of War, parliament indicated that it believed in giving the men who would command the troops in the field greater effective authority over them in time of peace. The possible political implications of such a system of command were discounted.[30]

A cabinet under Joseph Caillaux was formed to replace the government that had just fallen. The Minister of War in the new cabinet was Messimy. The Caillaux government had hardly been installed when the news reached Paris that the German gunboat *Panther* had dropped anchor at Agadir. This new Moroccan crisis once again raised the possibility of war and obliged the government to take stock of the military posture of the country. Except for certain material deficiencies

[27] *Journal des sciences militaires,* July 1911, p. 118.

[28] *J.O.C. Déb.* (1911), p. 2515.

[29] *Ibid.,* pp. 2514–2518.

[30] *R.D.M.,* July 1, 1911, p. 239.

in the army, nothing was more disquieting than the state of the high command. The new Minister of War was extremely dubious about Michel, the Generalissimo. In addition to finding him lacking in authority, Messimy also estimated that he was "ill-informed about questions pertaining to a mobilization . . . a poor fellow, crushed by the responsibility that could at any moment be his." [31] He, therefore, asked a number of men in the C.S.G., the future subordinates of Michel in case of war, for their opinions concerning his qualities as Commander in Chief. Generals Galliéni, Durand, and Dubail all agreed that he was incapable of effectively commanding the army, Durand going so far as to call him a "national danger." [32] Messimy then informed Michel that it was his opinion that he should resign as Vice-President of the C.S.G. and as Generalissimo. The Minister of War did agree to let him present his views about reorganizing the process of mobilization and about the artillery to the C.S.G. in order to ascertain if Michel had any support among his fellow generals.

Michel had drawn up a radical new plan for the mobilization and concentration of the army in case of war. This plan would place the reserve units in the front lines with the units from the standing army. The mobilized forces of the nation would thus be drawn up along the frontier, from the North Sea to the Swiss border, to meet the German assault. With regard to the artillery, Michel did not believe that there was need to have any piece heavier than the seventy-five, at least not on the army corps level. The C.S.G. rejected the views of Michel on both questions.[33] Repudiated by the men who would command the armies in time of war, Michel resigned forthwith. Messimy helped to ease the bitterness of the incident for him by suppressing at the same time the office of Vice-President of the C.S.G. Usually differences of opinion within

[31] Messimy, *op. cit.,* p. 74.

[32] *Ibid.,* p. 75.

[33] Conseil supérieur de la Guerre, "Procès verbaux" No. 12 (1907–1911), pp. 198–199.

the C.S.G. over technical questions were treated as secret or at least confidential, but in this case the press followed the affair closely. It is probable that Messimy had something to do with this.[34] Michel had important and potent political connections who felt that his treatment at the hands of the Minister of War had been a trifle brutal,[35] and Messimy may have taken prior precautions to see that he had as wide public support as possible.

The way was thus open for a reorganization of the high command, the necessity of which was becoming evident, and for which the political atmosphere was now propitious. Acting with great speed, Messimy had within ten days drawn up the requisite decrees. The single most important matter that he dealt with here was the dualism at the summit of the army, the chief defect in the old system of command. Messimy sought to remedy this by uniting the functions of Generalissimo and Chief of Staff in one man.

By the terms of the decree of July 28, 1911, this man, taking the title of Chief of the General Staff, was given extensive powers over the army. He was personally to direct the study of all questions relative to the general organization of the army with regard to war, including its mobilization and its subsequent deployment before the initial campaign. He would also oversee the work of the École de Guerre and the Centre des hautes Études militaires.[36] This last institution, baptized the "School for Marshals," was a recent innovation, a third year of studies for a few select graduates of the École de Guerre, during which the larger questions of strategy were taken up. Forty-one years after the defeat of 1870, the French military renaissance was climaxed by the creation of a post with approximately the same attributes as the Chief of the German

[34] J. Joffre, *Mémoires du Maréchal Joffre* (Paris: Plon, 1932), Vol. I, pp. 10–11.

[35] Messimy, *op. cit.,* p. 76.

[36] *Journal Officiel de la République française* (hereafter cited as *J.O.*), (1911), pp. 6444–6445.

General Staff. Having already derived so much from the Prusso-German experience, the French were to follow their mentors in setting in place the keystone to the whole military edifice.

With the creation of so eminent a position at the summit of the French military hierarchy, there naturally arose the extremely important question of who should occupy it. Several generals appeared to have the necessary qualifications. Caillaux as premier favored Galliéni. The son of a soldier, he had arisen from humble circumstances to become one of the outstanding officers in the colonial army, with a brilliant reputation both as a leader of men and as a just and humane administrator. Galliéni was also an undoubted republican. There were, however, a number of drawbacks to his nomination as Chief of the General Staff. For one thing, in 1911 he was sixty-two years of age. This meant that he would reach the mandatory age of retirement in early 1914, after less than three years in office, thus continuing the chronic instability in the high command. Since practically the whole of his military career had been spent in the colonies, his elevation to the post of supreme commander might not be well received by the officers in the army of the *Métropole*. Then, too, as one of those who had been instrumental in engineering the fall of Michel, he did not want to appear to have profited unduly from it.[37] So he refused the nomination.

The next choice was General Pau. Pau enjoyed a splendid reputation within the army as a tactician and as an administrator, but in the eyes of the politicians he was less attractive, being a practicing Catholic. In addition, Pau made it a condition of his acceptance of the post that the government formally agree to consult him at all times and under all circumstances as to the generals to be named to the various commands in the army. This would have given him virtual veto power vis-à-vis the other generals and would have made him,

---

[37] H. Contamine, *Le Revanche* (Paris: Berger-Levrault, 1957), p. 123.

and not the government, the final arbiter in the matter. In posing conditions such as these, Pau may have been acting at the behest of "influences whose origins can only be suspected. . . ."[38] Although Messimy agreed that he should have the largest possible say in the choice of his subordinates, he could not give a formal guarantee, nor could he commit his successors. Since Pau insisted on his own terms, the government had no choice but to look elsewhere. The next candidate was General Joseph Jacques Césaire Joffre.

Joffre was relatively unknown in 1911 even within the army. His career could be characterized as fortunate rather than brilliant. A graduate of Polytechnique in 1870, he had spent three extended tours of duty overseas, the first in Formosa and Tonkin, the second in the Sudan, where he had led the successful expedition to Timbuctoo, and finally in Madagascar, where under the orders of Galliéni he had supervised the construction of the naval base at Diégo Suarez. Because promotion came much more easily in the colonies and because he had performed his duties in commendable fashion, Joffre had risen quite rapidly, reaching the rank of divisionary general at the comparatively young age of fifty-four. After holding a series of respectable commands in metropolitan France, including the Sixth Division and the Second Army Corps, he was made a member of the C.S.G. in 1910. At the moment of his elevation to the post of Chief of the General Staff he was fifty-nine. Joffre thus had five or six years ahead of him before reaching the mandatory age of retirement. This would assure to the supreme command of the army a stability that had been lacking in recent years.

From a political point of view, Joffre was an excellent choice. He came from a petit bourgeois family, his father having been a prosperous manufacturer of barrels in the small town of Rivesaltes, near Perpignan. In his youth he had joined the Freemasons, though he was no longer associated with any

---

[38] Gen. Alexandre, *Avec Joffre d'Agadir à Verdun* (Paris: Berger-Levrault, 1932), p. 3.

lodge. Joffre considered himself to be a republican general,[39] but essentially he had no real political opinions. In his relations with his comrades and his subordinates, he held himself "above prejudices of caste, religion, and party." [40] During his successful military career, he had, unlike many of his fellow officers, received rapid promotion to the highest ranks "without effort, without intrigue." [41] His elevation to the supreme command of the army represented the victory of no particular faction, either reactionary or republican, within the officer corps, and he was thus free to choose his collaborators on the basis of military merit alone.

Joffre had enough native shrewdness and an acute enough sense of political reality to recognize that whatever their military capabilities, he would have to take into account the views of the government in his choice of the men to fill the subordinate commands. He could not be absolute master here as Pau had wanted to be. Even so, he intended to have his own way as often as possible. In his memoirs General Weygand reports that Joffre, as he was leaving Messimy's office after an interview on the subject, was heard to mutter: "I shall choose them even so. . . ." [42] Joffre had only one condition of this kind to make. He wanted as his immediate assistant someone who was expert in the intricacies of the work of the General Staff to compensate for his own admitted deficiencies in this area. On the advice of General Pau, Joffre requested that General de Curières de Castelnau be appointed as First Assistant Chief of Staff. Castelnau was a Catholic who was so ardent in his faith that he was known as the *Capucin botté,* or the "monk in boots." [43] He had been one of the three officers that General André had sacked in his trial of strength with the General Staff in 1900.[44] Although Castelnau was a fine soldier

---

[39] Contamine, *op. cit.,* p. 124.

[40] Alexandre, *op. cit.,* p. 8.

[41] É. Mayer, *Nos chefs de 1914* (Paris: Stock, 1930), p. 33.

[42] Gen. Weygand, *Mémoires* (Paris: Flammarion, 1950), Vol. I, pp. 63–64.

[43] B. Tuchman, *The Guns of August* (New York: Macmillan, 1962), p. 39.

[44] *Vide supra,* pp. 289–290.

with a profound knowledge of staff work, he had numerous enemies in parliament because of his pronounced religious views. Messimy notes that neither Caillaux nor Fallières, the President of the Republic, was happy about accepting Castelnau for so important a post but that reluctantly they acquiesced.[45]

In the decree of July 28, 1911, on the high command, Messimy also dealt at some length with the attributes of the members of the C.S.G. By the terms of the decree, it was once again stated that they were to make tours of inspection of the different army corps and that they were to enjoy very extensive powers for the carrying out of their assigned missions. That the members of the C.S.G. had considerable authority over the army corps under their inspection had been implicit in former decrees on the subject, but it had never been spelled out so precisely. Nor had it ever been stated before, as it was now, that those generals charged with the command of the wartime armies were to have permanently assigned to them the nucleus of their future staffs.[46]

One element alone marred the symmetry of the structure of command that was instituted in 1911. In making Joffre the Chief of the General Staff, Messimy was creating a new post in the military hierarchy, one with enormous prerogatives. At the same time he did not completely suppress the old post of Chief of Staff of the Army. Partly out of respect for the feelings of its present incumbent, General Dubail, Messimy retained it, though changing its functions.[47] There were also sound political reasons for not abolishing it. The sacrifice of Michel, a man with powerful political connections, had been facilitated by the suppression of the post he held, Vice-President of the C.S.G. To have removed Dubail in the same brutal fashion as Michel, in order to give his job to Joffre, would have created a tremendous scandal, especially since Dubail was performing his duties in a satisfactory manner. A

---

[45] Messimy, *op. cit.*, pp. 77–78.

[46] *J.O.* (1911), p. 6445.

[47] Alexandre, *op. cit.*, p. 13.

good soldier, he was also a *laic* in his political views.[48] Messimy therefore kept him on as Chief of Staff of the Army, while the official title of Joffre was Chief of the General Staff. Dubail was to collaborate with Joffre in the capacity of an adjunct chief of staff for the study of questions relative to the preparation of the army for war. In addition, he was directly responsible to the Minister of War for all matters dealing with the ordinary day-to-day life of the army in time of peace: personnel, troop movements, matériel, and supplies.

The maintenance of Dubail as Chief of Staff of the Army having been dictated more by personal and political reasons than by military necessity, the results were not entirely satisfactory. Even if it could be argued that he served to lighten the crushing load of work and responsibility that now rested on Joffre,[49] the confused attributes of his office—full power and authority in one field along with ill-defined subordination to the Chief of the General Staff in another—were such that Dubail faced difficulties from the start.[50] According to Joffre, there were no serious differences between himself and Dubail, with whom he was on very good terms, but Castelnau and Dubail disagreed continually over their respective prerogatives and authority.[51] Millerand, who succeeded Messimy as Minister of War, ended this last remnant of dualism in the high command through the decree of January 20, 1912.

By the terms of this decree the post of Chief of Staff of the Army was eliminated from the military hierarchy. Millerand reasoned that the distinctions between *service courant* and the preparation for war were extremely difficult to make. There were thus serious inconveniences in a system that deprived the Chief of the General Staff of responsibility for and authority over questions of personnel.[52] The post held by Dubail was

[48] Contamine, *op. cit.,* p. 125.
[49] Alexandre, *op. cit.,* p. 13.
[50] Gen. J. Revol, unpublished memoirs, p. 107.
[51] Joffre, *op. cit.,* Vol. I, p. 27.
[52] *J.O.* (1912), p. 711.

thus abolished, and he himself was given command of the Ninth Army Corps at Tours. The whole authority over the functioning of the army was thus placed in the confident hands of Joffre. There was to be no ambiguity about his responsibility or confusion over his attributes as the Commander in Chief in peace as in war.

By the decrees of July 28, 1911, and January 20, 1912, the final step was taken in providing the French army with a peacetime command structure that corresponded exactly with what it would have to be in war. Joffre now had a greater degree of control over the functioning of the French army than any general since Bonaparte. The difference between the situations of the two men was that the authority of Bonaparte with regard to the army stemmed from his position as the head of the French state, while Joffre received his extensive powers through governmental delegation. Even if the government would not and could not officially give him full powers over the army, Joffre came close to having them in effect, as can be seen from the estimate of one military author, General Regnault:

Having the ear both of parliament and of the successive governments, well considered by all factions, on the right as on the left, General Joffre was almost omnipotent in the three years that preceded the war. . . . The all but absolute master over promotion, it may be said of him that no one at this time was raised to the rank of general and that no general was assigned to a command unless he had given his approval.[53]

Certain of the stability of his situation and willing to assume responsibility for his actions, Joffre proceeded to purge the ranks of all those generals whom he found to be incapable of exercising the commands to which they had been assigned. Joffre was obliged to take some cognizance of the political

[53] Gen. Regnault, "Les leçons de la guerre: l'organisation du haut commandement," *Revue mondiale*, September 1, 1930, pp. 14–15.

connections of the general in question,[54] but in effect he had a free hand. Whenever he found a general who, in his opinion, was not up to the demands of the post he held, Joffre was ruthless. Here neither friendship nor camaraderie counted. Following the great maneuvers of 1912 in Poitou, Joffre took the occasion to sack the general commanding the Eleventh Army Corps, while the maneuvers of 1913 resulted in the dismissal of two out of the four corps commanders involved.[55]

So high was the rate of attrition and so great the number of generals placed in *disponibilité* that by 1914 a large number of billets normally held by divisionary generals had to be assigned to brigadiers. The magnitude of the task to be accomplished may be gathered from the fact that Joffre continued to relieve men of their commands down through the first six weeks of the war. On a number of occasions Joffre doubtlessly acted in hasty and arbitrary fashion, wrecking the careers of worthy officers, but in sum the caliber of the high command was much improved. Naturally enough, this brutal treatment of his subordinates aroused a storm of resentment both within the army and in political circles, but there was little that any government could have done. To have taken any positive measures to stop him would have provoked his resignation, and replacing Joffre at this juncture would have been difficult.

The military situation created for Joffre by the 1911 decree in the democratic and republican state of France was actually stronger than that of his counterpart in aristocratic, militarist Germany, the younger Moltke. Although Moltke exercised full powers over all matters pertaining to the preparation of the army for war, he was still responsible to the King-Emperor. The difficulty here was that the King-Emperor was also the *Kriegsherr,* or War Lord, whose prerogatives with re-

---

[54] Alexandre, *op. cit.,* pp. 92–94.

[55] Gen. Pichot-Duclos, *Au G.Q.G. de Joffre* (Grenoble-Paris: Arthaud, 1947), pp. 170–171.

gard to the army were not merely ceremonial. Indeed, William II took the military aspects of his office very seriously, despite the fact that he had no particular talents in that direction beyond a taste for dressing up in ornate uniforms. His desire to play the role of *Kriegsherr* meant that he was always interfering in military questions. One could generally get around the Kaiser, but the necessity of having to take William into his calculations complicated Moltke's task. There was also a considerable military terrain that was outside of the province of the German Chief of Staff. Promotion was handled through the Military Cabinet, whose chief reported directly to the Kaiser.[56] Moltke could affect such matters only indirectly, through the exercise of lateral influence.

In contrast, Joffre had virtually unlimited power with regard to the army. Even if he was, by the letter of the 1911 decree, still responsible to the Minister of War, that person had in fact been reduced to nothing more than the advocate of the high command before the government and before parliament. The Minister did not officially abdicate his prerogatives or his authority over the army, but all of the men who occupied the post during the next three years were politicians, and none of them would have ever considered trying to impose his views on the high command. Millerand at least was a man of some stature and force of character, but in the year that he served as Minister of War he set himself with single-minded zeal and determination "to follow the directives of the General Staff, without seeking either to control it or to correct those ideas where it was wrong. . . ."[57] Rather, Millerand made it his guiding principle to give full confidence to the military, "who, delighted to be neither contradicted nor brushed off, considered him an excellent Minister of War."[58] The role of

[56] H. Rosinski, *The German Army* (revised edition; Washington: Infantry Journal, 1944), p. 149.

[57] Paul-Boncour, *op. cit.*, Vol. I, p. 228.

[58] Contamine, *op. cit.*, p. 133.

the Minister at the top of the command structure of the army had been effectively nullified to the profit of the Chief of the General Staff.

Within the army the reorganization of the high command was greeted with great satisfaction. The whole tenor of the policies initiated by Messimy and continued and even intensified by Millerand, particularly the appointment of Joffre, had a tonic effect on the morale of the officer corps.[59] The problem of the high command, involving as it did long-standing republican suspicions of the army, had always been a difficult one to treat on its purely military merits. Now the government in the person of two successive Ministers of War had dealt with the problem, guided by military criteria alone and evidently unconcerned by any of the hypothetical political consequences of their decisions. This was in marked contrast to the way in which the government had approached such matters in recent years, and it did not pass unnoticed by the soldiers themselves.

These ultimate steps in the strengthening of the high command, which gave to the army almost complete autonomy within the state, were all accomplished through executive decrees. Parliament was not consulted at any point in the enactment of this vitally important reform. Still, the fact that the Chamber had repudiated the theories of General Goiran could be interpreted as indicating prior parliamentary approval of the reform that Messimy was about to undertake. In his report on the budget of 1912, Clémentel spoke for the majority of the deputies when he praised what Messimy had been able to accomplish. He considered that in a democracy above all there was need for a generalissimo, that is, "a *grand chef* who has full charge of and responsibility for preparing for war . . . ," and he felt that the new organization answered "the *desiderata* formulated by all the competent authorities. . . ."[60]

The only objection raised in parliament, and not a very serious one, concerned the legality of the reform in the light of

[59] Girardet, *op. cit.,* p. 277.
[60] *J.O.C. Doc.* (1911), pp. 1324–1325.

the 1873 law on the organization of the army. Like every other effort made by the government since 1888 to strengthen and to give stability to the high command, the measures sponsored by Messimy and Millerand were contrary to the spirit, if not to the letter, of the 1873 law. No one apparently noticed this long-standing illegality until 1912, when General Pédoya posed an interpellation on the subject. He objected primarily to those provisions in the recent decrees on the high command which dealt with the C.S.G. To state in a decree that the members of the C.S.G. were empowered to give instructions to the corps commanders was in formal contradiction to the law. The authors of the 1873 law expressly forbade the existence of any intermediate body between the Minister of War and the corps commanders. The fear was that such a body might end by "subalternizing" the corps commanders and hindering them in the development of individual initiative. According to Pédoya, "The very thing that the legislators did not want, the Ministers have done by means of decrees." [61] He objected less to what had been done than to the fact that it had been done illegally. If the members of the C.S.G. needed the powers given them by the various decrees since 1888, let a law on the subject be enacted.

Millerand, the Minister of War, declared in his reply to this interpellation that the decree in question was nothing more than the "conclusion, both logical and inevitable, to the work that has been underway for the past forty years. . . ." [62] Military necessity alone had led successive Ministers of War to strengthen the attributes and to increase the authority of the C.S.G. He closed by lauding the competence and devotion of the army, qualities that had helped the Republic to resolve "a problem that more than one person believed to be insoluble: how to maintain a large permanent army within the bosom of a democracy." [63] The only thing that Millerand did not do in

[61] *J.O.C. Déb.* (1912), p. 911.
[62] Millerand, *op. cit.,* p. 117.
[63] *Ibid.,* p. 128.

his highly patriotic oration was to give a direct answer to the objections of Pédoya about the legality of a ministerial decree that violated a law enacted by parliament. In a vote on the order of the day, the Chamber approved of Millerand's declaration by a majority of 338 to 7.[64] Possibly this could be taken as ex post facto approval by the Chamber of what past governments had done, a slightly tardy legalization of what was essentially a series of illegal, or at least unconstitutional, acts.

The efforts by the military to achieve and to maintain a high degree of independence within the state form an essential theme in the history of civil-military relations in France between 1871 and 1914. Throughout most of this period the government sought to retain some vestiges of the constitutional and legal forms that would assure the subordination of the army, while at the same time endeavoring to promote its military effectiveness. In the end, the Republic recognized that the military machine would function best if, to all intents and purposes, the soldiers were allowed complete autonomy in the management of their own affairs. Any legal measure taken by the government to reinforce or even to maintain civilian control tended automatically to hamper the army in the performance of its essential peacetime mission, to prepare itself for war. Only if the obedience of the soldiers to civilian authority was taken for granted, thus obviating the need on the part of the government to make certain of it by any specific legal means, was the defense of the nation most likely to be assured. A ministerial command structure was constitutionally correct but militarily inefficient. The government had a perfect legal right to keep itself informed about the political and religious opinions of the officer corps, but in doing so it displayed a lack of confidence in them that hurt military morale and rendered the army less apt to carry out its duties to the nation.

The key to the most fruitful possible relationship between the government and the army was a mutual sense of confidence. Because the government did not have that confidence

[64] *J.O.C. Déb.* (1912), p. 915.

in the military before 1911, full effective power over the army was not concentrated in one person but, rather, divided between several different organs. According to Revol, "Their interdependence, even if it was such as to relieve the government of all political fears, would certainly paralyze the initiative and the authority of the high command at the moment when it would have to act." [65] It could well be argued that to give any single general the power and the prerogatives that were bestowed upon Joffre by the decrees of 1911 and 1912 would be to place the regime in potential danger. This was doubtless an arguable and tenable hypothesis. The best reply to such an assertion could be found in the disciplined and subservient behavior of the military in the ten years that followed the Dreyfus Affair. Attacked in their most vital institutional interests and treated as suspects by the government, the soldiers never wavered or gave the civil authorities within the state any real grounds for doubting their sense of discipline toward the regime or their devotion to the nation. In this time of trial the military stood firm. Joffre was the first beneficiary of the renewed confidence and respect that the French army won from the government.

Military Necessity and the Three-Years Law

The change in the attitude of certain of the leading republican politicians toward the army that was one of the salient characteristics of the *Réveil national* was reflected in the military legislation of the period. Although there was nothing unusual about parliament following the lead of the soldiers in legislation specifically concerned with the army's organizational needs, such as the three laws on the cadres enacted between 1909 and 1912, the conscription law of 1913, on the other hand, represented a new departure. Contrary to earlier legislative acts on the same subject, the 1913 law was based primarily on military necessity as the soldiers understood and

[65] Revol, *op. cit.,* p. 102.

interpreted it, and it owed very little to the social and political theories of the republicans. In fact, these sociopolitical theories, which a few years before might have provided a perfectly sound basis for a conscription law, military opinion notwithstanding, now appeared insubstantial and chimerical, even in the estimation of many republicans.

The official republican view on military matters had always laid great stress on the importance of the reserves, but there was no coherent body of theory indicating how they should be organized in time of peace or utilized in time of war. The enactment of the two years' service, meant to be a decisive shift away from the standing army, was never implemented by any legislation specifically on the reserves.[66] Even though in the 1873 law on the organization of the army it was formally stated that a further law was to be enacted governing the constitution of the reserve units, its prescriptions were ignored. When, in 1912, a deputy sought to repair this deficiency by presenting a bill on the subject, the Minister of War refused to give it his backing, since he doubted that such a measure was either "prudent or useful." [67] With regard to this extremely vital matter, one could only refer to the Minister of War or, as one member of the Chamber put it, "the successive whims of different Ministers." [68]

With parliamentary initiative lacking for the implementation of an effective reserve program, it fell to the military themselves to organize the reserves as they saw fit. Monteilhet considers the military authorities of the period to have been "profoundly hostile" to the reserves; [69] but, even so, they did a great deal toward improving their state of readiness and giving them a significant role to play in the event of a war. Whereas the training periods had formerly been spent within

---

[66] *Vide supra*, p. 314.

[67] J. Monteilhet, *Les institutions militaires de la France* (Paris: Alcan, 1932), p. 264.

[68] *J.O.C. Déb.* (1912, sess. ext.), p. 2870.

[69] Monteilhet, *op. cit.*, p. 258.

the *caserne*, after 1908 the reservists were brought together in training camps as units under the men who would command them upon mobilization.[70] Plan XVI, which was introduced by General de Lacroix in 1909, represented a great advance over recent projects for the utilization of the reserves. The Plan envisaged the organization of 463 reserve battalions, instead of the 320 that had been projected before, which would bring the number of battalion-size units in the army at the moment of mobilization up to more than 1,000.[71] The military authorities naturally continued to see the organization of the armed forces of France primarily in terms of the standing army; but, nevertheless, within this framework they recognized the potential value of the reserves in the event of a war and made plans accordingly.

The lacunae in republican military theory with regard to the reserves were evident in the debate over the new laws on the artillery, infantry, and cavalry cadres. The officially stated motive for voting on a series of new laws to replace the one enacted in 1875 was the profound change in the army supposedly resulting from the two years' service.[72] Although the advocates of these measures went to considerable pains to show that they were endeavoring to reinforce the reserves, the laws in fact dealt exclusively with the needs of the standing army. Their argument would seem to be that the larger the proportion of reserves in the armed forces, the better organized and more effective the troops of the line would have to be, as they were the essential cadre of the nation in arms. Comparing the triumphs of the armies of the French Revolution with the failure of the mass levies of the Government of National Defense, Joseph Reinach explained the difference by the fact that in the former case the old royal army had supplied the cohesive element.[73] Millerand, in his capacity as Minister of War, said

---

[70] Contamine, *op. cit.,* p. 107.

[71] *Ibid.,* p. 117.

[72] *J.O.C. Doc.* (1909, sess. ext.), p. 344.

[73] *J.O.C. Déb.* (1912, sess. ext.), pp. 2862–2864.

that the recent maneuvers had shown that the reservists could become troops of an admirable solidity within a few days, but only if they were provided with a solid core of men from the regular army.[74] That the quality of the reserve units might also depend on their being well trained and organized in time of peace was not mentioned.

The assumption that the reserves would not be dependable troops unless they possessed a cadre of men from the regular army was used to justify the maintenance on active duty of many officers in excess of the real peacetime needs of the army. There were thus in every regiment a number of officers assigned to the so-called complementary cadre, who did not have much to do but who were to provide for the reserve units in the event of war. To spend half of one's years as a captain or major doing some vague auxiliary task while waiting for the chance to command a unit could be very dispiriting for the man involved. In response to the repeated criticism of the complementary cadre, the Minister of War suppressed it in the first draft of the projected law on the cadres, presented to parliament in 1907. He was, however, obliged to call for the creation in every regiment of a special staff to carry out essential auxiliary services.[75]

In the next version of the bill, drawn up by the Chamber Army Commission in 1909, both the complementary cadre and the special regimental staff had disappeared, to be replaced by a supplementary cadre. This reform, Messimy sardonically noted, amounted to a change of one syllable.[76] In the final version of the bill, the one ultimately debated in parliament and enacted in 1912, the complementary cadre reappeared. Whether the military authorities were concerned about the reserve units or not, the complementary cadre was far too necessary for the vital interests of the officer corps to be abolished. It represented a great many sorely needed billets; without them, promotion might grind practically to a halt.

[74] *Ibid.*, p. 2940.
[75] *J.O.C. Doc.* (1907, sess. ext.), p. 385.
[76] *J.O.C. Doc.* (1909, sess. ext.), p. 357.

Although the government had originally intended to enact one single over-all law on the cadres, the need for reorganization was felt to be acute only in one branch, the artillery. In this field, Germany had far outdistanced France with respect to the number of guns she would be able to put in line. So this section of the bill was separated from the rest and given comparatively urgent treatment. Even so, the law on the artillery cadres required some two years to be passed. The crucial issue in the discussion of the new law was whether there should be four guns per battery or six. A German battery contained six guns, but the artillery experts produced a variety of technical arguments to demonstrate that the traditional French system of four guns per battery was still more satisfactory, even if it did leave the French with fewer guns per army corps than the Germans, 120 against 144, but with a greater number of batteries, 30 to 24.[77] Since a captain was in command of a battery, it was obvious that the four-gun battery provided more billets per army corps for this particular rank. Possibly dubious about the validity of some of the arguments used by the technical experts consulted, the Chamber Army Commission had to remind them that, in their views on the reconstitution of the artillery, they should not allow themselves to be swayed "by considerations of promotion for their comrades." [78]

The military authorities were evidently determined that the vital interests of the officer corps be protected and, if possible, advanced by any new law on the cadres. This could be seen from the discussion in a 1907 meeting of the C.S.G. over the project being drawn up by the Ministry of War for presentation to parliament. Among other things, the bill provided for an increase in the number of colonels in the army, while reducing by approximately 1,150 the number of lieutenants. Noting that it would be the lieutenants who would be most needed by the reserve units at mobilization and also the ones most likely to fall in battle, General Millet, commander-designate of one of the wartime armies, could not understand

[77] *J.O.C. Doc.* (1908, sess. ext.), pp. 125–126.
[78] *Ibid.*, p. 124.

why their numbers should be decreased, especially when there was already a shortage of junior officers. Many a lieutenant's billet was now being filled by an N.C.O.[79] General Brun, at the time Chief of Staff, explained the anomaly simply enough, contending that the need was for "more captains, rather than lieutenants . . ." if the already deplorable situation regarding officer promotion was not to be further aggravated.[80]

Some four years later, the same kinds of questions were being raised in connection with the problem of reconstituting the infantry cadres. Messimy, by now Minister of War and therefore somewhat more sympathetic than formerly to the basic interests of the officer corps, had to defend the provisions he had made for a marked increase in the number of lieutenant colonels. To the objections made by one general that promotion to the rank of colonel would thereby be slowed down, Messimy replied that this was less relevant than the need to increase the number of officers retiring as lieutenant colonels rather than as majors.[81] It would seem that a military career terminating at the rank of major was, by definition, mediocre, while to retire as lieutenant colonel somehow indicated a degree of success.

The new laws on the cadres were extremely conservative measures. The result of about six years of leisurely and intermittent legislative effort was a series of laws, which, except for an increase in the size of the artillery, confirmed the existing state of things in almost every detail. The only people in parliament willing to give substance to the concept of the nation in arms were the Socialists led by Jaurès. In his remarkable work *L'armée nouvelle* and on the floor of the Chamber, Jaurès propounded a theory of military organization in which the reserves, representing the overwhelming majority of the mobilized armed forces of France, would be given the dominant role to play. The scheme proposed by the great So-

---

[79] C.S.G., "Proc. verb." No. 11 (1905–1907), p. 212.

[80] *Ibid.*, p. 213.

[81] *Ibid.*, No. 12 (1907–1911), p. 233.

cialist would abolish the usual "artificial, antiquated, and dangerous" distinctions that had been made between the men on active duty and the reserves. The whole virile youth of the nation would be grouped together in a coherent, homogeneous mass, to be mobilized in its entirety at the same hour for the defense of the country. This mass of men would be organized beforehand into territorial units, recruited and trained locally, thus merging "the life of the soldier with that of the citizen, the life of the army with the life of the nation, in such a way that there can never be a corporate military spirit distinct from the nation itself." [82]

By the abolition of the standing army, Jaurès could also claim to have solved the promotion crisis, the most pressing of the problems besetting the permanent cadre of officers, in much more effective fashion than was possible with such makeshift measures as the creation of a few more billets for the lieutenant colonels. According to his scheme, only one third of the officer corps would be professionals. They would receive their training, not in the great military schools, but in special sections of the universities. The remaining two thirds would be reserves, civilians who continued to receive military training. Because they were to represent so small a proportion of the total officer corps and because of their specialized, intensive training, the professionals would be quickly promoted and would thus soon arrive, while still "in their full active youth, at the command of the larger units." [83] Promotion would be much more likely to take place according to the military capabilities and the personal merit of the men in question than under the present system, while political and religious factors would count for less.

As logical and attractive as the theories of Jaurès may have been, they found few supporters among those in parliament most interested in the problem of national defense. The counterproject that he offered in opposition to the government

[82] *J.O.C. Déb.* (1912, sess. ext.), p. 3039.
[83] *Ibid.*

bill was voted down by a count of 481 to 93.[84] This lack of
response from even those on the left in parliament to the theories of Jaurès points up the ambiguity in republican military
thought about the reserves. The nation in arms, where the distinction between soldier and civilian had practically been
eradicated and where the reserves ceased to be an adjunct of
the standing army and became, in fact, the army itself, was
certainly more democratic than a military organization that
stressed the special nature of the army as a caste apart. On the
other hand, no one was ever quite convinced that the nation in
arms would be militarily very effective, despite the affirmations
of Jaurès to the contrary. If obliged to decide between the
theories of Jaurès and the opinions of the professional soldiers
with regard to a purely military question, the politicians instinctively chose the latter.

The basic assumption governing all military planning in the
years after 1871 was that the French army would have as its
mission the defense of the national soil against the inevitable
German invasion. The French plan of campaign was thus to
be a riposte to a prior German maneuver. All the recognized
authorities concurred that an army assigned this primarily defensive mission could contain a very large element, even a
majority, of reservists and still be adequate to the task. But as
the army regained confidence in itself in the years after 1910,
an influential segment of military opinion, particularly some
of the younger officers on the General Staff, began to doubt
the validity of this defensive strategy. With the courses of
Foch at the École de Guerre as their source of inspiration, a
number of them started to speculate on the greater efficacy of
the offense over the defense as a means to victory. Much of
what was written and said on the subject was no more than
common-sense reiteration of the truism that he who would be
the victor is ultimately going to have to attack—under most
circumstances, anyway—but some officers, soon to be nick-

[84] *Ibid.*, p. 3073.

named the "Young Turks," were carried away to the point of making a *mystique* of the offense. The most famous example of this approach was the two lectures given by Lieutenant Colonel Loyzeaux de Grandmaison in 1911. Chief of the prestigious Third Bureau of the General Staff, Grandmaison announced to the assembled luminaries of the army that the moral superiority of the offense was such that it alone supplied the key to victory. One of his phrases may be taken as summarizing his whole theory: "Imprudence is the best security." [85] Even if his vivid and paradoxical style made a great impression on many in the army, it would be a mistake to see in his lectures the authoritative statement of the military thought of the moment. Rather, the theories of Grandmaison should be considered as the extreme version of an idea that was gaining great currency.

This new stress on the primacy of the offense led people naturally to question the assumptions upon which French military plans were based. Even if the mission of the French army was to defend the country against attack, it was now argued that this mission could be best carried out through an offensive strategy. To assume a defensive posture and to let the Germans attack in order to parry their thrust would be to place the French army at a disadvantage from the very beginning. To be certain of the victory, France would have to have an army "geared for the offensive and for immediate attacks on the enemy." [86] This meant that the majority of the army would be men on active duty. Admirable as the French reservists might be, and the military authorities were willing to call them the best in Europe, it was still inconceivable that within a few days of their mobilization they would be in any state to take part in the vigorous offensive movement necessary to win a quick, decisive victory.

Talk about the virtues of the offense was not limited to the

[85] Quoted in Paul-Boncour, *op. cit.*, Vol. I, p. 216.
[86] R. D. Challener, *The French Theory of the Nation in Arms* (New York: Columbia University Press, 1955), p. 82.

military alone; it also found a ready echo in civilian circles. At a meeting of the Conseil supérieur de la Défense nationale in January 1912, Fallières, as President of the Republic, led a discussion of modifications in the plan for strategic concentration of the army. He noted with pleasure that France had renounced its plans for assuming a defensive posture, which for her constituted an admission of inferiority. "We are henceforth resolved to march straight at the enemy, without hesitation. The offense, which suits the temperament of our soldiers, shall assure us the victory. . . ." [87] In the discussion of the 1912 law on the infantry cadres, Joseph Reinach attacked the theories of Jaurès to the effect that the security of France could be assured through a purely defensive strategy. It was his contention, supposedly proved by the experience of the Revolution, that only an offensive strategy would permit the country to defend itself against an invader.[88]

Messimy wryly admits the way in which the current stress on the virtues and efficacy of the offense warped his own outlook in military affairs, blinding him to the significance of certain obvious phenomena on the field of battle. During the Balkan wars, he had gone to observe the victorious Bulgarian army in action against the Turks. After their great initial successes, the Bulgarian advance had become bogged down against the strongly fortified Turkish position at Chatalja. The general in command of the Bulgarian forces refused to attempt an assault that would needlessly sacrifice the lives of his men until he had brought up some heavy artillery. This led Messimy to conclude, not that a well-fortified and well-manned defensive position would be difficult to take by assault, but rather that the Bulgarian army was no longer so well prepared for offensive warfare. After six months of war it "had lost much of its initial dash." [89] The fact that many of the republican politicians most concerned with military affairs

---

[87] Messimy, *op. cit.,* p. 115.

[88] *J.O.C. Déb.* (1912, sess. ext.), p. 2866.

[89] Messimy, *op. cit.,* pp. 112–113.

so readily espoused the theories and attitudes currently in vogue with the professional soldiers was decisive for the enactment of the three-years law in 1913.

The military had never been very happy with the two years' service, but this would not have been a sufficient reason for its repeal if the German army had not been quite suddenly and rapidly increased in size. During the course of 1912 the Reichstag voted two laws whose ultimate effect would be to add some 150,000 men to the army, bringing the number of men on active duty to 860,000. The full effects of these two laws had not originally been expected to be felt before 1916 or 1917; but then at the end of 1912 and at the start of 1913, successive orders were given for their immediate implementation. According to Raymond Poincaré, President of the Republic from 1912 to 1919, the French intelligence services had learned of yet a third law, soon to be presented to the Reichstag and calling for a further increase of 143,000 in the size of the army.[90]

Against the 860,000 men soon to be under arms in Germany, France could muster no more than 480,000 men in the *Métropole*. Under the circumstances, French authorities had no choice but to consider ways of strengthening the armed forces of the nation, and for most people this meant an increase in their size. Here the growing disparity in population between France and Germany became an important factor. Germany could enlarge her standing army simply by inducting a larger percentage of each conscript class. It was not that simple in France, where all physically fit young men and many in questionable condition were being conscripted under the working of the two-years law. A larger army could be achieved only through a lengthening in the term of service. As the extent of the German increases were realized, the natural reaction on the part of the soldiers was therefore to call for a return to the three years' service in some form or other. In support of this

---

[90] R. Poincaré, *Au service de la France* (10 vols.; Paris: Plon, 1926-1933), Vol. III, pp. 144-145.

view, a number of arguments were adduced, some of them quite specious. Of these, the most notable one was based on the possible danger of an *attaque brusquée*.

The theory of the *attaque brusquée* was postulated on the assumption that on some future occasion when Germany enjoyed a massive, even if only temporary, military superiority over France she would be able to hurl her peacetime standing army across the frontier, without waiting to mobilize her reserves or to declare war. Before France could mobilize, her frontier-covering force, or *couverture,* would be overwhelmed, and she would be at the mercy of the invader. A military system in which the reserves played so large a role placed France at a real disadvantage against such a contingency. To call up and to incorporate the reserves required time, and as *France militaire* pointed out, "If you do not have *time* to carry out your mobilization, the best reserves in the world will be of no use.[91]

The first French author to speculate in terms of an *attaque brusquée* appears to have been Captain Gilbert, writing for the *Nouvelle revue* in the late 1880's and early 1890's.[92] Similar ideas were to be found in the works of such bellicose German theorists as Theodore von Bernhardi, who were often quoted as furnishing proof of Germany's willingness to resort to such a strategy. The most superficial examination of the military dispositions of the German Empire should have demonstrated the impossibility of a successful surprise attack, for in the one region from which it could be launched, Alsace and occupied Lorraine, there were only about as many full-strength battalions as on the French side of the frontier. Any German efforts to gain a preponderance there could be detected easily enough, while such an attack would also of necessity have to be made against the great line of fortresses built by General Séré des Rivières. As Jaurès pointed out during the debate

[91] "Vers le service de trois ans," *F.M.,* March 3, 1913.
[92] Col. J. Revol, *Histoire de l'armée française* (Paris: Larousse, 1929), p. 206.

on the three-years law, this line of fortresses obliged the Germans to mount any attack through the Ardennes, and then not before the sixteenth day of mobilization. He did not believe that the French army was in such a state of "disorganization and incapacity that in sixteen days we cannot lead to the frontier all the necessary forces." [93]

The competent military authorities certainly doubted the possibility of an *attaque brusquée*. General Percin wrote in an article for *Aurore* that while all the members of the C.S.G. favored a return to the three years' service, it was not for that particular reason.[94] The General Staff placed no credence in such theories, although it did little to refute them, thus leading many officers to believe in the myth. In the estimation of one authority, Henry Contamine, "Possibly it was happy to have a way in which it could shake up the electorate." [95] From the account given by Maurice Paléologue of the reestablishment of the three years' service, it would seem that the high command, in the persons of Joffre and Castelnau, evoked the specter of the *attaque brusquée* when discussing the need for a new conscription law in private conversations with members of the government.[96] They may have been practicing some discreet intellectual dishonesty in a good cause.

Even if the *attaque brusquée* were discounted, it could still be argued that the German increases obliged the French to do likewise. With so many men under arms at the moment of the outbreak of hostilities, Germany would be able to speed up her mobilization, thus getting an advantage of several days over France in the actual start of hostilities. An army in which the front-line units contained so large a proportion of men on active duty was simply better prepared to launch a vigorous offensive with the least possible delay.

[93] *J.O.C. Déb.* (1913), pp. 1996–1997.
[94] J.-L. de Lanessan, *Nos forces militaires* (Paris: Alcan, 1913), p. 100.
[95] Contamine, *op. cit.*, p. 144.
[96] M. Paléologue, "Comment fut rétabli le service de trois ans," *R.D.M.,* May 1 and 15, 1935, p. 316.

The military wanted the reestablishment of the three years' service for other reasons, quite apart from the possible contingencies of war. It also suited the peacetime institutional needs of the army in a way that the two years' service did not. Although the army was now officially considered to be a school where the nation in arms learned the rudiments of soldiering, the lack of parliamentary interest in implementing this theory meant that things could go on as before, with the military treating the conscripts as they always had. Despite the expectations of the authors of the 1905 law that each man would now be given a full two years of intensive training, thousands of soldiers were taken from their regiments to serve in the multitude of functions that the military considered to be necessary to the existence of the army. According to calculations made by Galliéni at the end of his tour of duty as the commanding general of the Thirteenth Army Corps, no less than 3,964 troops out of a total of 16,400 were employed in auxiliary tasks and thus lost to an effective and comprehensive program of military training. He estimated that for the whole French army some 112,000 men were in this situation, and in these figures he did not include the numerous men assigned to guard duty at public buildings and national monuments.[97]

The government sent out many directives and circulars to the effect that each conscript should be given two full years of training and that he should not be diverted into some semimilitary employment at the end of his first year. It was to no avail.[98] The military continued to follow their own traditional way of doing things, and there seems to have been little that the government could do to make them change. In the end, the government had to acquiesce in the solution proposed by the soldiers: to make certain that everyone received the two years of training still believed to be an indispensable minimum, all would serve a third year. The army could now, without fear of creating a scandal or of compromising the

[97] Lanessan, *op. cit.,* pp. 77–81.
[98] *J.O.C. Doc.* (1913), p. 325.

military proficiency of a conscript class, put as many men as it liked in the auxiliary jobs during their last twelve months in uniform. This also relieved the military authorities of the distasteful idea that civilians could handle many of the peripheral tasks that had always been done by soldiers. As *France militaire* put it, the time had come for people to let "the military run their own affairs a little bit more." [99]

The military had at least one somewhat more serious objection to the two years' service. As had been predicted before its enactment, the 1905 law did nothing to remedy the chronic lack of good N.C.O.'s.[100] In fact, it probably aggravated the situation. Although there had been an increased effort made to recruit and retain more professional N.C.O.'s, it had met with as little success as all prior attempts in this direction. The only recourse was to make corporals and even sergeants out of those in their second year of service. A conscript might be an adequate N.C.O. after two years in uniform, but he was not considered to have the requisite knowledge or authority over his comrades at the end of one year. Then, too, there were deficiencies in the more specialized branches such as the cavalry, where the Germans had retained the three years' service.

Despite its prior objections to the two years' service and despite the inconveniences that it created with regard to certain time-honored practices, the army had adapted itself to the new system of conscription with no great difficulty. Although there were many military writers who claimed that the two-years law was ruining the army and, in the words of General Cherfils, "placing France in mortal danger . . . ," there were others of equal authority, including Joffre, who declared that the French army in 1912 was in excellent condition.[101] Contamine notes that the splendid bearing of the troops in the maneuvers of 1912 was somewhat embarrassing to those offi-

[99] Quoted in Lanessan, *op. cit.,* pp. 153–154.

[100] Revol, *Histoire,* p. 207.

[101] G. Michon, *La préparation à la guerre: la loi de trois ans, 1910–1913* (Paris: Rivière, 1935), pp. 104–105.

cers who claimed that good soldiers could not be made in two years.[102] A military oracle such as General Bonnal, while preferring to see the three years' service introduced again, was still forced to admit that even with the two years' service the French army "would be, in case of a European conflict, a formidable instrument of war."[103] Whatever their opinion about the effect of the two-years law on the quality of the French army, this was not really the issue for most of the soldiers. Rather, it was their determination not to let the German standing army gain too great a numerical advantage that led them to advocate a return to the three years' service.

Within the upper echelons of the army, opinion was almost unanimously in favor of the reestablishment of the three years' service. Although Georges Michon, in his study of the enactment of the law, names six generals who were hostile to the project,[104] it should be noted that one of them, Pédoya, had retired from the army and was now in parliament, while three others, Percin, Peigné, and Goiran, were known as much for their ardently "republican" attitude as for their military qualities. According to General Legrand-Girarde, at the time Second Assistant Chief of Staff, Joffre was not in favor of abolishing the two-years law, and he was willing "only with great reluctance to propose an increase in the term of service."[105] Possibly Joffre, closer to the seats of political power than most generals in the French army, was aware of the difficulties almost certain to be encountered in the enactment of the three years' service and wished to avoid them, if it could be done. His aide-de-camp, Major Alexandre, states that Joffre saw the necessity of such a measure as soon as he learned of the projected increases in the size of the German army, though he

[102] Contamine, *op. cit.,* p. 133.
[103] Lanessan, *op. cit.,* p. 65.
[104] Michon, *op. cit.,* pp. 145–146.
[105] Gen. É. Legrand-Girarde, *Un quart de siècle au service de la France* (Paris: Presses Littéraires de France, 1954), p. 489.

was also certain that the law would prove so onerous that it would not be maintained for more than a few years.[106]

The weight of military opinion in favor of reestablishing the three years' service was of itself not necessarily a decisive factor. In 1905 parliament had by an overwhelming majority voted the two-years law, despite the nearly unanimous objections of the soldiers. The military authorities would first have to convince the government of the dangerous situation created for France by the rapid growth in the size of the German army. That this was accomplished with relative ease provides some indication of how the political atmosphere had changed over the past few years.

The politician who best personified the reawakened patriotism of the era was Raymond Poincaré. President of the Council of Ministers throughout most of 1912 and then elected President of the Republic in 1913, he could, unlike most of those called upon to serve in that office, be considered as "his country's strongest statesman." [107] Poincaré contends in his memoirs that during his term as premier, there was as yet no thought of lengthening the term of service, despite a general preoccupation with the actions of the German government,[108] but that his successor, Aristide Briand, grew alarmed at the tempo and the extent of the German increases and decided that France would have to reply by decisively strengthening her army.[109] Maurice Paléologue, future French Ambassador to Russia during World War I, reports a conversation with Briand in early February 1913, when, after a discussion of the troubled state of Europe, the Premier closed by saying: "If things are in this state—and I am afraid General Joffre thinks

[106] Alexandre, *op. cit.,* pp. 95–96. It should be noted that Alexandre is, of course, highly laudatory toward his former chief, while Legrand-Girarde, who was removed from his command in the first weeks of the war by Joffre, is not.

[107] G. Wright, *Raymond Poincaré and the French Presidency* (Stanford: Stanford University Press, 1942), p. 31.

[108] Poincaré, *op. cit.,* Vol. II, p. 78.

[109] *Ibid.,* Vol. III, pp. 145–146.

as you do—we will immediately have to reestablish the three
years' service." [110] A bill to that effect was forthwith prepared
by the government.

Just before it was presented to parliament, the government
project was discussed in a meeting of the C.S.G. attended by
both Briand and Poincaré. There was no question that the
assembled chiefs of the army would give their approval to the
reestablishment of the three years' service, because it was, from
a purely technical point of view, the most feasible way of
meeting the German threat. But here Briand had to remind
the generals of parliamentary realities. The three years' service
would constitute a heavy burden for the French people. Still,
the chambers would be willing to impose it if they could be
convinced of its necessity. To accomplish this, the government
would have to support its requests by impressive and striking
arguments, and "not only those of a technical nature, which
might not be understood." [111] Briand also noted that the law
would have to be founded on the principle of absolute equality.[112] Brought before the Chamber on March 6, 1913, the
government bill was sent to the Army Commission for consideration, where it remained for three months.

The bill that emerged from the Commission in the beginning of June fulfilled almost exactly the wishes of the military.
So complete an understanding was in itself remarkable, but
even more noteworthy was the fact that the whole tone of the
bill represented a repudiation of republican military ideas as
they had evolved over the past forty years. Republican
orators had always contended that a shorter term of service
was perfectly compatible with the conditions of modern warfare and that too long a stay in the barracks was probably
harmful to the military effectiveness of the average conscript.
Henry Paté, the reporter for the law, disagreed. In a conscript's third year of service, the military skills previously

[110] Paléologue, "Trois ans," p. 77.
[111] C.S.G., "Proc. verb.," No. 13 (1913–1920), p. 57.
[112] Ibid., p. 60.

acquired would be made automatic, something necessitated by the terrible new engines of war. "The more the reflexes of an infantryman are developed through daily exercise, the longer he will be able to hold out against the instinct of fear and will be both able and willing to fight, that is to say, advance. . . ." [113] The archetypal French soldier, with the qualities of initiative, intelligence, and gaiety under fire traditionally attributed to him in past conscription debates, was now to be superseded in favor of a uniformed automaton whose reflexes were to be trained and perfected through hours on the drill field.

Instead of lauding the qualities of the reservist, the reporter now cast doubts on them. He admitted that the older and more mature reservist, if compared to the young conscript on active duty, would possess admirable qualities of endurance and tenacity once he was back in good physical condition, but Paté nevertheless observed that he would have "less *élan,* less enthusiasm, less resiliency, and, it cannot be denied, less generosity than a few years before." [114] That he would sacrifice his life, if need be, went without saying, but he would still do so with more hesitation than the warmhearted, impulsive, yet disciplined conscript of twenty-one, who had less to lose. From this line of reasoning it naturally followed that the higher the percentage of men on active duty in a unit, the more vigorous it would be in battle, and thus more suited to offensive warfare.

Throughout the report on the bill the only issue under consideration was that of how to improve the military posture of France in the face of the growing might of Germany. In dealing with this problem, it was the opinion of the professional soldiers that was heeded at every point. As if to remind republicans of how little they really knew or understood about military questions, Paté evoked the memory of the debates in 1868 over the Niel Law. Then such republicans as Jules Favre and

[113] *J.O.C. Doc.* (1913), p. 331.
[114] *Ibid.,* p. 332.

Jules Simon had spoken out strongly against the measure. The events of 1870 made them repent their pacificst opinions. Paté asked that the lessons of history not be neglected. "It must not happen that in the future people will reproach the republicans of 1913 for the mistakes that still weigh so heavily on the memory of those who, unknowingly, paved the way for the disasters and caused our sorrow." [115] To blame the defeat of 1870 on the actions of the republican minority in the Corps Législatif was a perversion of history, one possibly to be expected from a fanatical Bonapartist but hardly from a republican, no matter how nominal.

The passage of the three-years law was extremely swift, hardly five months elapsing between the time it was first formally presented to the Chamber in March 1913 and the final vote of August 7, 1913. The speed of its enactment is particularly striking when compared to the years that were spent over the 1889 and 1905 conscription laws. Even so, the government was impatient that the debates consumed as much time as they did. In order to be sure that it would be voted on before the parliamentary holidays, it was decided that the Chamber should hold special extra sessions.[116] Despite the fact that the debate on the law was extremely spirited and at times quite fierce, with the opponents of the law giving a very good account of themselves, at the crucial junctures the government had the votes. In the Chamber the vote on the vital article concerning the length of service was 344 to 220.[117] This was certainly decisive, but the margin was much smaller than was usual in votes on conscription under the Third Republic.

Although the majority in the Chamber was oriented to the left, while the three years' service was championed above all by the Moderates and those on the right, there were enough defections among the Radicals and even among certain former

[115] *Ibid.*, pp. 385–386.
[116] Poincaré, *op. cit.*, Vol. III, pp. 211–212.
[117] *J.O.C. Déb.* (1913), p. 2514.

Socialists to provide the votes necessary for its enactment.[118] The vigorous and decisive leadership supplied by Poincaré doubtless had something to do with this. Even within the circumscribed attributes of the presidency there still was a considerable residue of power and influence which he exercised to the fullest.[119] At one point, Poincaré is reported to have gone so far as to threaten to request that the Senate dissolve the Chamber if it would not vote the three-years law. If the Senate were to balk, he planned to resign.[120] Paul-Boncour believes that Poincaré was instrumental in personally convincing Clemenceau of the necessity of the law, despite their mutual antipathy. Until then Clemenceau had had no very strong sentiments on the subject, either pro or con. Through him a sizable number of Radical votes were now won.[121]

The supporters of the law justified their stand primarily in terms of the nonpartisan issue of national security, but their opponents almost instinctively saw some ulterior political motive. When Étienne as Minister of War first broached the matter in a meeting of the Council of Ministers, one of his colleagues automatically accused him of wanting "to play the game of the reactionaries."[122] As the government officially laid the bill before the Chamber for the first time, it was greeted with cries of "Down with reaction!" and "Down with the Empire!"[123] The Socialists took the darkest view of the three-years law, considering it the veritable start of "a civil war waged against the working classes. . . ."[124] In an effort to escape this kind of stigma, Joseph Reinach stated that he and those of his friends who supported the bill were all good re-

---

[118] Challener, *op. cit.,* p. 88.
[119] Wright, *op. cit.,* p. 80.
[120] Paléologue, "Trois ans," pp. 318–319.
[121] Paul-Boncour, *op. cit.,* Vol. I, pp. 235–236.
[122] Paléologue, "Trois ans," pp. 81–82.
[123] *J.O.C. Déb.* (1913), pp. 815–816.
[124] Weber, *op. cit.,* p. 119.

publicans. They had favored the two years' service in 1905, but now, with the rapid increase in the size of the German army and the danger of imminent war, they had no choice but to vote for the three-years law.[125]

In the actual discussion of the bill, both within the Army Commission and on the floor of the Chamber, the opponents of the three years' service displayed great skill and determination. General Legrand-Girarde, who was delegate for the government to parliament in the preparation of the bill and in the debate over it, had to admit that the cogency of their arguments and their mastery of their material made his task very difficult.[126] Jaurès, in particular, attacked the government project with verve and authority. His speech presenting his own counterproject was one of the great oratorical achievements of his career.[127] That it was voted down 496 to 77 was not surprising, the Socialist leader having had few illusions about his chances of success. According to Paul-Boncour, "It was not so much a favorable vote that Jaurès sought, but rather propaganda." [128]

On the other hand, the chief supporters of the measure were somehow less impressive. Étienne, the Minister of War, for all his flashy patriotism gave evidence in the discussion of his "distressing mediocrity." [129] Legrand-Girarde claimed that some of these advocates actually hindered rather than promoted the passage of the law and that Paté was not up to the arduous task of defending it before the Chamber.[130] Joffre, speaking in the name of the army, was quite pedestrian. As his aide-de-camp noted, "He was not made for parliamentary discussions." [131]

---

[125] *J.O.C. Déb.* (1913), pp. 1676–1677, 1685–1686.
[126] Legrand-Girarde, *op. cit.,* p. 491.
[127] *J.O.C. Déb.* (1913), pp. 1991 ff.
[128] Paul-Boncour, *op. cit.,* Vol. I, pp. 230–231.
[129] J. Caillaux, *Mes mémoires* (Paris: Plon, 1947), Vol. III, p. 63.
[130] Legrand-Girarde, *op. cit.,* pp. 492–493.
[131] Alexandre, *op. cit.,* p. 99.

In its impatience to get the law voted, the government had a tendency to overstress the perilous situation in which France now found herself. The net impression was one of inconsistency and perhaps even confusion in the highest military circles. Only a few months before, during the debate over the 1912 law on the infantry cadres, the competent military authorities had stated that a company of 115 men was sufficiently strong for peacetime needs; now the cry was that with 115 men the company was a "skeleton unit . . . dying of exhaustion." [132] The only remedy, of course, was a third year of service. By the same token, though Millerand as Minister of War in 1912 had found the army to be in a generally satisfactory state of preparedness, his successor, Étienne, was very pessimistic. Since both Ministers of War received their information from the same General Staff, at least one deputy was led to wonder just where the truth lay and whether the government was justified in so suddenly presenting a bill and demanding that it be "supported by an immediate and blind act of faith." [133] Possibly the men who drew up the bill and managed its passage through parliament had heeded too well the admonition of Briand that it would have to be backed by dramatic and striking arguments in order to overcome the resistance of the legislators.

Despite the pressure brought to bear by the government, the enactment of the three-years law was by no means a sure thing. Its opponents might yet have been able to defeat it if they had concentrated all their efforts on one or two countermeasures, instead of dispersing their energies among the fourteen different projects introduced in the course of the debate.[134] Of these counterproposals, the one most dangerous to the government-sponsored bill was authored by Messimy and Paul-Boncour. They called for a development of the basic principles implicit in the two-years law—an intensification and

[132] *J.O.C. Déb.* (1913), p. 1744.
[133] *Ibid.*, p. 1632.
[134] Contamine, *op. cit.*, p. 149.

a better utilization of the periods of reserve training, along with a system of premilitary education. Until these measures could bear fruit, they planned a temporary increase in the term of service to thirty months.[135] So persuasive and forceful was Paul-Boncour's presentation of his scheme before the Chamber that Joffre felt that if the vote had been taken at the close of his discourse, the three years' service might well have been compromised.[136] The Chief of the General Staff later conceded to Paul-Boncour that it was a tenable project and that it might have been feasible if there had been more time.[137] It was rejected by the comparatively small margin of 312 to 266.

Much of the debate over the three-years law centered on the military capabilities of the reserves. The opponents of the measure condemned the chiefs of the army for not having shown more faith in them or organized them more solidly.[138] This allegation was not true according to the reporter for the law. "We declare once again that we have complete confidence in our reservists, that we can obtain from them all the devotion, all the courage that are the appanage of the French soldier." [139] As during the recent debate over the law on the infantry cadres, the official thesis of the government and the high command was that the reservists would make fine soldiers if they had with them a solid core of men from the standing army. In reply, one could well argue, as did one deputy, that a young conscript of twenty-one or twenty-two in his first or second year of service would, in fact, have less stamina and tenacity than the reservist, a grown man who had completed his full quota of military training.[140]

In their preoccupation with the reserves, the men of the Left tended to forget certain basic military realities. For one thing,

---

[135] Paul-Boncour, Vol. I, p. 233.
[136] Michon, *op. cit.*, pp. 163–164.
[137] Paul-Boncour, *op. cit.*, Vol. I, pp. 234–235.
[138] *J.O.C. Déb.* (1913), pp. 1992–1993, 1742–1743.
[139] *Ibid.*, p. 2116.
[140] *Ibid.*, p. 1814.

Germany actually had a greater number of trained reserves than did France, as General Pau explained to the Senate.[141] Since the stark demographic facts of life precluded competing with Germany in terms of numbers, a return to the old accent on quality, as opposed to mere quantity, was inexorably being imposed on the French. The usual arguments of the Left, stressing the military skill and cohesion of the reserve units, as witnessed in the annual maneuvers, ignored the fact that in battle sheer physical conditioning counted for a great deal, especially in an era when, despite the use of railroads for transporting men and supplies to their points of concentration, the troops would accomplish all other movements on foot and with a heavy pack on their backs. As one authority, Henri Contamine, has pointed out in his excellent study, *La Revanche,* long marches were considered by the Germans to be their particular specialty.[142] It would require a few weeks of intensive training before the French reserves were in the same physical condition as their comrades on active duty. In their strategic planning, the French did not make any allowance for such a delay.

In France the military authorities generally argued that the highest permissible ratio of reserves to men on active duty in a front-line unit was one to one.[143] A unit with a larger proportion of reservists than this was considered to be lacking in the solidity and cohesion necessary for it to stand up under fire. This was really nothing more than a rule of thumb, which, as Jaurès pointed out, had no historical support. During the Revolution the preferred proportion was two volunteers to one soldier from the old royal army. Furthermore, the *amalgame* took place, not within the companies, but on the level of the brigades, two battalions of volunteers to one of the regular troops of the line. This meant that the volunteers had been organized as individual units without a cadre of regulars.

[141] Contamine, *op. cit.,* p. 148.
[142] *Ibid.,* p. 120.
[143] Monteilhet, *op. cit.,* p. 287.

Jaurès quoted Dubois-Crancé, Minister of War in 1793, to
the effect that he hoped, not so much "to absorb the volunteers
into the army of the line, but rather to have the army of the
line absorbed by the volunteers.[144] This was precisely the
opposite of what the government was advocating in 1913.

Whatever their real attitude toward the reserves, the military authorities said nothing derogatory about them during
the debate. By declaring that the reserves would indeed have a
vital role to play in the event of war, they neatly robbed the
opponents of the three-years law of an excellent issue. To have
publicly doubted their military value would have been to vio-
late a republican shibboleth and would have provided a rallying cry for those still undecided. It might well have led to the
defeat of the law.

Apart from the three years, the other essential feature of the
law was the provision that the term of service be equal for all.
This in itself was one reason why the law was voted so
quickly. The social and political ramifications in prior conscription laws, especially that of 1889, had generated the real
debate and delayed their enactment for years. Since no one
seriously suggested going counter to the principle of absolute
equality already achieved in 1905, the sons of the rich and the
poor would have to be in uniform for three years. One might
even argue, as does Monteilhet, that the 1913 law, by making
the military burden heavier, actually "rendered equality more
tangible." [145] The Left had thus lost its most effective rallying
cry. Lacking a social issue and robbed of any kind of military
issue by the acquiescence of the soldiers in the need for the reserves, the opponents of the three years' service had no arguments to use against it, except to declare that it would lead to
no real improvement in the military posture of France while
resulting in huge supplementary expenditures. To this, the
soldiers could reply that it simply was not true. From either

[144] *J.O.C. Déb.* (1913), p. 2008.
[145] Monteilhet, *op. cit.,* p. 283.

instinct or intelligence, a majority of the legislators agreed with them.

The debate and the vote on the three-years law were accompanied by a wave of intense patriotism that bordered on chauvinism of the most extreme kind. References to Alsace-Lorraine were invariably greeted with cheers in the schools, and "lecturers now hardly dared to mention German methods or ideas for fear of the murmurs and catcalls." [146] Students applauded at the least mention of the "blue line of the Vosges." One teacher at Lycée Louis le Grand heard himself hooted by his pupils and accused in vivid terms of looking like a Boche for having dared to speak out against the three-years law.[147] A group of *lycéens* addressed a petition to the President of the Council of Ministers: "The undersigned, soldiers of tomorrow and the day after . . . are here to assure you that they are ready to sacrifice joyously, for the life and for the glory of France, three years of their youth." [148] In the theater, plays on a patriotic theme enjoyed a great success.[149] The press was generally in favor of the law. In a vigorous and often violent campaign that was launched on February 20, 1913, the nationalist papers all loudly called for a return to the three years. They were joined, though in more moderate tones, by the great dailies such as *Figaro, Le Matin,* and *Le Temps.* Only papers of the Left and Far Left, such as *Lanterne, Aurore,* and *Humanité,* were against the measure.[150]

The chauvinistic atmosphere in which the three-years law was debated, as well as the law itself, caused considerable alarm in Berlin. People wondered if the *Réveil national* had been carried to such lengths that France was now contemplating a war of revenge against Germany. Yet to see France as

---

[146] Weber, *op. cit.,* p. 107.

[147] Contamine, *op. cit.,* p. 147.

[148] Girardet, *op. cit.,* p. 239.

[149] Michon, *op. cit.,* p. 121.

[150] *Ibid.,* pp. 137–144.

Conclusion

In August 1914, France went to war with Germany. For the Republic and for the nation, it was to be the supreme test, one from which they would emerge victorious but seriously weakened. For the army in particular, it was the realization of a goal toward which two generations of soldiers had labored. That they were able to train and mobilize more than 8,000,000 men and then to lead this mass army to the ultimate triumph, *la Revanche,* was a tribute to the soundness and the efficacy of the military institutions of France under the Third Republic. Four decades of constant and unceasing effort had led the army from the shambles of a catastrophic defeat to a point where it could successfully measure itself against the Germans.

The great task of rebuilding and reform that was undertaken in the aftermath of the Franco-Prussian War was primarily the responsibility of the military, but the civilian leaders of the state also had a significant role to play. Recognizing that a strong army, able to defend the national soil, was a potent guarantee of the stability and the safety of the newly founded and seemingly feeble republican regime, the politicians willingly appropriated the huge sums that were demanded, enacted the necessary legislation, and generally did their utmost to create conditions favorable to carrying out the program of military reform. Between the civil and the military elements in the French state, there developed a pragmatic accommodation that was to prove to be remarkably durable and effective. Without this entente, the military renaissance of the years 1871–1914 and, perhaps, also the survival of the regime would have been impossible.

The government very early perceived that the army would best be able to carry through its program of reform and to prepare itself for an eventual war with Germany only if it were allowed a very high degree of autonomy and independence within the state. By granting such autonomy, the Republic was effectively relinquishing a vital prerogative: civilian control of the military. But one could argue that since the republican leaders of France were not prepared to offer a coherent alternate scheme of reform to replace what was being undertaken by the soldiers, too much government supervision over or intervention in technical military matters would only be detrimental to the interests of the army and the nation.

The only reason that the government might have for enacting any specific measures to ensure the subordination of the military, or even for rigidly enforcing such constitutional and legal provisions as already existed, was the fear that the army represented a danger to the Republic. Despite occasional assertions by certain republican politicians to this effect, the government was in general willing to place its confidence in the loyalty of the army. This confidence was fully justified. Whatever the personal opinions of even a majority of the officer corps on current social and political issues, in military matters they were the obedient servants and the willing collaborators of the Republic.

Motivated by an almost superstitious fear of "politics," the military were in no way involved in the great crises that punctuated the formative years of the Republic—the *Seize-mai,* Boulangism, and Panama. If during the Dreyfus Affair the army seemed to desert its traditionally nonpolitical role and to join those who were attacking the Republic, this was only illusory. In effect, the opponents of the regime seized upon an issue that directly concerned the right of the military to manage their own internal affairs and used it as the chief weapon in their campaign to overthrow the Republic. Loudly championing the authoritarian ideals of the army as against the apparently corrupt practices of the politicians, the antirepublican forces in France endeavored to recruit the soldiers as active participants in this campaign. Despite the anger that almost all men in the army may have felt at what they considered to be the gratuitous and unwarranted interference by the government in a strictly military concern and despite the overwrought utterances by certain officers, the military men would not forswear their nonpolitical role in the state. Had they done so, the Republic would certainly have fallen.

As long as the military adhered to the ideal of absolute obedience to the powers that be, civilian control was a fact, and neither legal measures nor specific institutional arrangements were needed to guarantee it. Indeed, it is difficult to see how the Republic could have asserted such control in any way that was consonant with the effective functioning of the French military machine since the preponderance of power was situated within parliament. The military problem facing the Third Republic was too complex, demanding too high a degree of technical *expertise,* to be readily handled by parliament. As a result, the competent military authorities were allowed to manage their affairs with only cursory supervision by the government. That such an abdication of effective responsibility did not conform to the spirit of the Constitution was regrettable but probably, under the circumstances, unavoidable. In any case, it in no way threatened the evolution of the regime during the period 1871–1914.

In the management of its relations with the army, the Republic was displaying one of its most characteristic features, its essential and necessary pragmatism. More than in any other regime in the history of nineteenth-century France, the government sought to avoid having to take a stand on matters of doctrine and ideology. From the casual nature of its constitutional laws to the willingness of the first generation of political leaders to assume the title of Opportunists, the Republic embodied a common-sense approach to the problems facing the country, and it survived because of that fact. The avowed practitioners of this political art, Gambetta, Freycinet, Waldeck-Rousseau, and even Clemenceau, were also the ones who best understood military reality, as France had to face it in these years, and hence the need for a strong, well-organized army. It is no coincidence that the periods of most fruitful cooperation between the army and the Republic were those of relatively undisputed dominance by the Moderates or Opportunists: the early 1890's, the era of the Freycinet reforms, and the years of the *Réveil national,* following the elections of 1910.

The fundamentally pragmatic spirit of the regime does not by itself provide the whole explanation for the successful relationship that existed between the army and the Republic in the years 1871–1914. The submissive and loyal attitude of the army was also a vital factor, and this was by no means a recent phenomenon. The tradition of obedience to the constituted powers was an old one in the French army, going back to the time of its founding as a permanent institution of state during the reign of Louis XIV. Under weak sovereigns as well as strong, in periods of revolutionary change and upheaval and in eras of calm, the military seldom deviated from the path of duty. The clue to this continuous sense of discipline lay less in the ideological currents of the times than in the fact that, for the most part, the governments of France, whether structurally weak or strong, ideologically sympathetic or antipathetic to the military ideal, assumed they had a mandate to rule the country and acted accordingly. Only when this mandate became questionable in the minds of both the people and the political leaders, as during the Directory and in the last days of the Fourth Republic, did any significant number of soldiers move to assert themselves politically. For three centuries, the military men were the docile and disciplined servants of any regime that knew how to govern, how to give orders, even if the soldiers disliked or disapproved of the orders in question.

This wholly pragmatic entente between the army and the Republic was eminently suited to the conditions of peace, but it had not been developed to meet the exigencies of war. With regard to the most efficacious way in which civil-military relations should be conducted in time of war, no more foresight was shown in France than in any other European country. The general theory to which everyone, civilian or military, subscribed was that the government should decide the ultimate goals of the war and that it should provide the means whereby the responsible military authorities might achieve these goals. It was understood, however, that the military would have full liberty to decide the purely technical question of how best to utilize these means.

Everyone, except a few extremely prescient persons, believed that the fate of the country would be settled in a relatively short time. That a long war would create problems of a peculiar nature, where technical military considerations, supposedly the domain of the commander in chief in the field, could not long be kept out of the realm of politics, was seen only dimly. In the 1911 debates over the high command, the Radical deputy André Hesse had declared before the Chamber that when the guns began to speak, it was best that "the politicians keep quiet." [1] It was an alluringly simple formula, one suited to a war that might last a month or two. It was of little help in a conflict that was to endure for more than four years and that soon came to demand almost the total energies of the French nation.

[1] *Vide supra,* p. 329.

Bibliography

Manuscript Sources

OFFICIAL FRENCH DOCUMENTS

Archives Nationales. "Police générale," series F7.

École militaire supérieure. "Cours de service d'état-major" (1879).

École supérieure de Guerre. "Cours d'administration et législation en temps de paix" (1896–1897).

Ministère de la Guerre, Bibliothèque, "Travaux d'études, No. 23," March 14, 1923.

Ministère de la Guerre. Conseil supérieur de la Guerre. "Registres des délibérations" and "Procès verbaux" (1872–1914).

Ministère de la Guerre. État-major de l'Armée. "Campagne contre l'Allemagne, 1914–1918." Cartons Nos. 4, 5, and 94.

Préfecture de la Police de Paris. Archives. Dossiers relating to the leading civilian and military figures of the period 1871–1914.

PERSONAL MEMOIRS AND PRIVATE CORRESPONDENCE

France, Bibliothèque Nationale. Cabinet des Manuscrits, Nouvelles acquisitions françaises, Vols. 13532, 13538, 24900.

Millet, General Charles. Unpublished memoirs. 2 vols. On microfilm at the Service historique de l'Armée, Château de Vincennes.

Revol, General Joseph. Unpublished memoirs. In the possession of General Revol.

"La vie du général Chanzy, 1823–1883. Lettre et documents." Six mimeographed volumes, privately prepared for Chanzy family. One copy in Archives Nationales, Paris.

Primary Printed Sources

OFFICIAL PUBLICATIONS

Annuaire de l'armée française (1873–1914).

France, Ministère de la Guerre. État-major de l'Armée. *Les Armées françaises dans la grande guerre,* Vol. I. Paris: Imprimerie nationale, 1922.

Journal Officiel de la République française (1870–1914).

PERSONAL MEMOIRS AND REMINISCENCES

Adam, Mme. Juliette. *Après l'abandon de la Revanche.* Paris: Lemerre, 1910.

Alexandre, General René. *Avec Joffre d'Agadir à Verdun.* Paris: Berger-Levrault, 1932.

André, General Louis. *Cinq ans de ministère.* Paris: L. Michaud, 1907.

Braibant, Charles. *Félix Faure à l'Élysée: Souvenirs de Louis Le Gall.* Paris: Hachette, 1963.

Brisson, Henri. *Souvenirs.* Paris: Cornély, 1908.

Caillaux, Joseph. *Mes mémoires.* 3 vols. Paris: Plon, 1942–1947.

Castex, General. *Ce que j'ai vu.* 2 vols. Paris: E. Capiomont, 1898.

Chalvet-Nastrac, Vicomte de. *Les projets de restauration monarchique et le général Ducrot, d'après ses mémoires et sa correspondance.* Paris: Alphonse Picard, 1909.

Choppin, Captain Henri. *Souvenirs d'un capitaine de cavalerie, 1851–1881.* Paris: Berger-Levrault, 1909.

Combarieu, Abel. *Sept ans à l'Élysée avec le Président Loubet.* Paris: Hachette, 1932.

Combes, Émile. *Mon ministère, mémoires, 1902–1905.* Paris: Plon, 1956.

Du Barail, General François. *Mes souvenirs.* 3 vols. Paris: Plon, 1894–1896.

Ferry, Jules. *Lettres de Jules Ferry.* Paris: Calmann-Lévy, 1914.

Fix, Colonel Nathanaël. *Souvenirs d'un officier d'État-major.* 2 vols. Paris: Juven (n.d.).

Freycinet, Charles de. *Souvenirs.* 2 vols. Paris: Delagrave, 1912–1913.

Grandin, General. *Dix-huit ans de généralat dans la cavalerie.* Besançon: Bossane, 1901.

Joffre, Joseph. *Mémoires du Maréchal Joffre.* 2 vols. Paris: Plon, 1932.

Legrand-Girarde, General Émile. *Un quart de siècle au service de la France.* Paris: Presses Littéraires de France, 1954.

Messimy, General Adolphe. *Mes souvenirs.* Paris: Plon, 1937.

Paléologue, Maurice. "Comment fut rétabli le service de trois ans," *Revue des deux mondes,* May 1 and 15, 1935.

————. *Un grand tournant de la politique mondiale, 1904–1906.* Paris: Plon, 1934.

Paul-Boncour, Joseph. *Entre deux guerres.* 3 vols. Paris: Plon, 1945–1946.

Pichot-Duclos, General. *Au G.Q.G. de Joffre.* Grenoble-Paris: Arthaud, 1947.

Pimodan, Comte de. *Simples souvenirs.* Paris: Plon, 1908.

Poincaré, Raymond. *Au service de la France.* 10 vols. Paris: Plon, 1926–1933.

Radziwill, Princess. *Lettres de la Princesse Radziwill au Général di Robilant.* 4 vols. Bologna: Zanichelli, 1933.

Thiers, Adolphe. *Memoirs of M. Thiers.* F. M. Atkinson, trans. London: Allen & Unwin, 1915.

Weygand, General Maxime. *Mémoires.* 3 vols. Paris: Flammarion, 1950–1957.

Zurlinden, General Émile. *Mes souvenirs depuis la guerre.* Paris: Perrin, 1913.

Newspapers and Periodicals Consulted

Année politique
Avenir militaire
Correspondant.
France militaire.
Gaulois.
Grande revue.
Le Jour.
Journal des débats.
Journal des sciences militaires.
Le Matin.

Moniteur de l'armée.
Nouvelle revue.
République française.
Revue des deux mondes.
Revue militaire suisse.
Revue politique et littéraire.
Spectateur militaire.
Le Temps.

Secondary Sources

Ameugny, Pierre d'. *L'âme de l'armée.* Paris: Nouvelle revue,
     1898.
Un ancien officier. *La puissance française.* Paris: Calmann-Lévy,
     1885.
Anon. *L'armée sous régime civil.* Paris: H. C. Lavauzelle, 1894.
Anon. (General Vanson). "Deux documents concernant la ré-
     organisation de l'armée," *Sabretache,* 1896.
Anon. *Pourquoi la France n'est pas prête.* Paris: Flammarion,
     1885.
Arbeux, Captain d'. *L'officier contemporain.* Paris: Grasset, 1911.
Avon, Commandant. *Notice sur le Ministère de la Guerre.* Paris:
     J. Dumaine, 1879.
Bayle, H. *De l'état des sous-officiers.* Paris: Rousseau, 1907.
Bédarida, François. "L'armée et la République: Les opinions
     politiques des officiers français en 1876–1878," *Revue
     historique.* Vol. 232 (July–September 1964).
Bidegain, Jean. *Le Grand Orient de France.* Paris: Librairie Anti-
     Sémite, 1905.
Bouchet, J. *Gouvernement et commandement.* Paris: Payot, 1930.
Boussel, Patrice. *L'Affaire Dreyfus et la presse.* Paris: A. Colin,
     1960.
Brogan, Denis. *The Development of Modern France.* London:
     Hamish Hamilton, 1940.
Bruun, Geoffry. *Clemenceau.* Cambridge: Harvard University
     Press, 1944.
Burnand, Robert. *Le Duc d'Aumale et son temps.* Paris: Hachette,
     1949.

Buthman, William C. *The Rise of Integral Nationalism in France.* New York: Columbia University Press, 1939.

Carnes, Jess Gale. "The French Army Officers and the Establishment of the Republic, 1876–1889." Unpublished Ph.D. dissertation, Cornell University, 1949.

Challener, Richard D. *The French Theory of the Nation in Arms.* New York: Columbia University Press, 1955.

Chalmin, Lieutenant Colonel Pierre. *L'officier français de 1815 à 1870.* Paris: Rivière, 1957.

Chapman, Guy. *The Dreyfus Case.* London: R. Hart-Davis, 1955.

Charnay, Jean-Paul. *Société militaire et suffrage politique en France depuis 1789.* Paris: S.E.V.P.E.N., 1964.

Cherfils, General Pierre. *Pour l'armée.* Paris: Berger-Levrault, 1913.

Choppin, Captain Henri. *L'armée française, 1870–1890.* Paris: Albert Savine, 1890.

Civrieux, Commandant de. *Du rêve à la réalité.* Paris: Belleville, 1908.

Clarétie, Jules. *Souvenirs du dîner Bixio.* Paris: Charpentier, 1924.

Un colonel. *La nation et l'armée.* Paris: A. Colin, 1900.

Contamine, Henry. *La Revanche.* Paris: Berger-Levrault, 1957.

Craig, Gordon. *The Politics of the Prussian Army.* London: Oxford University Press, 1955.

Dansette, Adrien, *Le Boulangisme.* Paris: A. Fayard, 1946.

Darrécagaix, General. *La guerre et l'armée.* Paris: Chapelot, 1901.

Daudet, Ernest. *Souvenirs de la présidence du Maréchal de Mac-Mahon.* Paris: Dentu, 1880.

Dilke, Sir Charles. "The French Armies," *Fortnightly Review,* November 1, 1891.

Dreyfus, Robert. *La République de M. Thiers.* Paris: Gallimard, 1936.

Du Saussois, E. *De Miribel.* Lyon: J. Gallet, 1894.

Earle, Edward Meade, editor. *Makers of Modern Strategy.* Princeton: Princeton University Press, 1943.

Epée, Jean d'. *L'officier français.* Paris: H.-C. Lavauzelle, 1907.

Freycinet, Charles de. *La guerre en province pendant la siège de Paris.* Paris: M. Lévy, 1871.

Gaulle, Charles de. *France and Her Army.* F. L. Dash, trans. London: Hutchinson, 1945.

Gheusi, Paul B. *La vie et la mort singulière de Gambetta.* Paris: Albin Michel, 1932.

Gilbert, Captain Georges. *Lois et institutions militaires: six études organiques.* Paris: Nouvelle revue, 1895.

Girardet, Raoul. *La société militaire dans la France contemporaine, 1815–1939.* Paris: Plon, 1953.

Goguel, François. *La politique des partis sous la troisième République.* 3rd ed. Paris: Éditions du Seuil, 1958.

Gooch, Brison D. *The New Bonapartist Generals in the Crimean War.* The Hague: N. Nijhoff, 1959.

Gooch, Robert K. *The French Parliamentary Committee System.* New York: Appleton, 1935.

Guérard, Albert. *Napoleon III.* Cambridge: Harvard University Press, 1943.

Haroué, Jacques. *La détresse de l'armée.* Paris: Havard, 1903.

Hautière, P. *Les dépenses du ministère de la guerre.* Paris: Jouve, 1914.

Hénin, Abbé. *Le Ministère de la Guerre.* Paris: L. Fournier, 1937.

Hervé, Gustave. *La conquête de l'armée.* Paris: "La guerre sociale," 1913.

Howard, Michael. *The Franco-Prussian War.* New York: Macmillan, 1961.

———, editor. *Soldiers and Governments.* London: Eyre & Spottiswood, 1957.

Humbert, Charles. *L'armée: sommes-nous défendus?* Paris: Juven, 1907.

Huntington, Samuel. *The Soldier and the State.* Cambridge: Harvard University Press, 1957.

Irvine, Dallas D. "The French Discovery of Clausewitz and Napoleon," *Journal of the American Military Institute,* Spring 1940.

Iung, General Théodore. *La République et l'armée.* Paris: Charpentier, 1892.

Katzenbach, Edward. "Charles Louis de Saulces de Freycinet and the Army of Metropolitan France." Unpublished Ph.D. dissertation, Princeton University, 1953.

Kovacs, Arpad. "French Military Legislation in the Third Republic," *Military Affairs,* January 1949.

Kuntz, François. *L'officier français dans la nation.* Paris: H.-C. Lavauzelle, 1960.

Lanessan, Jean-Louis de. *Nos forces militaires.* Paris: Alcan, 1913.
Lewal, Colonel Jules. *La réforme de l'armée.* Paris: J. Dumaine, 1871.
Manceau, Émile. *Notre armée.* Paris: Charpentier, 1901.
Marcère, Émile de. *Le seize-mai et la fin du septennat.* Paris: Plon, 1900.
Mayer, Émile. *Nos chefs de 1914.* Paris: Stock, 1930.
Messin, Claude. *L'armée française, ce qu'elle devrait être.* Paris: H.-C. Lavauzelle, 1891.
Michon, Georges. *La préparation à la guerre: la loi de trois ans, 1910–1913.* Paris: Rivière, 1935.
Millerand, Alexandre. *Pour la défense nationale.* Paris: Charpentier, 1913.
Miquel, Pierre. *L'affaire Dreyfus.* Paris: Presses Universitaires de France, 1959.
Mollin, Captain. *La vérité sur l'affaire des fiches.* Paris: Librairie universelle, 1905.
Monteilhet, Joseph. *Les institutions militaires de la France.* Paris: Alcan, 1932.
Un officier prussien. *La France, est-elle prête?* Paris: Henicksen, 1884.
Ornano, Roland d'. *Gouvernement et haut commandement sous le régime parlementaire français.* Aix-en-Provence: Pensée Universitaire, 1958.
Regnault, General. "Les leçons de la guerre: l'organisation du haut commandement," *Revue mondiale,* September 1, 1930.
Reinach, Joseph. *Histoire de l'affaire Dreyfus.* 7 vols. Paris: Revue Blanche, 1901–1911.
———. *La politique opportuniste.* Paris: Charpentier, 1890.
———. *La vie politique de Léon Gambetta.* Paris: Alcan, 1918.
Revol, Colonel Joseph. *Histoire de l'armée française.* Paris: Larousse, 1929.
Richard, Jules. *L'armée et la guerre.* Paris: Librairie Illustrée, 1896.
Rolland, H. de. *Galliffet.* Paris: Éditions de la Nouvelle France, 1945.
Rosinski, Herbert. *The German Army.* Revised edition. Washington: Infantry Journal, 1944.
Seignobos: Charles. *Le déclin de l'Empire et l'établissement de la troisième République,* Vol. VII of *Histoire de la France*

contemporaine, edited by Ernest Lavisse. Paris: Hachette, 1921.

———. *L'évolution de la troisième République,* Vol. VIII of *Histoire de la France contemporaine,* edited by Ernest Lavisse. Paris: Hachette, 1921.

Silvestre de Sacy, Jacques. *Le Maréchal de MacMahon.* Paris: Internationales, 1960.

Simon, Jules. *Le gouvernement de M. Thiers.* Paris: Calmann-Lévy, 1878.

Simond, E. *Histoire de la troisième République: Présidence de M. Loubet.* Paris: H.-C. Lavauzelle, 1922.

Stourm, René. *The Budget.* Thomas Plazinski, trans. New York: Appleton, 1917.

Thile, Lucien. *Pouvoir civil et pouvoir militaire.* Paris: Rousseau, 1914.

Thomas, Louis. *Le général de Galliffet.* 2nd edition. Paris: Aux Armes de France, 1941.

Thomas, Marcel. *L'affaire sans Dreyfus.* Paris: Fayard, 1961.

Thoumas, General. *Les transformations de l'armée française.* 2 vols. Paris: Berger-Levrault, 1887.

Trochu, General Louis. *Oeuvres posthumes.* 2 vols. Tours: A. Maine, 1896.

———. *L'armée française en 1879.* Paris: Hetzel, n.d.

Tuchman, Barbara. *The Guns of August.* New York: Macmillan, 1962.

Vagts, Alfred. *Militarism: A History.* New York: Norton, 1937.

Weber, Eugen. *The Nationalist Revival in France, 1905–1914.* Berkeley and Los Angeles: University of California Press, 1959.

Weygand, General Maxime. *Histoire de l'armée française.* Paris: Flammarion, 1953.

Wright, Gordon. *Raymond Poincaré and the French Presidency.* Stanford: Stanford University Press, 1942.

Index